Asian Diasporas

Asian Diasporas

New Formations, New Conceptions

edited by

Rhacel S. Parreñas and Lok C. D. Siu

Stanford University Press
Stanford, California
2007

Stanford University Press
Stanford, California

Printed in the United States of America on acid-free, archival-quality paper

Library of Congress Cataloging-in-Publication Data

Asian diasporas : new formations, new conceptions / edited by Rhacel S. Parreñas and Lok
C. D. Siu.
    p. cm.
  Includes bibliographical references and index.
   ISBN 978-0-8047-5243-5 (cloth : alk. paper)—ISBN 978-0-8047-5244-2 (pbk. : alk. paper)
  1. Asian diaspora. 2. Asians—Foreign countries. I. Parreñas, Rhacel Salazar. II. Siu, Lok C. D.

DS13.A75 2007
304.8095—dc22

                       2007026785

Typeset by Thompson Type in 10/14 Minion Pro

Contents

Acknowledgments   vii

Introduction: Asian Diasporas—
New Conceptions, New Frameworks   1
Rhacel Salazar Parreñas and Lok C. D. Siu

1 Latin America in Asia-Pacific Perspective   29
   Evelyn Hu-DeHart

2 Filipino Sea Men: Identity and Masculinity
   in a Global Labor Niche   63
   Steven C. McKay

3 "My Mother Fell in Love with Mỹ-Xuân First":
   Arranging "Traditional" Marriages Across the Diaspora   85
   Hung Cam Thai

4 The Queen of the Chinese Colony:
   Contesting Nationalism, Engendering Diaspora   105
   Lok C. D. Siu

5 Ritual in Diaspora: Pedagogy and Practice Among
   Hindus and Muslims in Trinidad   141
   Aisha Khan

6 "Our Flavour Is Greater"   161
   Sharmila Sen

7   Asian Bodies Out of Control:
    Examining the Adopted Korean Existence   177
    Tobias Hübinette

8   Diasporic Politics and the Globalizing of America:
    Korean Immigrant Nationalism and the
    1919 Philadelphia Korean Congress   201
    Richard S. Kim

9   When Minorities Migrate: The Racialization
    of the Japanese Brazilians in Brazil and Japan   225
    Takeyuki (Gaku) Tsuda

10 Legal Servitude and Free Illegality:
    Migrant "Guest" Workers in Taiwan   253
    Pei-Chia Lan

    COMMENTARIES

11 Asian Diasporas, and Yet . . .   279
    David Palumbo-Liu

12 Beyond "Asian Diasporas"   285
    Ien Ang

    List of Contributors   291
    Index   295

Acknowledgments

PEOPLE OFTEN SAY that putting together an edited volume can be a nightmare, with so many people involved and with the supposed lackluster sales that has kept many publishers away from committing to such projects. We are fortunate that our experience has been exactly the opposite. First, we had wonderful contributors, none of whom missed the deadline either for the first or second round of revisions. Second, we immediately found a very supportive press at Stanford University, which we have both worked with in our own previous projects. Finally, we could not have found a better partnership in working on this volume.

Our collaboration was incredibly productive, intellectually stimulating, and most of all, pleasurable. We shared the work equally. We each read every chapter of the volume repeatedly and commented on each of them. Our introduction shifted hands dozens of times as we each revised, conversed, reformulated, and rewrote multiple drafts. It was truly a shared endeavor. The process of working together was not at all difficult, perhaps because we have a longstanding friendship that began many years ago during our freshman year of college at the University of California, Berkeley. Our intellectual exchange formally began in a seminar with Trinh T. Minh-ha on the Politics of Difference in spring 1991. This class fundamentally shaped us, as years later we are completing this project that brings together disparate experiences and builds a framework of alliance across those differences.

This project emerged from a panel entitled "Asian Diasporas" at the Asian Studies Association meeting in San Diego in 2003. We initially organized this panel to put into conversation scholars working on various contemporary migratory movements in various parts of the world. We were delighted that the panel received a warm reception at the conference, with senior scholars and publishers encouraging us to produce a volume on this topic. Building on our preliminary presentations and discussions at the conference, this volume addresses the question of similar racial displacements among different ethnic groups from Asia across geographical space. We have included all the papers of the panel in this volume, along with other essays that showcase a diverse range of Asian diasporic experiences. Included in the latter category are Evelyn Hu-DeHart's essay, previously published in Arif Dirlik's, *What is in a Rim? Citical Perspectives on the Pacific Region Idea* (1998), and Lok Siu's essay previously published in Chapter 2 of *Memories of a Future Home* (SUP 2005). The first group we would like to thank, then, is the contributors to this volume. Without their scholarship, this book would not have been possible. In particular, we appreciate their heroic effort at always getting their materials to us in a prompt and professional manner.

In addition to the individual contributors, conversations with many people have helped us develop the theoretical framework of this book. We want to thank Celine Parreñas Shimizu, David Eng, Vicente Rafael, Juno Parreñas, and students from Lok Siu and Aisha Khan's fall 2006 graduate seminar on "Comparative Diasporas." We are grateful to Evelyn Hu-DeHart for giving us the opportunity to formally present our ideas for this project at the Freeman Center at Wesleyan University in spring 2006. The Center for Gender Studies at Ochanomizu University in Tokyo provided institutional support. The staff at New York University's Department of Social and Cultural Analysis also provided administrative assistance.

Our editor, Kate Wahl, deserves special thanks. Her sustained investment in and commitment to this project kept us going as we revised and reformulated the theoretical foundation of this book. She guided us through the timely completion of the volume. To put it simply, she was "on top of it" always. Additionally, the production of this book benefited immensely from the editorial assistance of Kirsten Oster and Margaret Pinette at Stanford University Press and the research assistance of Pauline Chu and Rachel Ferrer at the University of California, Davis. Pauline Chu's amazing management skills kept this project together during its production stage. We are also grateful for the readers' reports that gave us constructive comments for further developing our introduction.

Finally, we want to thank Andre Bertrand, who tolerated our hours-long conversations with the utmost patience and support a partner could ever give, and also Aisha Khan and Malou Babilonia for their steadfast friendship.

RSP and LCDS
New York City, NY

Asian Diasporas

Introduction: Asian Diasporas— New Conceptions, New Frameworks

Rhacel Salazar Parreñas and Lok C. D. Siu

DIASPORA, TRANSNATIONALISM, AND GLOBALIZATION have become central issues of our time (Cohen 1997; Kearney 1995; Safran 1991; Sassen 1996; Toloyan 1991). While they are historical processes that reach back more than five hundred years, their reemergence in popular and academic discourse in recent decades addresses the dramatic transformations of the last quarter of the twentieth century—transformations brought about by incredible technological and communication developments; global political and economic shifts characterized by the end of the cold war; the adoption of neoliberal policies and principles of deregulation, privatization, and marketization; and both the increase and extensive reach of global migration. While it is impossible to discuss any one of these terms without referencing the others, it is equally untenable to address all of them at once. This book takes diaspora as its central problematic. Given that much has been written on this concept, it is likely that we hold different understandings of diaspora. We begin, then, with a working definition (which we will further elaborate throughout this chapter). We define *diaspora* as an ongoing and contested process of subject formation embedded in a set of cultural and social relations that are sustained simultaneously with the "homeland" (real or imagined), place of residence, and compatriots or coethnics dispersed elsewhere. More precisely, we view the experience of diaspora as entailing (1) displacement from the homeland under the nexus of an unequal global political and economic system;[1] (2) the simultaneous experience of alienation and the maintenance of affiliation to both the country of residence and the homeland; and finally (3) the sense of collective consciousness and connectivity with other people displaced from

1

the homeland across the diasporic terrain. Necessary in sustaining these simultaneous relations are everyday practices of sociality, collective memory, economic exchange, and the work of cultural imagination and production, to name a few.

Using Asian diasporas as the organizing framework of this book, we invite the reader to explore with us the linkages, disjunctures, and contradictions among different ethnic groups that claim Asia as their site of dispersal, real or imagined. In doing so, we encourage critical and constructive dialogue about the relevance, usefulness, and pitfalls of using the concept of Asian diasporas. Let us state from the outset that this is not some kind of master narrative we seek to promote but rather an experiment in assessing the intellectual and political potential of such a concept. As a theoretical tool, Asian diasporas should be treated as an open and flexible framework that is inductively formulated and, therefore, always being produced and revised with new research findings.

Our goal for this book is simple. We want to make an argument for Asian diasporas as an intellectual and political project. Extending current debates on diaspora, we make three interventions. By bringing together a collection of historical and ethnographic studies, we underscore diaspora as human experience, first and foremost, and emphasize the value of examining the relationship between larger social structures and people's everyday lives. While much of the literature on diaspora has been primarily theory focused, this volume offers important insight into how people experience, interpret, and give meaning to diaspora.

Second, we broaden current discussions of Asian diasporas by including mostly new research by emerging scholars and selecting essays that offer a different geographical coverage than is conventionally found in either Asian or Asian American studies. It is not altogether coincidental that while the re-emergence of diaspora studies in the late 1980s has brought Asian and Asian American studies closer together, discussions of diaspora within these two fields have focused primarily on the relationship between Asia and Asian America. To expand our field of vision, we highlight works that explore sites outside the United States. Asian migration, after all, has always been global, and it has become even more so in the past few decades. Our point is to make visible and give voice to communities that, because they fall outside the privileged discourses of and about the United States and Asia and therefore also Asian American and Asian studies, would otherwise be left unacknowledged or, at best, given only a customary nod. We suggest that the framework of Asian diasporas offers a rare but sorely needed opportunity for communities in marginalized or intersectional areas of study to assert their presence.

Finally, we further disrupt the tendency in Asian and Asian American studies to think of diaspora solely in binary terms of homeland and place of residence. The concept of Asian diasporas we propose entails comparative analysis on two scales concurrently: the place-specific / cross-ethnic (e.g., racialization of Indonesians and Filipinos in Taiwan) and the ethnic-specific / transnational (e.g., racialization of Chinese in Nicaragua and Panama). This two-prong approach will provide us with the means to compare not only the specific conflicts, negotiations, and solidarities that form in different locations but also how they shift and reconfigure when examined through the transnational frame. Asian diasporas facilitate analysis of interlocking relationships that are at once local, national, and transnational. It seeks to explore global connections from different angles.

Situating Diaspora in Asian American Studies

Diasporas, as phenomena and experience, are centuries old. However, diaspora, as an analytical category of discussion and debate, only gained significance in Asian American studies in the early 1990s. A combination of factors converged at this historical juncture to enable this to happen. To a large extent, demographic shifts in the Asian American population combined with technological advancements and global economic changes made the concept of diaspora particularly meaningful to the study of Asian America. Since the 1965 Immigration Reform Act, the Asian American constituency has shifted steadily from a primarily American-born population to a mostly foreign-born one. The legislation was also class biased, so that aside from those coming into the United States as political refugees or for family reunification, it favored skilled and educated immigration applicants. Intersecting with developments in communication technologies, especially the Internet and all its associated services, these post-1965 immigrants and their descendents were the first group that was truly able to sustain communication on a regular and timely basis with relatives and friends dispersed in Asia and other parts of the world.[2] By the 1990s, this demographic shift in Asian American college- and university-level student bodies had become increasingly apparent, and the area of Asian American studies was confronted with the challenge of making the field relevant to them. Diaspora, which offers a framework to study relations among the adopted home, the ethnic homeland, and geographically dispersed coethnics, provided a meaningful way to address the experiences of this new student body and population.

The end of the cold war, along with celebratory proclamations of a more interconnected world and increasingly porous national borders, ushered in questions about the established approaches of area studies, which had separated the world into neat, bounded regions (Appadurai 1986; Guyer 2004). Conferences were convened to explore possible new paradigms that would be more appropriate to study this changed world environment[3] (Ford Foundation 1999). These global political and economic shifts, then, were also played out in the academy. The once well-funded area studies were faced with budget cuts. (This was the trend until after September 11, 2001, when government funding once again poured into the study of select world regions.) Faced with changing times, both intellectually and materially, Asian studies were compelled to redefine their research agendas. Meanwhile, the second wave of ethnic studies movements in the 1990s mobilized for the formation of Asian American studies in universities in the Midwest and on the East Coast. In response, many institutions adopted the Asian–Asian American studies model. The study of diaspora and transnationalism served as the theoretical framework that facilitated the coming together of these two previously antagonistic fields of study.

By the mid-1990s, the combination of all these factors led to the predominance of diaspora and transnational approaches in Asian American studies. Of course, Asian American studies were not the only ones affected. Diaspora —along with discussions about the future of the nation-state, the effects and processes of transnationalism, and the porosity of borders and boundaries —became the central concern of the time across the social sciences and humanities disciplines as well as in ethnic studies. And with any paradigm shift, there was also tremendous unease and skepticism.

In Asian American studies, a number of scholars raised critical questions about this theoretical crossroads (Dirlik 1999). However, no one articulates the concerns of the field better than literary scholar Sau-ling Wong. Her 1995 article served as a wake-up call to Asian Americanists about the possible pitfalls of what she has coined the "denationalization" of Asian American studies, or the displacement of the United States as the field's proper unit of analysis. Pointing to what she saw to be an uncritical shift toward the adoption of the diasporic approach at the expense of the domestic U.S. focus, Wong was concerned about the intellectual and political implications of this shift. At a time when most scholars willfully adopted the concept of diaspora, Wong asked some halting questions: What would be gained by denationalizing Asian American studies or broadening the scope of analysis beyond the U.S. nation-state? How would adopting a diasporic approach that takes ethnicity as the common denominator affect the U.S.-based, panethnic (i.e., shared racialization) agenda that has long defined Asian American studies?

To a large extent, the project of Asian American studies, both as an area of study and as a social movement, has been defined around the practice of claiming America as home and asserting Asian belonging in the United States. It seeks to build a panethnic coalition based on shared experiences of racialization in the United States. Inarguably, studies of transnational processes and diasporic formations inherently call into question the boundedness of the nation-state, and by extension, they also challenge the United States as the privileged site of analysis. This, of course, strikes at the core of how the field has defined itself. According to Wong, taking a diasporic approach, with its ethnic-specific premise and homeward gaze, actually threatens the panethnic coalition-building spirit of Asian American studies. Taking it one step further, she suggested that the diasporic perspective may lead to the disembodiment of Asian American constituents, diffusing their political potential as a people who claim America as home and whose political commitments should be locally and nationally defined.

As Asian Americanists, we are very much invested in the coalition-building project of the field and therefore also mindful of Wong's incisive cautionary insights. At the same time, our disciplinary training in anthropology (Siu) and sociology (Parreñas) cultivated our particular understanding of diaspora, which is ethnographically grounded and historically informed. Moreover, both of us were greatly influenced by British cultural studies approaches, which emphasized diaspora as a political positioning and identification (Hall 1990) as well as a process of constructing links based on shared history and experience among geographically dispersed diasporic communities (Gilroy 1987, 1993). Similarly, we were informed by political economic approaches that emphasized the structural and material effects compelling migrations as well as by ethnographic approaches that focused on people's everyday lives and interpretations. As we pursued our own research projects that centrally engaged the framework of diaspora and that, in fact, were made possible by the growing interest in this approach, we came to a different conclusion than Wong about the limitations and potentials of diaspora studies. What led to our divergent conclusions, we suggest, is our understanding of what diasporic analysis entails and what it can bring to Asian American studies.

Within Asian American studies, diaspora has been used primarily to refer to ties and relationships between Asians in the United States and their respective ethnic homelands in Asia. Diaspora research in this field, therefore, has focused on this binary relationship between homeland and place of settlement. As mentioned above, this focus on Asia–Asian American relations emerged at a time when the disciplinary borders between Asian and Asian American studies were becoming more porous (see, for instance, Chuh and Shimakawa 2001). Diaspora provided an intellectual framework that both facilitated and legitimated their coming together as one institutional program or department. Given the history of antagonism between the two fields—one founded by cold war imperatives and the other by student activism—not only was their institutional relationship fraught with ideological tension and looked upon with suspicion but (for many) so was the concept that facilitated their merging. The entry of diaspora approaches into Asian American studies, then, was quite contested.

To date, the emphasis on homeland–Asian American ties still dominate discourses of diaspora in Asian American studies. This certainly keeps our field of vision narrowly focused on ethnic ties between two locations, Asia and the United States. We wish to expand that field of vision by proposing Asian diasporas as a research agenda that encourages not only ethnic-specific studies of ties between the homeland and place of settlement and ties among geographically dispersed communities but also comparative analysis of different ethnic diasporas, both in terms of their two sets of ties and in terms of their interaction with one another in specific locations. This involves both ethnic-specific / geographically dispersed and place-specific / comparative ethnic research. Moreover, it does not restrict investigation among ethnic Asians but also between Asians and other racial groups, including blacks, Latinos, and indigenous peoples. What the study of Asian diasporas aspires to do is articulate an intellectual and political agenda that makes possible the forging of not only locally and nationally based alliances but also translocal and transnational coalitions across the globe. Doing so, we emphasize, does not mean the elision of tensions, inequalities, and conflicts but rather the confrontation of those issues with the goal of achieving social equality.

We suggest that the framework of Asian diasporas, as we define it, does not necessarily threaten or contradict the coalitional spirit of Asian American studies. We argue, instead, that it helps extend it. The study of Asian diasporas, we suggest, offers a synthetic approach that brings together the important lessons learned from the nation-based, panethnic framework and the potential links offered by the diaspora approach. To a certain degree, our proposal to join these two approaches is not completely new. In fact, the Asian American studies movement of the late 1960s and early 1970s framed the institutionalization of Asian American studies as an effort toward self-determination that rejected both American colonialism in Asia and internal colonialism of Asian Americans in the United States. It articulated a transnational politics that underscored their interconnected experience of racialization, exploitation, and colonial violence. It is in this same spirit of seeking dialogue and mutual exploration and understanding that this volume is created. Without overdefining the term and thereby restricting its flexibility as a theoretical tool, this chapter, and more generally this book, provides a working definition of what we mean by Asian diasporas.

Defining Asian Diasporas

In proposing the concept of Asian diasporas, we recognize that not all Asian migrations are diasporic in nature; we do not presume that all Asians living outside of their so-called homelands have a diasporic sensibility, take a diasporic position, or assume a diasporic identity. For instance, some migrants—people who physically relocated from one area to another regardless of their settlement—are better described not as diasporic but as transnational because they maintain relations only to the home and host societies and do not share a connection or history with compatriots living in other locales[4] (Basch, Schiller, and Blanc 1994). Others may choose to adopt a singular national identity and reject the double consciousness or dual identification inherent in diasporic living (Gilroy 1993). As such, we do not claim the formation of an all-encompassing or singular Asian diaspora that is universal in scope and relevance to Asian migratory experiences. To do so would be to deny the multiplicity of experience and to make meaningless the very category we seek to define. In other words, we are *not* proposing a panethnic Asian diaspora but rather insist on referring to Asian diasporas in the plural. This is to underscore the multiple and varied formations of Asian diasporas as well as the fragmentation of ethnicity, gender, race, nation, sexuality, and class in and across diasporas.[5] Hence, diasporic connections do not universally include the entire globe but instead are composed of fragmented, multiple connections that emerge from historically specific conditions.

Consequently, our discussion of diasporas does not disregard the ethnic differences and conflicts that mar relations in Asia. We are deeply aware of the unequal relations within and between nation-states as well as the historical and contemporary conflicts in this region. We therefore avoid constructing Asia as a homogeneous homeland. (Wong 1995). In fact, given the active manner in which some Asian states pursue their respective diasporas, as with the cases of Taiwan, Japan, Korea, India, and the Philippines, it is impossible to imagine Asia as existing as a singular homogenized continental homeland for all Asians. In promoting diasporic identifications, each state reconstructs its own distinct historical narrative and uses culturally specific discourses and practices to arouse and bolster sentiments of ethnic belonging and loyalty. For instance, and as illustrated in essays in this volume, the Philippines bolsters the masculinity of Filipino men to promote the global dispersion of its seafarers (Chapter 2); Korea has begun to embrace its once rejected crop of Korean adoptees as their own children (Chapter 7); and Japan assumes an essential notion of culture when limiting its low-wage migrant workforce to coethnic Nikkei-jin (Chapter 9).

Indeed, the last two decades of the twentieth century witnessed an intensification of efforts by certain Asian homeland states to reach out to their diasporas for political, economic, and labor support. For instance, while mainland China has called upon its diaspora for economic contributions to strengthen the Chinese nation (Louie 2004), Taiwan has reached out for political support in its efforts to establish sovereignty (Siu 2005a, 2005b). Meanwhile, India has instituted the Non-Resident Indian status to encourage diasporic economic investment in India, and Japan has recruited its diaspora in Latin America for labor resources (Lesser 2003; Linger 2001; Raj 2003; Roth 2002; Shukla 2003; Tsuda 2003). The active role of Asian states in producing and sustaining diasporic connections and identifications with their respective homelands is perhaps the single most important factor that distinguishes Asian diasporas from most other diasporas (Israel being a notable exception).

Despite our epistemological construction of Asian diasporas, we also recognize the danger of reiterating Asia as a singular unit bounded by conventions of geographical proximity and cultural-racial sameness. Indeed, we are profoundly aware of the internal differences, antagonisms, and hierarchies that exist within Asia. Yet, without ignoring them, we understand Asia to be a homogenizing category that is historically produced through a set of discourses and imaginaries and whose parameters have been drawn and redrawn by the shifting agendas of various intellectual and political projects (Said

1978). While there is no singular or uncontested version of what Asia represents, the dominant perception of Asia still evokes a set of orientalized images and concerns. We cannot deny the legibility of Asia as a recognizable geographical region and "Asianness" as the cultural component in both popular imagination and academic discourse. Moreover, the conflation of place, culture, and race continues to persist: even as people move from Asia, they cannot be disassociated from being Asian. Asian diasporas, hence, call attention to the racializing-gendering process involved in diaspora making. As much as Asia has been constructed as a distinct "oriental other" against which the neoliberal West has defined itself (Chuh and Shimakawa 2001), we insist that *Asia* also serves as a powerful term of identification against the West. Hence, our intention in using Asian diasporas as the organizing framework is strategic. While the word *Asian* in Asian diasporas forces us to think critically about the racializing-gendering processes involved in diaspora making, *diasporas*—in its plural form—insist that we examine the links and disjunctures within and between this assemblage of collectivities. What we want to accomplish in this volume, then, is to facilitate two sets of comparative analysis at once: the place-specific, cross-ethnic study of how racializing-gendering processes affect different diasporic groups in one location, and the transnational relations and interactions among the geographically dispersed communities of each diaspora. Taking this dual approach moves us beyond the denationalization debate that situates the national in opposition to the diasporic. This volume seeks to formulate a new politics that is informed by transnational connections while recognizing the specific disciplinary regimes of local-national emplacement.

While it is important to examine the constantly shifting discursive formation of Asia in relation to the West, it is not enough to stop there. To fully grasp the production of Asian diasporas, we also emphasize the uneven political and economic relations that have formed between Asia and the West, as well as within Asia, and discuss their implications in facilitating Asian emigration as well as in shaping the conditions of their displacement. Again, we understand Asia to be tremendously diverse, embodying different cultural histories and political economic realities. What we want to emphasize is that as much as Asia, as imagined construct, has occupied a critical place in the West, so too has Asia as political and economic territory.

A quick glance at the colonial history of Asia will show its significance as prized territory of numerous resources. It is worth reminding that, almost all territories in Asia[6] have been subjected to various forms and degrees of

Western colonialism, and in fact some places have been colonized more than once. The British, Dutch, French, Portuguese, Spanish, and Americans all had colonized different parts of Asia, extracting natural resources and facilitating labor migrations from the region. As illustrated in Evelyn Hu-DeHart's (Chapter 1) seminal piece on the history of Chinese labor migration to Latin America, European colonialism was the main medium through which migrations, indentured and otherwise, dispersed from Asia to elsewhere in the world. Some went as indentured laborers to other colonized territories: hundreds of thousands of Chinese laborers were taken to Cuba and Peru in the late nineteenth century, and the same was true for Indians sent to Trinidad, Guyana, and Surinam. For the most part, despite the end of formal colonialism, the unequal relations between Asia and the West prevail, albeit with some exceptions and appearing in different forms and guises. These relations continue to be reflected in contemporary Asian migrations. An aim of this volume is to examine the historical threads and divergences between the earlier migrations of the nineteenth century with those of the twentieth century. What are the specific political and economic conditions that frame these different migrations? And what are the cultural and social factors that compel and enable the production of diasporic identifications? The essays in this volume offer multiple answers to these questions while illustrating the diasporic processes shared by Asian migrant groups across time and space. They also illustrate the dialectic relationship between structures that frame diasporas and the efforts of diasporic subjects to construct ties to more than one place and culture.

In studying diasporic processes rather than treating diaspora as a stable object, this volume seeks to establish bases of cross-national and cross-ethnic alliances for marginalized migrants. While it may be true that Asian diasporas emphasize ethnic-specific identifications, it does not preclude other forms of identification. Contrary to the idea that the transnational ethnic-specific focus of diaspora loses sight of cross-racial politics (Wong 1995), we insist there is nothing inherent in diasporic identifications that prevents the formation of broader political alliances. It does not have to be one or the other, but both forms of collective identification can coexist. In fact, we suggest that diasporic consciousness and identifications emerge and grow stronger from local processes of racialization, be it in the form of exclusion or affirmation. It is a strategy of resistance, though we recognize that it may not always have a progressive agenda. Recognizing diaspora as resistance offers a basis for examining larger structures of domination at work. Herein lies the potential for mobilizing cross-ethnic and cross-racial political alliance. Like other forms of identity—be it racial, gender, or national—diasporic identity "comes out of very specific historical formations, out of very specific histories and cultural repertoires of enunciation, that it can constitute a 'positionality'" (Stuart Hall 1996: 502). Using diaspora as a means of investigating these histories comparatively offers the possibility of articulating a larger collective positioning and politics.

Lastly, we insist on the epistemology of Asian diasporas in order to situate various diasporic formations in the world system that ties nations in a relationship of unequal dependency, especially in relation to the West. The notion of Asian diasporas underscores the global and engenders the development of a multinational collective politics of Asianness that accordingly acknowledges inequalities between nation-states. Moreover, reminiscent of Caren Kaplan and Inderpal Grewal's (1991) idea of scattered hegemonies, this concept underscores the shared displacement of migrant exclusion that various Asian migrants encounter in different local contexts across varying locations. In other words, we use the rubric of diaspora to emphasize the similar experiences of exclusion in multiple domestic contexts across nations. To give a few examples, the psychic injuries of displacement from the homeland described by Tobias Hübinette (Chapter 7) of Korean adoptees resonates, for instance, with Sharmila Sen's (Chapter 6) want for a cultural authenticity long lost by the transformations forced by geographical displacement. Similarly, experiences of national exclusion are shared but operate differently, for instance, socioeconomically or culturally. While Takeyuki Tsuda (Chapter 9) speaks about the double displacement of being cultural outsiders experienced by Japanese Brazilians in Japan and Brazil, national exclusion is illustrated socioeconomically by Pei Chia Lan (Chapter 10). Specifically, she illustrates how the exclusion of provisional migrants in Taiwan minimizes their wages and labor bargaining power. In so doing, she demonstrates how the operation of global capitalism depends on the erection of borders. Nationalism is at the heart of diasporic displacements. As such, our reference to diaspora is not a mere acknowledgment of the transnational forces that shape race relations but instead include the local manifestations of social inequalities such as racism and xenophobia.[7] Moreover, our project distinguishes those Asians who can move, especially to the West, from Asians who are left immobile by the forces of global capitalism and those who choose not to move because of their privileged access to global capitalism. Hence, we do not wish to establish the sameness in experiences of Asians in relation to global capitalism and instead maintain the distinction between those Asians located in Asia to Asians in the West.[8]

The Making of Diasporas

Being diasporic is "to know [one's homeland and place of residence] intimately, but [neither be] wholly of either place" (Hall 1996: 490). It is this process of continual displacement that serves as our springboard to categorically situate Asian migrations under the rubric of diasporas. Our point of comparison, hence, does not begin with a search for diasporic "origins." Being diasporic is not a static, monolithic identity, nor does it denote an unchanging past or some kind of preserved ethnicity or primordial essence that needs to be rediscovered or untapped. This perspective assumes that diasporas exist in a vacuum removed from external forces and protected from social, economic, and cultural transformations. In our view, being diasporic requires continual reproduction of certain conditions and identifications. The essays in the volume illustrate this process well from the turn to Vietnam for brides by diasporic Vietnamese men confronting the rise in nontraditional dual wage-earning households in the West to the use of religious rituals from the homeland by economically subjugated Hindi and Muslims in Trinidad and Tobago. In going home, however, diasporic subjects do not excavate an authentic ethnic self but instead reproduce cultures in inevitably altered forms.

Our approach to understanding Asian diasporas, then, is to focus on the *making* of diasporas and the *experience* of diasporization. Thus, essays in this volume highlight the multiple forms of displacement that cause diasporization, including political economic inequities in the globe, social inequalities in multiple host and origin societies, and cultural barriers that impede belonging to the place diasporic Asians inhabit and the place they call homeland. These processes of marginalization are the underlying threads that tie the multiple diasporic communities we present in this volume.

Hence, we establish the triadic relationship that captures the essence of diasporic experiences by illustrating the efforts of diasporic subjects to reproduce their connections to more than one place and culture in the context of various systems and forces of local and global inequalities. In other words, this volume explicitly addresses both the marginalizing factors as well as the liberating aspects of diaspora as it illustrates the making of diasporas in the actions of subjects. Rather than treating diaspora merely as a form of identification, this volume also draws out the sociopolitical and material conditions that produce, sustain, and perpetuate diasporic formations. For instance, we stress that the diasporic condition is produced by the partial belonging of subjects to both their place of residence and the homeland, and more specifically by the displacement caused by their placement outside the logic of the racially and culturally homogenous and territorially bounded nation-state.[9] In this sense, we view diaspora as much more than a cultural identity; rather, it is as is racism a condition of living in displacement. It is as much an embodied experience as it is a way of understanding one's personhood.

In the past two decades, diaspora has served as a liberatory concept to refute one's subordinate status as "ethnic minority" and second-class citizen in the host nation (Ang 2001; Gilroy 1987). To be part of a diaspora is to reference one's relationship and belonging to some larger historical cultural-political formation—a people, a culture, a civilization—that transgresses national borders. It is a way of reformulating one's minoritized position by asserting one's full belonging elsewhere. It seeks to redefine the terms of belonging. In focusing on its liberating potential, however, scholars of diaspora have often deemphasized the negative and confining aspects of diasporic identification. This volume offers a corrective to this tendency and insists on examining the marginalizing forces that work to produce and sustain diasporic formations. As described earlier, racism and xenophobia are two such marginalizing forces that impede the full belonging of diasporic groups not only in their place of settlement but also in their place of origin. This is, for instance, illustrated in Tsuda's vivid illustration of the cultural in-between space inhabited by Japanese Brazilians. They neither fully belong in Japan nor in Brazil. Similarly, Korean political leaders during the Japanese occupation experienced a similar double displacement from *place*. As Richard Kim (Chapter 8) illustrates, they were displaced from political participation and representation not only in the homeland but also from host societies that only recognized the government of the occupying force of Japan. Such displacements tell us that being diasporic is not always a matter of choice.

Consequently, we emphasize the exclusionary practices that confront migrants upon settlement and the alternative forms of belonging and community that they inspire. Sociologist Yasmin Soysal fears that the reduction of migrant identity to "ethnic arrangements, transactions, and belongings" in diaspora could disregard the affiliation of migrants to the host society (2000: 13). Not in disagreement with Soysal, we believe that migrants *always* experience a process of acculturation and belonging to their host societies. However, acculturation does not necessarily occur in opposition to diasporization. Ien Ang similarly notes, "Migrants always inevitably undergo a process of cross-cultural translation when they move from one place to another, from one regime of language and culture to another . . . But the process of cultural translation is not a straightforward and teleological one: from the 'old' to the 'new'" (2001: 4). The routine of everyday life and daily interactions propel the hybrid, syncretic, and uneven formation of migrant cultures and identities that mixes old and new. Our approach to Asian diasporas, then, is not concerned with excavating the old or reconstructing diasporic subjects' one-sided relationship with the homeland. Instead, we are interested in how shifting configurations of power and resistance in the local impel and enable alternative imaginaries and practices of belonging in displacement.

Thus, we consider how strained relations with the host society could engender diasporic consciousness. For instance, the underclass may reclaim their loss status via return migration, while those integrated to ethnic economies could potentially maximize capitalist accumulation by acquiring multiple passports, and likewise those who assimilate into the dominant spaces of the middle class may increase their cultural cache by leading a cosmopolitan lifestyle that cannot exist without their contacts within the diaspora.[10] We do not view diasporas and immigration to be mutually exclusive categories of settlement, but instead note that similar to the transmigrants, migrants with the resources to do so are those who may opt to lead more diasporic lives so as to smoothen their process of "assimilation" or more accurately integration— whether permanent or temporary—in their particular host society. Thus, we insist on the conceptualization of Asian diasporas to underscore not only the marginal inclusion experienced by Asian migrants in various local contexts but also the way they utilize diasporas to resist their experience of marginal inclusion. At the same time, and as noted earlier, we recognize the subaltern who is without resources to cross or align across borders. We therefore give emphasis to the resources that enable diasporic subjects to cross borders.

Diasporic Condition in Relation to Home

Essays in this volume illustrate the ongoing social relations, memories and imaginaries, and cultural production of diasporic Asians that construct multiple links to places, cultures, and communities. In so doing, they bring out the tensions that underlie notions of home in diasporas. Indeed, the question of home serves not only as a source of anxiety but also as a site of creativity and refuge. It is both a place one left behind and a place one currently inhabits. "Home" is situated in both as well as somewhere in between. Being diasporic involves the simultaneous *affiliation* and *disidentification* with both the place one occupies and "back home." These two seemingly contradictory forms of relating to home, in fact, emerge from and are constituted by the *marginal inclusion* of diasporic subjects to both places. While affiliation and disidentification reference the affective and subjective experiences of diasporic people, marginal inclusion describes the external factors that shape their partial incorporation into society.

Working in tandem, the marginal inclusion in and affiliation / disidentification with the place of residence and homeland help perpetuate and reproduce the continual displacement of diasporic subjects from home. Migrants negotiate a different set of social structures and experience a distinct racializing process in varying historical-local contexts. Their experiences of migration and settlement shift according to a number of factors. To name a few, migration policies, the make-up of the ethnic community, and the labor market structure that awaits them (Portes and Rumbaut 1996) all play roles in the process of settlement. Indeed, it is one's positioning in the local that helps define one's relationship to an "elsewhere." Usually, diasporic affiliation to homeland (real or imagined) is very much inspired by the disidentification with the host society. They index the tensions, anxieties, and desires of asserting full belonging somewhere. In other words, diasporic affiliations to homeland are part of the process of constructing a new home in a place that one cannot fully (yet) call home.

Referring to more than just the forced dispersal of peoples from "home"-lands, diasporas have come to refer also to the dual affiliation and loyalty that migrants and their descendents maintain to the places they occupy and "back home" (Lavie and Swedenburg 1996). Yet, as the essays in this volume show, being diasporic involves not only being connected to more than one place at once, but it is also a positioning. More specifically, diasporic subjects often express feelings of *situated loyalties*. By this we refer to how migrants express a greater sense of affinity and loyalty to the place from which they are geographically displaced and which provides the imaginary space of an idealized home. Yet, this imaginary space is always in flux and changing, and it can represent more than one place. For instance, an Indonesian Chinese in Australia could construct home as both China and Indonesia (Ang 2001). A

Japanese Brazilian may feel more Japanese in Brazil and more Brazilian in Japan (Tsuda, Chapter 9 in this volume). Similarly, a Filipina domestic worker in Hong Kong continuously longs to return to the Philippines but comes "home" only to hasten her return to Hong Kong (Constable 1999). As Constable describes, she is perpetually in a state of being "at home but not at home" (Ibid.). Home is what diasporic subjects yearn to locate but from which they are continuously displaced by the dual processes of migration and marginal inclusion.

The essays in this volume speak to one another in dynamic and multifaceted ways, but five major themes emerge as critical axes that connect and cut across the essays in this collection. They include the recognition of inter-Asian strife in past and present; the persistence of the nation state; the salience of race, ethnicity, gender, and sexuality; the forces of labor, colonialism, and globalization that maintain relations of inequality within Asia as well as Asia in relation to the West; and the centrality of culture. By discussing each of these separately, we bring the essays into creative tension and conversation with one another.

Inter-Asian Strife and Conflict   Although we strategically use Asia as a shared point of origin that brings together various diasporic formations, this volume neither ignores differences and tensions between Asians nor disregards the uneven political and economic relations within Asia. Inequities that mar ties within Asia do not engender the formation of an Asian diaspora but instead produce discrete diasporic movements and communities of Asian ethnic groups and nationalities. These inequities include but are not limited to Japan's colonization of Korea, the Philippines, and parts of China; the displacement of ethnic Chinese from Malaysia and Indonesia; political and economic inequities between the economic tigers of the region and the still underdeveloped economies in Southeast Asia; and the unequal flows of goods and labor that tie richer and poorer nations in the region.

Various chapters in this volume, although not all, illustrate how the category of Asian diasporas does not overlook the conflicts, competitions, conquests, and dominations that shape relations between various Asian groups in the past and present. For instance, Pei-Chia Lan's important discussion of the political status of foreign domestic workers shows how relations of economic inequality in the Asian region plays out in the restrictive border policies that Taiwan imposes on the migrant workers whose labor they need from Indonesia and the Philippines. Not exclusive to Taiwan, other host societies in Asia

including Japan, Singapore, and Hong Kong impose similar restrictive policies on temporary labor migrants *within* the region. As much as political economic inequities do, the history of colonization between modern nations of
Asia also jars the possible formation of cross-national alliances among Asians.
Inter-Asian colonization engenders diaspora as it figures prominently in the
formation of diasporic identities. For example, Richard Kim's lucid discussion of the political activities of Korean farm workers in California and their
rejection of their political status as Japanese nationals brings to the forefront
inter-Asian conflicts as it questions the idea of the singular formation of an
Asian diaspora.

Finally, as Steven McKay's (Chapter 2) essay demonstrates, the state actively promotes ethnic-national distinction between Filipinos and other
seafarers. By emphasizing their ability to speak English and their American-
standard certification, the Phillippine state arms Filipinos with a competitive
advantage over seafarers of other nationalities, expecially Asian seafarers
who are their most direct competitors. (In his larger project, MacKay shows
how Filipino seafarers measure their masculinity against other Asians in the
sea trade—specifically Indians, compared with whom they view themselves
as more diligent, and Korean officers, whose authority they question by
mocking their poor command of the English language.) The state further distinguishes Filipino seafarers by ascribing certain "innately Filipino" qualities
to them, such as hard-working, harmonious, and compliant—qualities that
strongly appeal to shipowners. What we learn from McKay's research is that
the state actively promotes Filipino ethnic-national distinction in order to
fashion the most competitive seafaring laborers in the industry. This suggests
that interethnic and international competition within Asia (and beyond) is
alive and well.

The Persistence of the Nation-State   By now, a postnational world is hardly
imaginable. In place of earlier predictions that suggest the blurring of national
borders and the diminishing power of the state, we see instead the continuing,
if not increasing, significance of nationalism and the vitality of the state in re-
defining its citizens and national borders. Many of the essays in this volume
show the entangled relationship between the nation-state and diaspora. For
instance, Takeyuki Tsuda shows the contestation by Brazilian Japanese of the
ethnically homogeneous identity of Japan, which restricts its migrant labor
force to coethnics and encourages the "return" to Japan of diasporic subjects
but does not account for their distinct cultural practices and consequently the

cultural clashes engendered in their return. Steven McKay's discussion of Filipino seafarers clearly illustrates not just their self-construction as masculine
subjects but also how the Philippine state actively constructs Filipino men as
the ideal ethnomasculine subject for seafaring, thereby facilitating their participation in this global migrant labor market. The state, therefore, is directly
involved in encouraging the out-migration of its citizens via their entry into
the seafaring industry and the formation of this labor diaspora.

Playing out a contrasting scenario, the Taiwanese state in Pei-Chia Lan's
study is involved in the production of diaspora from a different angle. By in-
stituting stricter policies against provisional labor migrants, who are entering
Taiwan in response to heightened labor demands, Taiwan is in effect creating
the paradoxical condition in which labor migration is encouraged at the same
time that full political integration of these migrants is made impossible. This
condition inspires a mode of diasporic formation that is based on economically inspired migration combined with politically restricted settlement. This
contradiction of "partial citizenship" (Parreñas 2001) in their lives tells us
that "a global market space is constrained by the territorialized regulations of
both sending and receiving governments." Moreover, the increase of migrant
labor has also contributed to the rise of Taiwanese nationalism, one that defines its national identity and character against this group of ethnically and
class-marked "other."

From a different perspective, Richard Kim shows how diasporic Koreans
exercise "long-distance nationalism" (Glick-Schiller and Fouron 2001) and
underscores that the diaspora, despite its geographical distance from the
ethnic homeland, still engages in political activities that help shape and determine the fate of the Korean nation-state. In fact, it is their collective participation in Korea's independence movement that gives rise to a distinct diasporic
Korean consciousness, one that inspires an enduring link to the homeland at
the same time recognizing one's displacement from it. Involvement in homeland nation building, then, has been crucial to the formation of the Korean
diaspora, both culturally and politically.

In the case of diasporic Chinese in Central America and Panama, Lok Siu
(Chapter 4) shows how their shared sense of being in diaspora (living outside
of China) is fractured by the very placedness of their national location, so that
even within the diaspora and despite their shared sense of being ethnically
Chinese, national difference matters. Not only do nations of residence shape
the manner in which diasporic Chinese subject formation is articulated, but

the unequal political and economic status of these nations in relation to one another also influences the differentiated power among diasporic Chinese to determine the cultural politics within the diaspora. Moreover, the homeland Chinese state, the Republic of China, in this case, plays a significant role in the diaspora. By cosponsoring the annual conventions in which the Chinese in this region come together, the homeland Chinese state ensures its influence in the social and cultural reproduction of the Chinese diaspora. The nation and the state, as all these articles underscore, are very much alive and kicking. More importantly, these articles help demystify how the nation and the state play an integral role in diasporic formation.

The Salience of Race, Ethnicity, Gender, and Sexuality   As Gupta and Ferguson (1992), among others, have pointed out, cultural difference has become even more prominent as the world moves toward greater interconnectedness. Far from being culturally homogenous, the world in fact is embedded in difference —racial, ethnic, gender, and sexual (among other axes of difference). Many of the essays illustrate not only how these differences are experienced intersectionally but also how they are central to processes of diaspora making. Displacement in diaspora is often experienced as marginality, second-class citizenship, or the lack of full belonging. These various experiences of marginalization are often mediated and facilitated by processes of racialization. In the case of Japanese Brazilians, Takeyuki Tsuda describes how their identities shift according to their racialization in the different local contexts of either Japan or Brazil. He demonstrates their "situated ethnic identities" by showing how Japanese Brazilian negotiate the different regimes of racialization and ethnicization as they migrate from Brazil to Japan. While their sense of identity in Brazil is largely defined by their Japanese ethnic difference, it is, to their surprise, their Brazilianness that places them in the margins of Japan and that they reclaim as their own cultural identity. Being diasporic, hence, requires constant negotiation of one's racial and ethnic identity in relation to places of settlement. Ethnic identities, he reminds us, are not only imposed but also actively constructed.

Addressing the performance of whiteness, Tobias Hübinette poignantly discusses the forced integration of Korean adoptees into pockets of white communities in the West. To the question of whether racialization affects the subject formation of transracial adoptees, Hübinette answers with a resounding "yes." Drawing on writings by Korean adoptees, he shows how their racial difference within the family and community has shaped their self-perception and their relationship to whiteness. Their sense of displacement from their ethnic homeland, Hübinette continues, has also had consequences on their psychic well-being. While adoptees have not been the conventional subject of diaspora studies, our intention in including the experiences of Korean adoptees in our analysis has to do with the way in which they articulate their shared sense of dispersal from Korea (their ethnic homeland) as well as their shared history and experience of displacement.

The intersectionality of ethnicity, gender, and sexuality emerges vividly in the essays of Hung Thai (Chapter 3), Steven McKay, and Lok Siu. Hung Thai looks at contemporary arranged marriages between Vietnamese men in the diaspora and women in Vietnam and shows how they negotiate gender, sexuality, and status within the homeland-diaspora framework. He shows how gender ideologies intersect with class to shape the cultural parameters defining marriage suitability. On another level, the gender configuration of these arranged marriages, in which the men from diaspora are seeking brides from the homeland, helps reinscribe the metaphor of gender relations between the feminine peripheral nation and the masculine metropole. Gender and sexuality, hence, operate on two registers in Thai's work.

As mentioned above, McKay directly addresses the state's mobilization of Filipino masculinity, an ethnically gendered and sexualized construction, in securing a place for Filipino men in the seafaring industry. In Siu's work, her examination of a beauty contest shows how the contestants embody, perform, and challenge idealized notions of diasporic Chinese femininity. Through their performances and the discussions that ensue, we come to see how race, ethnicity, gender, and sexuality intersect to determine the criteria for becoming queen of the diaspora.

The Forces of Labor, Colonialism, Globalization   As we noted earlier, it is impossible to discuss the formation of Asian diasporas without addressing their relationship to labor, colonialism, and globalization. All the essays in this volume either directly or indirectly speak to these issues. Evelyn Hu-DeHart challenges our understanding of Asian migration to the Americas in both historical timeline and geographical dispersion. She dates the earliest Asian community in the Americas in 1630's Mexico, and she documents the massive indentured labor migration of ethnic Chinese to Cuba and Peru in the mid to late nineteenth century. Of course, their migration was not limited to just these two countries but also the West Indies, Panama, Central America, and the United States. What Hu-DeHart captures are the twin forces of globalization and its insatiable demand for cheap labor. The history of the Chinese in Panama and Central America, then, must be understood within this historical context. The Chinese, however, were not the only Asians to play a central role in the expanding agricultural economies of the nineteenth century. Via British colonialism came people from the Indian subcontinent. Their indentured labor migration to the British West Indies provides the backdrop to the essays by Aisha Khan (Chapter 5) and Sharmila Sen. In fact, the legacies of colonialism are still palpable in the everyday lives of Indo-Trinidadians.

In the case of the Korean diaspora, we see that their transnational movement for Korean independence was thoroughly entwined with their rejection of Japanese colonization. On the other hand, American imperialism has also made its mark on the lives of not only the Filipinos—whose country was part of the American empire until World War II—but also the Korean adoptees—whose massive displacement occurred after the Korean War—and the Vietnamese—whose displacement was caused by the Vietnam War. Not to be lost is the way in which American intervention in Panama and Central America has caused decades of civil unrest and political instability throughout this region. In these examples, we see the shadow of American empire setting the basis for mass emigration and the formation of diasporas.

While it is important to recognize colonialism as a critical factor in the displacement of people, it is also essential to not stop there but to examine their enduring and divergent effects on the (trans-) formation of these diasporas. For instance, for the Korean adoptees and diasporic Vietnamese living in the United States, their idea of and relationship to "America" may not be so easily defined but may be filled with ambivalence and ambiguity.

If the labor migrations of the Chinese and Indians to the New World characterize mid-nineteenth-century globalization, then the transnational dispersal of Filipino laborers may very well epitomize late-twentieth-century globalization. As illustrated by Pei-Chia Lan's and Steven McKay's essays in this volume, as well as by Rhacel Parreñas's (2001) earlier work with domestic servants, Filipinos are quickly becoming the most visible migrant Asian workers in the global market. The case of Brazilian Japanese also offers an interesting twist in late-twentieth-century globalization. While the Japanese in the nineteenth century had encouraged emigration to the Americas, Japan is now finding itself in need of labor and has turned to diasporic Japanese in

Latin America to fulfill its domestic labor demands. The goal in recruiting diasporic Japanese labor was to minimize cultural conflict; the assumption was that diasporic Japanese share the same ethnic-racial and cultural characteristics as the Japanese in Japan. As Takeyuki Tsuda expertly shows, this was not the case. The "return" migration of Brazilian Japanese presents a complicated reworking of identity within this new labor context. As other essays in this volume also document, culture is constantly being made and remade.

The Centrality of Culture   We think of culture as a heuristic devise to examine a dimension of everyday life that "attends to situated and embodied difference" (Appadurai 1996, 13). Culture is not a laundry list of properties that make up a bundle we characterize as X culture or Y culture. It is not a thing but a process by which differences are mobilized to articulate boundaries between and within groups. It is a process that is ongoing, contested, and constantly changing; it involves negotiation, production, and transformation. This fluid and dynamic process of cultural production is prominently illustrated in the works of Sharmila Sen, Aisha Khan, Lok Siu, and Takeyuki Tsuda. Each traces the various and multifaceted ways in which the meaning of being in diaspora is actively constructed through memory and forgetting, performance, and ritual.

Sharmila Sen's essay asks how the Indian diaspora remembers; forgets; and reconstructs tastes, aromas, sentiments, and affiliations in the twenty-first century. She introduces the concept of diasporic amnesia as a way of thinking about the cultural rupture caused by displacement, a rupture that facilitates the production of diasporic culture based on remembering and forgetting, on continuity with the homeland and modification in the new context. Using the metaphor of "doubles," Sen elegantly captures the sameness and difference of diasporic cultural formation among geographically dispersed Indians. Their uncanny similarities of being part of the larger Indian diaspora exist alongside their distinct differences based on place and location. Diasporic cultural formation—both in cultural production, meaning, and affect as well as social affiliations and relations—is an ongoing process of negotiating between "here" and "there" and among the past, present, and future.

This theme of sameness and difference in diaspora (drawn from Stuart Hall's work) also emerges in Siu's discussion of the beauty contest of Chinese in Panama and Central America. In their performance of diasporic Chineseness, the contestants powerfully convey both their cultural similarities stemming from their shared history of displacement and their differences eminating from their particular local-national contexts. The beauty contest provides the site of performing, contesting, and negotiating what it means to be diasporic Chinese. Similarly, the active process of negotiating identity is evident in Tsuda's treatment of the Brazilian Japanese, whose identification with being Japanese and Brazilian shifts as they move from Brazil to Japan, respectively.

In her essay on religious practice and diaspora, Aisha Khan highlights the mutually constitutive relationship between diasporic consciousness and ritual practice, both in its performative execution and intellectual interpretation. By showing how diasporic Hindu and Muslim Indians in Trinidad and Tobago use ritual practice as a mechanism for producing and sustaining diasporic consciousness, we come to see the dynamic relationship between religious ritual and identity formation. Reminiscent of Sen's essay, the production of diasporic Indian consciousness involves a turn to the homeland and the appropriation of its cultural traditions as a means to interpret their collective displacement from India and to negotiate their subsequent experience of subjugation in the New World. Within this dialogue between ethnicity and religious identity lies the struggle to understand and define the diaspora's relationship to tradition, modernity, and colonialism. Collectively, these chapters underscore culture as a central dimension in diasporic formation.

In keeping our intention of treating Asian diasporas as an experiment, we have invited literary scholar David Palumbo-Liu and cultural studies scholar Ien Ang to offer commentaries to this volume (Chapters 11 and 12). Our hope is that their comments and questions will lead to more critical engagement with the concept of Asian diasporas as well as engender new directions for broadening this conversation.

The contributors of the volume address a wide variety of Asian diasporic experiences and in no way seek to provide an overarching definition of the diasporic experience or, for that matter, a singular definition of Asian diaspora. Their essays, individually and collectively, do not merely add to our empirical knowledge of diasporic experiences. Each in its own way contributes and extends our theoretical conceptualization of diaspora. From Sen's theorization of diasporic amnesia to Tsuda's illustration of situated identies to Lan's explication of legalized indenture of temporary migrants to McKay and Kim's discussion of the dialectical relationship between the state and the diaspora, the essays lead us to a number of theoretical directions that enhance and refine our understanding of diasporic experiences and diaspora-making processes. As we have noted, these processes include but are not limited to negotiating the forces of labor, colonization, and globalization; confronting national borders and exclusions; navigating racial, ethnic, gender, and sexual systems among other axes of difference; and producing and transforming culture. Such processes inform and shape the triangulating realtionship that subjects sustain with the homeland, the country of residence, and the dispersed communities of coethnics and nationals globally. Focusing on these processes within and across nations as well as regions places our understanding of Asian migrations, in the past and present, in a global terrain. It brings to the forefront global processes such as geopolitical formations and neoliberalism in our understanding of muliple migratory movements from and within Asia. Finally, it underscores not only the multiple impacts of the unequal processes that embody globalization and their influence in determining the limits and possibilities of diasporic subject formation, but also the ways in which diasporic subjects experience and construct identity, home, and belonging.

Notes

1. We agree with Wanni W. Anderson and Robert G. Lee (2005) that studies of diaspora must be examined within the context of displacement.

2. While earlier migrants were able to keep regular communication with family and friends abroad with mail and telegrams, our point is that recent technological advances in the speed, variety, and accessibility of communication devices have opened up vastly more opportunities to maintain steady and regular communication with people abroad.

3. The Ford Foundation, through its initiative "Crossing Borders: Revitalizing Area Studies," funded scholarship and teaching in thirty universities throughout the United States to innovate new approaches in area studies.

4. While transnational studies historically have focused on the social, economic, and political ties that people form between two sites (the homeland and place of settlement), diaspora studies have emphasized the cultural, imaginative, and affective bonds that displaced people form with the homeland and their coethnics living elsewhere. Over the years, however, the distinction between transnational and diaspora studies has become more blurred.

5. It is important to note that our conception of Asian diasporas considers both the political and economic conditions that produce diasporas as well as the subjective positioning that is actively constructed through memory, imagination, and practice. These dual forces of materiality and cultural production are intertwined and form the bases of defining Asian diasporas.

6. Thailand is the only exception. It has never been colonized by a Western power.

7. Insisting on the global linkages of Asian migrants does not diffuse but instead only situates the political struggles of Asians against racial exclusion in a cross-national setting. We agree with Jonathan Okamura who insists that "a transnational perspective does not elide race as a significant category of analysis" in Asian American Studies (2003: 172). Looking at the United States, Okamura notes that transnational factors influence race relations, for instance, through the orientalization engendered by the continuous flow of Asian immigration and the bilateral ties that Asian migrants maintain to the homeland, as well as the disadvantages caused by unequal relations between the United States and Asian countries.

8. In the anthology *Orientations,* Chuh and Shimakawa situate Asia/Asian American in a global context specifically by positing a postcolonial, transnational, and postnational framework for understanding their experiences. As they state, "transnationalism . . . both describes and interrogates the possibilities for inhabiting and co-opting this cross-border mobility for the sake of envisioning communities bounded not principally by national identifications and investments" (2001: 5). The anthology *Orientations* establishes constructions of "Asian" in Asian Studies and Asian American Studies. They posit that the possibilities for sameness in the construction of Asian in both fields could lead to new epistemologies or critiques that could lead to alliances.

9. Paul Gilroy's discussion of the "new racism" illustrates how ideas of national belonging are bound up with racial ideologies. "The politics of 'race' in [Britain] is fired by conceptions of national belonging and homogeneity which not only blur the distinction between 'race' and nation, but rely on that very ambiguity for their effect" (1987: 45).

10. These illustrations directly respond to the construction of Alejandro Portes and Min Zhou of the different trajectories of immigrant assimilation. They enumerate three possible patterns of adaptation among contemporary immigrants and their offspring. As they state, "One of them replicates the time-honored portrayal of growing acculturation and parallel integration into the white middle-class; a second leads straight into the opposite direction to permanent poverty and assimilation into the underclass; still a third associates rapid economic advancement with deliberate preservation of the immigrant community's values and tight solidarity" (1993: 82). Differences in human capital, social capital, and structures of opportunities that welcome migrant ethnic groups shape the trajectory of immigrant assimilation.

References

Anderson, Wanni W. and Robert Lee, eds. 2005. *Displacements and Diasporas: Asians in the Americas.* New Brunswick, NJ: Rutgers University Press.

Ang, Ien. 2001. *On Not Speaking Chinese.* New York: Routledge Press.

Appadurai, Arjun. 1986. "Theory in Anthropology: Center and Periphery." *Comparative Studies in Society and History* 28, no. 2: 356–361.

——. 1996. *Modernity at Large.* Minneapolis: University of Minnesota Press.

Basch, Linda, Nina Glick Schiller, and Cristina Szanton Blanc. 1994. *Nations Unbound.* Amsterdam: Gordon and Breach Publishers.

Chuh, Kandice, and Karen Shimakawa, eds. 2001. *Orientations: Mapping Studies in the Asian Diaspora.* Durham, NC: Duke University Press.

Cohen, Robin. 1997. *Global Diasporas.* Seattle: University of Washington Press.

Constable, Nicole. 1999. "At Home but Not at Home: Filipina Narratives of Ambivalent Returns" *Cultural Anthropology* 14(2): 203–29.

Dirlik, Arif. 1999. "Asians on the Rim: Transnational Capital and Local Community in the Making of Contemporary Asian America." In *Across the Pacific: Asian Americans and Globalization,* ed. Evelyn Hu-DeHart. Philadelphia: Temple University Press.

Gilroy, Paul. 1987. *"There Ain't no Black in the Union Jack": the Cultural Politics of Race and Nation.* Chicago: University of Chicago Press,

——. 1993. *The Black Atlantic: Modernity and Double Consciousness.* Boston: Harvard University.

Glick-Schiller, Nina, and Georges Eugene Fouron. 2001. *Georges Woke Up Laughing: Long-Distance Nationalism and the Search for Home.* Durham, NC: Duke University Press.

Gupta, Akhil, and James Ferguson. 1992. "Beyond 'Culture': Space, Identity, and the Politics of Difference." *Cultural Anthropology* 7, no. 1: 6–23.

Guyer, Jane I. 2004. "Anthropology in Area Studies." *Annual Review of Anthropology* 33: 499–523.

Hall, Stuart. 1990. "Cultural Identity and Diaspora." *Identity: Community, Culture, Difference.* ed. Jonathan Rutherford. London: Lawrence & Wishart.

——. 1996. "The Formation of a Diasporic Intellectual. An Interview with Stuart Hall by Kuan-Hsing Chen." Pp. 484–503 in *Stuart Hall: Critical Dialogues in Cultural Studies,* eds. David Morley and Kuan-Hsing Chen. New York: Routledge.

Kaplan, Caren, and Inderpal Grewal. 1991. "Introduction: Transnational Feminist Practices and Questions of Postmodernity." Pp. 1–35 in *Scattered Hegemonies: Postmodernity and Transnational Feminist Practices.* Minneapolis: University of Minnesota Press.

Kearney, Michael. 1995. "The Local and the Global: The Anthropology of Globalization and Transnationalism." *Annual Review of Anthropology* 24: 547–65.

Lavie, Smadar, and Ted Swedenburg. 1996. "Introduction: Displacement, Diaspora, and Geographies of Identity." Pp. 1–26 in *Displacement, Diaspora, and Geographies of Identity,* eds. Smadar Lavie and Ted Swedenburg. Durham, NC: Duke University Press.

Lesser, Jeffrey, ed. 2003. *Searching for Home Abroad.* Durham, NC: Duke University Press.

Linger, Daniel. 2001. *No One Home: Brazilian Selves Remade in Japan*. Stanford, CA: Stanford University Press.

Louie, Andrea. 2004. *Chineseness Across Borders: Renegotiating Chinese Identities in China and the United States*. Durham, NC: Duke University Press.

Okamura, Jonathan. 2003. "Asian American Studies in the Age of Transnationalism: Diaspora, Race, Community." *Amerasia Journal* 28(2): 171–93.

Parreñas, Rhacel Salazar. 2001. *Servants of Globalization: Women, Migration, and Domestic Work*. Stanford, CA: Stanford University Press.

Portes, Alejandro, and Min Zhou. 1993. "The New Second Generation: Segmented Assimilation and Its Variants." *ANNALS of American Academy of Political and Social Science* 530: 74–96.

Portes, Alejandro, and Rumbaut, Ruben. 1996. *Immigrant America: A Portrait*. Berkeley: University of California Press.

Raj, Dhooleka. 2003. *Where Are You From? Middle-Class Migrants in the Modern World*. Berkeley: University of California Press.

Roth, Joshua. 2002. *Brokered Homeland: Japanese Brazilian Migrants in Japan*. Ithaca, NY: Cornell University Press.

Safran, William. 1991. "Diasporas in Modern Society: Myths of Homeland and Return." *Diaspora* 1(1), pp. 83–99.

Said, Edward. 1978. *Orientalism*. New York: Pantheon Books.

Sassen, Saskia. 1996. *Losing Control? Sovereignty in an Age of Globalization*. New York: Columbia University Press.

———. 2003. "Global Cities and Survival Circuits." Pp. 254–274 in *Global Woman: Nannies, Maids and Sex Workers in the New Economy*, eds. Barbara Ehrenreich and Arlie Hochschild. New York: Metropolitan Books.

Shukla, Sandhya. 2003. *India Abroad: Diasporic Cultures of Postwar America and England*. Princeton, NJ: Princeton University Press.

Siu, Lok. 2005a. "Queen of the Chinese Colony: Gender, Nation, and Belonging in Diaspora." *Anthropological Quarterly* 78(3), pp. 511–542.

———. 2005b. *Memories of a Future Home: Diasporic Citizenship of Chinese in Panama*. Stanford: Stanford University Press.

Soysal, Yasmin. 2000. "Citizenship and Identities: Living in Diasporas in Post-War Europe?" *Ethnic and Racial Studies* 23:1 (January): 1–15.

Toloyan, Kachig. 1991. "Preface." *Diaspora* 1(1), 3–7.

Tsuda, Takeyuki. 2003. *Strangers in the Ethnic Homeland*. New York: Columbia University Press.

Wong, Sau-ling. 1995. "Denationalization Reconsidered: Asian American Cultural Criticism at a Theoretical Crossroads," *Amerasia Journal* 21(1/2): 1–27.

1 Latin America in Asia-Pacific Perspective

Evelyn Hu-DeHart

ALTHOUGH LATIN AMERICA ENJOYS a long Pacific coastline, because of its relative economic and political insignificance in the late twentieth century, it can be overlooked easily in discussions of the Asia-Pacific region. In point of fact, from Mexico to Peru, and across the South American continent to Brazil, there has been a long and continuous historical connection between this large region of first Iberian America and Asia and later Latin America and Asia. Asians had established small communities in Mexico at the beginning of the seventeenth century, and most recently in 1990, a Peruvian of Japanese descent, Alberto Fujimori, was elected president of his adopted homeland.

Here I sketch out a history of the relationships between Latin America and societies across the Pacific, especially China. The discussion focuses on the most prominent aspect of these relationships: Chinese immigration into Latin America beginning in the mid-nineteenth century, first as coolies, then from the late nineteenth century, as free labor. Labor migrations, I argue, were initially tied in with developments in Latin America as part of a larger world economy, specifically, the need for labor in plantation economies once the abolition of slavery cut off sources of labor in the Atlantic region. The migrations themselves contributed to the formation of a "Pacific" and encouraged further flows of population. By way of conclusion, I will say a few words on Asian immigrants' contribution to Latin America in spite of a social and cultural environment that was frequently hostile to their presence.

Spanish America and the Initial Formation of the Pacific

In 1513, Spanish explorer Vasco Núñez de Balboa's "discovery" of the Mar del Sur (the Southern Sea), the first European name for the Pacific Ocean, set in motion Spain's discovery and exploration of the Pacific coast of South America. By mid-sixteenth century, Spanish conquistadores had conquered the Inca empire, renaming it the colony of New Castille, or Peru.

In 1518, Hernán Cortés arrived on the Atlantic coast of Mexico near present day Veracruz, sailing not directly from Spain but from the already established Spanish foothold in Santiago de Cuba. Three years later, the Aztec empire collapsed from the combined weight of internal disintegration and external pressures; from its ashes arose the Spanish colony of New Spain, or Mexico. Together, the silver-producing colonies of Peru and Mexico constituted the core of the extensive and long-lasting Spanish empire in the New World.

In 1540, the Spanish Crown sent its first viceroy to New Spain, which extended from today's U.S. Southwest to today's Central America. During the preceding two decades, Cortés and other early conquistadores sent expeditions north from Acapulco and other points along the Pacific coast to Baja California and California, culminating with Vázquez de Coronado's exploration (1540–42) of the Colorado River and the Gulf of California (then known as the Sea of Cortés) and Juan Rodríguez de Cabrillo's long voyage to present day San Francisco in 1542.

By the end of the sixteenth century, the Spanish finally figured out how to accomplish what Columbus failed to achieve—finding a way to the Orient by sailing westward. Spain established the Manila galleon trade, which lasted some three centuries, linking China and Japan via the Philippines (which Spain had also acquired as a colony) to Europe in an exchange of Mexican silver for Oriental luxury goods. Acapulco on Mexico's Pacific coast was developed specifically for this purpose.

Not long after the Manila trade was established, the first Asian colony in the Americas appeared. In 1635 a group of Spanish barbers in Mexico City complained about excessive competition from Chinese barbers in that colonial capital city. They petitioned the viceroy to remove these bothersome Asian barbers to special quarters at the outskirts of town, so that they, the Spaniards, would not have to compete with the *chinos de Manila* for business.[1] Although this early settlement of Asians never grew into a large colony during the colonial period, it left legacies now firmly entrenched in Mexican folklore, notably the embroidered blouse known popularly as the *china poblana*, worn by Mexican women in central Mexico.[2]

Thus, it can be said that long before any Northern Europeans laid eyes on the Pacific coast region of what is now the United States, the "Spanish-Pacific" was already a well established geographical and political entity. Moreover, the Spanish-Pacific was the result not only of Spanish settlement along the Pacific coast from California to Chile, a settlement sparse at both ends but dense and intense in the middle (Mexico and Peru)—it established an early continuous link to Asia through trade and some migration across the Pacific.

Asian Labor in Latin America

After Mexico and Peru's independence from Spain in the early nineteenth century, the reality of a Spanish-Pacific, though briefly interrupted by the cessation of the Manila galleon trade in the early nineteenth century, was renewed by first Peru and Cuba, and later Mexico. In the creation of a "Latin American-Pacific" in the nineteenth and twentieth centuries, material trade continued to play a role, but this time it was secondary to international labor migration and other forms of population movements from Asia across the Pacific. Chinese labor was initially most prominent in these population movements, starting around the turn of the twentieth century and later joined by Japanese labor. Peru, among the countries of Spanish America, took the lead in attracting Japanese labor, but the largest number of Japanese immigrants in Latin America would end up not in Spanish America but in Brazil on the Atlantic coast.

Chinese Coolie Labor in Cuba and Peru

In the middle of the nineteenth century, Peru, which became independent of Spain, and Cuba, which remained a Spanish colony in the Caribbean, both actively promoted the importation of Chinese coolies or contract laborers to work on sugar plantations. Known in Spanish as *la trata amarilla* (the yellow trade), it bore remarkable resemblance to the African slave trade, which both countries, especially Cuba, had practiced extensively. From 1847 to 1874, as many as 250,000 Chinese coolies under eight-year contracts were sent to Peru and Cuba, with 80 percent or more destined for the plantations. In Peru, several thousand coolies also helped build the Andean railroad and worked in the offshore guano mines south of Lima. In the 1870s escaped coolies and free Chinese were among the pioneers who penetrated the Peruvian Amazon building settlements, introducing trade activities, cultivating rice, beans, sugar, and other crops, manufacturing on a small scale, and brokering communication between the native Amazonian peoples and later European arrivals. Finally, although demand for cheap plantation labor remained high, international outcry against this brutal human traffic abruptly terminated the coolie trade in 1875, with the last contracts expiring by the 1880s.[3]

The British were the first to experiment with the exporting of Chinese, then East Indian, laborers under contract to their overseas colonies. As early as 1806, at precisely the time when the British ended the slave trade, 200 Chinese were sent to Trinidad. Although this experiment was a failure, British entrepreneurs continued to press for the export of Asian labor, turning from China to India by the 1830s. By 1838, some 25,000 East Indians had been exported to the new British East African colony of Mauritius and successfully adapted to the plantation system there. In 1845, the first cargo of East Indians was shipped to British Guiana, Trinidad, and Jamaica in the West Indies. They were under contract to the plantations for five years, a period known euphemistically as "Industrial residency," after which they could presumably ask for passage home or remain in the colonies as free men and women. During the same time, the French also acquired East Indians who were indentured to French colonies in East Africa and the Caribbean.[4]

Between 1763—the year the British captured Havana, occupied the city for ten months, and opened this Spanish colony to international trade and the emerging North American market—and 1838, when the Cuban industry mechanized significantly, Cuban society was transformed from "the relatively mixed economy based on cattle-ranching, tobacco-growing, and the small-scale production of sugar" to the "dominance of plantation agriculture based on the large-scale production of sugar and coffee."[5] Cuba surpassed its British West Indian neighbors to become the preeminent sugar producer in the world. Along with new markets, improved technology, capital availability, a responsive political climate, a modern entrepreneurial spirit among the planters, and other factors, African slave labor was crucial to the success of the plantation economy. The slave population had grown from 38,879 (22.8 percent of the total population) in 1774, to 436,495 (43.3 percent of the total population) by 1841. Despite British efforts already underway to end the international slave trade, Cuba continued to import large numbers of Africans during the early nineteenth century, as many as 25,841 in 1817.[6]

The transformation of Cuban society was not just an economic phenomenon, it was social as well, for the population became not only increasingly slave and colored, but the planter class—often *hacendado* (landowner), *esclavista* (slave owner), and *negrero* (slave trader) all in one—reigned supreme, with its interests driving most policymaking, and its authority, particularly on the estates, largely unquestioned.

In Peru, the coastal sugar economy declined after independence due to the ravages of war and labor shortage brought on by the end of African slavery. The slave trade to Peru ended in 1810, and slavery itself was formally abolished in 1854. But the guano trade of the 1840s generated new capital, some of which was transferred to agriculture, and revitalized the agrarian economy. Referring to the rise of this new *burguesía agraria*, Peruvian historian Jorge Basadre stated:

> El poderío económico de la nueva plurocracia costeña tuvo su base en parte en contratos de individuos aislados con el Estado enriquecido por el guano, en especulaciones bursátiles o en dividendos en bonos, as como también en propiedades urbanas y, a la vez, en el auge que supieron dar a sus haciendas trabajadas principalmente por los chinos.[7] (The economic power of the new coastal plantocracy had its base in part in isolated individual contracts with the state, enriched by guano, stock market speculations, and dividend earnings, as well as in urban properties, and at the same time, in the economic surge that they knowingly gave their plantations as worked principally by the Chinese [my translation].)

Together with the guano merchants, coastal planters went in search of cheap labor overseas, unable to find it among the small coastal peasantry or the faraway *serranos*. When slavery was officially abolished in Peru in 1854, there were only 17,000 slaves left. Even if they were willing to remain as salaried workers, there were hardly enough to meet the growing labor demand. Between 1839 and 1851, the Peruvian government paid 450,000 pesos in premiums to encourage importation of foreign labor to replace slaves.[8] Two-thirds of this money was directly invested in labor for the sugar plantations.

In Cuba, planter interests were represented by the powerful *Real Junta de Fomento y de Colonización,* presided over by the eminent landowner and international businessman Julián Zulueta. An agency of the junta was the *Comisión de Población Blanca,* charged at first with promoting immigration of free European workers to Cuba, as these farsighted planters were already preparing for the imminent end of Africa as their source of labor and the need to adjust to white labor. But free men and women in Europe were not attracted to the plantation society with slave labor. So, in 1844, when the British coolie trade was in full swing, the junta sent an agent to China to study the possibility of importing Chinese coolies. The Spanish government was also familiar with Chinese agricultural labor in the Philippines. An agreement was concluded in 1846 between Zulueta in London and the British in Amoy, a treaty port in Fujian Province, South China. On June 3, 1847, the Spanish ship *Oquendo* docked in Havana with 206 Chinese on board, after 131 days at sea. Six died at sea and another seven shortly after arrival. Nine days later, a British ship, the *Duke of Argyle,* arrived with 365 Chinese on board, after 123 days at sea.[9] Thirty-five persons had died at sea. Both human cargoes were consigned to the Junta de Fomento, which proceeded to distribute the coolies in lots of ten to the island's most prominent planters and a railroad company.

Shortly after the Cubans initiated the Chinese coolie trade, Peruvian planters emulated their Cuban counterparts. An immigration law of November 1849 granted exclusive license (called *asiento* as in the African slave trade) for four years to two planters, Domingo Elías and Juan Rodríguez, to introduce Chinese into the departments of Lima and La Libertad after they had imported an initial experimental group of 75 Chinese *colonos* in October 1849. During the Elías-Rodríguez license period and continuing until 1854, 4,754 Chinese were imported.[10]

Initial response to the Chinese as workers in both Cuba and Peru was not enthusiastic. The Peruvian government suspended the trade in 1856, although a few hundred more trickled in between 1857 and 1860. Cuba also suspended the trade after the first contract with Zulueta and spent the next few years promoting other forms of immigrant labor, including Yucatecos (Mayan Indians) from Mexico and Gallegos, Catalans, and Canary Islanders from Europe. But these failed to meet the ever-growing labor demand. The Chinese trade was officially resumed in 1853 to Cuba and in 1861 to Peru. By then, in response to harsh international criticism of an already infamous human experiment, the British prohibited their subjects from participating in the particularly notorious passage to Cuba and Peru, forcing the trade to the Portuguese colony of Macao off the China coast, where Portuguese colonial authorities for the right price fully cooperated with the European coolie traders until 1874, when even Portugal succumbed to international pressures to end it. By then, over 200,000 Chinese had been sent from Macao, although of course, the ultimate origins of Chinese remained in South China, in Guangdong and Fujian Provinces. Table 1.1 summarizes the figures for the duration of the trade to Cuba and Peru, correlated with slave importation for Cuba and sugar production for both Peru and Cuba.

Table 1.1 Coolie imports and sugar production in Peru and Cuba, 1847–1878

Year	Peru		Cuba		
	Coolies	Sugar (metric tons)	Slaves	Coolies	Sugar (metric tons)
1847				571	
1848	4,754				
1853			12,500	4,307	391,246
1854			11,400	1,711	397,713
1855	2,355		6,408	2,985	462,968
1856	4,220		7,304	4,968	416,141
1857	405		10,436	8,547	436,030
1858	300		19,992	13,385	426,274
1859	321		30,473	7,204	469,263
1860	1,092	618	24,895	6,193	429,769
1860	2,116	885	23,964	6,973	533,800
1862	1,691	1,257	11,254	344	454,758
1863	1,620	1,615	7,507	952	445,693
1864	6,562	2,864	6,807	2,153	525,372
1865	5,943	1,463	145	6,400	547,364
1866	6,725	5,111	1,443	12,391	535,641
1867	3,360	3,431		14,263	585,814
1868	4,307	9,352		7,368	720,250
1869	2,861	12,479		5,660	718,745
1870	7,544	13,175		1,227	702,974
1871	11,812	13,141		1,448	609,660
1872	13,026	14,022		8,160	772,068
1873	6,571	21,696		5,093	742,843
1874	3,827	31,940		2,490	768,672
1875		56,102			750,062
1876					626,082
1877					516,268
1878					553,364

SOURCES: Peru, coolies—Humberto Rodríguez Pastor, *Hijos del Celeste Imperio en el Perú (1850–1900): Migración, Agricultura, Mentalidad y Explotación* (Lima: Instituto de Apoyo Agrario, 1988), Table 4 and Anexo 1, pp. 27, 296; Peru, sugar—Rodríguez Pastor, *Hijos del Celeste Imperio*, p. 269; Cuba, slaves—Rebecca Scott, *Slave Emancipation in Cuba: The Transition to Free Labor, 1860–1899* (Princeton, NJ: Princeton University Press, 1985), p. 10; Cuba coolies—Scott, *Slave Emancipation*, p. 29; Cuba, sugar—Scott, *Slave Emancipation*, pp. 36, 240.

In the case of Peru, about half of the total number of coolies arrived during the first twenty years of the trade, 1849–69. The other half arrived during the last five years, 1870–74. This was also a time when sugar production mounted rapidly, from 13,475 metric tons in 1870, to 31,940 metric tons in 1875. Although the trade had ended by then, most of the Chinese were still under contract. During this time, the Chinese constituted almost the exclusive labor force on the plantations, as Peru had no slaves and few other forms of labor. It is undeniable, therefore, that coolie labor was a significant factor in the growing success of sugar production.

A similar correlation can be observed in the case of Cuba. As the African slave trade wound down and ended with the last shipments in 1865 of just 145 and in 1866 of 1,443 slaves, the size of the coolie imports rose markedly, reaching as many as 12,391 and 14,263 in 1866 and 1867. From 1865 to the end of the coolie trade in 1874, 64,500 coolies arrived, constituting over 50 percent of the total number imported. During this period, sugar production climbed steadily, reaching a high of 768,672 metric tons in 1874. Coolies constituted the source of labor replenishment, delaying the crisis that would have set in with the end of the slave trade and making it possible for the plantation economy to continue to prosper. It is also noteworthy that after 1875, when both the slave and the coolie trade had ended, sugar production displayed a pattern of general decline, a crisis brought on certainly in large part by the shortage of labor.

When the coolie trade was cut off to Cuba and Peru in 1874, many of those already in these two countries still had to work off their terms of servitude. Moreover, in both places mechanisms were put in place to extend the term of service by forcing or enticing the Chinese to continue working under some kind of contract primarily on the plantations, where demand for labor continued to be high.

In Cuba, forced recontracting began early, with the *Reglamento* of 1860, which obligated those coolies who had completed their first eight years to recontract (for an unspecified period of time) or leave Cuba at their own expense. Only those whose contracts expired before 1861 were exempt. To critics such as Cuban historian Juan Pérez de la Riva, recontracting simply further confirmed his conclusion that the coolie system was slavery, in that compulsory and successive recontracting perpetuated servitude to the point that the legal distinction between indenture and slavery became blurred in practice.

There is no doubt that the Cubans issued the recontracting regulation in order to keep as much as possible of this captive foreign labor force on the plantations, knowing full well that very few of the coolies could have saved enough from their meager wages to pay for their passage home. Equally undeniable a factor was racism, for the question of race definitely figured in this decision to keep the Chinese unfree. Cuban slavers and abolitionists alike had trouble dealing with a free nonwhite population and were concerned about the further mongrelization of Cuban society with the admission of another undesirable colored race—more on this point later. Recontracting succeeded well as a device to keep Chinese labor in agriculture. The 1872 Cuban census noted 58,400 Chinese, of whom 14,046 were "free," that is, had completed their original contracts. Nevertheless, of this number, 10,044 remained in agriculture.[11] Records uncovered by historians in the People's Republic of China revealed that from 1880 to 1885, a period when many of the coolies sent to Cuba and Peru during the height (also the last thrust) of the coolie trade in the first half of the 1870s would have completed their original contracts, only 1,887 Chinese managed to make their way back home to China. This was an insignificant number, given that over 100,000 left China in the 1870s for Cuba and Peru.[12]

In Peru, recontracting began in the early 1870s, a time of many expired and expiring contracts. No laws per se forced the coolies to recontract, although compulsory recontracting was proposed by Peruvian lawmakers in 1870. The planters resorted to debt or other forms of coercion. One frequent practice was the *sobretiempo,* or *yapa,* an extension attached to the original term on grounds that the coolie had not worked all the days due the *patrono* (some planters argued that work was due them on Sundays, in spite of the contracts consistently exempting Sunday work) or owed money to the *patrono,* which then had to be paid off by more work. The debt could have been incurred as a result of loans, advances, or even costs involved in recapturing coolies who ran away.[13] More likely, however, the wages offered and the short term of the recontract—ranging from as short as six months to no more than one or two years at the most, with the option of recontracting several times under these terms—enticed many coolies to recontract voluntarily in their desire to accumulate more savings and ultimately break free from the plantations. What made savings more feasible under the recontracting system was the planter's offer to pay the wages in advance, up to one year's worth, as incentive. In the late 1870s and 1880s, as the trade came to a close but demand for labor remained high, planters offered other concessions to lure the Chinese to remain longer on the estates. As early as the 1870s, in Santa Province, in the labor force of twenty haciendas that relied almost exclusively on

Chinese labor, 930 laborers or 77.1 percent, were under contract; 117 (9.7 percent) were recontracted, and 160 (13.2 percent) were *libres* (free), living and working in nearby pueblos.[14]

In both Peru and Cuba, recontracting took a significant new turn, beginning as early as 1870 in Cuba and appearing around 1880 in Peru. Although the original recontracts were between the individual coolie whose contract had just expired and the planter or estate administrator, usually the same person who made the original contracts, a new contracting system involved a free Chinese—operating as an *enganchador* (labor contractor or broker)—who engaged and organized fellow free Chinese (*chinos libres*) into *cuadrillas,* or gangs. This entire group of *cuadrilleros* was then hired out to a plantation for a specified period of time or a specific piece of work, such as the evaporating room (*casa de calderas*) in the *ingenios* (sugar factory on the estate) of Cuba.[15]

In Peru, the Chilean invasion in 1880 during the War of the Pacific created chaos along the coast and led to the destruction of numerous estates. The displaced Chinese, both those still serving out contracts and those already freed, became readily available clients of the Chinese *enganchadores.* The Chinese enganchador negotiated all terms of work for a squad and handled all aspects of employment for the workers, including obtaining advances from the planters to pay them; handing out tools; arranging for lodging and food; and being responsible for discipline, control, and supervision. The enganchador, who also assumed the risks of all losses and damages, was likely once a coolie, but was now an independent merchant trading in goods and people. Michael González, who studied the Aspíllaga planter family and their estate Cayaltí, found that the Aspillagas also offered their Chinese contractors the right to operate small stores on site to cater to the needs of the Chinese workers, who were each paid sixty centavos per day without rations.[16]

In Cuba, by the census of 1872, 14,064 coolies had completed their original contract and naturalized or registered as foreign residents. Under contract were 34,408 coolies; 7,036 were runaways still missing, 864 were captured runaways, and 684 were sentenced criminals. Awaiting recontracting in the *depósitos* (pens where slaves were held awaiting sale) were only 864.[17] Thus, the planters welcomed the Chinese cuadrillas in 1870 as an innovative device to keep the Chinese working on the estates after their contract expired. But the planters also realized that the presence of these chinos libres posed a severe problem of control over slaves and especially coolies still under contract. An editorial in the *Boletín de Colonización,* an official organ of the colonial government that represented sugar interests, concerned about the high rate of *marronismo,* or runaways, charged that the cuadrillas were the principle cause of flight. The writer asserted that the runaways could easily hide among the cuadrilleros, and that their presence "demoralized the workers."[18] Thus, the colonial authorities banned the use of cuadrillas, seeing the need for control as more important than economic flexibility. But the system was revived in 1879 at the end of the Ten Years' War, when the coolie trade as well as slave imports had been terminated for several years and labor was in short supply.[19]

For the Chinese, given the 1860 regulation forcing them to recontract or leave the island, joining one of these cuadrillas was one way to stay in Cuba without resorting to the much-hated individual contract with a planter. And as in Peru, the Chinese contractor accumulated capital for business through this process.[20]

As the decade of the 1880s drew to a close, both Peru and Cuba saw the end of dependence on slave and coolie labor on the plantations. Very simply, after 1885, an aging Chinese population whose ranks were not being replenished by younger immigrants was increasingly replaced by Peruvian *peones libres;* Chinese disappeared almost entirely from the plantations by the end of the century. By then, Peruvian hacendados had learned how to entice and keep native Peruvian workers with the use of advance wages and debts, much the same way they had enticed and coerced free Chinese to work for them. In Cuba, the old plantation system gave way to the colonos, or independent small farmers, who cultivated and supplied the newly modernized mills with the raw canes. Many of these colonos were new immigrants, mostly Canary Islanders and Gallegos.

During the chaos of the War of the Pacific, when the invading Chilean army sacked a number of Peruvian coastal haciendas and liberated coolies (whether under original contract or recontracted), other hacendados eagerly hired the Chinese, usually by agreement with a Chinese contractor, "incorporating them as peones," or wage workers, to supplement the coolies that remained under contract on the estates. "It would not be exaggerated to say that for a period of time, very short to be sure, the great sugar estates depended on these Chinese contractors and those Chinese engaged by them, that is, the same people who years before had worked as forced laborers and been treated like slaves." These outside-contracted Chinese workers (*chinos enganchados*) became an "embryo" of Peru's "rural proletariat," and an initial form of "peonage" or wage labor.[21]

The *enganche* system in Peru gave way entirely to a free, or wage, labor system, involving many Chinese until these died or moved out of agriculture into commerce and other urban occupations. They were succeeded in the field by Peruvian serranos contracted by labor brokers emulating the example of the Chinese.

An official inspection of the coastal provinces of 1887 located 8,503 Chinese, of whom the vast majority of 6,245 were ex-coolies now free, who worked in agriculture, and whose condition "was similar to that of the *peon libre nacional*." They received the same wages and rations as other workers, although wages varied from hacienda to hacienda. Another 1,182 Chinese on the coast were individually recontracted, and only 838 were tied to a labor contractor. There were also 40 *yanaconas,* or sharecroppers, 193 *arrendatarios,* or renters, and 5 shopkeepers and innkeepers. The commission of inspection even located one ex-coolie who had become an hacendado himself and who hired 80 or 90 free Chinese to work for him.[22] The workforce of one important plantation as early as 1883 had become predominately Peruvian and Chinese wage laborers—373 of the total 550, or 68 percent.[23] The transition to an authentic free labor system was clearly in progress. If coolies—that is, Chinese workers during their eight-year term—were more slave than free in the way they were treated, ex-coolies earning a wage did become the country's early free workers, paving the way for other peones.

Although the major imprint of the Chinese in Peru was unquestionably on the coastal export economy (guano and sugar) and later in retail commercial development, they also ventured into the largely Indian *sierra* as well as joined the pioneer efforts into the Peruvian Amazon.[24] It is for their contribution to Amazon settlement and resource development that the Chinese have been least known, more neglected, and as one new study suggests, deliberately suppressed in official Peruvian historiography due to a prevailing nineteenth-century Peruvian attitude that only European pioneers were capable of bringing "civilization" to the jungle.[25]

As early as 1873, Chinese colonies were established in the Amazon. By the end of the century, Chinese had built colonies in major towns such as Iquitos, Huánuco, Chanchamayo, and Pucallpa, as well as scattered all over the Amazon region. Some of these first pioneers and settlers very likely were fugitives from coastal masters, joined later by coolies who had completed their contract and were free immigrants.

These early colonies were small—around one hundred persons each—but prosperous, and in the sparsely populated underdeveloped Amazon region, assumed a significance above their size. The Chinese acquired urban lots as well as rural land; they manufactured basic consumer items as well as growing food to provision the towns. In the towns and regional markets, as itinerant peddlers (muleteers) and shopkeepers, they not only sold their own crops (principally rice, but also beans, peanuts, and sugar cane) and manufactured goods (clothing and shoes), but also took on an intermediary role in the exchange of natural, artisanal, and agricultural products between the highland and the jungle. When cash was not available, they bartered.

In these activities, the Chinese covered a lot of territory, occasionally suffered Indian attacks, and also became much sought after as expeditionary guides and interpreters. Not only did the Chinese adapt with alacrity and facility to the Amazon environment, but as early pioneers and trailblazers, they acted the role of the cultural broker between the "uncivilized" Indian natives and the Peruvian and European settlers.

Rubber and gold in Loreto Province, with its capital in Iquitos on the Amazon River, attracted Chinese from all over Peru, directly from China, and from California. They spread over the vast jungle to tap wild rubber trees; they washed for gold in the tributary rivers; and they established themselves in business in Iquitos. By 1899, the Chinese community of Iquitos, numbering 346, was the largest of many foreign groups in that most cosmopolitan of Peruvian cities, isolated to be sure from the national capital of Lima, but well connected to Europe, the United States, and especially Brazil.

Chinese Immigrants in Mexico

After the coolie trade, some Chinese continued to go to Peru and Cuba, now as free immigrants, but a much larger number voluntarily migrated to Mexico, particularly to the northern frontier zone bordering the Untied States. Not coincidentally, this new immigration occurred just when the United States enacted the first Chinese Exclusion Act in 1882, by which the Chinese became the first group specifically designated by race to be barred from entering the country.

Chinese immigrants, mostly young males, began arriving on the west coast of Mexico in 1876, coinciding with the military coup of Porfirio Díaz, who ruled Mexico with an iron hand for thirty-five years and promoted its rapid economic development by foreign investors. This immigration accelerated following the passage of the Chinese Exclusion Act in the United States. Entering through the Pacific coast ports of Mazatlán and Guaymas, the Chinese spread throughout Mexico but primarily in the northern border states, no doubt attracted by their proximity to the United States. An initial tendency to cross illicitly into the United States abated, however, as the Chinese perceived and moved swiftly into a widening economic space in the rapidly developing frontier region, where the bulk of U.S. investment in Mexico was concentrated. Unlike the Chinese north of the border, those in northern Mexico did not take up laboring jobs, which were filled by Mexicans, but rather entered commerce as small independent entrepreneurs or occasionally in partnership with U.S. mine and railroad owners in the company towns. Chinese shopkeepers followed the trail of Yankee capital.

Nowhere was this pattern clearer than in the northwestern state of Sonora, which bordered the then territory of Arizona. Astutely avoiding competition with established European Mexican merchants in old towns such as Guaymas and Hermosillo (the state capital), the Chinese ventured into some remote villages of the interior, but mostly into new working-class settlements that sprang up along railroad and mining sites, and later, modern agricultural colonies. These were the new towns that grew in the wake of foreign, mainly U.S., investment in northern Mexico during the last quarter of the nineteenth century. The Chinese were often the first *comerciantes* to reach these new localities, thus the first shopkeepers to cater to the needs of the workers.

Within two generations, they succeeded in monopolizing the small commercial sector of the state's economy. Far from being a hindrance, the Mexican Revolution of 1910–17 actually furthered their commercial growth in several ways. First, with most Mexicans engaged in the civil conflicts, the revolution retarded the emergence of Mexican small businesses to compete with the Chinese. Second, even during these turbulent times, towns, including mining and railroad centers that continued to operate, needed to be supplied with goods and services. Third, the various revolutionary armies needed to be provisioned. As aliens, the Chinese remained officially "neutral" and willing to do business with all revolutionary factions. Although some of the sales were on "forced loan" bases, whereby Chinese merchants were given a credit slip for future payment by revolutionary generals who commandeered goods and supplies, the Chinese figured these inconveniences to be part of the cost of doing business in the midst of chaos. Fourth, further solidifying the Chinese position in Sonoran commerce was the weakening of traditional commercial links between Mexico and Europe during World War I, which coincided in time with the Mexican Revolution. Some of the departed German, French, and Spanish commercial houses were replaced by Chinese firms, which turned to U.S. suppliers, thereby forging new Mexican-U.S. commercial ties. This in turn strengthened the existing symbiotic relationship between Chinese merchants and U.S. interests in Sonora and explains the actions frequently taken by U.S. consuls to protect Chinese persons and businesses when they came under violent attack by Mexicans.

Most of the Chinese immigrants were young males, who arrived in Mexico nearly penniless, armed with only a willingness to work long and hard. However, a small number of Chinese capitalists also went early to Mexico to set up merchant houses in Guaymas and Hermosillo, with branches in important new towns such as Magdalena along the Sonoran railroad and Cananea of the Greene Consolidated Copper Company. In some cases, they added factories next to the stores to manufacture cheap shoes and clothing. These large merchants hired almost exclusively fellow Chinese in stores and factories. They also, significantly, extended goods on credit to enterprising but poor compatriots to peddle in small, remote mining towns and to set up new stores throughout the state. By the twentieth century, the Chinese controlled the trade in groceries, dry goods, and general merchandise. Some Chinese truck-farmed on land they leased, then carted the fruits and vegetables to local markets, which were often dominated by Chinese-owned stalls. Other Chinese worked as artisans and small-scale manufacturers, producing shoes, clothing, brooms, masa for tortillas, pasta, and sweets. In these multiple ways, the Chinese succeeded in creating a production, purchasing, supply, and distribution network among themselves, a closed system with characteristics of vertical integration that in effect became the state's first commercial infrastructure. This remarkable system endured until early 1931, when most of the Chinese were expelled from Sonora and their businesses nationalized.[26]

By the end of the Porfiriato, in 1910, the Chinese population in Sonora had reached 4,486, in a total population of 265,3883, making them the largest foreign colony in the state, surpassing the 3,164 U.S. nationals by over a thousand and well above the 259 Spaniards and 183 Germans. In 1910, according to Mexico's official census, there were 13,203 Chinese throughout Mexico, in every state except Tlaxcala. Table 1.2 summarizes demographic data for Chinese immigration to Mexico, by state, from 1900 to 1930.[27] The Chinese colony in Sonora—as in all of Mexico—was almost exclusively male. Even as late as 1930, the census noted only 412 women among the 3,471 Chinese recorded for Sonora. Not even all these four hundred or so women were necessarily Chinese, for Sonoran law had begun to strip Mexican women married to Chinese men of their citizenship and nationality, consigning them to their husband's ethnic group.

Table 1.2　Chinese population in Mexico, 1900–1930

State	1900	1910	1921	1927	1930
Aguascalientes	102	21	14	31	47 (18)
BC Norte	188	532	2806 (14)	5889	2982
BC Sur		319	175 (3)		139 (3)
Campeche	5	70	61 (1)	108	113 (38)
Coahuila	197 (5)	759 (14)	523 (16)	707	765 (153)
Colima	5	80 (2)	32 (1)	43	38 (14)
Chiapas	16	478 (1)	645 (30)	1261	1095 (238)
Chihuahua	328 (2)	1325 (9)	533 (16)	1037	1127 (229)
Méx. D.F.		1482 (5)	607 (18)	1062	886 (141)
Durango	147 (1)	242 (2)	46	197	229 (33)
Guanajuato	11	102	21 (3)	37	37 (12)
Guerrero	3	27	3	7	10 (3)
Hidalgo		38	50 (1)	98	70 (18)
Jalisco	20	70 (1)	53 (1)	192	151 (48)
México	15	58 (1)	25	78	24
Michoacán	4	26	5	8	12 (1)
Morelos	5	18	3	9	3
Nayarít			152	164	170 (27)
N. León	90	211	89 (2)	216	165 (4)
Oaxaca	81	262	158 (6)	254	158 (50)
Puebla	11	31	17 (1)	22	44 (12)
Querétaro	1	5	1	1	2
Quin. Roo		3	3	2	10 (4)
San Luis P.	32	109	105 (2)	288	271 (18)
Sinaloa	233 (1)	667 (4)	1040 (4)	2019	2123 (438)
Sonora	850 (9)	4486 (37)	3639 (66)	3758	3571 (412)
Tabasco	2	36 (1)	48 (4)	67	64 (23)
Tamaulipas	38	213 (2)	2005 (21)	2916	2117 (242)
Tepíc	29	173			
Tlaxcala					
Veracruz	116	434 (1)	847 (10)	1908	1238 (162)
Yucatán	153	875	773 (5)	1726	972 (153)
Zacatecas	19	41	19	113	142 (25)
Total	2,719	13,203	14,498	24,218	17,865
	(18)	(80)	(185)	(1,772)	(2,522)

NOTE: Women in parentheses.

SOURCES: Mexican Censuses for 1900, 1910, 1921, 1930. For 1927, see "Extranjeros residents Estados Unidos de México. Resúmen del censo practicado por la Sria de Gobernación en 1927, y extranjeros, distribución por estados, 14 marzo 1928." Archivo Histórico del Gobierno e Estado de Sonora (AHGES), vol. 50, 1930.

The highest number of Chinese in Sonora was recorded in 1919, when the Chinese colony itself supplied the count of 6,078. The sharp drop to the 3,571 noted for 1930 can be explained in a number of ways, aside from unreliable statistics. It reflected declining new immigration into the state at a time when Sonora had begun expulsion proceedings against established residents, many of whom were nationalized Mexican citizens. During the 1920s, as anti-Chinese campaigns mounted in intensity and frequency, many Chinese fled the state—back to China, illegally across the border to the United States, south to Sinaloa, and it appeared, especially across the gulf to Baja California, which recorded 5,889 Chinese in 1927 compared to 3,785 for Sonora.

When the Chinese first began arriving in Sonora in the last quarter of the nineteenth century, they congregated in Guaymas, the port of entry, and in the capital of Hermosillo. They moved to newer towns, notably the railroad hub of Magdalena north of Hermosillo, and to the state's leading mining town of Cananea on the northwest corner of the state close to the U.S. border. By 1904, Chinese could be found in all nine districts of the state, although unevenly distributed. Still prominent in Guaymas, Hermosillo, and Magdalena, by far the largest number had gone to Arizpe district, which included Cananea as well as a number of smaller mining camps and border towns. Of Arizpe's 1,106 Chinese, 800 resided in Cananea. In contrast, the districts of Altar, Sahuaripa, and Ures, which had no significant mining or railroad activities, had only a few Chinese residents each. The informative 1919 census, the data for which was provided by the Chinese Fraternal Union to the federal Department of Labor, noted 6,078 Chinese distributed across all nine districts and in fifty-eight of the state's sixty-two municipalities. Only four very small towns in Sahuaripa and Ures districts had no Chinese at all.

The 1919 community was composed overwhelmingly of young to middle-aged men, that is, men of working age. Eighty-four percent were between twenty-one and forty-five, the percentage increasing to an astonishing 91 percent if the upper limit is raised to fifty. Only 33 individuals, or less than 1 percent, were under twenty, and only 170, or 2.8 percent, were older than fifty-one. In years of residency in Mexico as of 1919, 41 percent had been in Mexico for ten to fifteen years, and another 37 percent for five to ten years. Thus the vast majority, almost 80 percent, had at least five years experience in Mexico. The data also suggest that a significant number, 1,459 or 24 percent, had entered Mexico during the active revolutionary years of 1912–15.

The first year for which there is good commercial data on the Chinese was 1913, published by the International Chinese Business Directory.[28] For Sonora,

279 Chinese businesses were noted, most of them in general merchandise or groceries, located in twenty-six towns. There were also forty restaurants, sixteen laundries, four hotels, two dry goods businesses, two clothing factories, one shoe factory, and two pharmacies (probably Chinese herbal goods).

In 1919, of the 6,078 Chinese residents in Sonora, 70 percent (4,258) were listed as *comerciantes* by occupation, which probably included store owners, partners, and clerks (see Table 1.3). Common or day laborers, *jornaleros,* were a distant second, with 12.8 percent. There were very few cooks or launderers. Artisans and craft workers of various kinds—tailors, shoemakers, jewelers, carpenters, bakers, and tanners constituted another 2 percent.

By 1925, although the Chinese population had declined sharply as noted earlier, the Chinese maintained a solid hold on local small businesses throughout the state.[29] Only a handful of traditional communities in Ures, Altar, and Sahuaripa districts had no Chinese presence. What is important is that these towns had *probably no stores whatever.* In other remote communities, such as Atil, Tubutama, and San Pedro de Cueva, with only one or a few commercial outlets, *all* were Chinese owned and operated. Even more significant, the commerce of certain mining towns, such as Nacozari de García near Cananea, was also exclusively in Chinese hands. The same was true for rapidly developing commercial agricultural towns in the southern part of the state, such as

Table 1.3 Chinese occupations in Sonora, 1919

District	(1)	(2)	(3)	(4)	(5)	(6)	(7)	(8)	(9)	(10)
Moctezuma	514	25	75	5	6	8	2	4	5	75
Guaymas	1156	50		5	15	8	2	1	9	65
Sahuaripa	46	2		1	1				1	6
Altar	146	15	1	4	2	1	1		3	15
Alamos	492	2	15	5	6	5	2		2	100
Ures	51	3		1	1			1	1	8
Arizpe	758	20	120	15	18	15	8	6	10	287
Magdalena	516	66		15	12	8	4		7	147
Hermosillo	579	24		7	8	24	4	3	1	75
Total	4258	207	196	58	69	69	23	15	39	778

NOTE: (1) Merchant (fixed or traveling); (2) Truck farmer; (3) Mine worker; (4) Cook; (5) Launderer; (6) Shoemaker (or repairer); (7) Tailor; (8) Confectioner, butcher, tanner; (9) Baker; (10) Day laborer. In addition, there were 8 "industrialists" (probably meaning someone who owned some kind of manufacturing business); 3 jewelry maker/repair, carpenter; 100 "minors"; and 255 "vagrants" (probably meaning someone without a fixed or stable occupation).

SOURCE: Departamento de Trabajo. Sección de Conciliación. "Informe que rinde el Jefe de la Sección sobre la situación de las colonias asiáticas en la Costa Occidental de la República," 1919 (E. Flores, Commissioner). Archivo General de la Nación/Trabajo, México, D.F.

Cócorit in the Yaqui Valley, with forty-two Chinese merchants, and Etchojoa and Huatabampo in the Mayo Valley.

The widespread distribution of Chinese businesses must also be noted in the context of their capitalization. In 1919, only fifteen Chinese businesses were capitalized at $20,000 pesos or above, for a total of $721,830, compared to 238 non-Chinese businesses, with a total of $18 million.[30] The average Chinese in this group had capital of $48,797, compared to $75,630 among the others. Only three of the Chinese had over $50,000. If this group can be characterized as Sonora's "grande bourgeoisie," then the Chinese were only an insignificant part of it. Chinese participation at this level of economic activity did not grow with time. From 1917 to 1920, Chinese entrepreneurs formed some eighty "mercantile societies," or companies.[31] The vast majority of the eighty were capitalized under $5,000 pesos. Mexican, European, and U.S. companies, by contrast, were typically capitalized at $25,000, $50,000, in the hundreds of thousands, and up to one or two million for the big mining, railroad, land, and agricultural enterprises.

The detailed report prepared by the Mexican Labor Department on capital invested in the Sonoran economy in 1919 further confirms the low Chinese presence among the large enterprises and the fundamentally petit bourgeois nature of the Chinese business community. Total Chinese-owned capital did not lag far behind all other capital combined, $2,186,935 pesos compared to $2,813,540 (see Table 1.4). However, there were almost twice as many Chinese

Table 1.4 Commercial establishments and capital in Sonora, 1919

District	Chinese		Mexican and All Others	
	No.	Total Capital	No.	Total Capital
Moctezuma	81	$220,520.00	28	$522,270.00
Guaymas	248	854,110.00	54	936,805.00
Sahuaripa	6	27,000.00	29	40,550.00
Altar	30	61,404.00	42	73,810.00
Alamos	102	185,100.00	44	104,400.00
Ures	25	48,900.00	28	45,400.00
Arizpe	110	196,320.00	67	546,555.00
Magdalena	107	320,621.00	54	168,400.00
Hermosillo	118	272,960.00	88	375,350.00
Total	827	2,186,935.00	434	2,813,540.00

SOURCE: Departamento de Trabajo. Sección de Conciliación. "Informe que rinde el Jefe de la Sección sobre la situación de las colonias asiáticas en la Costa Occidental de la República," 1919 (E. Flores, Commissioner). Archivo General de la Nación/Trabajo, México, D.F.

establishments as all others combined—North American, German, French, Arab, Japanese and other foreigners, and Mexican. The average Chinese business capital was $2,644, compared to $6,482 for others. Of the 827 Chinese businesses distributed over sixty communities, 740 were capitalized under $5,000.

Finally, in 1925, in the midst of a vigorous anti-Chinese campaign that called for their expulsion from Sonora, the state government once again took stock of the Chinese business profile, this time comparing it to Mexican industrial and commercial holdings.[32] By this time, it should be noted, a Mexican industrial and large commercial bourgeoisie had firmly established itself in Sonora, home to President Plutarco Elías Calles and former President Alvaro Obregón as well as many other revolutionary leaders who all laid claim to land and other properties in the state except for what the Chinese still held. Mexican-owned enterprises can be characterized as falling within the medium to large range: twenty-seven capitalized at $5,000 to $10,900 pesos; twenty-eight at $11,000 to $99,000, and five over $100,000. Among the Chinese, a considerable forty-one fell in the $5,000 to $10,900 range, but only four between $11,000 and $99,000, and only one above $100,000. The vast majority of Chinese businesses were capitalized under $5,000, with most of them actually worth $1,200 to $2,500. There was only one Mexican-owned business in that modest category. Moreover, the 517 Chinese businesses were spread over sixty-five of the state's seventy municipalities; the sixty-one Mexican firms were to be found in only fourteen towns.

In short, this commercial / industrial survey conducted by the state government conclusively demonstrated the Chinese monopoly of the small business commercial sector, to the practical exclusion of Mexicans. The situation was not particularly alarming to the large Mexican capitalists who in turn controlled the large commercial industrial sector of the economy, but it would provide fodder for the average Mexican who could, and did, aspire to the small commercial sector that was firmly in Chinese hands. The ubiquitous nature of these Chinese comerciantes, although providing a necessary service to all Sonorans, also became a thorn on the side of middle- and working-class Mexicans. Modest in fact, but prosperous in comparison to ordinary Sonorans still struggling to improve their lives well after the revolution in which many of them fought in the name of social justice, the Chinese also reminded Sonorans just how much foreigners had historically controlled their destiny, and how much farther they would have to go to reclaim Mexico for the Mexicans. Understandably, Mexican workers, landless peasants, and their families formed the backbone of the campaigns to remove the Chinese from their midst.

Where did the expelled Chinese go? It is hard to trace their steps. Some tried to enter the United States surreptitiously; some returned to China; others resettled in more hospitable parts of Mexico, notably Baja California Norte, a territory and Mexico's last frontier.

Like Mexico's other frontier and border regions, such as Sonora in the north, the Yucatán and Tapachula in the south, Baja California also experienced an influx of Chinese. But well before Sonoran Chinese fled to Baja California in the late 1920s and early 1930s, Chinese workers had been brought there under rather unique circumstances at the beginning of the twentieth century to develop the virgin land of the fertile Mexicali Valley. U.S. landowners and entrepreneurial Chinese formed partnerships to clear the rich valley, an extension of California's Imperial Valley, for large-scale cotton cultivation. U.S. landowners leased land to California Chinese merchants and labor contractors who brought in the workers to do the backbreaking work. By 1920, Chinese lessees and their Chinese workers were raising 80 percent of Mexicali's cotton crop. Details of the relationship between Chinese labor contracts and workers have been recounted elsewhere.[33]

Other Asia-Pacific Labor in Latin America

My concern in this discussion is primarily with Chinese immigrants. I would like to note here, however, Chinese were not the only Asia-Pacific people to end up in Latin America. Equally important in numbers and activity have been Japanese immigrants. In contrast to Chinese labor, the emigration of Japanese labor into Latin America, as into the United States, was much more closely regulated and supervised by the Japanese government. The first Japanese laborers began to arrive in Latin America—in Mexico and Peru—just around the turn of the twentieth century and increasingly after 1908, in Brazil. By the second and third decades of the twentieth century, Peru and Brazil were the foremost recipients of Japanese labor in the Western Hemisphere. By 1940, there were 234,574 immigrants of Japanese origin in Latin America, nearly 48 percent of all Japanese living abroad outside of Asia. By far the largest number were in Brazil (around 200,000), followed by Peru and Mexico. Also noteworthy is the fact that among Japanese immigrants to Latin America were large numbers of Okinawans and Ryukyu Islanders.[34]

The majority of Japanese immigrants to Latin America arrived initially also as contract laborers on coffee plantations in Brazil, sugar plantations in Peru, and rubber plantations in Bolivia. Although Japanese, like the Chinese in Peru, Cuba, and Mexico, would gradually move into urban small businesses (and after World War II, the professions), in Brazil in particular they were to achieve prominence as independent landed proprietors ("middle-class farmers," as James Tigner describes them) pioneering settlement in frontier regions, which made them a crucial sector of the agrarian economy of Brazil.[35]

One other group must be mentioned here not because it played any significant part in the development of Latin America, but because of what its presence in Latin America reveals about the underside of an Asia-Pacific formation. These are the Easter Islanders, who were nearly exterminated by labor needs in Peru. In 1862–63, for a period of a few months, private entrepreneurs "recruited" by force and guile Easter Islanders (among other Polynesians) to work in the guano fields in Peru. In the end, the islanders proved not suitable for the job. Many perished on the voyage or of disease and suicide after arrival. In a few months, the population of Easter Island came to the verge of extinction, about to follow the wake of the Arawaks of the Caribbean and the Tasmanians of the Pacific. Luckily for the Easter Islanders, their labor proved "useless," and the trade created such disgust in Peru that it came to an end while some of them still lived.[36]

Asian laborers contributed in significant ways in Latin America's development. As coolies and workers, they provided much needed labor in mines, guano fields, and plantations. As free laborers and small entrepreneurs, they opened up new frontiers of settlement and contributed to the vitality of urban economies.

As the earliest modern agriculturalists in Baja California who cleared the land for commercial crops, as coolies who moved progressively from semi-slavery to wage labor in Peru, the Chinese in Latin American agricultural and labor history have not been adequately recognized and fully documented. Yet the prosperity of both Baja California Norte and the Peruvian coast could not have been realized without Chinese sweat. The exact relationship of various categories of Chinese workers to production systems needs further research and more in-depth analysis.

As free immigrants to northwest Mexico and the Amazon, the Chinese proved adaptable to strange physical and cultural surroundings as well as harsh work regimens. They demonstrated an uncanny ability to detect and move swiftly into new economic spaces, often in "untamed" and under-developed frontier and border regions, where they usually found little or no competition from locals. They also tended to avoid conflict with entrenched, more powerful white or Europeans interests. Rather, they were instrumental in both Mexico and Peru's frontiers in clearing land to grow food for local consumption and crops for export. And with their production and distribution system and their widespread retail network, they in effect helped create in both countries a modern commercial infrastructure.

Latin America and the Asia-Pacific

The fragility of the small Easter Island population nearly drove it to extinction in a short period of recruitment for labor in Peru. There was no such danger for Chinese and Japanese. The experiences of immigrant laborers from China and Japan, however, were also revealing of the economic exploitation, racist discrimination, and cultural suppression of Asia-Pacific people that attended the formation of the Asia-Pacific region,

Although the coolie labor of the nineteenth century must be distinguished from slavery, it is quite clear that Chinese laborers were imported to Cuba and Peru to substitute for African labor that was lost with the abolition of slavery, and at least initially, they were barely distinguishable from slaves in the conditions of labor as well as in the treatment to which they were subjected.

The eventual success of Chinese in converting themselves into small urban business proprietors and the influx of free Asian immigrants to Latin America in ensuing decades were accompanied everywhere by anti-Asian agitation and mob action, as well as more organized state campaigns and persecution. In emulation of the U.S. Exclusion Act, Latin American governments in the early twentieth century enacted laws to severely limit further Asian, especially Chinese, immigration.

In Mexico, again echoing what had occurred earlier in California, anti-Chinese persecution culminated in 1929–31, the onset of the Depression, with mass expulsion from Sonora and to a lesser extent Baja California. The once ubiquitous and relatively prosperous Chinese community of Sonora never recovered, although Chinese have continued to be a viable commercial force in Baja California.

In Peru, at the end of the twentieth century, Chinese Peruvians remained a visible minority, their presence illustrated by the numerous and popular *chifas*, or Chinese restaurants, in Lima and other Peruvian towns big and small.

Shortly after the triumph of the Cuban revolution of 1959, a large number of the Cuban Chinese left the island as part of the massive exodus of the Cuban middle class.

Although Japanese communities in Latin America survived more intact than Chinese communities, in some ways, anti-Japanese persecution in Latin America reached even greater heights. In Peru, anti-Japanese sentiments led to the government's willingness to allow the U.S. government during World War II to round up and transport 1,429 Japanese Peruvians to the United States for internment in special concentration camps. In spite of this infamy, Japanese immigration resumed after World War II to Peru and especially Brazil. Significantly, from the beginning and throughout its history, Japanese migration to Latin America included more women and children. New immigration and natural reproduction allowed Japanese communities in both Peru and Brazil to continue to grow, until in both countries they came to constitute the largest immigrant community in the postwar period, numbering over 50,000 in Peru and 700,000 in Brazil by the 1970s.[37]

Against this historical background, Alberto Fujimori's election to Peru's presidency is truly extraordinary. On the other hand, the Japanese Peruvians are only cautiously proud of their fellow son of immigrants, fully aware that in the extremely difficult economic condition and volatile political situation of the country, Fujimori could well fail to govern effectively. Should that happen, another round of anti-Asian violence would not be beyond question.

In sum, the Latin American Pacific from the mid-nineteenth to the late twentieth century has been a mixed and often bitter experience for most Asian immigrants. Until Fujimori's election in 1990, Asian Latin Americans led a mostly quiet existence, trying hard not to call excessive attention to themselves.

For the past 150 years, from the California Gold Rush days on, the Pacific has been defined by another kind of Latin American migration. Led by Mexicans, but since the 1960s increasingly joined by Central and South Americans, legal but mostly undocumented Latin Americans have been streaming across the Mexican border into the United States. Largely in search of better economic opportunities, they also come to escape from civil war and political persecution at home.

At the time of Mexican independence from Spain in 1820, both the United States and Mexico had wide and sparsely settled frontiers rich in natural resources and open land. Both frontiers were also inhabited by hostile indigenous peoples determined to protect their distinctive way of life, land, and environment, and whose resistance to white encroachment made colonization difficult for Euro-Americans in both countries.

With a series of disastrous territorial losses by Mexico (amounting to three-fifths of its national territory) to the United States in the mid-nineteenth century—Texas independence in 1836, the Treaty of Guadalupe Hidalgo in 1848, the Treaty of La Mesilla (Gadsden Purchase) in 1853—the U.S. frontier expanded greatly at the expense of Mexico, and the U.S. government increasingly assumed responsibility for pacifying this broad zone. The long and violent process culminated with the pacification of the Apaches in the 1880s, opening up the final chapter of U.S. conquest of the West and Mexico's colonization of its by then much reduced north.

When the two frontiers finally met along the Rio Grande, they were also transformed into an international border.[38] But far from separating two countries, this border functioned to integrate Mexico and the United States far more closely than they had ever been before. For twentieth-century Mexicans, this border and the land beyond is known as *El Norte*.[39] The El Norte phenomenon has created in Los Angeles the second largest Mexican-populated city in the world, second only to Mexico City.

Driven from their homeland by landlessness and unemployment, twin results of dependent capitalist development, and by revolutions and civil wars, Mexicans have been going north since the days of the California Gold Rush. They continued crossing the border when mining gave way to agriculture, factories, manufacturing, assembly, and service industries in the late nineteenth and throughout the twentieth century. With jobs and economic opportunities constantly beckoning on the other side of the border, Mexicans have become the reserve labor force of the U.S.-Pacific. For Mexicans, this border has also been porous, a legal fiction never intended to keep them out permanently, but merely to control their movement to conform to vicissitudes of the U.S. economy and its changing labor demands.[40]

Although population movements back and forth across the border have involved mostly Mexican laborers, equally significant since the 1880s has been the massive flow of U.S. capital investment into Mexico and the resultant trade with Mexico. Initially concentrated in mining and railroads, since the 1940s it has diversified into commercial agriculture—culminating in the highly technified Green Revolution—and manufacturing. More recently, since 1965, U.S. capital has erected labor-intensive border plants known as *maquiladoras,* which utilize mostly young female labor to assemble products from parts imported duty free into Mexico; the finished products are then shipped back into the United States, also duty free. Touted as an ingenious mechanism to contain surplus Mexican labor within Mexico and hence stem the flow of Mexican workers across the border, the maquiladoras have actually served to integrate the Mexican economy even more closely with that of the United States and further consolidate Mexico's dependent status.

Any current and future conceptualization of the Asia-Pacific must contend with the El Norte phenomenon and integrate at least Mexico, if not the rest of the Pacific Rim of Latin America, into its configuration. With an equally massive post-1965 migration from Asia, Mexicans and Asians have transformed the demographic makeup of the U.S.-Pacific. According to the 1990 census, these two ethnic/racial minorities already exceed 35 percent of California's total population of nearly thirty million. Through continuous immigration and high reproductive rates, their growth will continue to outstrip that of other Euro-Americans, and their presence severely challenge the preservation of the dominant ethnic composition of U.S. society.

Postscript: Latin America and Asia-Pacific in the 1990s

On January 1, 1994, the Indian peasants of Chiapas, Mexico's southern-most province, rose up in rebellion, timing their action to coincide with the first day of implementation of the North American Free Trade Agreement (NAFTA) eagerly signed by the governments of the United States, Canada, and Mexico to consolidate neoliberal economic policies and practices in the hemisphere. Grandiosely named the Zapatista National Liberation Front (FZLN, for *Frente Zapatista de Liberación Nacional* in Spanish) and quickly popularized as Zapatistas, the rebels aimed their protest directly at outgoing President Carlos Salinas de Gotari and against NAFTA's certain acceleration of inmiseration of the country's rural poor.

Dubbed the world's first postmodern uprising because the rebels professed no interest in seizing state power while demonstrating uncanny sophistication in generating and maintaining international media interest in their just cause, the Zapatistas had been joined less than two years later by other indigenous peasant insurgencies in at least six other poverty-stricken states in southern and central Mexico loosely organized under the banner of the Popular Revolutionary Army (ERP, or *Ejército Popular Revolucionario,* organizationally distinct from the FZLN).

What all these rural rebels have in common is their vociferous objection to one of Salinas's most controversial preparatory moves for NAFTA: undoing Article 27 of the constitution of the Mexican Revolution, which had created thousands of pueblos with inalienable community land holdings called *ejidos,* the centerpiece of Mexico's postrevolutionary land reform and primary symbol of social justice for the peasants. Much to the shock of observers in Mexico and worldwide, Salinas violated an unspoken, sacrosanct principle that even his most corrupt and venal predecessors had kept, when he allowed the communal land holdings of the ejidos to be broken up, sold off, and privatized.[41]

This fateful decision indicated just how far Salinas and Mexico's governing elite in the officially party PRI (*Partido Revolucionario Institucional*) were willing to go to mortgage Mexico's most vulnerable citizens to neoliberalism's New World Economy. For over eighty years, peasants were assured of at least a minimum safety net; now even this threadbare net was yanked out from under them, leaving Mexico's forty-plus million already living in poverty (half of Mexico's total population) to sink deeper into misery. In the ten years of neoliberal policies that preceded the formal implementation of NAFTA in 1994, more than two million new rural poor were produced in the countryside.[42]

Nowhere is the poverty more visible or more entrenched than in Chiapas, Mexico's poorest state, where the insurrection has been converted into an "armed critique" of Salinas's neoliberal policies, designed to modernize Mexico through international economic integration based on export-oriented production and removal of all trade barriers, protective tariffs, and central government regulation of the economy. To demonstrate his commitment to the free market, Salinas also had to maximize privatization of Mexico's wealth, its resources and infrastructure. Not even communally owned land was immune to this onslaught.[43]

While the Zapatistas launched their protest in Mexico's south, all was seemingly quiet on the northern front. The maquila-driven border economy has been recently embellished and enhanced by capital investment from Asian "tigers" big and small—Japan, Korea, and Taiwan. In March 1996, Samsung of Korea opened a new $212 million TV assembly plant. Together with Daewoo, Sony, and Matsushita, these three giant conglomerates employ twenty-four thousand Mexican workers in the Tijuana area (border with San Diego), producing nine million TV sets a year, 90 percent of which are sold in the United States. Also operating in Mexico are some sixty Taiwan plants, soon to be joined by many more.[44] Given its abundant, increasingly disciplined and still cheap workforce of mostly willing women, and its gateway location to both the U.S. and Pacific markets, Mexico's advantage as the manufacturing center of the continent was firmly sealed in place by NAFTA.

Never explicitly stated but increasingly obvious is that Asian capital has become an unnamed partner of the North American Free Trade project. Salinas's secret plan was to diversify Mexico's economic relations with the world while lessening its dependence on U.S. capital and markets. To do so, Mexico needs to attract more capital from Asia and even Europe. For this to succeed, Mexico must be seen as an equal partner with Canada and the United States in the North American regional economy. By the same token according to this "trilateral strategy," expanded relations with industrial powers such as Japan may enhance Mexico's negotiating leverage with its powerful northern neighbor.[45]

By the early 1990s, Japan had become Mexico's second largest international economic partner. This relationship actually took off in the late 1970s, when Japan turned Mexico into a key supplier of its petroleum needs. During this past decade, Mexico saw a threefold increase of Japanese manufacturing investment in Mexico. Almost 180 Japanese maquiladoras were doing business in Mexico in 1990, most in automobile and electronics. Japanese firms are investing in Mexico for a variety of reasons. Nissan, for example, moved some operations to Mexico initially to survive the contraction of its domestic market. By contrast, Sanyo (electronics) and Yasaki (automobile) invested in Mexico as part of their globalization strategy within the larger North American market. By 1989, Mexico was exporting over $3 billion worth of auto parts, engines, and automobiles, mostly to the United States.

What has attracted Japanese investors to Mexico is Mexico's abundance of cheap labor and its close proximity to the United States. The maquiladora program allows plants to import raw materials, components, and capital equipment to Mexico duty free, while assembled products exported to the United States are subject only to duties on value added. The aggressive growth of the Japanese maquiladora sector can be further explained by Japan's policy of linking production in Mexico more to their U.S. investments than to the Mexico market. In other words, when Japanese auto makers opened plants in the United States to counter charges of U.S.-Japan trade imbalance, the Japanese concurrently established plants in Mexico to produce parts and components for the U.S.-based factories. For example, Honda opened a parts plant in Jalisco, Mexico, in the mid-1980s for $41 million; the operation has been exporting goods to the United States worth $100 million annually.[46]

In recent years, neoliberalism has been spreading beyond Mexico and the confines of NAFTA to Central America, where labor is even cheaper. In the San Marcos Free Trade Zone of San Salvador, capital of the densely populated, extremely poor country of El Salvador, Taiwanese businessmen such as David Wang have been sewing for such well-known U.S. clothing brands such as Gap, J. Crew, Eddie Bauer, and Liz Claiborne, among others. When women workers tried to organize, Wang apparently fired them.[47]

We can now make abundantly clear that far from being unconnected, the Zapatistas and other peasant rebels of Mexico on one side, and the maquiladora workers on the other, actually weave together one narrative, the underside of NAFTA. This narrative, furthermore, has an Asian-Pacific dimension. If in the distant past of the Spanish colonial period, Europeans went via Mexico and Central America across the Mar del Sur to extract the Orient's luxury goods for export, and if in the more recent past of the nineteenth century Latin American and Caribbean economies imported Asian coolie and family labor for plantations and factories, most recently, at the beginning of the twenty-first century and the dawn of neoliberalism's New Global Economy, these critical relationships have reconfigured. Today, Latin America imports capital from Asia, and exports parts as well as finished products to the United States, in turn supplying cheap labor to Asian entrepreneurs. Bearing the brunt of the cost are the poorest of the poor in Mexico, for whom NAFTA is, in the words of the enigmatic Zapatista leader, *Subcomandante* Marcos, "a death certificate for the Indian peoples of Mexico."

Notes

1. H. H. Dubs, "The Chinese in Mexico City in 1635," *Far East Quarterly* 1 (1942): 387–89.

2. The popular historian Stan Steiner asserted that a Chinese from Mexico City helped found Los Angeles in the eighteenth century. A seductive idea undoubtedly, but I believe he made a mistake, based on a misreading of colonial Spanish terminology, specifically a reference to a *chino* named Antonio Rodrigues who was a member of a motley crew of marginalized, mostly mixed-race individuals—eight Indians, three mulattos, two Blacks, one mestizo, and two Spaniards—seeking their fortune on New Spain's far northern frontier and founding a settlement they named "Ciudad de Los Angeles" (City of Angels). In colonial Spanish terminology, the term *chino*

by itself did not refer to a Chinese or an Asian, but rather, a dark-skinned person of mixed racial heritage. To refer to a Chinese or a person from Asia, the colonial records used the term *chinos de Manila,* Stan Steiner, *Fusang: The Chinese Who Built America* (New York: Harper & Row, 1979).

3. Watt, Stewart, *Chinese Bondage in Peru: A History of the Chinese Coolie in Peru, 1849–1874* (Durham, NC: Duke University Press, 1951); Evelyn Hu-DeHart, "Coolies, Shopkeepers, Pioneers: The Chinese of Mexico and Peru (1849–1893)," *Amerasia* 15 (1989): 91–116. During this period, about 1.5 million Chinese went overseas, to Southeast Asia, North America, as well as South America and the Caribbean, and other parts of the world. See Arnold Joseph Meagher, "The Introduction of Chinese Laborers to Latin America and the 'Coolie Trade,' 1847–1974" (Ph.D. dissertation, U. C. Davis, 1975), p. 55 (This is an excellent piece of research that should have been published as an important contribution to an aspect of the international migration of labor in the nineteenth century.)

The approximately 225,000 Chinese who went to Cuba and Peru were almost exclusively males. So few women went under contract that they were statistically insignificant. A few women went as prostitutes (possibly sent from California by enterprising California Chinese) or free women. The Cuban census of 1872 noted 58,400 Chinese, of whom only 32 were females, 2 under contract, and 30 free. Of the 34,650 noted in the 1862 census, 25 were females. Of the 24,068 in the 1877 census, 8 were female (some possibly born in Cuba and Peru). These figures were taken from C. M. Morales's papers, vol. 3, no. 19, Biblioteca Nacional José Marti, Havana: Vidal Morales y Morales, "Immigración de chinos en la Isla de Cuba. Datos que ha proporcionado el que suscrita a Mr. Sanger, Inspector General del Censo" (Collection of clippings, n.d.). The Peruvian census of 1872, which is incomplete, notes 12,849 Chinese in the four coastal provinces of Pacasmayo, Trujillo, Chiclayo, and Lambayeque where the Chinese population was concentrated; only 15 of them were females (*Censo de 1872,* Archivo General de Peru [AGP]).

4. After experimenting briefly with Chinese coolies in the early nineteenth century, the British exported massive numbers (1–2 million) of East Indian coolies to the West Indies and East Africa; for a comprehensive study of this coolie trade, see Hugh Tinker, *A New System of Slavery: The Export of Indian Labor Overseas: 1830–1920* (London: Oxford University Press, 1974).

5. Franklin Knight, *Slave Society in Cuba during the Nineteenth Century* (Madison: University of Wisconsin Press, 1970), p. 6.

6. Ibid, p. 22.

7. Cited in Humberto Rodríguez Pastor, *Hijos del Celeste Imperio en el Perú (1850–1900): Migración, Agricultura, Mentalidad y Explotación* (Lima: Insituto de Apoyo Agrario, 1988), p. 32.

8. Michael J. Gonzáles, *Plantation, Agriculture and Social Control in Northern Peru, 1875–1933* (Austin: University of Texas Press, 1985), p. 23.

9. Archivo Nacional de Cuba (ANC), Junta de Fomento, 147 / 7282. Also, Juan Jiménez Pastrana, *Los Chinos en la historia de Cuba, 1847–1930* (Havana: Ed. Ciencias Sociales, 1983), pp. 13–17.

10. Watt Stewart, *Chinese Bondage in Peru*, pp. 13–17; he gives the number of Chinese imported in 1849–1854 as 2,516. The figure of 4,754 was taken from Rodríguez Pastor, *Hijos del Celeste Imperio*, p. 24, Cuadro no. 4.

11. *Boletín de Colonización*, I: 18, 15 October 1873. The *Boletín*, published in 1873 and 1874, was the official organ of the powerful *Junta* (or *Comisión*) *de Colonización*, which had jurisdiction over the coolie trade and the coolies, whom it always and consistently termed *colonos* or *immigrantes*. The president of the junta was the prominent planter and international businessman, Julián Zulueta, the same one who introduced the first coolie cargo to Cuba in 1847. Zulueta exemplified what might be termed vertical integration in the sugar industry of Cuba.

12. Zhang Kai, "Guba huagong yu Zhong Guo jianjiao shimo" (Chinese Labor in Cuba and Establishment of Sino-Cuban Diplomatic Relations), *Huaqiao Huaren Lishi Yanjiu* (Overseas Chinese History Review) 4 (1988): 3–11.

13. Rodríguez Pastor, *Hijos del Celeste Imperio*, p. 39; Stewart, *Chinese Bondage in Peru*, pp. 117–23.

14. "Actas de las comisión inspectora de asiáticos en la provincia de Santa," *El Peruano*, 29 April 1870; Rodríquez Pastor; *Hijos del Celeste Imperio*, p. 52. Many examples of recontracts in Cuba can be found in the ANC, Misc. de Exp., e.g., 4193 / Cs, which contains several for 1868. The Archivo del Fuero Agrario account books for Peruvian plantations also contain much information on recontracted Chinese in the 1870s and 1880s.

15. Antonio Chuffat Latour, *Apunte histórico de los Chinos en Cuba* (Havana: Molina y Cía., 1972), p. 93; *Boletín de Colonización* I:9, 30 May 1873, contains editorial on the *cuadrillas*, describing them as dedicated "colectivamente a las faenas de la finca."

16. Gonzáles, *Plantation, Agriculture and Social Control*, pp. 71, 93.

17. *Boletín de Colonización* 1:9, 30 May 1873. By law, anyone residing in Cuba but not naturalized must be registered as an alien or foreign resident. As most Chinese in Cuba embarked from Macao, they registered generally with the Portuguese consul in Havana. Beside, there was no representation of the Chinese government in Havana at the time of the census (1872).

18. *Boletín de Colonización* 1:9, 30 May 1873 (Editorial); Denise Helly, *Idéologie et ethnicité: Les Chinois Macao à Cuba, 1847–1886* (Montreal: Les Presses Universitaires de Montréal, 1979), pp. 231–37.

19. Rebecca Scott, *Slave Emancipation in Cuba: The Transition to Free Labor, 1860–1899* (Princeton, NJ: Princeton University Press, 1985), pp. 99–100, 110, 120.

20. Helly, *Idéologie et ethnicité*, pp. 237–40.

21. Rodríguez Pastor, *Hijos del Celeste Imperio*, pp. 108, 121.

22. "Expediente sobre la averiguación practicada por la Comisión China asesorada por funcionarios del gobierno, respecto al la situación de sus connacionales que prestan sus servicios en las haciendas," Lima, 9 de mayo 1887–diciembre 1888. Biblioteca Nacional, Lima, Peru. This document, also based on testimonies taken from the Chinese (in this case, mostly ex-coolies, given the late date), is the Peruvian equivalent of Chinese Commission to Cuba.

23. Rodríguez Pastor, *Hijos del Celeste Imperio,* pp. 145–46, 165.

24. A study of a small but important Chinese community in a sierra town is contained in Isabel Lausent, *Pequeña propiedad, poder y economía de mercado. Acos, Valle de Chancay* (Lima: Instituto Estudios Peruano, 1983).

25. Lausent is also the one who has published on the Chinese in the Peruvian Amazon: "Los inmigrantes chinos en la Amazonía Peruana," *Bulletin Institut François d'Etudes Andines* 15 (1986): 49–60.

26. Elsewhere I recount more fully the establishment of the Chinese community in Sonora and Mexican reaction: "Immigrants to Developing Society: The Chinese in Northern Mexico, 1875–1932," *Journal of Arizona History* 31 (Autumn 1980): 49–86; "Racism and Anti-Chinese Persecution in Mexico," *Amerasia* 9 (1982): 1–28. Also see Charles Cumberland, "The Sonoran Chinese and the Mexican Revolution," *Hispanic American Historical Review* 40 (1960): 191–211; Leo H. D. Jacques, "The Anti-Chinese Campaign in Sonora, Mexico, 1900–1931" (Ph.D. dissertation, University of Arizona, 1974).

27. The demographic discussion is based on the following sources: Mexican censuses for 1900, 1910, 1921, and 1930; "Extranjeros residentes Estados Unidos de México. Resúmen del censo practicado por la Sría de Gobernación en 1927; "Extranjeros, distribución por estado, marzo 1928," Archivo Histórico del Gobierno e Estado de Sonora (AHGES), vol. 50, 1930; Consul A. Willard to State Department, Guaymas, 31 December 1887, U.S. National Archives, General Records of the Department of State, Record Group 59, M284, Roll 4, no. 851; Willard to State, 8 May 1890, RG59/M284/Rool 4, no. 983; Ramón Corral, *Memoria de la administración pública del estado de Sonora* (Guaymas, 1981), vol. 1, pp. 586–602; "Comisión oficial encargado del estudio de la inmigración asiática en México, 18 noviembre 1903," reports submitted by district prefects in 1904, AHGES, vol. 1900; Sonora State Government, Census of Chinese residents, submitted by municipal presidents, 1919, AHGES, vol. 3345; Estado del Sonora, Sección de Estadística, Abril de 1925, "Censo Chino," AHGES, vol. 3741; Departamento de Trabajo. Sección de Conciliación. "Informe que rinde el Jefe se la Sección sobre la situación de las colonias asiáticas en la Costa Occidental de la República," 1919, Archivo General de la Nación/Trabajo, México, D. F.

28. International Chinese Business Directory, 1913.

29. Estado de Sonora, Sección de Estadística, Año de 1925, "Censo Chino," AHGES, vol. 3741.

30. "Lista de los causantes sujetos a la contribución directa ordinaria que tienen capitales de $20,000 en adelante," AHGES, vol. 2968.

31. "Sociedades civiles y mercantiles en Sonora, 1912, 1917, 1918, 1919, 1920," taken from the *Registro Público de la Propiedad* (property registration) of each district, AHGES, vol. 432.

32. "Noticia de estadística comparativa de los giros comerciales e industriales con especificaciones de su capital invertido, de Nacionales y Chinos establecidos en el Estado de Sonora," 2 junio 1925, AHGES vol. 3758.

33. For a fuller discussion of the Chinese in Baja California Norte see my article, "The Chinese of Baja California Norte, 1910–1934," *Baja California and the North Mexican Frontier,* Proceedings of the Pacific Coast Council on Latin American Studies, vol. 12 (San Diego, CA: San Diego State University Press, 1985–1986). This pattern of Chinese leasing land from U.S. landowners and contracting Chinese labor gangs to work the land is similar to what happened in California as described by Sucheng Chan, *This Bittersweet Soil: The Chinese in California Agriculture, 1860–1910* (Berkeley, CA: University of California Press, 1986).

34. James L. Tigner, "Japanese Immigration to Latin America: A Survey," *Journal of Interamerican Studies and World Affairs* 23, no. 4 (November 1981): 457–82. Despite their number and importance little has been published in Spanish or English on the Japanese in Brazil and Peru (though more may be published in Japanese). Among available works, in addition to Tigner are the following: José Tiago Cintra, *La Migración Japonesa en Brasil* (1908–1959) (México. El Colegio de México, Centro de Estudios Orientals, 1974); C. Harvey Gardiner, *The Japanese and Peru, 1873–1973* (Albuquerque: University of New Mexico Press, 1975); Amelia Morimoto, *Los Inmigrantes Japoneses en el Perú* (Lima: Taller de Estudios Andinos, Universidad Nacional Agraria, 1979); C. Harvey Gardiner, *Pawns in the Triangle of Hate: The Peruvian Japanese and the United States* (Seattle: University of Washington Press, 1981).

35. Tigner, "Japanese Immigration," p. 476.

36. Grant McCall, "European Impact on Easter Island: Response, Recruitment and the Polynesian Experience in Peru," *Journal of Pacific History* II, pt. 1 (1976): 90–105. See also H. E. Maude, *Slavers in Paradise: The Peruvian Slave Trade in Polynesia, 1862–1864* (Stanford, CA: Stanford University Press, 1981).

37. Evelyn Hu-DeHart, "Spanish America," The Encyclopedia of the Chinese Overseas. General Editor: Lyan Pan. (Singapore: Archipelago Press, 1998), pp. 254–60.

38. For an elaboration of this thesis on the first two frontiers becoming an international border, see Friedrich Katz, *The Secret War in Mexico: Europe, the United States and the Mexican Revolution* (Chicago: University of Chicago Press, 1981), chapter 1.

39. Since the 1960s, Mexicans have been joined by increasing numbers of Central Americans going to El Norte. A good depiction of this migration is the film *El Norte*.

40. For a fuller discussion of Mexican labor immigration into the United States and the idea of the border as legal fiction, see James D. Cockcroft, *Outlaws in the Promised Land: Mexican Immigrant Workers and America's Future* (New York: Grove Press, 1986).

41. Andrew Reding, "Rebellion in Mexico," *Washington Post,* January 11, 1994; Reding, "Chiapas is Mexico: The Imperative of Political Reform," *World Policy Journal* (Spring 1994), pp. 11–25; "NAFTA and the Chiapas Crises," *Latin American Labor News,* Issue 9 / 1993–94, pp. 1 and 4; Greg Campbell, "The New Manifest Destiny: NAFTA and Oil Threaten Future of Chiapas Indians," *Boulder Weekly,* July 4, 1996, p. 8.

42. Julio Moguel, "Salinas's Failed War on Poverty," in Fred Rosen and Deidre McFadyen, eds., *Free Trade and Economic Restructuring in Latin America.* New York: Monthly Review Press, 1995, p. 210.

43. Gerardo Otero, "Mexico's Political Future(s) in the Globalizing Economy," *The Canadian Journal of Sociology and Anthropology* 32: 3 (August 1995), pp. 315–39. See also Otero, ed., *Neo-Liberalism Revisited: Economic Restructuring and Mexico's Political Future.* Boulder: Westview Press, 1996.

44. Anthony DePalma, "Economic Lesson in a Border Town," *New York Times,* May 23, 1996, p. C1; Kelly Her, "Mexico's Luring Taiwan Investors," *Free China Journal,* September 13, 1996, p. 8.

45. Barbara Stalling and Gabriel Szekely, "The New Trilateralism: The United States, Japan, and Latin America," in Stalling and Szekely, eds., *Japan, the United States, and Latin America: Toward a Trilateral Relationship in the Western Hemisphere.* Baltimore: Johns Hopkins, 1993, pp. 33–34.

46. Gabriel Szekely, "Mexico's International Strategy: Looking East and North," in Stalling and Szekely, eds., *Japan, the United States,* pp. 159–160.

47. Bob Herbert, "In Deep Denial," *New York Times,* October 13, 1995, p. A15.

2 Filipino Sea Men: Identity and Masculinity in a Global Labor Niche

Steven C. McKay

THE FILIPINO LABOR DIASPORA is arguably the largest in the world. Over eight million Filipinos—nearly 10 percent of the entire Philippine population—toil abroad in 140 countries, funneling ten billion U.S. dollars back into the Philippines each year.[1] Yet beyond sheer volume and diffusion, these "new heroes" of the transnational nation are nevertheless channeled into highly stratified, gendered, and racialized occupations. This channeling has led to particular—and sometimes peculiar—labor market niches: from nurses in the United States, to maids in East Asia, to hotel house bands around the world (Bowe 2005; Choy 2003; Constable 1997). But the niche Filipinos arguably most dominate is also the one most overlooked: merchant seafaring. In one of the world's most globalized industries, it is a curious fact that nearly one in every three workers at sea is from the Philippines. Over 255,000 Filipino seafarers, by far the largest national group, ply the world's oceans and seas, primarily as deck hands, engine room oilers, cabin cleaners, and cooks aboard container ships, oil tankers, and luxury cruise liners.

I take up the rise and reproduction of this largely invisible occupational niche to explore how labor diasporas shape—and are shaped by—race, class, gender, and history. Ships and sailors have been central in forming theories of diaspora. Paul Gilroy (1993) uses the image of the ship as a "chronotope" or optic to understand cultural systems operating beyond national boundaries. For Gilroy, ships "were the mobile elements that stood for the shifting spaces in between the fixed places that they connected . . . a means to conduct political dissent and possibly a distinct mode of cultural production" (Gilroy 1993: 16–17). Yet in celebrating alternative "third-spaces" such as ships, diaspora studies has tended to downplay the multiple structures that continue to constrict and shape diasporic subjects (Auge 1995; Cheah 1999). In fact, rather than spaces of mobility and dissent, contemporary ships—as detailed below—are suffused with the forces and inequalities of the international world, often reproducing, not transcending, a highly stratified order.

Another neglected area of diaspora studies is the active role of nation-states, both imperial and postcolonial. As Stuart Hall argues, contemporary diasporic subjects can only be understood in their specific political and historical contexts (Morley and Chen 1996). For Filipino seafarers, their emergence in today's shipping industry owes much to American colonial policies that molded Philippine education, while also racializing Filipino incorporation into labor markets abroad. The postcolonial Philippine state has played an equally important role, seeding the diaspora through official policy and projecting a particular image of Filipino migrant labor to boost the returns of the country's number one export.

Finally, the case of Filipino seafarers helps highlight the construction and negotiation gendered identities in diaspora. Recent migration scholars have tended to treat gender primarily as an added variable or given social category and focus almost exclusively on women (Pessar and Mahler 2003; Thompson 2003). Below, I use gender as a lens to examine masculinity among Filipino seafarers and how among migrants it can serve as both a disciplinary regime as well as a site of creative resistance.

My analysis is thus located in the dialectic between nation and diaspora and throws into sharper relief the political processes of identity and niche formation at such "transnational edges" as oceangoing ships (Smith 2003; Yeoh, Willis, and Fakhri 2003). I argue that the construction of *Filipinoness* and exemplary styles of masculinity, forged despite subordinate racial and class positions both onboard and in the labor market, help Filipino sea men endure the harshness of workplace conditions, while at the same time reproducing their niche. I also argue that the overlapping but at times contradictory meanings of *Filipinoness* as defined by both the Philippine state and by seafarers themselves highlight the constructed nature of diasporas and the need to analyze and theorize diasporic formations less as stable, bounded entities and more as contested political projects (Brubaker 2005).

The chapter first presents a brief history of Filipino seafarers and an overview of recent changes in the global shipping industry that have spurred labor demand. It then focuses on the Philippine state and manning agencies, which have helped construct particular discourses on national identity and masculinity in order to match the needs of the global market. In the final section, I focus on Filipino seafarers themselves and how they construct and navigate multiple masculinities at work and at home to maximize the benefits of migration and reassert their status and social roles in their communities.

The essay draws on two months of field research in the Philippines, conducting interviews and gathering data from state officials, manning agencies, ship management firms, training centers, and seafarer advocacy groups. With the assistance of local researchers, I collected some 100 two-hour interviews with seafarers onboard training and commercial ships visiting Manila Bay, in two sea men's dormitories, and at the spot labor market for seafarers on the streets of Manila. Interviews focused on how seafarers were drawn into shipping, their relations with seafarers of other nationalities, and their national, occupational, and gender identities as Filipino sea men.

Changes in International Shipping and the Rise of Filipino Crews

Filipino seafarers on Western merchant ships have a long history: from forced labor aboard Spanish galleons from the sixteenth to the nineteenth century, to crew members on British trading and American whaling ships in the nineteenth century, to a brief stint as stewards in the American merchant marines in the early twentieth century (Aguilar 2003; Borah 1995 / 1996; Melendy 1977). In fact, Filipinos became so identified with crewing that the term *Manilamen* —a reference to the capital of the Philippines—became an entire category for "Asiatic" seafarers on Western ships, including Filipinos, Chinese, Malays, Oceanians, South Asians, and those of mixed race (Chappell 2004). The presence of Filipinos in the world's ports also led to small but stable communities of Manilamen strewn across the globe, from Shanghai and Singapore to London, Cape Town, and New York (Aguilar 2003; White 1972 [1861]).

Yet Filipinos virtually disappeared from international commercial shipping after 1936, when the United States barred foreigners from their vessels. So how did Filipinos reemerge to dominate crewing by the turn of the twenty-first century? To understand their contemporary resurgence, it is important to understand labor markets more generally. The seafarer marketplace, like all labor markets, is not a frictionless arena in which labor supply automatically adjusts to labor demand, and all players—employers, recruiters, and job seekers—have equal power, mobility, or access to information. Rather, the seafarer labor market is a socially organized and often highly segmented matching process in which clusters of jobs of differential quality (that is, "good," stable, and well-paying jobs versus "bad," low-paying, and insecure jobs) are often categorically fitted to different *groups* of workers seen as best suited to these jobs (Grannovetter and Tilly 1988; Peck 1996). This is most clearly illustrated by the sexual division of labor and the gender labeling of different jobs and occupations, leading to gendered labor niches and, consequently, women receiving—on average—less pay, lower positions, and less authority than men (Padavic and Reskin 2002; Waldinger 1994).

In the seafarer labor market, Filipinos exploded back onto the scene in the 1970s, but were channeled into specific (lower) positions due to two key structural factors: first, changes in global demand for seafarers and second, the character of Filipinos' labor supply. After a post-World War II boom, the oil crises of the 1970s and the subsequent slump in world trade left the shipping industry with too many vessels, too few orders, and intense pressure to cut costs (International Labor Organization [ILO] 2001). In response, shipping firms and their home governments reorganized the industry and crafted new regulations that radically restructured the labor market. Until the 1970s, shipowners registered or "flagged" their vessels in their home country, requiring them to employ their own nationals and observe domestically negotiated labor laws and wages. However, the rising competitive pressures led shipowners looking to lower their costs to flag their vessels in countries that promised minimal interference, little or no taxes, and few industrial or labor regulations (Alderton et al. 2004). Known as flags of convenience (FOC), these thirty or so countries—led by Panama and Liberia—allow both foreign ownership of vessels and crewing by nonnationals. By design, they have little or no regulatory capacity to impose either national or international regulations over these foreign-owned ships (International Confederation of Free Trade Unions [ICFTU] et al. 2002). Some countries, such as Norway, the United Kingdom, and Germany, also created "second registers" that mimic the unregulated conditions of FOC states. Today, over 64 percent of all shipping is done under FOC or secondary registers, and more than half of the over 1.2 million seafarers worldwide sail on such lightly regulated ships (ILO 2001).

The move to FOC and secondary registers has had an enormous impact on the seafarer labor market. In 1960, only 15 percent of the world's sea men were Asians. By 1987 Asians—mainly from the Philippines, South Korea, India, and Indonesia—constituted 67 percent of the seafaring labor force (Turnbull 2000). The primary reasons for the shift were to lower wage bills and circumvent national regulations. For example, a Norwegian ship owner in 1987 claimed he could save one million dollars per ship per year on crew costs by moving to an FOC state (ILO 2001).

Crucially, the creation of secondary registers was done in conjunction with European and Japanese seafarer labor unions. These unions sought to retain their key positions at the higher officer and engineering levels, while allowing foreign crewing for "ratings" or positions in the lower ranks of the deck and engine room. Thus the ship owners opened up the labor market, but only at the bottom. As one captain from the Norwegian Training Center in the Philippines noted: "Norwegians were just getting too expensive, so [the Norwegian ship owners] started looking around for replacements . . . But they did some horse-trading with the Norwegian unions . . . the agreement let senior officers and specialized workers keep their top positions."

Although the conditions in the global labor market were ripe for the entrance of lower cost seafarers from developing countries, the question remains, how did *Filipinos* come to both enter and later dominate the lower echelons of international crewing? Here, the influence of American colonial institutions and language loom large. As early as 1899, the American colonial government in the Philippines helped set up the Philippine Nautical School (PNS), creating a maritime training curriculum and making all instruction in English, which today remains the *lingua franca* of shipping. Following World War II and Philippine independence, PNS remained the only public maritime academy, setting the national standard. When PNS was reorganized in 1963 and renamed the Philippine Merchant Marine Academy (PMMA), it modeled its newer curriculum, training, and certification directly along the lines of the U.S. Merchant Marine, which dominated international shipping in the early postwar period (PMMA 2003). Thus in the early 1970s, when foreign shipping firms were being squeezed by industry crises and began looking for cheaper labor, they were attracted to Filipinos for their English-language training and certifications based on the American standards.

Still, as with many ethnic labor niches, the path to Filipino dominance began somewhat serendipitously. According to Peter Toundjis, a Greek ship manager, it all started by accident: in 1966, a Greek ship came to Manila needing an emergency replacement crew. His company, which usually only helped restock provisions, nevertheless agreed, sparking the first placement of Filipinos on Greek ships. Toundjis (1975: 7–8) writes: "word quickly spread in Piraeus, New York and other international maritime centers that Filipinos were good and dependable. El Greco [Toundjis's company] thereupon launched an information campaign to sell the Filipino seaman, undertaken through brochures distributed to more than 2,000 shipowning companies all over the world. The brochures generated inquiries from all directions and helped put the Philippine crewing industry firmly on its feet."

Indeed, as the word spread, other major shipping firms that were experimenting with foreigners in their lower-rank positions began trying out Filipinos. One Norwegian captain interviewed noted: "The Norwegians knew seafarers worldwide through experience . . . They liked Filipinos because they spoke English and had certificates to sail. Indians were 'snotty' and wanted higher positions, but Filipinos were cheaper, willing to be ratings [lower level, nonofficers] and were willing to take orders. Hoegh [shipping lines] was the first big Norwegian company to start using Filipino ratings. They swapped the Norwegians in one day."

Hoegh was not alone. Whereas in the late 1960s only about 2,000 Filipino seafarers served on foreign ships a year, by 1975, 23,534 seafarers (over 65 percent of all overseas workers) were sailing internationally (National Seamen Board [NSB] 1982). In the 1980s, recruiting took another big leap; in a single year, Filipinos on European-owned ships went from 2,900 to 17,057, and overall there were over 57,000 Filipinos aboard some 4,000 foreign ships (ILO 2001; NSB 1982). The numbers have continued to rise steeply, reaching over 255,000 seafarers in 2001 (Philippine Overseas Employment Administration [POEA] 2001). Filipinos are now by far the largest national group in the global labor market—making up 28.1 percent. The next closest national groups—Russians at 6.8 percent, Ukrainians at 6.3 percent, and Chinese at 6.2 percent—together make up only about half that of the Filipinos (Amante 2003). Today, in large part because seafarers must by law remit at least 80 percent of their base wages to the Philippines, seafarers send home some two billion U.S. dollars *each year,* or nearly 30 percent of all official remittances from overseas Filipino workers (Amante 2003).

Yet while their numbers and remittances have grown dramatically, their positions on the occupational ladder have not substantially improved. Filipinos were recruited initially to serve as lower level ratings or nonofficers on deck and in the engine room. In 1976, of the 45,000 registered sea men, only 10 percent were officers, and these were at the junior rank of fourth engineer and third mate (NSB 1976). By 2000, only 15 percent of registered Filipino seafarers were officers, and in 2003 only 8.5 percent had reached the senior officer level (Amante 2003; POEA 2001). Stratification by nationality is also evident when comparing Filipinos to other seafarers. For example, while there are over eight lower level Filipino ratings for every senior Filipino officer, among Indians, there are only two and a half ratings for every senior officer, and among Ukrainians, only two ratings for every senior officer (Wu 2004). Some studies of the global seafarer labor market have pointed out that historical deficiencies in Philippine officer training standards and questionable licensing procedures in the past have led to their under-representation at the officer level (Alderton et al. 2004). However, while competence can be an important factor, there is also clear evidence that the labor market remains segmented and that some shipping companies maintain distinct preferences for different positions by nationality. For instance, both Japanese and Greek ship owners fill the majority of their lower level ratings positions with Filipinos. Yet while Japanese also fill 40 percent of their senior officer positions with Filipinos, Greek ship owners fill only about 14 percent of their senior officer positions with Filipinos (Wu 2004).

The segmented labor market, then, can obviously reduce access for "out-groups" such as Filipinos. A continuing problem, as noted by Anthony Lane "is the low number of Filipino officers who gain promotion to senior ranks" (2002:9). But for "in-groups," segmentation can also help limit competition and secure a stable position in competitive markets. So once they broke into the lower positions, Filipinos—and their national government that relies on their dollar remittances—have tried hard to differentiate themselves from other nationalities in order to set Filipinos apart in the labor market and defend their existing (albeit lower) niche.

The Philippine Migration Industry and Narratives of Masculinity

To explore how Filipino seafarers have become differentiated and on what basis, it is important to understand how labor market segmentation intersects with the construction of national and gendered—in this case masculine —identities. As in other labor markets, the least desirable jobs often go to the most marginal groups, usually sorted along gender, national, and ethnic lines. Crucially, the main requirement for jobs at the bottom of the labor market, where workers have the least bargaining leverage, is tractability. Thus in filling such "secondary" jobs, employers tend to prefer groups that they feel are best suited to subordination, then ascribe this character to members of the group itself (Waldinger and Lichter 2003). Although in commercial shipping rigid authority structures have been somewhat relaxed, social relations are still much more hierarchical than in most workplaces, due in large part to their military origins and the fact that captains are still literally referred to as *masters* (Lane 1996). In shipping, Filipinos have taken up such lower or "secondary" positions and have also been ascribed with the characteristic of being "good subordinates."

Yet this characterization is not simply imposed by foreign shipowners. A key player in promoting and differentiating Filipinos has also been the Philippine government. Through its explicit development strategy based largely on the export of Filipino labor, the state—along with Philippine manning agencies—works hard to both reproduce the Filipino niche in seafaring and keep remittances flowing. But they have often done so by constructing particular narratives of *Filipinoness*, national heroism, and subordinate masculinity that reinforce existing racialized and gendered stereotypes used in the hiring process.

Government-sponsored marketing abroad has been critical to the success of Filipinos in international shipping. The key state institution that began promoting seafarers was the NSB, created in 1974, with three main goals: employment creation, the protection of sea men, and generating foreign exchange (NSB 1976). Captain Benjamin Tanedo, the NSB's assistant executive director commented: "[I]n 1975 I started traveling all over the world, marketing in Europe—to Germans, Greeks—also to Americans and Japanese to try to sell our sea men . . . They had a need for sea men, so it wasn't like I was selling something they didn't want, like some cheap shoes. I was selling something they needed!"

The NSB and later the POEA, in their materials and in interviews with officials, have always been careful to point out the strong training and English-speaking abilities of Filipinos.[2] Yet in order to set Filipinos apart from their competitors, the state and the manning agencies also constructed an image of Filipino seafarers to best fit the requirements of the segmented labor market. This entails endowing the "natural" Filipino seafarers with the "innate" qualities of pliability. One POEA brochure from the early 1980s boasts: "[W]hat truly makes a Filipino the most dependable shipmate are certain inherent traits. He is adaptable and hard-working. The Filipino's charm and friendliness makes for a harmonious relationship essential to the working situation on board. He is neat and disciplined. Reflective of household breeding, the Filipino is particularly observant of clean surroundings and good grooming. Moreover, he keeps within set rules and regulations" (POEA n.d.).

Interestingly, while nearly all the demand was for male workers in the 1970s and 1980s, today the fastest growing area in crewing is in the luxury cruise liners, which hire a substantial portion of women as housekeepers; entertainers; and kitchen, restaurant, and wait staff. This shift has somewhat altered the marketing of Filipino seafarers. For example, the marketing materials of the Philippine Seafarers Promotion Council (PSPC)—a group of leading manning agencies, labor unions, shipowners, and government agencies—emphasize that Filipinos are "reliable, resilient, well-trained and loyal." They also project a more "feminine" character of Filipino seafarers proclaiming: "Filipinos go the extra mile and serve with a smile . . . When you employ Filipinos, you have access to SKILL with a HEART. Filipinos are by nature a warm people who exude a high standard of customer service. They are also happy to work even under challenging conditions at sea" (emphasis in the original). Thus Filipino seafarers not only remain in subordinate positions, but there is a growing emphasis on their feminine and willingly subservient character.

While the state and private players promote Filipinos externally to employers, they are also concerned *internally* with keeping seafarers cheap and tractable. Despite their external rhetoric of pliability, in order to win the consent of migrants, the state and the migration industry craft particular understandings of *Filipinoness* and masculinity that help obscure tensions both in the workplace and in the state's own development strategy.

To keep Filipino seafarers cheap, the POEA, which determines the minimum standard contract terms, has delayed implementing the ILO's wage recommendations for three years, using in their 2003 standard contract the 2000 ILO rate of $385 per month for an able-bodied seaman, which remains $50 below the 2003 ILO rate and $915 below the unionized rate set by the International Transport Workers' Federation. In terms of "pliability," the Promotion Council and other industry groups have been concerned with the rising individual and collective actions of seafarers in drawing attention to their plight and winning redress. The PSPC has responded, lobbying the government and cautioning, "we must urgently reverse the emerging reputation of the Filipino seafarer as a troublemaker . . . This reputation has come about because of the practice of some Filipino seafarers . . . to file [legal] cases in other jurisdictions." The statement, contained in an industry development plan, also calls for "a reversal of the tendency of our seafarers to be litigious" (Maritime Industry Cluster Secretariat [MICS] 2003: 83–84).

The state has also been active in heading off migrants' collective complaints and the broader concerns of the Philippine public over well-publicized migrant abuse and subordination as "servants of globalization" (Constable 1997; Parreñas 2001). In response the state constructs overseas workers as

Bagong Bayani or "new heroes" of the nation, to recognize—but not necessarily relieve—the suffering of overseas workers and draw attention to their contributions to the state's domestic economic development (Guevarra 2003; Okamura 1998). What is interesting is the ambivalent gendering of the term *hero* as the gender balance of the migrants has shifted. While in the 1970s and early 1980s migrant laborers were overwhelming male, by the 1990s over half of the migrants were women (Parreñas 2001). As Connell (1995) notes, the idea of a national hero has long been associated with masculinity. But in this case, the Philippine government, needing to address both male and female migrants, has broadened the idea of national hero to be less gender specific, focusing more on sacrifice and economic provision for one's family. The POEA has used the term since 1984, giving out annual *Bagong Bayani* awards to outstanding overseas workers. In 1995, President Fidel Ramos declared National Seafarers Day in order to recognize seafarers as among these new heroes.

The term *new hero* and its gendered ambiguity must be understood within the particular cultural repertoire of Philippine nationalism. The term derives its power and cultural meaning from the suffering and martyrdom of the "first Filipino" and nationalist hero José Rizal at the hands of Spanish colonizers (Rafael 2000). As Rafael (2000: 211) has argued, the potency of Rizal's heroic legacy draws from his connection to the narrative of Christ's *Pasyon*, with both Rizal and Christ "at once pathetic and prophetic . . . forced to undergo humiliation at the hands of alien forces." Thus in evoking the term *new hero* the state taps into particular cultural understandings of heroism steeped in the ability of an individual—male or female—to sacrifice and suffer for the nation. These values are inscribed in the annual *Bagong Bayani* awards for overseas Filipinos. In a 2002 speech to award overseas workers, President Arroyo appealed to the idealized national character of sacrifice and delayed gratification: "to all our honorees, I say, congratulations and thank you for what you do for our country. You epitomize the seven million great Filipino workers . . . who labor patiently in the great Filipino tradition of *pagsusumikap* (working hard) and *pakikipagkapwa* (getting along with others)."[3]

When the state directly addresses seafarers, it incorporates similar sentiments in its hero rhetoric to deflect potential conflicts at work and depoliticize their plight. But since seafarers are still overwhelmingly men, it tends to reemphasize the masculine representation of seafaring and the traditionally male gender role of breadwinner and family provider (Burton 1991). For example, in addressing the potentially thorny issue of "empowerment" the former secretary of the Department of Labor and Employment sidesteps workplace issues, workers' rights, or even citizen's rights. Rather he stresses the traditional male role of provider and patriarch:

> what we need to focus . . . on is economic empowerment . . . [T]o be considered as economically empowered, a Filipino seafarer should wield purchasing power to have command of resources sufficient to give him and his family comfort, luxury and stature in the community . . . What does it take . . . ? I believe discipline and determination . . . Discipline not limited to the seafarer, but also his wife and family.[4]

Seafarer industry organizations have also appealed to the breadwinner ideal of new heroism. For example, one leading private training center opens its training materials this way: "Modern day heroes, consistent dollar earner. For decades, our seafarers braved seven seas and brought honor and recognition to the country. A steadfast sacrifice for the sake of uplifting circumstances for his family and at the same time contributes to the improvement of the Filipino life in general."

Thus the state and the migration industry are involved in shaping an understanding of *Filipinoness* aimed at both external actors in the global labor market and internal members of the nation in order to reinforce and reproduce the niche and continue the flow of much-needed remittances. In addressing seafarers, the state and the manning agencies combine enforceable state policies with more subtle discourses on *Filipinoness* and masculinity that emphasize traditional Filipino family values and male gender roles. At the same time, in order to play down a more aggressive masculinity that might lead to collective complaints or organization, the state sanctifies a kind of subordinate new heroism that stresses sacrifice, delayed gratification, and the ability to get along without complaint.

Navigating Masculinities and Writing Their Own Narratives

Like the Philippine state, Filipino seafarers act to defend their niche from incursion by asserting their superiority. But while the Philippine government works hard to promote a particular image of its citizens abroad, Filipino maritime workers themselves contest the construction of Filipinos as simply willing subordinates and criticize their government for its often vacuous claims about empowerment and heroism. Instead the seafarers actively accommodate, resist, and go beyond such constraints, forging their own identities to make sense of their secondary status onboard ships and in the labor market.

Active Filipino sea men are on average thirty-eight years old or two years older than sea men of all nationalities, with Filipino junior officers averaging over forty years of age. The high average age of these officers reflects their limited access to both senior-level positions and their often long tenure as lower-level crew. Filipino sea men are also overwhelmingly from the southern islands within the Philippines—a region with a long history of seafaring but also the area with highest domestic poverty rates, ranging from 38 to 46 percent of the region's population. Finally, sea men come mainly from rural, working-class backgrounds, with over 50 percent from farming or fishing families and only 2 percent being the children of professionals (Amante 2003).

Although they come primarily from poor, rural, and provincial backgrounds, Filipino sea men are nevertheless able to carve out a positive self-image as Filipino sea men, with gender and masculinity again playing key roles. Few occupations can match seafaring for its distinct and historically gendered identity, which seems to date from the very inception of merchant shipping in the Mediterranean and in East and Southeast Asia (Connell 1995; Hohman 1956; Reid 1993). Like many other types of manual labor, constructing work at sea as particularly masculine and even heroic helped sailors survive historically exploitative relations onboard, while at the same time allowing them some measure of self-esteem and agency (Kimmel 1996; Reid 1993; Willis 1977). Sea men, in many ways, represent what Connell (1995: 185) calls "exemplars of masculinity": heterosexual, competitive, homosocial, and able to dominate women as well as other men. But Connell (1987: 183) also stresses that such "hegemonic masculinity" is always constructed in relation to at least three other types of masculinity: complicit masculinity, derived from men's general advantage over women; subordinate masculinity—the opposite of the hegemonic heterosexual ideal—linked to homosexuality and femininity; and marginalized masculinity, which represents race- and class-based variations, such as Black and/or working-class masculinities. The production of these four types of masculinity intersects with the processes of labor market segmentation, helping explain both stratification within seafaring and the existence of different masculinities among groups of seafarers.

Filipino seafarers experience the racial discrimination and subordinate or marginal masculinities embedded in the segmented labor market most viscerally while onboard. Those interviewed had a clear understanding of a racial division of labor, with the nationalities of sea men often directly related to their rank. One seafarer commented, "In my experience, all the Japanese seafarers whom I had worked with were all officers and the Filipinos were at the lowest ranks. In other cases, officers are composed of British, Germans, etc. and the ratings are Filipinos." Another commented, "So far, I have rarely seen or have not seen 'whites' in the lower positions. They are always at the higher ranks. Filipinos must go through the eye of the needle before they get promoted to higher positions."

In mixed nationality crews that are racially segmented along authority lines, questions of masculinity get similarly segmented. In one study aboard two cargo ships with Norwegian officers and Filipino crews, the Norwegian sailors constructed themselves in terms of a hegemonic masculinity in direct contrast to the subordinate masculinity of the subordinate Filipino crew:

> The discourse among Norwegians was mostly about being a good sailor, meaning *physically strong, masculine, conscientious* and *responsible* . . . the Norwegians were expressing their self-categorizations . . . mainly through contrasting themselves against the Filipinos. The Norwegians' view of the Filipinos was . . . stereotyped as being *physically weak, feminine, negligent* and *irresponsible* . . . Filipinos are regarded as feminine and quite often labeled as homosexual. (Ostreng 2000: 7)

But Filipino seafarers themselves, in defending their niche, resist their construction by both the state and dominant groups as subservient or pliable. Rather, they navigate multiple masculinities both at home and onboard and fashion themselves an occupational identity as masculine exemplars. First, Filipino seafarers express a pride in their work, emphasizing their experience, ingenuity, and improvisation / creativity [*diskarte*], which set them apart from their "educated" white officers. For example, one Filipino engineer stressed the superiority of their hands-on skills: "When I was on board I had a chief mate who was a foreigner [German]. When we were doing trouble shooting he handles a book and gives instructions on what he reads. The Filipinos are laughing at him, because the problem is too simple and he consulted a book. . . . They rely too much on books but they don't hold tools."

Filipinos also cited their ability to creatively repair machinery [*remedy-oneering*]: "When you are a Filipino seaman, they say you are industrious, have initiative and perseverance. Other nationals are more of the 'by the book' type. When it comes to problems, for example, machine problems, and it is not stated in any book, they cannot troubleshoot it anymore. Filipino sea men are more ingenious, they can find ways to solve problems."

Here, the Filipinos' "marginal" masculinity that celebrates manual dexterity and hands-on experience challenges the normally "hegemonic" masculinity of formal education and "book" knowledge.

Despite the often harsh working conditions, many seafarers continue to view their jobs in masculine terms, reinterpreting their exploitative and dangerous work, "into a heroic exercise of manly confrontation with the task" (Willis 1977). This is clear in the gender typing of the job's unique characteristics. A third mate noted:

> this is a man's job [*barako talaga*] . . . You are away from your family, you are in the middle of the sea and you see nothing but the sea and the sky for one month . . . If you want adventure, seafaring is your type of job. But given the heavy work, loneliness and the waves, seafaring is really a difficult job . . . Most land-based jobs are safe, [but] when a seaman boards a ship, one foot is already in the grave.

While the workplace has long been recognized as a production site for masculinity, other social locations—such as the household and local community—are equally important, creating the possibilities for contested and multiple masculinities (Connell 1995; Pessar and Mahler 2003). This is particularly true for labor migrants, since migration allows an even greater separation between the home and work spheres, providing migrants more control over their distinct gender performances and a way to conceal their lowly workplace status. Thus exploitative and even emasculating labor relations experienced in host settings do not *necessarily* carry over when migrants return home (Margold 1995). This is most clearly demonstrated when male migrants return to the Philippines as "one day millionaires," able to obscure the exploitative conditions under which their wealth was created by asserting their exemplary masculinity through conspicuous consumption and narratives of adventure (Osella and Osella 2000; Pelez 1995).

Seafarers onshore were particularly selective in their appropriation of the new heroism language. While they pointed out the yawning gap between the state's rhetoric and the helpfulness of its actual policies, they nevertheless generally embraced the new hero label to boost their image as exemplars of masculinity. In particular, seafarers embraced the emphasis on financial contributions to one's family and personal sacrifice. For example, one seafarer noted, "Sea men are *Bagong Bayani* [new heroes] because on-board, you cannot really be sure of your life there. . . . We are called *Bagong Bayani* because we sacrifice, we think of other people. And we are happy helping our family.

We also help the government because of the remittance that we provide for the country." Another stated, "It is true. You go to other countries to help your family. What you do for your family makes them proud of you. You are a hero because you are willing to sacrifice for them."

But while many welcomed public acknowledgment, some also took a quite jaundiced view of the state's use of heroic language. One seafarer noted, "Maybe they are projecting the sea men as saviors of this country because we bring in dollars. But . . . the government does not help us . . . They just flatter the sea men and project us as valuable to other people." Similarly, a chief mate noted, "[w]e should be called *Gagong Bayani* [stupid heroes] because even if we contribute significantly to the country, the government fails to help unemployed sea men . . . I pity my fellow seafarers."

Nevertheless, seafarers interviewed take advantage of and help propagate the exemplary masculine images of the heroic seafarer—as seasoned adventurer, as sexually experienced, as provider and patron, as father and husband—to boost their status in their families and wider communities. If living with their extended families, many experience a clear change in status. As one young seafarer reflected:

> [I]t is a nice feeling when you are at your own house because you see things which you bought for them. And when you are asleep, you hear your mother telling your siblings not to eat the food because that is saved for you or you hear her telling your siblings not to make noise because you are sleeping. Sometimes my siblings would also fight over washing my pants because they know that whoever washes it would get 500 Pesos from me. The way my family treats me has changed. And I am happy.

Others tell about their higher status locally. Discussing his neighbors, one noted, "They have high regard for sea men because they know that they have high incomes. You try telling stories in your town; nobody would pay attention to you. But if you are a seaman, before you open your mouth to tell a story or joke, everybody would already be laughing. That means, *bilib sila sa iyo* [they believe you / have faith in you]." Another added:

> People in the neighborhood in the province tend to idolize you because you always have many stories to tell, about certain experiences, women, etc. . . . For example, surviving a storm in the middle of a sea is a big thrill which you can share with other people . . . [neighbors] think that going abroad means being rich . . . that is why some sea men tend to be so proud.

Their material well-being, often on display through conspicuous consumption, also enhanced their standing. An older, chief engineer boasted, "I am proud because seafaring enabled me to build a house, buy a vehicle and buy all the things for inside the house . . . They [the townspeople] idolize you because they can see that you have a good life and your children can wear good clothes. And our tuition fees are no longer a problem. In other families, these are difficult to pay."

Seafaring also provides men with the status of being dominant and sexually experienced, but also a good marriage match. A young married second officer stated:

> Women nowadays look for security and they know that with seafarers, they are already secure. When they say "seaman" its twin would be "dollar." They would appreciate you because of the dollars you are earning. Even abroad, Filipino seafarers are popular because they are very *galante* (generous). An example is that an American officer would give a woman $50 while a Filipino chief cook would give her $100. That is true. South American women would say that Filipino seafarers are not only *romantiko* but also *galante*.

One married steward also exclaimed, "for Filipina DHs [domestic helpers], we are perceived as 'papa' [prospective partners/lovers]. In my experiences in Taiwan and Hong Kong, Filipina DHs would approach the sea men and invite them to discos. The DH would pay for everything."

Finally, their subordinate masculinity onboard and their ascription by the dominant group of seafarers of being "homosexual" can be turned around and made a point of agency for Filipino men, while also a point of subordination for their spouses. A thirty-year-old married seafarer stated:

> We cannot deny the fact that there is "macho" culture because we are all men. They say that there are only two things that the seafarers would tend to do: *bumigay* (to have gay sex); or *maghanap* (to seek sex with women). That is why wives are asked about their preference between these two choices: to catch her husband in a date with a fellow man; or to catch him in a date with a woman.

Conclusions

Filipino seafarers today have quietly carved out a dominant niche for themselves in one of the most global labor markets. But to explain how this particular national group came to populate the bowels of the world's merchant fleet requires an understanding of the structural changes in the industry, the legacy of American colonial institutions, and the role of the Philippine state that actively intervenes to secure niche closure. Furthermore, the Philippine state—together with its allies in the Philippine migration industry—also operate on the ideological front to construct Filipinos as particularly well suited to these lower labor market positions. With the overall feminization of Filipino out-migration since the 1980s, the state has constructed a less gender-specific notion of national heroism, but one that still allows for the elevation of Filipino masculinity in order to both reinforce the commitment of Filipino seafarers to the state-led project and to regulate the reactions of Filipino seafarers to harsh workplace conditions. Thus through its external marketing, disciplinary policies, and gendered narratives, the Philippine state has manufactured Filipino seafarers as symbolic yet subordinate new heroes, ones that can celebrate—but not directly challenge—their marginal masculinity.

Despite their clearly subordinate relations onboard, Filipino seafarers have nonetheless constructed particular meanings around their work and masculinity that helps them invert—or at least obscure—their secondary or marginal status. The combination of a segmented labor market analysis with a theory of multiple masculinities helps us begin to make sense of the contradictory character of Filipino seafarer masculinity. It can be argued that Filipino sea men face a problem of double masculine consciousness: trying to assert themselves as men, but within a context of being both racially marginalized in the labor market / workplace and often labeled effeminate by dominant groups of seafarers. It is the added analysis of the gendered migration process that helps us better explain how Filipino sea men make sense of their contradictory social locations. The process of migration, the physical separation of work and home, and the ability of seafarers to move between these transnational spaces of masculinity make it possible for Filipino seafarers to straddle their double masculine consciousness and fulfill multiple masculinity roles. Thus their conspicuous consumption, reputation as hypermasculine adventurers, and their ability to endure hardships, all give Filipino seafarers a chance to transform a marginalized and subordinate masculinity on the job into a model of exemplary masculinity at home, emphasizing the ideals of fatherhood, economic provision, sacrifice for one's family, and the machismo of manual work.

However, while these tactics help Filipino sea men endure their subordinate positions and reclaim some agency and dignity, it must also be noted that their constructions of exemplary masculinity do not directly challenge the exploitative relations and often blatant racism onboard and in the labor market. Thus their predicament is similar to that of other migrant workers in diaspora struggling to secure "their" niches in the global marketplace: both challenging yet at the same time often complicit in their own subordination.

Finally, the competing definitional claims on *Filipinoness* by seafarers and the Philippine state highlight important lessons for diaspora studies. Scholars have often theorized diaspora as a liberatory concept, a way to go beyond essentialized notions of national belonging (Gilroy 1993). In this case, Filipino seafarers would seem to epitomize the extraterritorial diaspora, a globally dispersed group literally floating between places. Yet as we have seen, diasporas themselves are not immune from the tendency to essentialize group identity. Even in such "third spaces" as ships, physically outside *any* territorially bounded nation-state, we find the representation of *Filipinoness* not only heavily influenced by the particular logic and the reach of the Philippine state, but also constructed in different, often strategic ways by the Filipino workers. Thus diaspora might be better understood as a dynamic process of intersecting, often competing, diasporic projects rather than as a singular entity. As Brubaker (2005: 12) has commented, "[w]e should think of diaspora in the first instance as a category of practice . . . used to make claims, articulate projects, to formulate expectations, to mobilize energies." In this sense, the emergence of the Filipino niche in shipping and the competing claims to *Filipinoness* demonstrate that the boundaries of belonging remain highly contested, with the state and migrant workers struggling not only over access to resources, but over the very symbols and ideas of what it means to belong to a Filipino diaspora at both a group and a subject level.

Notes

1. The ten billion U.S. dollars in remittances to the Philippines makes up nearly 10 percent of the country's gross domestic product (GDP), a far higher percentage than remittances to Mexico (1.73 percent of GDP) or to India (1.65 percent of GDP), the only two countries that have more in total remittances than the Philippines (International Organization for Migration [IOM] 2005).

2. The NSB was absorbed into the POEA in 1982 to combine the regulation of both land- and sea-based migrant workers into one agency.

3. Transcript from Awarding Ceremonies of the 2002 Presidential Awards for Filipino Individuals and Organizations Overseas accessed from http://www.op.gov.ph/speeches.asp?iid=264&iyear=2002&imonth=12.

4. Comments made by former Department of Labor and Employment Secretary Bienvenido Laguesma on September 28, 2002, on the occasion of the Filipino Seafarer's National Convention.

References

Aguilar, Filomeno. 2003. "Global Migrations, Old Forms of Labor, and New Trans-border Class Relations." *Southeast Asian Studies* 41(2): 137–61.

Alderton, T., M. Blorr, E. Kahveci, T. Lane, H. Sampson, M. Thomas, N. Winchester, B. Wu, and M. Zhao. 2004. *The Global Seafarer: Living and Working Conditions in a Globalized Industry.* Geneva: International Labor Organization.

Amante, Margtas. 2003. "Filipino Global Seafarers: A Profile," Draft Report. Cardiff, UK: Seafarer International Research Center, Cardiff University.

Auge, Marc. 1995. *Non-places: Introduction to an Anthropology of Supermodernity.* London: Verso Press.

Borah, Eloissa Gomez. 1995 / 1996. "Filipinos in Unamuno's California Expedition of 1587." *Amerasia Journal* 21(3): 175–183.

Bowe, John. 2005. "How Did House Bands Become a Filipino Export?" *New York Times Magazine,* May 29: 41–45.

Brubaker, Rogers. 2005. "The 'diaspora' diaspora." *Ethnic and Racial Studies* 28(1): 1–19.

Burton, Valerie. 1991. "The Myth of Bachelor Jack: Masculinity, Patriarchy and Seafaring Labor," in C. Howell and R. Twomey (eds.) *Jack Tar in History: Essays in the History of Maritime Life and Labor.* Fredericton, New Brunswick: Acadiensis Press, 179–98.

Chappell, David A. 2004. "Ahab's Boat: Non-European Seamen in Western Ships of Exploration and Commerce," in B. Klein and G. Mackenthun (eds.) *Sea Changes: Historicizing the Ocean.* New York: Routledge Press, 75–90.

Cheah, Pheng. 1999. "Spectral Nationality: The Living on [sur-vie] of the Postcolonial Nation in Neocolonial Globalization", *Boundary 2* 26(3): 225–52.

Choy, Catherine Ceniza. 2003. *Empire of Care: Nursing and Migration in Filipino American History.* Durham, NC: Duke University Press.

Connell, R. W. 1987. *Gender and Power: Society, the Person and Sexual Politics.* Cambridge: Polity Press.

———. 1995. *Masculinities.* Berkeley: University of California Press.

Constable, Nicole. 1997. *Maid to Order in Hong Kong: Stories of Filipina Workers.* Ithaca, NY: Cornell University Press.

Gilroy, Paul. 1993. *The Black Atlantic.* Cambridge, MA: Harvard University Press.

Granovetter, Mark, and Charles Tilly. 1988. "Inequality and the Labor Process" in N. Smelser, (ed.) *Handbook of Sociology.* Newbury Park, CA: Sage, 175–221.

Guevarra, Anna. 2003. Governing migrant workers through empowerment and sustaining a culture of labor migration: the case of the Philippines. Paper presented at the American Sociological Association 2003 Annual Meeting, Atlanta.

Kimmel, Michael. 1996. *Manhood in America: A Cultural History.* New York: Free Press.

Hohman, Elmo Paul. 1956. *History of American Merchant Seamen.* Hamden, CT: Shoe String Press.

International Confederation of Free Trade Unions (ICFTU) et al. 2002. "More Troubled Waters: Fishing, Pollution and FOCs." Submission for 2002 World Summit on Sustainable Development in Johannesburg, South Africa.

International Labor Organization (ILO). (2001.) *The Impact on Seafarers' Living and Working Conditions of Changes in the Structure of the Shipping Industry.*, Geneva: ILO.

International Organization for Migration (IOM). 2005. *World Migration 2005: Costs and Benefits of International Migration.* Geneva: IOM.

Lane, Anthony. 1996. "The Social Order of the Ship in a Globalized Labor Market for Seafarers," in R. Crompton, D. Gallie, and K. Purcell (eds.) *Changing Forms of Employment: Organization, Skill and Gender.* London: Routledge Press, 83–206.

———. 2002. Philippine Seafarers: Realities, Opportunities and Challenges. Paper presented at the Filipino Seafarers' National Convention, Manila, Philippines.

Maritime Industry Cluster Secretariat (MICS). (2003.) *A Primer for the Maritime Industry Development Action Strategy 2003.* Manila: MICS.

Margold, Jane. 1995. "Narratives of Masculinity and Transnational Migration: Filipino Workers in the Middle East," in A. Ong and M. Peletz (eds.) *Bewitching Women, Pious Men.* Berkeley: University of California Press, 274–98.

Melendy, H. Brett. 1977. *Asians in America: Filipinos, Koreans and East Indians.* Boston: Twayne Publishers.

Morley, David, and Kuan-Hsing Chen (eds.). 1996. *Stuart Hall: Critical Dialogues in Cultural Studies.* London: Routledge Press.

National Seamen Board (NSB). 1976. *Annual Report.* Department of Labor, Republic of the Philippines.

National Seamen Board (NSB). 1982. *Annual Report.* Department of Labor, Republic of the Philippines.

Okamura, Jonathan. 1998. *Imagining the Filipino American Diaspora: Transnational Relations, Identities, and Communities.* New York: Garland Press.

Osella, Filippo, and Caroline Osella. 2000. "Migration, Money and Masculinity in Kerala," *Journal of the Royal Anthropological Institute* (N.S.) 6: 117–33.

Ostreng, Dorte. 2000. Does togetherness make friends? Stereotypes and intergroup contact on multiethnic-crewed ships, unpublished paper.

Peck, Jamie. 1996. *Work-Place: The Social Regulation of Labor Markets.* New York: Guilford Press.

Padavic, Irene, and Barbara Reskin. 2002. *Women and Men at Work.* 2nd ed. Thousand Oaks, CA: Pine Forge Press.

Parreñas, Rhacel Salazar. 2001. *Servants of Globalization: Women, Migration, & Domestic Work.* Stanford: Stanford University Press.

Peletz, Michael. 1995. "Neither Reasonable nor Responsible: Contrasting Representations of Masculinity in a Malay Society" in A. Ong and M. Peletz (eds.) *Bewitching Women, Pious Men.* Berkeley: University of California Press, 76–123.

Pessar, Patricia, and Sarah Mahler. 2003. "Transnational Migration: Bringing Gender In," *International Migration Review* 37(3): 812–46.

Philippine Merchant Marine Academy (PMMA). 2003. "History of PMMA" available at: http://www.pmma.gov.ph.

Philippine Overseas Employment Administration (POEA). 2001. *Overseas Employment Statistics*. Mandaluyong City: Planning Branch, POEA.

Rafael, Vicente. 2000. *White Love and Other Events in Filipino History*. Durham NC: Duke University Press.

Reid, Anthony. 1993. *Southeast Asia in the Age of Commerce 1450–1680: Volume Two: Expansion and Crisis*. New Haven, CT: Yale University Press.

Smith, Robert C. 2003. "Migrant Membership as an Instituted Process: Transnationalization, the State," *International Migration Review* (37) 2: 297–43.

Thompson, Eric. 2003. "Malay Male Migrants: Negotiating Contested Identities in Malaysia," *American Ethnologist* 30(3): 418–38.

Toundjis, Peter. 1975. *The Philippine Crewing Industry: Jobs and Dollars the Philippines Might Lose*. Quezon City, Phillipines: El Greco Shipping Company.

Turnbull, Peter. 2000. "Contesting Globalization on the Waterfront," *Politics & Society* 28(3): 367–92.

Waldinger, Roger. 1994. "The Making of an Immigrant Niche," *International Migration Review* 28(1): 3–30.

Waldinger, Roger, and Michael Lichter. 2003. *How the Other Half Works: Immigration and the Social Organization of Labor*. Berkeley: University of California Press.

Willis, Paul. 1977. *Learning to Labor: How Working Class Kids Get Working Class Jobs*. New York: Columbia University Press.

White, Walter. 1972 [1861]. "Reflections of a Sailor's Life in India, China, Japan, South America, Borneo, Sumatra, Etc.," Greenwich, U.K.: *National Maritime Museum, Maritime Monographs and Reports* No. 3.

Wu, Bin. 2004. Segmentation of global labor market for seafarers: Quantitative evidence, unpublished statistics from the Global Seafarer Database, SIRC.

Yeoh, Brenda S. A., Katie Willis, and S. M. Abdul Khader Fakhri. 2003. "Introduction: Transnationalism and Its Edges," *Ethnic and Racial Studies* 26(2): 207–17.

3 "My Mother Fell in Love with Mỹ-Xuân First": Arranging "Traditional" Marriages Across the Diaspora

Hung Cam Thai

ARRANGED MARRIAGES HAVE BEEN AROUND throughout global history. And although they are still the norm in large parts of contemporary Africa, Asia, and the Middle East (Ahuvia 1992; Applbaum 1995; Batabyal 2001; Blood 1967; Goode 1963), the idea of marriage through arrangement often disturbs Westerners for it is often presumed to involve complete strangers and no sense of individual choice. Mainstream media such as the *New York Times* and the *New Yorker* (Dugger 1998; Gourevitch 1999) have published stories depicting how Westerners often simply cannot fathom how practical strangers can be married to each other and settle down for a life together in the name of family. Yet, arranged marriages vary in different parts of the world, in patterns related to social class, family ties, and historical contexts (Applbaum 1995; Batabyal 2001). As Sunaina Marr Maira (2002) argues, the trope of arranged marriages "fits too neatly with Orientalized understanding of Asian cultures that sacrifice personal freedom to inexplicable but ancient traditions and collectivist control, unlike the individualist liberty of the rational, enlightened West" (p. 153).

In this chapter, I examine the interactions between personal freedom, cultural traditions, and material motivations to shed light on arranged marriages in the Vietnamese diasporic context. Vietnamese mass out-migration and the formation of a diaspora was part of a specific historical phase in global history that ended on April 30, 1975, with the fall of Saigon when U.S. troops pulled out of Vietnam. One of the most profound results of this phase in history has been the movement of a large population of Vietnamese to Western countries over the past three decades. Post-1975 Vietnamese international migrants first came as refugees directly to the United States as part of the airlift effort that evacuated more than 130,000 Sàigònese who were mostly from the urban middle class (Freeman 1995). Subsequent waves of refugees included a large number of "boat people" from diverse regions of Vietnam who spent some time in refugee camps in another Southeast Asian country (most notably in Hong Kong, Thailand, and the Philippines) before they were sponsored by a country in the West. Since April 1975, over two million people emigrated from Vietnam, about 3 percent of the country's current population of eighty million. Approximately 60 percent left as boat refugees; the remaining 40 percent departed from Vietnam and went directly to resettlement countries. Ninety-four percent of those who left Vietnam eventually resettled in Western countries. Between 1975 and 1995, the United States accepted 64 percent of that group; 12 percent went to Australia and 12 percent to Canada. Among European countries, France received the largest number, although this represents only 3 percent of total resettlements (Merli 1997).

As the refugee influx declined over time, family reunification and family sponsorship, such as family-forming migration, have dominated Vietnamese out-migration at the beginning of the twenty-first century. In 1986, after having no contact with most of the outside world for over a decade, Vietnam adopted a new socioeconomic policy called *doi moi*[1] (renovation) which, although it did not end state ownership or central planning, moved the country from complete state-sponsored socialism to partial free market capitalism (Ebashi 1997; Morley and Nishihara 1997). The normalization of economic and social ties by 1995, the year that former U.S. President Bill Clinton established full diplomatic relations with the country, gradually increased the number of individuals from the Vietnamese diaspora who returned as tourists or to visit family members.[2] The traffic of Vietnamese diasporic goods, people, and ideas has manifested itself in profound gendered ways, one of which is the ability for overseas Vietnamese men and women in Vietnam to globalize their marriage options.

The recent formation of a transpacific marriage market in this "aging" diaspora is not just a matter of an emigration history nor is it simply a matter of demographic skews. It has emerged in the context of global forces and kinship ties across the diaspora that have changed Vietnamese society on many levels, as well as consequences of changing gender relations in postmigrant overseas Vietnamese communities that are partly related to demographic skews (Kibria 1993). In the larger project, I argue that transpacific marriages involve men and women who are pioneers in what I call the Vietnamese double gender revolution, a revolution among men in the diaspora and women in Vietnam to postpone or resist marriages with their local counterparts and to subsequently globalize their marriage options. In Vietnam, some single women are resisting marriages with local men who they believe are still held back by outdated gender traditions. At the same time in overseas Vietnamese communities, some single men are resisting marriages with women who they believe have undermined Vietnamese traditions that the men want to preserve (Thai 2003b). To explain some variations in this double gender revolution, this chapter focuses on a situation where there is little "revolt" on the female side of this transpacific marriage market. I present a case study of one anomalous couple in which the successful arrangement of a "traditional" marriage has much to do with individuals' decisions to bargain with patriarchy (Kandiyoti 1988) and the ways in which kinship politics play a role in retaining traditions across the diaspora.

During fourteen months of fieldwork done in phases in Vietnam and in the United States, I got to know sixty-nine Vietnamese transpacific arranged marriages between women in Vietnam and overseas Vietnamese men living in the diaspora. The contemporary Vietnamese transpacific marriage market is demographically gendered because very few overseas women return to Vietnam for husbands as I have discovered in my investigation of case studies and in my confirmation with marriage registration lists at the Department of Justice in Vietnam. The basis of this gendered pattern is that a high male mortality rate during the Vietnam War and the larger number of men than women who emigrated during the last quarter of the twentieth century has produced what demographer Daniel Goodkind (1997) calls the "double marriage squeeze," a situation resulting in a "surplus" of women of marriageable age in Vietnam and a "surplus" of men of marriageable age in Vietnamese overseas communities, especially in Australia and in the United States.[3]

In this distinct and emergent global marriage market, overseas Vietnamese men typically go to Vietnam to marry through arrangement and subsequently return to their places of residence in the diaspora (most are from the United States, Canada, France, and Australia) to initiate paperwork to sponsor their wives as immigrants. The couples I got to know in these marriages were, therefore, in a "migration waiting period." That is, they were transnationally separated as the women were waiting to be united with their husbands through migration. During this waiting period, I came to know them by first entering the lives of the brides in Vietnam and later the U.S.-based grooms. In 1999, the Vietnamese Department of Justice provided two randomly generated lists of 200 names of couples whose marriages were registered in Saigon and 120 names of couples whose marriages were registered in a Mekong Delta province I call Se Long (220 kilometers southwest of Saigon). These lists contained names of both grooms and brides who registered their marriages between September and December 1999. Although a few of the transpacific wives do not eventually migrate abroad to join their husbands for various reasons that I detail elsewhere (Thai, 2003b), marriage registration at the Department of Justice in Vietnam is the first step a transpacific couple must make in order to begin the paperwork to sponsor the wives as immigrants. From the two lists of names, I systematically selected every fourth name from top to bottom of each list and literally went to the brides' houses, knocked on their doors, and invited them to participate in the study. To underscore the diasporic nature of Vietnamese emigration, I note that the overseas grooms in the original two lists of married couples came from over thirty-five countries, although in my probability sample, the men came from a total of eight countries. In the United States, they came from sixteen states. For the scope and feasibility of this project, once I captured the experiences of brides in Vietnam, I was able to only interview the U.S.-based grooms in the metropolitan areas of San Francisco, Los Angeles, Seattle, and Boston.[4]

In my interviews with grooms and brides, I found that their conceptions of Vietnamese migration through the prism of transpacific marriages were diasporic in scope and not simply a transnational connection between Vietnam and one other country. In other words, like Siu and Parreñas (this volume), I found that diasporic ties entailed displacement from the homeland, experiences of alienation and maintenance to both the country of residence and the homeland, and a sense of collective consciousness and solidarity with other people across the diaspora. To illustrate this point, the brides in Vietnam often asked me, "where are you from *over there*?" This question indicates that they conceptualized overseas Vietnamese locations on a global terrain and not just one particular country. Grooms, on the other hand, understood diasporic ties by often referring to their knowledge of many overseas men from "everywhere" who return to Vietnam for wives. I suspect that one of the reasons why grooms conceived the transpacific marriage market as a diasporic phenomenon was because some of them felt stigmatized for returning to Vietnam for wives, often because they were labeled as "unmarriageable" upon their return to Vietnam. In response, they often made claims about the "normative" nature of this transpacific marriage market because Vietnamese men were coming from "everywhere."

This chapter offers a glimpse into the complicated interplay of what Mahler and Pessar (2001) call the "gendered geographies of power," a framework for analyzing "people's social agency—corporal and cognitive—given their own initiative as well as their positioning within multiple hierarchies of power operative within and across many terrains" (p. 447). For analytical clarity, I present an anomalous marital case study of Joe Ngô and Mỹ-Xuân Quốc in my sample of sixty-nine marriages. The successful matchmaking of Joe and Mỹ-Xuân was unexpectedly unique to my sample of marriages, because they represent the "highly marriageables," and were the only couple from my sample of sixty-nine marriages in which a high-wage man married a woman without at least a high school degree. In the larger project, I found that most couples involved the "unmarriageables"—low-wage men and highly educated women (in their own national contexts), a topic I cover elsewhere (Thai 2002, 2003a, 2005). Unlike cases involving the unmarriageables in my study, the anomalous case of Joe and Mỹ-Xuân fits the ideal "traditional" arranged marriage whereby a man marries "down" and a woman marries "up." In the following pages, I make two implications. First, the marriage of Joe and Mỹ-Xuân shows that even as contemporary transpacific arranged marriages differ from traditional arranged marriages in crucial ways, they resemble them in some ways. Second, notions of tradition and particularly traditions along gender lines are often preserved because of the interplay between kinship politics and the decisions of individual couples to "bargain" with patriarchy (Kandiyoti 1988) within complicated "geographies of power" across the diaspora.

The Intimate Details of Diasporization

Joe Ngô, a thirty-six-year-old software engineer, had changed his name from "Cường" when he went to college in the United States because that was when he realized that it bothered him when people had difficulty pronouncing "Cường."[5] The changing of his name was not a racialized issue for Joe, for people's mispronunciation of his name was not something he particularly noticed while growing up in the suburbs of the San Francisco Bay Area. As a child, Joe had many white friends, and he said that that "made life easier." Joe was proud that he was able to navigate in the many racial worlds that characterize the Bay Area. Yet, although the multicultural Cường dated white girls in high school, he was more racially exclusive in college. With a near perfect American accent that distinguished him from most of the men in my study,

Joe had neat model-minority hair, the sort of hair that some men in Asia refer to as 7–3: 70 percent on one side and 30 percent on the other. Just under six-feet tall, but clearly above average size for a Vietnamese man, Joe spoke Vietnamese with a sense of confidence and properness that I rarely got a chance to hear during the course of pursuing this research project.

On the coffee table in his living room, Joe had a faded picture of his family when Joe was in high school, which included his parents and older brother, Lâm, all of whom migrated with Joe to the United States when he was eleven. They were part of the first large cohort of Vietnamese migrants who were evacuated directly out of Vietnam days before the fall of Sàigòn. Shortly after they arrived in the United States, Joe's father worked in a middle-class job as an accountant while his mother worked as an instructional assistant for the local school district. Few of the men in my study had parents with such respectable postmigration jobs. The sorts of jobs most parents of the men in my study took after migration were most often in the secondary or enclave labor market, jobs in the service sector with relatively low pay. Because his father had a middle-class job, Joe explained, his parents had high expectations for him and his brother. And the two young men met those expectations by going to the local University of California campus. Both majored in electrical engineering, and both were active in the Vietnamese Student Association (VSA).

Unlike his brother who met his wife in the VSA club, Joe was somewhat disillusioned with the ethnic organization, and he eventually worked his way out of the club. He said he initially ran for leadership positions, but often did not like the cliques that formed. "Most of them," Joe said, "were interested in looking pretty and wearing nice clothes." Joe was turned off by what he described as the "material performances" that many of his Vietnamese peers participated in, and after two years in the club, Joe ended his membership. When I asked if there were gendered patterns in performances of material differences, Joe explained:

> Of course, the women were especially materialistic. They wanted boyfriends who they could brag about, and the guys would spend all their money to get a trophy girlfriend. It was all a game of good looks and spending, and I knew many other Vietnamese students who did not join because of that. You can say that it was a marriage market for many of those people, but I did not like it. I did not like to compete with people and date girls who cared only if a guy could spend all of his financial aid package in one week. It was stupid.

This did not mean that Joe was not interested in meeting Vietnamese American women at his university, but he avoided those in the ethnic club, a place where students celebrated history and culture, but which Joe felt was too pretentious. Yet, Joe was conscientious about maintaining his sense of being Vietnamese, while embracing the middle-class privilege that he seemed to identify with while growing up as a product of the 1975 cohort of Vietnamese refugees. For example, he proudly spoke about his love for music produced by Vietnamese American singers living in Southern California like Hương Lan and Thế Sơn, two well-known performers in overseas Vietnamese communities. Yet, when he spoke of his childhood in the United States, he evoked his middle-class background, and by extension, did not talk much about the migration experience, an experience marked by poverty for most Vietnamese refugees regardless of what social class background they came from in Vietnam. "My parents were involved in the PTA and my brother and I did everything our white friends did," he said, as if to demonstrate his family's exceptionalism in the refugee experience. Often, as with other studies done on adult children of immigrants (Kibria 2002; Pyke 2000), men like Joe in my study referred to whiteness as middle class and vice-versa, and instances of parents participating in their school life were markers of being middle class. Such men viewed white "mainstream" families, particularly in television sitcoms (Pyke 2000), as emblematic of middle-class life. And it was often class privilege, although rare, that made up for racial marginality among some of my informants.

Joe was very proud of his role model middle-class family—two parents and a good brother—who he said "all worked hard." For him, as it is the case for many young adult children of immigrants, the family is a place where "normative structures" of American life are enacted (Pyke 2000). Pride in his family meant that Joe had transplanted some of those normative structures—like a nuclear family, middle-class status, and the American Dream ideology—into his personal life. Joe recalled memories about how his parents defied stereotypes of Asian people as not being publicly affectionate. He said that his parents were "emotionally healthy" and often displayed their love for each other in front of him and his brother. Joe also evoked nostalgia of his nuclear family. He said they were protected from the pressures of pooling resources that he had heard many other Vietnamese families experienced, since his family had no extended relatives around. And when I inquired about the gender practices between his parents, particularly how they divided household chores as he grew up, Joe said he was proud of his mother. "She never complained."

Unlike most early waves of Vietnamese refugees who relied on public assistance regardless of their social class, Joe's parents were employed in good jobs that enabled them to almost immediately buy a house not too far from San Francisco where Joe and his brother attended good public schools. Even though both of his parents worked, Joe recognized that his mother did the bulk of household labor. She also took responsibilities for Joe's and Lâm's schooling. The fact that this setup "worked" for Joe's parents led him to associate it with a Vietnamese ethnic model that he felt many of his friends' families lacked, especially those who came from "broken" homes. "Most of the friends I had who come from divorced families," he said, "were people whose parents fought because their mothers were resentful about their roles [*phận*] as mothers." Joe saw a good figure in his father, someone who peacefully commanded authority over the family. He recalled that his brother and he gave great respect to his father:

> Both of my parents are good people. They worked hard. My mother never complained about being a mother. And my father was always in control, but not mean about it. He knew that it was important for him to be in charge of the house, to make sure that my brother and I listened to him. And if we were to listen to him, my mother had to make sure that she also showed him respect as the man of the house. I admired him for that. That he never made life difficult for my mother, I think mostly because my mother just never complained. That makes life very easy on children, you know.

Joe said that prior to being married, he was concerned about stability in family life. He drew on his ethnic identification to critique mainstream America's practice of individualism to family and kinship, a practice he felt could cause problems in the family. Joe also felt his middle-class background was central to his sense of self. "I think that success and a good life means that a man is able to financially support his wife and children. If you can't support a family as a man, you should not get married," Joe explained. Middle-class life for Joe also meant that a husband and wife are able to neatly divide what is traditionally thought of as "women's work" and "men's work." To assert masculinity, Joe needed to feel that he could easily support his family (Kibria 1993), and if he could not, then he had not reached middle-class life. As an immigrant child and a child of immigrants, Joe lived in the context of traditional gender arrangements that he saw his parents lived by despite the fact that his mother worked. Because his father enjoyed the label of being the "provider," even as his mother also contributed to that role, Joe did not see the social "costs" to men and women—both physical and psychological—as men seek to take on the provider role (Farrell 1975). Thus, Joe aspired to be the provider, and he said he yearned for a life that his father enjoyed: two sons with a wife whose work did not interfere with her role at home.

When Joe entered college and subsequently thought about marriage, he was caught in a gender, class, and ethnic paradox: he was in a marriage market in search of Vietnamese women where most women were receiving an education so they could work to partially become part of the provider in family life. Had he sought a blue-collar occupation like some of his friends from high school, he may have been able to find a marriage partner who would be happy with staying at home. "If I met a woman with a horrible job, she would definitely want to be a housewife," Joe explained. Because Joe went to a prestigious university, he had few outlets to meet young women who had prospects of having "horrible jobs" or who did not want to work or who did not go to school in order to work. "I think it is hard to find someone like my mother," Joe said, "she took good care of her children and she worked and it was no problem."

But the *problem* was that Joe wanted to marry a Vietnamese woman (of which there were a limited number, in part because many Joe knew dated white men) who shared in his conception of family and marriage. His conception of a good family and a good marriage involved a man doing paid work and a woman "taking care of the house." Most of the women he knew in college were children of immigrants whose parents worked hard in low-wage jobs to earn their way up in order to send their children to college. Joe acknowledged that few people he knew, women or men, were as lucky as he was. "Most of my friends had parents who worked very hard while they were growing up, worked in minimal wage jobs for very long hours. So I think most people I know saw college as truly a way to move up economically." Yet, Joe was hopeful that he would find a woman in college he would marry and who may or may not work, but who would be happy with her role as a housewife, too.

After graduation in the late 1980s, such a woman never entered Joe's life. His excuse was that the university he attended had too many overachievers. "They all wanted to be superstars," he said, "and most of them wanted to get the best job possible which meant that they had to work really long hours." Joe is no exception. His electrical engineering degree earned him a very nice job with all the long hours and stress that it entailed. He worked for a start-up company not too far from the university he had attended, and at the age of twenty-five, he bought a house near his parents. After the house purchase, Joe's parents pressured him to "acquire" a wife and some children to fill the house.

The Politics of Kinship in Marital Choice

Shortly after he bought his house in 1990, Joe and his mother took their first trip back to An Hội, the Mekong Delta village they had left fifteen years earlier for a life that they had admittedly achieved in the United States. For Joe's mother, Mrs. Bụi,[6] bringing home her youngest educated son was an opportunity to display the success for which she and her husband had taken the risk of migration. Many Vietnamese immigrants I met throughout various corners of the diaspora, particularly in Europe, Australia, and the United States, delayed the trip back to the homeland because they did not have the material or the symbolic capital to show for their migration. In some ways, migration is like a contest. Losers are those who do not have the material evidence to show that they competed well in the migration game. As Mrs. Bụi explained to me when Joe took me to his parents' house one day:

> That's how you should live if you left Vietnam, like my sons. They worked hard and they got a good education at a very good university. There are too many men their age who have nothing to show for their trip. They should have just stayed in Vietnam. They wasted a space that many hardworking men in Vietnam would die to have. You know in Vietnam, if you go back to visit, you really have to have something to show like a big house or you have to have children who were educated well. We are lucky. We worked hard and my children have good jobs. We have what we came to America for.

On the first trip back to their hometown in Vietnam, neither Mrs. Bụi nor Joe intended to look for a potential marriage partner for Joe. "We joked about it," Joe said, "but I never considered it seriously the first time. It was just talk for fun [*nói cho vui*]." Thus, the trip was simply to be part of the first groups of Việt Kiều, a term referring to Vietnamese people living overseas, to return home after many years of migration. Mrs. Bụi said she knew about the discourse that circulated throughout overseas Vietnamese communities about the danger of international marriages between Việt Kiều men and women in Vietnam, in particular, the reputation of "bad girls" who just wanted to have a good life abroad.[7] Yet, she believed that if done carefully, transpacific arranged marriages can "succeed" [*thành công*]. She explained, as if to also warn me:

You really have to be careful, you know. Vietnam is very poor, and everyone wants to leave the country if they can. Many of these young Việt Kiều men do not know that those young girls in Vietnam only want to marry them for money or the chance to go to the United States. They might love each other for a time period, or they can pretend to love, but it can always change. If they discover that their husbands cannot afford to buy them this and that, they will leave the husbands very soon.

Because Joe had the ability to fulfill the provider role, to buy "this and that," Mrs. Bụi had confidence, as she said, that "Joe's wife would not go anywhere." This reflects the usual first thought many families in bride-receiving communities expressed to me, the fear that "passport chasers" would leave men once they migrated abroad. Some families looked into the bride's "credentials," that is to say, her family's background, to make sure she was not simply using marriage as a bridge to a Việt Kiều community. Few people like Mrs. Bụi relied on their son's ability to provide in order to secure a stable marriage. But aside from her confidence in Joe's ability to "afford" a stable marriage, Mrs. Bụi also had a special affinity for her new daughter-in-law, Mỹ-Xuân Quốc. Mrs. Bụi was the key person in arranging the transpacific marriage for Joe, and as he told me, "my mother fell in love with Mỹ-Xuân first."

At nearly sixty-years, Mrs. Bụi came of age in An Hội in postcolonial and prewar Vietnam. She was from a poor family and was married off to the son of a wealthy farmer in a neighboring village. Her father was a teacher of French and his education combined with her good looks gave them the matching currency to compete for her husband, someone who came from the prewar propertied class. From her own experience, Mrs. Bụi believed in arranged marriage, as she agreed to her own, and saw good things in it. "It takes away a lot of thinking for young people," she said. "Older people know what their children need."

Indeed, Mrs. Bụi knew, if only from her own arranged marriage, what a *man* needs to be successful and what it takes to make a family harmonious: a wife who "bargains" with patriarchy by exchanging submissiveness and propriety for economic protection (Kandiyoti 1988). For Mrs. Bụi, just as for the women in Nazli Kibria's study (1993) of new Vietnamese refugees, preserving traditional gender arrangements ensured male economic protection. Mrs. Bụi felt she got what she bargained for in the family, and her traditional family system gave her the status to exercise considerable authority over her two sons. So if, in the eyes of Joe, their family setup "worked" for his parents, in the eyes of Mrs. Bụi, it was "necessary" for her children. And in Mrs. Bụi's world of two sons, where the idea of "feminism" or *thuyết nam nữ bình quyền* did not exist in her vocabulary, she was not impressed by women with an education. "You know the Vietnamese phrase, *trai tài gái sắc* [boy success, girl beauty]?" It means that a girl does not need to be successful, she needs to be beautiful and she needs to be a good wife."

Moment of Encounter

When Mrs. Bụi held a celebration for her and Joe's homecoming in An Hội, a socially required event for Việt Kiều returning home for the first time, she instantly "fell in love" with Joe's wife. "She was proper, a very polite girl," Mrs. Bụi explained. "She reminded me of when I was a young single woman, quiet, spoke well, but very considerate of older people." And if twenty-four-year-old Mỹ-Xuân competed for a daughter-in-lawship in An Hội, she probably would have been highly ranked. Although she did not have any formal college education, Mỹ-Xuân respectfully finished eleventh grade in the provincial high school, a marker of being at least "good enough" [*cũng đủ*], if not excellent, in the Vietnamese village world of educational mobility for women. And in the same line of logics, many villagers told me "girls don't need too much education or they will become unmarriageable [*con gái học nhiều qúa thì sẽ ế*]." Mỹ-Xuân was thus highly marriageable not only because she had limited education, but also because she was blessed with attractive features, the least of which was long, dark, and straight black hair that exemplified popular conceptions of Vietnamese beauty.

Mỹ-Xuân had never thought much about going abroad until she was proposed for marriage by Joe and his mother. This made sense because Mỹ-Xuân did not have much contact with the overseas world; all of her immediate relatives were in Vietnam. One cousin, who she said she was not particularly close to, was living and working in construction in Korea. When I asked Mỹ-Xuân why she delayed marriage, because, after all, twenty-four was considered beyond the marriageable age in village life, she explained that her parents had not "approved" of anyone:

My father has high expectations. He is a rather difficult man, and he told me that I could not find a boyfriend because he and my mother would try to find a husband for me. Because my father has many friends and he does business often in the city, he said that I could trust him to find a suitable groom for me. [Did you believe he could?] I think my father could, probably better than I can. My parents are really smart people, especially my father. He knows how to be diplomatic and he has a lot of contact people.

Mỹ-Xuân was an "obedient daughter"—apparently a declining population even in villages, according to some of the older village folks I spoke to. As Vietnam continues to rely on the West and on overseas capital, many locals place the "feminine subject" under moral surveillance, and young rural women who embrace overseas opportunities like taking English classes, engaging in advanced education, or making friends with Việt Kiều and Westerners easily become objects of critique. And those who maintain the traditional inscriptions of the "authentic" Vietnamese female subject celebrate this ideal as a reminder that not all of Vietnam had been abducted by the West. Thus, Mỹ-Xuân was a celebrated figure in the eyes of fellow villagers and her parents. Mỹ-Xuân, according to Mrs. Bụi, embodied all that the true Vietnamese woman should be. She had long, straight, black hair and she regularly wore *đồ bộ*, the Vietnamese colorful matching blouse and trousers that the younger generations are beginning to see—and reject—as emblematic of a Vietnamese past. Desires of the present mean that the younger generations, both men and women, are now opting for commodities of the West, in part, because notions of "cool," which are critiqued by the older generation, have also arrived on the scene, all symbolizing a new, modern Vietnam.

Mỹ-Xuân offered a striking contrast to most of the women in my study, because she had a strong identification with being an "authentic" Vietnamese woman, a label that rendered her traditional, and thereby, *hiền*, a Vietnamese word used to describe gentle people. For wives and daughters, it often means that they are submissive. "Mỹ-Xuân is very *hiền*," as Mrs. Bụi emphasized to me. "I have never seen her talk loudly, she always uses the right term to address me, and she never speaks out of turn. I know many of the villagers around there who said that she does whatever older people ask her to do. She respects *and* listens to older people."

Listening to and respecting people were two activities of the everyday that Mỹ-Xuân had done well all her life. As the middle daughter (she had one older brother and one younger sister), Mỹ-Xuân always deferred first to her father, then to her older brother and mother in the decisions they made concerning her life. And when I spoke to neighbors in An Hội about Mỹ-Xuân, they almost always referred to her as *đúng là con gái Việt nam* [truly a Vietnamese girl]. This echoed the "listen and respect" repertoire that is often expected of Vietnamese women. The identification of an imagined feminine authenticity, organized by family, fellow villagers, and recent overseas actors, had normalized the gendered vision that Mỹ-Xuân managed for herself and her "role" as a daughter, wife, and daughter-in-law. So when I asked Mỹ-Xuân how she felt about *her* recent decision to marry a Việt Kiều, she abstractly explained: "In Vietnam, a duty of a woman [*bổ phận của đàn bà*] is to care for her family and her husband. She has to respect her parents and husband and her husband's family. If a woman wants happiness, she has to listen to her husband and her family. For me, my duty is to listen to my husband and to respect my husband."

Although she considered her family's financial situation as "just enough," compared to many families in the provincial capital of Se Long, Mỹ-Xuân's family was probably living somewhere near "middle" class in their cultural contexts. Her father, Mr. Thông, had a position in the local government in the district [*huyện*] where they lived, serving on several councils that made decisions about things like when a foreign company could move a factory into district boundaries. This meant, according to Mỹ-Xuân, that her father commanded a lot of respect in public life. "Sometimes, he could earn 'gift' money from people to get their permits approved quickly," she said. Her mother ran a small shop selling watches in the provincial capital, a thirty-minute motorcycle ride from their house. Despite having no overseas remittances, with local incomes from two people and many years of savings, they were able to buy a fairly decent house with some of the amenities that are usually only found in remittance-receiving homes.

Mỹ-Xuân's father's level of public respect had a lot to do with how Mỹ-Xuân got to know Mrs. Bụi and Mrs. Bụi's subsequent encouragement for Joe to marry Mỹ-Xuân. When Mrs. Bụi and Joe held their homecoming celebration back in Vietnam Mỹ-Xuân's parents were invited along with many other relatives that Joe did not recall knowing. At the celebration, according to Joe and Mrs. Bụi, where there were over 100 guests, Mỹ-Xuân's father had been highlighted as a key village leader, someone whom virtually everyone held in high esteem. His reputation was followed by an impressive meeting with Mrs. Bụi and Joe, which Joe described: "Everyone told us we had to meet him, that he was fair, smart, and a very respectable person. We felt special that he genuinely welcomed us home . . . he never talked badly about Việt Kiều as everyone had something bad to say about Việt Kiều being stuck up, and he did not talk about money, which everyone seemed to ask about."

The fact that money was never a topic of conversations between Mrs. Bụi and Mr. Thông served as a compelling confirmation to Mrs. Bụi that Mr.

Thông was a person of respectability. "In Vietnam, everything is about money [*Ở Việtnam, cái gì cũng là tiền*]." For many Việt Kiều, the subject of money, especially the explicit request to remit after the initial visit, is a common source of dispute with the very families they visit. Often, relationships tragically disintegrate or simply end when expectations are too high or too unreasonable for Việt Kiều to fulfill. Some people in Vietnam claim that Việt Kiều have "forgotten" their familial obligations, and those who do not remit or fail to remit sufficiently are often socially indicted for having "lost" their culture. Those who remit sufficiently are often called *chính cống* or "real" Việt Kiều.

If there is a "realness" that characterizes Việt Kiều, then there is a Vietnamese "realness" that Việt Kiều search for themselves when they go to Vietnam on their visits. For Mrs. Bụi, authentic Vietnamese was clearly in Mỹ-Xuân's family, not only because Mỹ-Xuân represented authentic Vietnamese femininity, but also because her father knew how, according to Mrs. Bụi, to *tôn trọng người nước ngọai* or "respect those from overseas." Respect for those in Vietnam means that Việt Kiều fulfill their obligation of kinship by remitting, while respect for Việt Kiều means that local Vietnamese do not make the topic of money explicit. For Việt Kiều, gift giving is done without explicit requests. For the Vietnamese, Việt Kiều need to be "reminded."

But Mrs. Bụi explained, "*Khi người ta nói tới tiền, là đòi hỏi*" or "when they talk about money, it is to demand." Mrs. Bụi admired Mr. Thông not only because of the respect he had from her relatives and former fellow villagers (which included one sister), but also because Mr. Thông had an honorable presentation of a Vietnamese self: he never talked about money. Her judgment of Mr. Thông combined with a peculiar identification and affinity for Mỹ-Xuân led her to propose marriage for Joe for which Mr. Thông agreed after he had "*điều tra*" or "investigated" Mrs. Bụi's background.

Like many overseas Vietnamese who return, especially to small villages that often remain unchanged over many years, Mrs. Bụi eventually connected a past to her present. Mr. Thông had been a neighborhood friend of one of Mrs. Bụi's male cousins in the 1960s when they were young men coming of age during the war. Mrs. Bụi learned that the two family's history went as far back as the 1940s when Mr. Thông's father and Mrs. Bụi's father were fellow landowners [*chủ đất*]. This history marked a peculiar nostalgia for Mrs. Bụi, and she helped to persuade Joe to agree to a marriage with Mỹ-Xuân. The marriage of Joe and Mỹ-Xuân was a way for Mrs. Bụi to reclaim a geographical identity, an identity that she left behind more than twenty-five years ago. Her support of patriarchy because it "worked" for her and her children, combined with an absence of feminist consciousness in Mỹ-Xuân, will ensure that Joe's marriage will not include "complaints."

The marriage Joe entered was anomalous and will most likely "work" for him because, in contrast to most of the women in my sample, his wife had not entered the quiet feminist revolution in Vietnam among women who resisted local marriages, the main reason that, unlike Mỹ-Xuân, most of the women in my sample opted for a transpacific marriage. Most women resisted local marriages because they are participating in a version of what Shere Hite (1988) calls a "female revolt" in Vietnam against traditional and patriarchal marriages. Mỹ-Xuân, however, participated in the Vietnamese transpacific marriage market because of traditions of familial piety. She "listened" to her father's encouragement and of other adults who she came to respect, including Mrs. Bùi and numerous other villagers who urged her that Joe was "the most suitable groom" she could ever marry. She was not particularly drawn by the potential material advantage of marrying an overseas man, but she knew that it would immensely help her family. "I want to help my family in the future," Mỹ-Xuân explained. "Even though we are not poor, we should always aspire to be better." And while mobility in her family had never come from remittances, *their* marriage to a high-wage overseas family meant that they had a bright future to anticipate. "If you have children overseas," as Mr. Thông explained in a polite, yet matter-of-fact, demeanor, "they have to help their families [*có con ở nước ngoại thì phải giúp đỡ gia đình*]."

Notes

This is a slightly different version of a chapter in my forthcoming book, tentatively titled, *For Better or for Worse: Marriage and Migration in the New Economy,* forthcoming from Rutgers University Press. I wish to thank the editors of this volume, Rhacel Parreñas and Lok Siu, for their helpful feedback on this chapter.

1. Literally, "changing for the new."

2. Incentives provided by the state for the overseas population, like the ability to purchase land and provisions for investment opportunities, have created an extraordinarily important Việt Kiều, or overseas Vietnamese, economy. For instance, remittances grew dramatically from only $35 million in 1991 to more than $2 billion by 2002 (Nguyen 2002). The Vietnamese government estimates that currently more than one million Việt Kiều return annually for tourism and to visit relatives, a dramatic increase from the 87,000 who came in 1992, and from the only 8,000 who visited in 1988.

3. A shortage of one sex or the other in the age group in which marriage generally occurs is often termed a marriage squeeze (Guttentag and Secord 1983). The Vietnamese double marriage squeeze specifically refers to the low ratio of males to females in

Vietnam and the unusually high ratio of males to females in the Vietnamese diaspora, especially in Australia and in the United States. Among the fifteen most populated nations in 1989, Vietnam had the lowest ratio of men to women among those at the peak marrying ages. By 1999, among people between the ages of thirty to thirty-four years in Vietnam, statistically speaking, there were approximately 92 men for every 100 women. In 1990, for Vietnamese Americans in all age groups, there were about 113 males for every 100 females (Zhou and Bankston 1998). By 2000, among Vietnamese Americans between twenty-five to twenty-nine years, there were 129 men for every 100 women; for the age group of thirty to thirty-four years, there were about 135 men for every 100 women. These calculations are based on Goodkind's (Goodkind 1997) 1990 data. I simply added ten years to each cohort, though I acknowledge that mortality for either sex as a whole may have caused a shift in sex ratios since 1990.

4. The final analysis in this project is based on a sample of sixty-nine marriages. In the bride phase in Vietnam, I conducted multiple formal tape-recorded in-depth interviews with ninety-three individuals, including sixty-six wives and twenty-seven of their family members. In the groom phase, based primarily in the United States, I interviewed thirty-six individuals, including twenty-eight husbands and eight of their family members. I did not meet three of the wives who were included in my sample because I discovered that they had already left Vietnam to join their husbands abroad. Two of these wives emigrated to France, and the third went to Australia. In Vietnam, many people, including officials from the U.S. embassy, told me that compared to other Western countries, the United States had the strictest and slowest process for clearing paperwork for family reunification migration. I decided, nevertheless, to include the marriages of the three women whom I did not meet in my analysis because interviews with their families who were still in Vietnam gave me extensive information about their marriages. In addition to formal tape-recorded interviews with brides, grooms, and their families, I was a participant observer of eight families in Saigon, maximizing variation (e.g., by age, level of education, income, and contexts of transnational networks). I transcribed and translated about half of the interviews, and the rest were done by two research assistants in the United States.

5. To protect the privacy of informants, all names have been changed. As well, I have changed the names of peasant villages in Vietnam and small towns in the United States; I have kept the real names of all metropolitan areas. I have also placed diacritic / accent marks on all Vietnamese names of my informants as well as any Vietnamese words I translated into English. However, all scholarly references remain as they are used in the original source (most do not have diacritic marks). Finally, while full Vietnamese names are usually indicated in the order of last, middle, and first names, I will use "American" standards of referencing names since I used this format when I got to know informants.

6. The reader will note that Joe does not share the same surname as his mother; this is because it is uncommon for women in Vietnam to take their husbands' surname.

Children generally take their father's surname. I have kept this pattern throughout to maintain the authenticity of identities. In addition, to make generational distinctions, I refer to brides and grooms by their first names; and I refer to their "elders" using proper titles, although when I spoke to these individuals, I employed Vietnamese kinship terms since all titles of address are kinship terms.

7. Indeed, Mrs. Bui's anxiety echoed the concerns that U.S. immigration officials had pertaining to foreign wives of American citizens, which prompted the Marriage Fraud Amendment Act of 1986. This act allowed the Immigration and Naturalization Service to impose conditional permanent resident status after the migration of foreign brides. This act stipulated that an immigrant spouse could be deported if she left the marriage before two years elapsed. As Constable (2003) notes, although immigration laws are theoretically gender neutral, legal scholars have argued that the Marriage Fraud Amendment Act was fueled by concerns surrounding foreign brides, particularly mail-order brides from Asia.

References

Ahuvia, Aaron C. 1992. "Formal Intermediaries in the Marriage Market: A Typology and Review." *Journal of Marriage and the Family* 54: 452–463.

Applbaum, Kalman D. 1995. "Marriage with the Proper Stranger: Arranged Marriage in Metropolitan Japan." *Ethnology* 34: 37–52.

Batabyal, Amitrajeet A. 2001. "On the Likelihood of Finding the Right Partner in an Arranged Marriage." *Journal of Socio-Economics* 33: 273–280.

Blood, Robert O. 1967. *Love Match and Arranged Marriage: A Tokyo-Detroit Comparison*. New York: Free Press.

Constable, Nicole. 2003. *Romance on a Global Stage: Pen Pals, Virtual Ethnography, and "Mail-Order" Marriages*. Berkeley: University of California Press.

Dugger, Celia. 1998. "In India, an Arranged Marriage of Two Worlds." Pp. A1, B6–B7 in *New York Times*. New York.

Ebashi, Masahiko. 1997. "The Economic Take-Off." Pp. 37–65 in *Vietnam Joins the World*, edited by J. Morley and M. Nishihara. Armonk, NY: M. E. Press.

Farrell, Warren. 1975. *The Liberated Man*. New York: Random House.

Freeman, James M. 1995. *Changing Identities: Vietnamese Americans, 1975–1995*. Massachusetts: Allyn and Bacon.

Goode, William J. 1963. *World Revolution and Family Patterns*. New York: Free Press.

Goodkind, Daniel. 1997. "The Vietnamese Double Marriage Squeeze." *International Migration Review* 31: 108–128.

Gourevitch, Philip 1999. "A Husband for Dil: Can Tradition Make a Young Woman Happy?" *New Yorker*, February 22–March 1, pp. 78, 80, 93–94, 98–102.

Guttentag, Marcia, and Paul F. Secord. 1983. *Too Many Women?: The Sex Ratio Question*. Beverly Hills: Sage Publications.

Hite, Shere. 1988. *Women and Love.* New York: Knopf.

Kandiyoti, Deniz. 1988. "Bargaining with Patriachy." *Gender & Society* 2: 274–290.

Kibria, Nazli. 1993. *Family Tightrope: The Changing Lives of Vietnamese Americans.* Princeton, NJ: Princeton University Press.

Kibria, Nazli. 2002. *Becoming Asian-American: Second Generation Chinese and Korean American Identities.* Baltimore: The Johns Hopkins University Press.

Mahler, Sarah J., and Patricia R. Pessar. 2001. "Gendered Geographies of Power: Analyzing Gender Across Transnational Spaces." *Identities* 7: 441–459.

Maira, Sunaina Marr. 2002. *Desis in the House: Indian American Youth Culture in New York City.* Philadelphia: Temple University Press.

Merli, Giovanna M. 1997. "Estimation of International Migration for Vietnam 1979–1989." *Center for Studies in Demography and Ecology.* Working Paper Series 97–04. University of Washington, Seattle.

Morley, James W., and Masashi Nishihara. 1997. "Vietnam Joins the World." Pp. 3–14 in *Vietnam Joins the World,* edited by J. W. Morley and M. Nishihara. Armonk, NY: M. E. Press.

Nguyen, Hong 2002. "*Viet Kieu* Remittances Set to Top $2 Billion Target." *Vietnam Investment Review,* December 9, 2002.

Pyke, Karen. 2000. "'The Normal American Family' as an Interpretive Structure of Family Life Among Grown Children of Korean and Vietnamese Immigrants." *Journal of Marriage and the Family* 62: 240.

Thai, Hung Cam. 2002. "Clashing Dreams: Highly Educated Overseas Brides and Low-Wage U.S. Husbands." Pp. 230–253 in *Global Woman: Nannies, Maids and Sex Workers in the New Economy,* eds. B. Ehrenreich and A. R. Hochschild. New York: Metropolitan Books.

Thai, Hung Cam. 2003a. "For Better or Worse: Gender Allures in the Vietnamese Global Marriage Market." Pp. 275–286 in *Feminist Frontiers,* eds. L. Richardson, V. Taylor, and N. Whittier. Boston: McGraw Hill.

Thai, Hung Cam. 2003b. "The Vietnamese Double Gender Revolt: Globalizing Marriage Options in the Twenty-first Century." *Amerasia Journal* 29: 51–74.

Thai, Hung Cam. 2005. "Globalization as a Gender Strategy: Respectability, Masculinity, and Convertibility Across the Vietnamese Diaspora." in *Critical Globalization Studies,* edited by R. P. Appelbaum and W. I. Robinson. New York: Routledge.

Zhou, Min and Carl L. Bankston. 1998. *Growing Up American: How Vietnamese Children Adapt to Life in the United States.* New York: Russell Sage Foundation.

4 The Queen of the Chinese Colony: Contesting Nationalism, Engendering Diaspora

Lok C. D. Siu

ALL THE BEAUTY CONTESTANTS had performed their roles brilliantly—parading gracefully across the stage several times, modeling their national dresses and variations of traditional Chinese gowns, and performing their respective national dances.[1] They had introduced themselves in Spanish and sometimes in Cantonese and/or Mandarin. Finally, they had offered their eloquent responses to the questions asked by the master of ceremonies. The audience of diasporic Chinese from Central America and Panama anxiously waited to hear the final decision of the judges.

Half an hour went by, then an hour, then two. The banquet hall was by now only half full, with about a hundred restless people energized by gossip and suspicion. Why were they taking so long? What was the problem? Finally, the emcee took the podium and proclaimed Miss Honduras 1996's "Reina de la Colonia China" (Queen of the Chinese Colony).[2] But before Miss Honduras could reach the stage, the vice president of the Convención de Asociaciones Chinas de Centroamérica y Panamá (Convention of Chinese Associations of Central America and Panama) interjected and announced that there had been a mistake—that, in fact, Miss Costa Rica was the winner, not Miss Honduras.

The audience was confused. They looked around at one another, not knowing how to react, wondering what to make of what had just happened. Judging from the looks on their faces, I could see this was not a common outcome, that something had clearly gone wrong.

Then, suddenly, out of this confused silence, a man in his sixties marched onto the stage. The contrast of his angrily flushed face with his graying hair and formal dark gray suit attracted the crowd's rapt attention. Without a moment's hesitation, his body rose as if preparing for battle, and he unleashed a passionate tirade denouncing what had just happened: "This event is supposed to be a joyous celebration for all those attending this convention. Why do you newcomers insist on betraying the spirit of this convention and break the community in this way?"

As reflected in this scene, the annual contest for the "Queen of the Chinese Colony" is not just about beauty, femininity, or friendly competition. The fact that the contest evokes such passionate interest suggests that other issues are at stake. As the anthropologists Colleen Ballerino Cohen, Richard Wilk, and Beverly Stoeltje have argued, "Beauty contests are places where cultural meanings are produced, consumed, and rejected, where local and global, ethnic and national, national and international cultures, and structures of power are engaged in their most trivial but vital aspects" (Cohen et al. 1996, 8). Wilk proposes that, as sites where multiple struggles for power and representation are publicly debated, beauty contests mediate difference in order to produce a "structure of common difference" and suggests that "the process of judging beauty is always a process of negotiation, a process of reconciling difference or at least accepting the terms of the disagreement" (Wilk 1996, 117).

I want to extend Wilk's argument further by asserting that not only can this "structure of common difference" be created through beauty contests but, more important here, diasporic communities contest, forge, and reaffirm their identities through gender itself. Moreover, I argue that the contest over who is to be the Queen of the Chinese Colony is a microcosm of broader issues at play among diasporic Chinese in Central America and Panama. Indeed, what is at stake in this beauty contest is the struggle for diasporic citizenship or for full belonging within the diaspora. By mediating debates about diasporic Chinese femininity, the contest seeks to establish the criteria for idealized diasporic subjectivity, criteria against which belonging in the diaspora is measured. With the beauty contestants embodying and performing specific ways of being diasporic Chinese, their divergent representations not only reflect the wide spectrum of diasporic Chinese in this region but also reveal and disrupt hegemonic constructions of what it means to be "Chinese" and "Central American" or "Panamanian." Furthermore, the contest provides a window onto the regional differences among diasporic Chinese communities, thereby disrupting the simple binary formula of "nation of residence" and "homeland" in understanding diaspora. The contestants' varied presentations and performances reflect the tension not only between their emplacement in specific local contexts and their ongoing engagement with Chineseness but also between their national difference and shared regional affiliation. Overall, their performance helps mediate debates of belonging and cultural identity, and the elected queen becomes the symbol and representative of the Chinese diaspora.

But what happens when there is no agreement, or even acceptance of the terms of disagreement, as in the case I describe above? What does the disputed result of this beauty contest tell us about the tensions and contradictions within the diaspora and the cultural politics of diaspora? Furthermore, what does it tell us about the nature of diaspora that makes diasporic identifications so contingent and tenuous, yet so provocative and powerful? The ensuing debates about who should be queen and why reveal not only the politics of belonging within the diaspora, but also the shifts in identifications among diasporic Chinese. The question of belonging in diaspora is highly contested and, as we shall see, contingent on local-transnational dynamics.

In the discussion that follows, I briefly outline the historical context of the Federation of Chinese Associations in Central America and Panama, the organization that sponsors the beauty contest and the annual convention, before returning to a more detailed discussion of the 1996 convention and its controversial beauty contest. The final section turns specifically to Panamanian Chinese and examines their interpretations and responses to these debates. By using gender as a category of analysis (Scott 1999) and taking the beauty contest as a focus, I examine how racial-cultural purity, migration, and homeland politics intersect in setting the terms of diasporic citizenship.

Transnational Networks and Diasporic Identifications

The Queen of the Chinese Colony beauty contest takes place at the annual Convention of Chinese Associations of Central America and Panama, which is hosted by the Federation of Chinese Associations of this region. Its participants include Chinese from Panama, Costa Rica, Nicaragua, Guatemala, Honduras, and El Salvador. This transnational organization was founded in 1965, amid intensifying regional instability, by the presidents of the six national Chinese associations of this region. Shortly after its founding, the association leaders requested financial help from the Republic of China (ROC) embassies in order to make the organization a permanent institution of the diaspora. Since then, the organization has become a joint venture between diasporic Chinese and the ROC government, solidifying both their sociopolitical ties and their symbolic ones.[3]

According to the Chinese Panamanian Association's president, Alberto Lee, the Federation of Chinese Associations of Central America and Panama decided to host an annual convention that would bring together representatives of the six nation-based associations to discuss economic and political issues confronting their respective communities. The founders intended this organization to provide additional resources and support for diasporic Chinese beyond what was available within the borders of their nation-states. For instance, during the Sandinista Revolution in Nicaragua, when diasporic Chinese who had supported the Somoza regime were being systematically captured and imprisoned, the organization raised funds and lobbied government officials on their behalf. As a result, a number of Chinese were able to escape to other parts of Central America. The organization has also provided relief funds for victims of natural disasters and scholarships for underprivileged Chinese.

Given that these Central American countries have been relatively poor and—until recently—politically volatile, it was understandable that diasporic Chinese of the region would pool their resources on a transnational scale to form a safety net for themselves. The fact that diasporic Chinese have experienced long histories of persecution in Central America (and throughout the world), and the realization that they could not rely on China for protection, further motivated the formation of the organization to help ensure their safety and survival.[4]

It is also important to remember that there is not a simple binary relationship between the nation-state and the diaspora. On the contrary, diasporas are not only embedded in the system of nation-states but also partially constituted by the conditions within those nation-states. In other words, the marginalization of diasporic Chinese, manifested in their lack of cultural and political acceptance in Central America and Panama, has everything to do with their desire to maintain ties with a distant homeland and to form transnational organizations that create "safe spaces" and a sense of community. Indeed, their inability to participate as full citizens of the nation-state has inspired many to participate in diasporic politics, where their voice is heard and their presence matters.

Gender, Patrilineality, and the Reproduction of the Diaspora

Six years after the founding of the Convention of Chinese Associations, its annual gatherings were expanded to include women and youth, and new activities were initiated, one of which was the beauty contest. As Alberto Lee frankly explained to me, "[We] started these activities because the second generation was marrying out. [I] want my kids to meet other Chinese people and since my wife and I were working so hard, [we] never had time to do things with [our] children." By bringing his family to these conventions, he had hoped his children and, later, his grandchildren would meet other "like-minded Chinese." Lee continued, "In order to convince the kids that these conventions are not just a bunch of old men talking about boring business, I thought a beauty contest would attract both young men and women to participate, to 'mingle,' and you know, to build 'friendships.'" He then proceeded to list several marriages that have resulted from these conventions: so-and-so's daughter from Panama had married so-and-so's son in Guatemala, and so on and so forth. He stopped in the middle of his narrative and abruptly turned to me, asking, "Are you married?" When I answered "No," he paused and smiled mischievously, as if to say that his scheme works and perhaps it could also work for me.

Lee's emphasis on encouraging diasporic Chinese youth to meet and mingle reflects the dominant sentiment favoring endogamy or marrying within one's ethnic group. Parents often stated that ideally they want their children to marry "Chinese," claiming that such unions promise a greater possibility of both spouses speaking the same language (Cantonese) and sharing the same cultural values, such as respect for elders, honesty, a strong work ethic, and commitment to family. What is suggested is not merely their preference for maintaining racial and cultural purity but, more important, a desire for shared cultural expectations that leads to familial intimacy rather than division. While this preference for "marrying within" has historical roots that link reproduction of racial and cultural purity with class distinction, Chinese parents are primarily expressing their profound anxiety over the possibility of "losing" their children through exogamy. They assume that marrying "Chinese" will reinforce familial bonds, while marrying out will lead to their deterioration. In fact, it is rather telling that their preference for marrying Chinese overrides their concern about geographical separation.

The emphasis on endogamy is less consistent among diasporic youth. In fact, the question of marriage in general is less a concern for them than for their parents. The youth attend the convention because they want "to travel," "to meet new friends," or "to have a good time." Amelia, the beauty contestant from Panama, asserted, "I came because I wanted the opportunity to meet people outside of Panama. I thought it would be fun to see how different their experience [of being diasporic Chinese] is from mine. Besides, I wanted to visit Costa Rica." Many of the youth, including the contestants, offered similar answers, and for most, finding a marriage partner was not a priority.

Getting to know one another is precisely what the youth did while attending the convention. Local Costa Rican Chinese youth organized trips to shopping malls, movies, and dance halls. I often went with them. During the day, we would explore the city, window-shop in malls, walk around tourist sites, and relax over a meal or a cup of coffee and snacks. Our conversations concerned family, experiences of discrimination, things we wanted to do, and the futures we imagined. We returned to the convention only to have dinner, and then off we went to the dance halls. By the end of the convention, we had made promises to one another to keep in touch via e-mail and phone, to continue attending these conventions, and to visit one another whenever possible. The intensive interaction we shared over the course of three days created strong bonds; most of us made meaningful friendships, and a few romances also developed.

The purpose of the beauty contest, quite explicitly described by Alberto Lee, is to encourage youth participation and interaction. In fact, the contest has become the highlight of the convention, with the contestants embodying idealized qualities of diasporic subjectivity, qualities that are to be reaffirmed, emulated, and reproduced. In essence, the contestants represent both the source of encouraging youth participation and the medium through which the diaspora is reproduced. The trope of women as social and cultural reproducers of the nation is here reconfigured into the trope of women as reproducers of the diaspora (Cohen et al. 1996; Yuval-Davis and Anthias 1989). And constitutive of this gendered discourse of reproduction is the assumption and reification of heterosexuality.

Diasporas have been described as masculinist projects of transnational community formation (Brown 1998; Helmrich 1992). Extending this, I suggest that patrilineality structures diasporic organizations from local to transnational contexts. Benedict Anderson's idea of the nation as "a horizontal comradeship" between men—in the sense that the nation is imagined not as a hierarchical structure but as one in which men see one another as equals within the nation—is likewise useful as a way of thinking about the Chinese diaspora (1992). In moving from nation to diaspora, however, this horizontal comradeship becomes what I would call a "brotherhood of patrilineages"—a nonhierarchical relationship among men of the same generation and among their respective generations of ancestors and descendants who reach beyond the temporal and territorial space of the nation. In other words, men are to nation as patrilineages are to diaspora. We can see this phenomenon at work in the relationships among this regional organization, the national Chinese associations, and the various native place associations that link together the diaspora.

As I mentioned earlier, this umbrella organization is comprised of the various Chinese associations in Central America and Panama, and its voting members are representatives of each of the national Chinese associations. In Panama, and I suspect in the Central American countries as well, members of the Chinese Association are elected representatives of the various native place associations, which are the most basic unit of formal organization of the ethnic Chinese community.[5] In fact, native place is arguably the most significant form of identification, aside from clan and family groupings, among ethnic Chinese in Panama.

Historically, Chinese immigration to Panama has been disproportionately male, and native place associations were formed as a kind of fraternity that aimed to provide mutual aid and protection for immigrant men. Like other native place associations that have developed throughout the Chinese diaspora, these organizations serve as support networks, minigovernments, and mechanisms of control and discipline (King 1994; Lai 1998).[6] In Panama, native place associations serve two major functions. They help immigrants maintain a sense of connection to and relations with their native places in China and give them access to "kinship" networks in Panama that provide them with support. In short, the associations link immigrants to their native villages in China and regroup them into quasi-kinship networks in Panama based on that linkage.

Moreover, native place identifications and kinship networks are traced patrilineally. Each generation identifies with the father's native place and kin group. Hence, these kinship networks are sustained and reproduced through male descent, thereby making men their nodes and primary guardians. For example, people who are from Chungsan (Zhongshan)[7] Province or whose patrilineal ancestry can be traced to that province are presumed to belong to the same kinship network and are therefore related. Those who share the same surname can claim even closer relations. In this manner, native place associations extend the geographically defined kinship networks beyond the territorial space of China, replicating patrilineality and kinship relations in the diaspora.

Over time, however, as people create their own family and social networks in Panama, these native place associations become less and less important. Also, people's connections to their native places tend to weaken over generations. For instance, native place identifications do not conjure up the same nostalgic memories or feelings of attachment for Panamanian-born Chinese as they do for immigrants. Indeed, these associations were created for and are mostly nurtured by immigrants, and their existence, therefore, depends on immigration flows from their respective regions in China. It is not surprising, then, that the founding members of the Chinese Association in Panama were all men and that the association remains an all-male organization to this day. In addition, meetings are conducted in Cantonese, which further limits participation. For these reasons, the membership of the Chinese Association consists mostly of immigrant men and is extremely vulnerable to changes in patterns of immigration. Up until the 1980s, the Chinese Association, along with native place associations, had been diminishing in importance and power because of the low rate of Chinese immigration to Panama. Organizations headed by Panamanian-born Chinese were slowly eclipsing the Chinese Association in providing leadership. However, the sudden and dramatic influx of immigrants in the 1980s revitalized both the Chinese Association and the native place associations. In fact, these organizations are now wracked by struggles for control between the early immigrants and the recent immigrants.

Patrilineality, then, structures gender bias into these various diasporic organizations. It ensures an (almost) all-male membership, which gives men control of these organizations and thereby also of the formal politics of the diaspora. In Panama, with the exception of two organizations that were founded and are run by women, all the organizations are dominated by men. It is important to note that the expansion of the Convention to include women and youth by no means opened the official meetings to them. On the contrary, it reinscribed and reenforced the division between the masculinized space of the "official meetings" and the feminized arena of the beauty contest and other "recreational" activities. For example, while men attended their two-day-long meetings, women were taken on tour buses around the city for sightseeing and shopping. Although there was no formal or explicit rule excluding women from these official meetings, there was no encouragement for them to participate either. When I sought permission to attend these meetings, I encountered mostly surprised looks and some resistance. Out of thirty attendees at these official meetings, only five were women (not counting myself); and out of these five women, three were translators and note takers. Only two were voting members. The stark gender imbalance clearly indicates male dominance in these official meetings. Indeed, since this regional organization ultimately draws its members from native place associations, it directly inherits its androcentric premises of belonging.

Tourism and the beauty contest are the two arenas within the convention where women are the key participants. Tourism, the shared experience of exploration, facilitates the formation of social ties among women. Spending all day together, women build affective bonds through conversation, exchange knowledge about one another, and create shared memories of their experience. Often, the ties they create in these informal arenas are stronger and longer lasting than those formed between the male participants. In fact, these feminized arenas of sociality serve an important role in generating and reaffirming the social bonds among diasporic Chinese. Several women I interviewed commented on their lasting friendships with one another. While some had met each other outside this context, their participation in the convention over the years has sustained their relationship. Luana, who is now in her sixties, explained, "Carmen and I have been friends since we were teenagers in Nicaragua. However, since I moved to Guatemala twenty years ago, the annual conventions are the only chance we get to see each other. And every time we meet, it is like it was just yesterday that we were together."

The beauty contest is another arena where young women bond with one another, their mothers, and other women relatives. The contestants often draw on their female kinship networks for advice and support. Most are accompanied by their mothers and at least one other female relative, who work behind the scenes to make sure the contestants appear their best. Their intimate and honest interactions, their emotional reliance on one another, and their overall shared experience all engender strong social bonds. One contestant commented, "I have never felt so close to my mother. She was so proud of me and so supportive throughout the whole process. I never saw that side of her until then." Another contestant claimed that she and her cousin have become closer because of this experience, stating that "without [her] cousin's constant support and attention to detail," she would have never been able to compete or have the strength to go through the contest. The beauty contest, then, provides an important site where intergenerational and lateral relations among women are affirmed and strengthened.

The beauty contest is also the only arena where women are expected to assert their identities publicly. Certainly, the structure of the beauty contest limits the kind of agency they are allowed. Nonetheless, the contestants have creative license to shift established norms, offer new versions of what it means to be diasporic Chinese, and provoke discussion about their performances. In fact, the beauty contest itself offers an intersubjective space where the interaction between the contestants' performances and the audience's reception makes possible certain interventions. I shall return to this discussion shortly. For now, I underscore that the gendering of arenas, such as the masculinization of formal diasporic politics and the feminization of informal interactions and the beauty contest, has reproduced gendered practices and ways of belonging to this diasporic organization.

Negotiating Homeland State and Diaspora Relations

To grasp the full significance of the Chinese Association, one has to see it in its global context and examine its role in Chinese diasporic politics. The Republic of China (ROC) and the People's Republic of China (PRC) have debated the right to claim Chinese state legitimacy since 1949, and the issue is far from having been resolved today. While the PRC continues to insist that Taiwan is a province under its jurisdiction, the ROC argues that Taiwan should have sovereignty.[8]

Panama has been a strong supporter of the ROC and continues to be part of the small minority of nation-states that maintain diplomatic relations with it.[9] Critical to maintaining the good relations between Panama and the ROC has been the work of Chinese Panamanians, who have fostered a mutually beneficial relationship with the ROC embassy. Part of the ROC's strategy in garnering international support has been to increase the awareness and involvement of diasporic Chinese in the PRC-ROC conflict. Historically, the Chinese diaspora has played a significant role in Chinese political, economic, and cultural developments, and it continues to do so today (Duara 1997). By institutionalizing diasporic networks such as the Federation of Chinese Associations of Central America and Panama, the ROC has demonstrated its commitment to sustaining relations with diasporic Chinese. In fact, this organization is part of a much larger structure of networks that tie the diaspora to the ROC. These networks include the Chinese associations on the national level, this organization on the regional level, the Federation of Chinese Associations in the Americas on the continental level, and, finally, the Global

Association of Cantonese. Through this sophisticated structure of organizations, the ROC seeks to nurture a well-informed, highly connected, and politicized Chinese diaspora that can lobby on its behalf in both the national and the international arenas.

A closer examination of the discussions that take place in the "business" meetings of the Convention reveals the complex relationship between diasporic Chinese and the ROC government. One Panamanian representative described a typical meeting as follows:

> We discussed two major topics: each country's political and social matters, and our [collective] relationship with Taiwan. Basically, each country reports their annual activities and discusses their community's needs. This year, we talked about the budget for [Chinese school] teachers and eventually passed a joint resolution to increase the allocation. In terms of our relationship with Taiwan, well . . . this year, the Taiwanese wanted us to support, morally mostly, a KMT (Kuomintang) member and his political position. We agreed to support a political framework but not a particular member of the KMT. The Taiwanese often ask the six countries for political support; in exchange, they give us support, whether it is economic or moral or whatever.

This only hints at the intricate symbiotic relationship between the diasporic Chinese of this region and the ROC government. It clearly shows the influential role of diasporic Chinese in negotiating geopolitical relations between the ROC and the PRC. In exchange for the ROC's financial support, diasporic Chinese lend moral-political affirmation. Anthropologists Linda Basch, Nina Glick Schiller, and Cristina Szanton Blanc (1994) have coined the term *deterritorialized nation-state* to underscore the manner in which a state can exert influence over people living both within and outside its national territory. More recently, Glick Schiller and Georges Fouron (2001) have extended Benedict Anderson's notion of "long-distance nationalism" (1992) to describe the process by which transnational migrants continue to participate in homeland politics. The difference between long-distance nationalism and diasporic Chinese-ROC relations is that the latter are based less on nationalism or nationalist sentiment than on mutual exchange. In fact, diasporic Chinese are concerned with Chinese politics only to the extent that it affects or benefits their local situation in the diaspora. The promise of funding to hire local Chinese schoolteachers in exchange for moral-political support is only one example. Given the ROC's economic wealth in comparison to the collective wealth of diasporic Chinese in this region, what it has done via cosponsor-ship of this transnational organization is to translate economic capital into political capital. Clearly, the ROC cosponsors this organization and its annual convention in order to sustain relations with diasporic Chinese, to reinforce diasporic identifications and relations among Chinese in this region, and to recruit their political support. The ROC understands that this organization helps generate a collective consciousness among diasporic Chinese, which in turn helps build a community base from which to mobilize political support. The stronger and more organized the community, the more influence and power diasporic Chinese can wield in national and international politics. And it is precisely the dual relations that diasporic Chinese maintain with their place of residence and the ROC that can help its cause in the international arena. Hence, it is in the interest of the ROC both to nurture the economic, social, and political growth of diasporic Chinese in their local contexts and to maintain strong ties with them. Similarly, it is also in the best interest of dia-sporic Chinese to maintain relations with the ROC embassy, which provides significant material support for the development of the community. For both parties, then, the emphasis is on strengthening local development in the dias-pora and not direct intervention in Chinese/Taiwanese national politics. This is what differentiates diasporic citizenship from long-distance nationalism.

The Convention provides a transnational venue for the ROC and the lead-ership of the Chinese communities to reinforce their mutual support. While it draws diasporic Chinese into the sphere of PRC-ROC politics, it simultane-ously provides a structure to reproduce a collective consciousness and contin-ued alliance with the ROC. Furthermore, by making its annual gathering a family-friendly event, it engages multiple generations of diasporic Chinese and ensures the continuation of the organization by grooming the next generation of participants. For instance, the cohort of friends I met during the 1996 con-vention continues to maintain social relations through periodic visits, e-mail, and telephone calls. Moreover, the annual convention provides both a venue and a purpose for reunions. Hence, while these conventions help forge social networks among ethnic Chinese, those networks in turn increase participa-tion in them.

The Convención de Asociaciones Chinas de Centroamérica y Panamá is thus clearly and unabashedly a diaspora-building project. By providing a transnational structure that meets annually and pools their resources, the Convention builds alliances among the different Chinese communities and enables the formation of social networks and a sense of collective identity among diasporic Chinese. It also engages diasporic Chinese in the PRC-ROC struggle and reinforces the relationship between the diaspora and the ROC. Finally, it helps recruit and socially reproduce convention participants and ROC supporters by reaching to several generations of diasporic Chinese, thereby also ensuring the effectiveness of the organization in the diaspora.

The 1996 Convention

In August 1996, I traveled with eighty-four Chinese Panamanians by plane to San José, the capital of Costa Rica. Miss Costa Rica and a few leaders of the Chinese Costa Rican community greeted our delegation as we deplaned and boarded the tour buses that would take us to the convention. With approximately two hundred participants in total, the Panamanian group was by far the largest, reflecting the relative size of Panama's Chinese population with respect to the other countries. It may be useful to note that Costa Rica has the second largest Chinese population, estimated at 47,000, followed by El Salvador with 18,000, and Guatemala at 16,800 (Commission on Overseas Chinese Affairs, ROC 1997). With less than 5,000 Chinese, exact figures for Nicaragua and Honduras are not available (Ibid.). Overall, the participants were mostly men and women between the ages of forty and eighty. Most of the men came as representatives of their Chinese associations and were accompanied by their wives. A few brought their children who were in their teens and twenties; there were no more than thirty of these young people, and they were evenly divided by gender. Generally speaking, the participants belonged to either the petite bourgeoisie or the professional class. Most people of the older generation were small business owners, while the younger generation consisted primarily of college-educated professionals.

With the exception of the Nicaraguan and Honduran delegations, the majority of the representatives were from the immigrant generation and were bilingual in Spanish and Cantonese, with some also speaking Mandarin and/or English. Latin American-born participants, especially the younger generation, tended to be fluent in Spanish and at least proficient in English and sometimes Cantonese. In addition to the Chinese Latin Americans, about thirty ROC officials from the Overseas Chinese Affairs Office in Taiwan and in Central America and Panama also attended the convention. Most of these officials were men between the ages of forty and sixty; all of them spoke Mandarin, and some also spoke English. Very few spoke Spanish.

The convention hotel was spacious enough to host several small conventions at once. There were at least two large banquet rooms for hosting our lunches and dinners. After registration, there was no set schedule for our first day there, so we disbanded. While the more senior groups of men and women went shopping around the city, the twenty-something participants met and relaxed in the hotel. We introduced ourselves and discussed our different backgrounds and experiences. People were friendly and accepting, and we soon established rapport with one another. By the afternoon, we were ready to explore the city, and we all packed into several cars and headed toward the mall, where we window-shopped, ate, and took pictures.

The convention officially convened the following day, and for the next two days, the delegates of each country met in the mornings and the afternoons, while most women participants shopped and toured the city, and the youth were free to do whatever they pleased. The last day of the convention was reserved for recreation. A group trip was organized to Mi Pueblo (my town), a tourist attraction where important scenes from the history of Costa Rica are reenacted. The group spent the remainder of the afternoon at an amusement park, which was open only to our private party. Each night after the dinner banquets, the younger participants gathered and planned their excursions to nightclubs and dance parties. Within those few days of the convention, we became good friends and promised to keep in contact in the years to come. In fact, during my thirteen months of field research in Panama from 1996 to 1997, we were able to meet twice as a group, once in Guatemala and another time in Panama.

The costs of attending these annual conventions were kept to a minimum, with travel and hotel expenses subsidized by the respective Chinese associations and the ROC Overseas Affairs Office. A few participants informed me that the delegates from each country attend these conventions at no cost to them. All other participants paid only airfare and hotel expenses. The dinners were Chinese-style banquets and were sponsored by different organizations. For instance, the Chinese Association of Costa Rica hosted the inauguration dinner, while the ROC embassy in Costa Rica sponsored the second dinner banquet. The following day, it was the ROC Ministry of Overseas Chinese Affairs that sponsored the dinner, and the Kuomintang Chinese Affairs Commission hosted the closing banquet. At each of the dinner banquets, entertainment was provided. The first dinner banquet featured mostly student performances of Chinese and Latin American dance forms. The second night showcased mostly Chinese folk dance and music, and the beauty contest was the scheduled entertainment for the concluding banquet.

These dinner banquets were formal affairs, and everyone was elegantly dressed in semiformal or formal attire. In fact, before departing for this trip, I was explicitly told that I should bring my best outfits. The Chinese travel agent with whom I registered for this convention made it a point to warn me: "I know Americans tend to be casual. But here in Latin America, we are more formal, and in these banquets, we really do it up." Indeed, every evening men showed up in dark suits, and women wore evening gowns. People of all ages took time to plan their outfits, and they looked simply spectacular. For most participants, these conventions provided one of the few occasions on which they could dress up, catch up with friends and family, and have a grand time. A look around the banquet hall showed new friendships forming, romances developing, and old friends reuniting. Whether through migration, marriage, kinship networks, or social relations formed at these conventions, people had strong transnational ties that made this regional convention seem almost neighborly. Indeed, looking around the room, I recognized a few people whom I had met in Nicaragua a few years ago. I walked over to reintroduce myself and was greeted with welcoming smiles and open arms. In that moment, I glimpsed why it was that people kept returning to these conventions.

The Beauty Contest:
Performing Nation/Performing Diaspora

Throughout the four days of the convention, the beauty contestants were at their best. They knew all too well that their performance began the moment they arrived and that they were judged not only on their onstage presence but also on their overall demeanor and comportment throughout the convention. Since the beauty contest took place during the last dinner banquet, people were by then already familiar with the contestants, and many had chosen their favorite. What follows is a discussion of the various categories of the beauty contest, with a particular focus on the two contested queens, Miss Costa Rica and Miss Honduras, and their different strengths in the "national dance" and "self-introduction" categories. As the contestants performed, not only did they present hegemonic constructions of Central American/Panamanianness and Chineseness, they also disrupted them by revealing the tensions and contradictions inherent in diasporic subjectivities. Moreover, their very embodiment of difference within the diaspora also incited discussions of idealized diasporic subjectivity, unveiling in public debate competing notions of diasporic citizenship.

The beauty contest was divided into four categories. The contest began with the contestants adorned in their respective national dresses.[10] Carrying their respective national flags and marching to their national anthems, the contestants slowly entered the banquet room and walked onto the stage. The reigning queen, who also happened to be my cousin from Guatemala, marched with the contestants; but instead of wearing her national dress, she wore the traditional Chinese cheongsam and marched to the ROC national anthem. The symbolism of her Chinese dress in contrast to the national dresses worn by the contestants encapsulates the process by which the winner of the beauty contest shifts from representing the nation to representing the Chinese diaspora (and its connection to the Chinese homeland). The beauty contest in this sense serves to abstract the differences between the national communities and reconstitutes them into a queen whose image emphasizes a shared Chinese identity. Once all the contestants and the queen were on stage, the audience applauded, and the two masters of ceremony briefly introduced the contestants in Mandarin and Cantonese.[11]

Following this segment, the contestants took turns performing their respective national dances. While a couple of the national dances used indigenous dance forms popularized as official representations of national culture, the others were drawn from colonial contexts. This category of performance underscored diasporic identification with the nation of residence. Yet, even as the contestants performed these dances, they inherently disrupted the very message they sought to convey—that of homogenizing the nation. Their embodiment of racialized difference articulated their disidentification with the nation. José Muñoz defines disidentification as the process of recycling and rethinking encoded meaning, stating that disidentification "scrambles and reconstructs the encoded message of a cultural text in a fashion that both exposes the encoded message's universalizing and exclusionary machinations and recircuits its workings to account for, include, and empower minority identities and identifications" (1999, 31). As the contestants performed their national dances, they not only made visible the exclusionary practices that continually denied their right to full citizenship but also simultaneously inserted themselves and insisted on their belonging.

In this category, Miss Honduras definitely outperformed her competitors. In general, the dance routines tended to be rather repetitive, but Miss

Honduras displayed extraordinary originality and poise. Carrying a basket of roses, she sang along with the music and danced with ease and grace, prancing around the stage, rippling her dress, and tossing roses into the audience. Her supporters responded happily, clapping, chanting her name, and catching the roses she threw to them. Without any sign of exhaustion or tentativeness, she exhibited a playfulness and ease with the dance steps that projected a sense of complete "at-homeness."

Miss Costa Rica was less adept. With her eyes fixed on her feet, she seemed overly concerned with the dance steps, reflecting a lack of skill and confidence. Her steps seemed more prepared, more tentative, as if she were performing them by rote. Focusing on her dance steps, she was unable to engage the audience, and near the end of her performance, one could see the exhaustion in her face and her relief as the music came to an end. The two juxtaposed performances illustrated the contestants' contrasting degrees of expertise and comfort. As one audience member commented, "Miss Honduras looked comfortable . . . as if she owned [the dance] . . . Miss Costa, on the other hand, needed more practice." If this category were meant to establish one's relationship with the nation, Miss Honduras seemed to embody Honduranness, whereas Miss Costa Rica showed far less familiarity with her national identity.

The third category, the "self-introductions," featured the contestants in cheongsams. With Chinese music playing in the background, the contestants glided elegantly across the stage and introduced themselves in whatever languages they chose. Coming after the national dance category, this segment showcased performances of Chineseness. Overall, the rhythm and pace were slower; the contestants assumed a more reserved and more subtly coquettish demeanor. In contrast to the dance category, this one focused on overall comportment, gestures, and speech. It was in the stylized movements (the tilt of one's head, the swaying of hips and arms, the poses one strikes) and ways of presenting oneself (dress, hair, makeup, intonations, and content and pattern of speech) that people discussed and judged their Chineseness. The seemingly simple act of walking across the stage took on immense meaning. According to my cousin, the reigning queen, the walk itself required arduous practice. She explained, "I watched videos of Hong Kong pageants to see how the women moved, walked with books on my head to check my balance. And once I learned the actual movements, I had to learn to be natural doing it." The subtle movements of the arms, hips, hands, and face, along with particular ways of looking and smiling all played a role in presenting a particular style of feminine sexuality. In their introductions, most of the contestants spoke in Spanish and Cantonese, but a couple of them also spoke in Mandarin. The use of different languages and the information they included and excluded all reflected their strategies of self-representation (cf. Besnier 2002).

Miss Costa Rica, dressed in a classic cheongsam, presented an archetypical image of idealized Chinese femininity. Slender, tall, with her hair tied in a bun and a few loose strands playing around her cheeks, she displayed an elegant, classic, and reserved femininity that clearly captivated the immigrant Chinese in the audience. Miss Honduras, with more voluptuous curves and wearing a less popular variation of the cheongsam, was less able to reproduce the conventional ideal of Chinese femininity. Despite this disadvantage, her performance was no less powerful.

Most contestants introduced themselves in Spanish and spoke at least a few words in Cantonese. Not surprisingly, since most were Latin American born and/or raised, all of them spoke perfect Spanish. In the area of Chinese-language competency, Miss Costa Rica had an advantage. She spoke fluent Cantonese and Mandarin, while it was clear that the others had learned specific phrases for the purpose of the contest. When introducing herself, Miss Costa Rica spoke in Spanish, then repeated herself in both Cantonese and Mandarin. She had firm control of all three languages, coming across as truly multilingual. Miss Honduras, who clearly did not speak any Chinese, used her fan as a prop from which she read phonically a few words in Mandarin. As she struggled with pronunciation, audience members reacted with either mocking smiles or enthusiastic applause. A number of her supporters whistled, clapped, and shouted her name in support. To most Chinese speakers, her attempt was almost indecipherable. To monolingual Spanish speakers, her performance was courageous and commendable. In the intersubjective process between performance and reception, her sincere attempt to speak Chinese was interpreted as either mimicry or parody, as either "trying to be but not quite succeeding" or as criticizing and subverting the absurd notion that equated *being* Chinese with *speaking* Chinese. In my conversations with various audience members, I learned that most Chinese of the immigrant generation interpreted her attempt as an honest but failed effort, while most Panamanian-born Chinese saw it as a courageous act of subtle critique. In speaking with Miss Honduras after the contest, she commented, "I did what I could, what I was expected to do, but I am who I am, and there is nothing I can do to change that. People will judge me accordingly." Keenly aware of the judges' expectations, Miss Honduras understood both the possibilities and limits of performance. She knew all too well that one's socialization and embodiment also play a role in the contest.

Miss Honduras's performance highlighted the long-standing divide between immigrant Chinese speakers and Latin American-born Spanish speakers and enabled the latter to express openly their collective rejection of marginalization based on linguistic ability. As one audience member resentfully remarked, "Immigrant Chinese-speaking men dominate the leadership of this organization. They are the gatekeepers of the Chinese colony and determine the agendas and set the criteria of belonging in the diaspora. It is time to change that." Clearly, Miss Honduras's insistence on speaking Chinese, however distorted it was, disrupted the dominant expectation that all contestants (and more generally, all diasporic Chinese) *should* speak Chinese with some degree of mastery. Her performance articulated disidentification. It created a break, a rupture, in representations of diasporic Chineseness, thereby allowing non-Chinese-speaking diasporic subjects to vocalize and confront the unspoken and unacknowledged marginalizing practices of the diasporic leadership. Indeed, diasporic formations are in part produced in response to the exclusionary practices of nation-states. Yet, in practice, diasporas often generate their own set of exclusions. In this particular case, the close relationship between diasporic Chinese and the ROC government undoubtedly shapes the manner in which idealized diasporic subjectivity is formulated and reproduced. Remarkably present throughout the contest, and the convention more generally, is the insistence on strong Chinese identifications, the ability to speak Chinese being the most significant of these. Speaking Chinese is also crucial for relations with the ROC, whose representatives are primarily monolingual Chinese speakers. The fact that business meetings in the annual conventions are conducted only in Mandarin and Cantonese further substantiates the importance of Chinese in sustaining diasporic communication and relations with the ROC.

The final segment of the pageant featured the contestants in Western-style evening gowns, and they were asked one question each, to which they gave impromptu answers. The questions varied: Who is your female role model? What would you say to your fellow contestants if you were to win the contest? Which of three—intelligence, wealth, beauty—is the most important to you, and why? Most of the contestants answered in Spanish only. In 1996, the two exceptions were Miss Costa Rica, who answered first in Cantonese and then in Spanish, and Miss Honduras, who answered in Spanish and then in English. By displaying their ability to speak at least two languages, they performed and simultaneously affirmed the value of biculturalism. Miss Costa Rica re-emphasized her ability to speak Cantonese and Spanish, and Miss Honduras surprised the audience with English. When I asked her later why she had answered in English, she responded, "I really wanted the judges to hear what I have to say. I know that some of them, especially the Taiwanese representatives, don't speak Spanish,[12] so I thought it would be a good idea for me to answer in English. I know most of them speak at least some English. Also, I wanted to show the judges that I can speak a language other than Spanish. I don't speak Chinese, but English has to count for something. I mean, just because I don't speak Chinese doesn't mean that I am closed-minded or provincial." While knowing that speaking Chinese is a quality valued in this competition, Miss Honduras also understood the significance of communication, and her strategic performance of English questioned the qualities associated with diasporic Chineseness.

In play here were the complexities of geopolitics. By speaking English, Miss Honduras subtly called attention to the role of American imperialism as the basis for relations between the ROC and Central America and Panama. America's Cold War campaign from the 1950s to the 1980s not only made impossible a mainland Chinese presence in this region but, in fact, encouraged and nurtured ROC relations with it and also with the diasporic Chinese there. While it may be difficult to assess Miss Honduras's intentions, her comment at the end of the contest reflects her understanding of politics in culture: "We [the beauty contestants] are mere pawns in their game of politics. It does not matter who we are or what we do. It's all about them and their political agendas." Succinctly, she unveils the beauty contest as a platform for political posturing and maneuvering.

Embodied Difference:
Miss Costa Rica and Miss Honduras

The contestants' contrasting strengths in the beauty contest, conveying their degrees of cultural identification with the nation and Chineseness, were reinforced by their identity construction. Miss Costa Rica and Miss Honduras exemplified very different ways of being diasporic Chinese. Miss Costa Rica was born in mainland China and immigrated to Costa Rica about ten years ago. Both her parents are Chinese from the People's Republic. She speaks fluent Mandarin, Cantonese, and Spanish. Given these characteristics, she was considered the "most Chinese," both in racial and cultural terms. Light-skinned, svelte, and the tallest of all the contestants, she reminded me of a Hong Kong movie star. Her appearance, gestures, and mannerisms epitomized Chinese cosmopolitanism: her speech pattern and language abilities reflected a sense of worldliness, her choice of contemporary classic styles of dress marked her fashion consciousness, and her subtle yet effective makeup replicated contemporary Hong Kong aesthetics. She projected a reserved, slightly aloof aura of refinement and elegance. In addition, I was told that her father has strong ties with the Taiwanese in Costa Rica, and a few people complained that she seemed arrogant because she did not mingle or "hang out" with the other participants in the convention. In her defense, however, another person responded that she has very protective, "traditional" parents and that she is not allowed to go out at night.

Miss Honduras is almost the polar opposite of Miss Costa Rica on the spectrum of Chinese Central Americans. She was born in Honduras and is racially mixed, her father being Chinese and her mother *mestiza* Honduran. Her facial features are unmistakably *mestiza,* and her shoulder-length brown hair is slightly wavy. Her style of dress was distinctively Latin American. Her outfits were vibrant in color and snug-fitting, so that they accentuated her feminine curves. She exuded a certain sensuality, confidence, and maturity that the other contestants had not yet developed. There was a quality of openness, warmth, and sincerity about her. She spoke neither Cantonese nor Mandarin but was fluent in Spanish and had a firm grasp of English. Furthermore, she was eloquent, thoughtful, and reflexive, qualities that came across not only in casual conversation but also throughout the beauty contest. She was very popular among her peers, who generally described her as friendly, warm, outgoing, and witty.

With the two women projecting such contrasting identities, one may ask how the winner could possibly have been in dispute? Unless, of course, there was little consensus to begin with, and, as a result, the votes were extremely polarized, with one group in favor of Miss Costa Rica and the other in support of Miss Honduras.

What is at stake in the beauty contest involves not only who gets to represent the Chinese diaspora, but also what qualities are deemed to be idealized characteristics of that diaspora. Which of the women best embodies Chinese

Central American beauty, femininity, and community? What characteristics, standards, and values are being projected, affirmed, and reinforced? That the two winners occupy two extremes of the Chinese diasporic spectrum is hardly accidental. Chineseness, after all, is a homogenizing label whose meanings are multiple and constantly shifting (Ang 1994, 5). To understand the concerns negotiated on stage, I suggest we examine the larger debates among diasporic Chinese in this region. First, however, I want to highlight the tensions and contradictions inherent in diasporic formations and, more specifically, in the Chinese diaspora, in hopes that this may help clarify the persistence of certain irreconcilable struggles for diasporic citizenship.

Between "Here" and "There": Irreconcilable Tensions in Diaspora

In its simplest formulation, diaspora refers to the condition of a people who share a common "homeland," real or imagined, and who are dispersed throughout the world, either by force or by choice. Diaspora most commonly refers to "the doubled relationship or dual loyalty . . . to two places—their connections to the space they currently occupy and their continuing involvement with 'back home'" (Lavie and Swedenburg 1996, 15). It is precisely this dual relationship, this tension between "where you are at" versus "where you are from" (Ang 2001; Gilroy 1990; Hall 1990) that constitutes the condition and the idea of diaspora and gives diasporic identifications the potential to be empowering as well as disempowering. In a sense, diaspora embodies a third space where the "here and there," "now and back then" coexist and engage in constant negotiation, and it is within this time-space continuum that diasporic subjects interpret their history, position themselves, and construct their identity.

The Chinese diaspora has its distinct set of histories and complex relations with the Chinese "homeland." Three particular factors—China's immense presence in the global political economy, China's image as the "Other" in the Western imagination, and the symbolic construction of China as the cultural and geographical core of "Chinese identity"—together exercise an extraordinary pull on diasporic Chinese to always look to China for identity and a sense of belonging (Ang 1994). While such identification can provide a sense of pride and serve as a tool for empowerment, it also reconfirms the "impurity," the "lack," and/or the "inauthenticity" of diasporic Chinese. Measuring Chineseness by one's imagination and romanticization of China and at the same time recognizing the cultural difference that is informed by one's current location fuels the debates over what constitutes Chineseness in the diaspora. Furthermore, the situation for diasporic Chinese is rendered more complicated by the existence of two political entities—the PRC and the ROC—espousing two different official narratives and imaginaries of the Chinese nation-state and homeland. (The conflict between the PRC and Taiwan, not explicitly apparent in this essay, became much more significant after 1996.)

Most diaspora literature has focused on the predicament of trying to maintain dual relations with the nation of residence and the homeland (Axel 2001; Louie 2004; Raj 2003), with few exceptions.[13] In the case of diasporic Chinese, while it is certainly true that both the Chinese homeland and the nation of residence exert tremendous cultural-political influence, it is also important to recognize the interactions and relations among diasporic communities. Moreover, diasporic Chinese are not a homogenous group; distinctions in status and influence are evident within the diaspora (Tu 1994). As nation-based collectivities, each group's place of residence tends to determine its relative power in the diaspora. For instance, diasporic Chinese in the United States wield more influence and have higher status than those in Ecuador or Kenya simply because the United States is a wealthier and more powerful nation, which in turn lends diasporic Chinese living there more weight within the larger diaspora. As shown in this essay, nationality serves as a primary identifier of difference among diasporic Chinese, because people are associated with their countries of residence. Nowhere is this clearer than in the beauty contest, where contestants represent and perform their national differences. As mentioned earlier, the Convention of Chinese Associations in Central America and Panama facilitates social ties and intimate relations that the Chinese across this region sustain and actively seek to reproduce. In recognizing these lateral relationships between diasporic communities, however, I also want to underscore their unequal power relations in relation to one another. Heterogeneity and unevenness within diasporas have not received sufficient attention; those of us engaged in diaspora studies would do well to shift our analysis to include conversations and interactions among diasporic subjects across national—as well as class, racial, gender, and generation—groupings.

National Differences and Inequalities Within the Diaspora

Despite their common colonial histories and geographical proximity, Panama and these Central American countries each confront very different political and economic conditions. Consequently, in spite of their common ethnic status in this region, the Chinese communities have developed in contrasting ways. To a large extent, the beauty contestants reflected certain national differences. Just as Miss Honduras, Miss Nicaragua, and Miss Guatemala were Central American born, racially mixed, and limited in their Chinese-speaking abilities, so are the majority of Chinese youths in these countries. Chinese immigration to El Salvador, Honduras, Nicaragua, and Guatemala has not been significant in the past few decades due to volatile political and economic situations in these countries. Therefore, the Chinese population in these countries has dwindled, with more emigration from than immigration to these countries. Furthermore, Chinese cultural practices and institutions such as Chinese-language schools, Buddhist temples, and native place associations have become almost obsolete. The leadership of the Chinese associations of Honduras and Nicaragua is now composed mostly of Spanish-speaking, Central American-born Chinese. In contrast, Chinese immigration to Panama and Costa Rica has increased tremendously in recent decades. While the influx of Chinese immigrants to Costa Rica has largely been from Taiwan, most of Panama's immigrants are from the southern region of mainland China.

These differences are not free of power asymmetries. For one thing, all the formal meetings at the convention are held in Mandarin and Cantonese. This is so largely because the Taiwanese delegates from the Overseas Chinese Affairs Office do not speak Spanish. Also, members of the immigrant generation often feel more comfortable speaking Cantonese or Mandarin than Spanish. Hence, while these meetings can be empowering experiences for Chinese immigrants, they often exclude the non-Chinese-speaking population from participating. Let me draw on one ethnographic example to illustrate this point.

The official meetings of the Convention I attended were held in the following manner. The presiding officer would read an item of discussion in Mandarin, followed by open discussion in either Mandarin or Cantonese. After these discussions, the membership would vote. Throughout the meeting, the most outspoken members were from Panama, Costa Rica, and Guatemala. The Nicaraguan delegation sat there restlessly, looking around the room as representatives from different countries stood up and offered their opinions. It became clear that none of the Chinese Nicaraguans could understand the discussion. They were completely lost, unable to participate in any real way. The presiding officers, who had known about this problem, chose not to address it. Instead, a trilingual Chinese Panamanian, noticing the situation, walked over to the Chinese Nicaraguans and began translating for them.

Language has always been a central problematic in the politics of diaspora.[14] Ien Ang argues that her inability to speak Chinese has become "an existential condition that goes beyond the particularities of an arbitrary personal history. It is a condition that has been hegemonically constructed as a lack, a sign of loss of 'authenticity'" (Ang 1994, 11). The privileging of Chinese languages in the official meetings of the Convention clearly reinscribes certain characteristics and even certain peoples as more Chinese and therefore more legitimate as participants than others. The Chinese Nicaraguan predicament also reminds us to be attentive to unequal power relations between the different Chinese communities in Central America and Panama in relation to the larger diasporic organization. Although Chinese Nicaraguans are part of this network, they by no means participate to the same extent, with as much influence, as Chinese Panamanians or Chinese Costa Ricans, who are often bilingual. Similarly, the beauty contestants confront these same criteria for being diasporic Chinese. It is not surprising, then, that all the contestants attempted to say at least a few words in Chinese, with, of course, varying degrees of success. Clearly, the ability to speak Chinese is a salient factor in determining the level of participation in this diasporic organization, and more specifically, in gaining more leverage in the politics of diaspora.

Immigration and Competing Claims of Belonging

Aside from national differences, one of the most pronounced divisions within these communities, especially in Costa Rica and Panama, is between the recent immigrants, on the one hand, and the earlier immigrants and their descendants, on the other. It is important, moreover, to note that the category of "recent immigrants" is different in Costa Rica than in Panama. The controversy over the crowning of the queen brings these overlapping debates to the surface, as an examination of the Panamanian response to the pageant's outcome makes clear.

Ricardo, a Panamanian-born Chinese in his forties who had been attending these conventions for the past twenty years, offered this analysis of the 1996 beauty contest:

Everyone wanted Miss Honduras to win. That was the talk around town the next morning. It's not that they felt pity [for her for what had happened], but it was the right thing to do. It has always been that a full Chinese, a Chinese-speaking girl, has the preference. In this case, that was Miss Costa

Rica. Further[more], the vice president of the Costa Rican association, the one who organized the event, is Taiwanese. He leaned toward a more traditional Chinese outlook, so to speak. Behind all this, there is an old infight between the old [immigrants] and the new [immigrants] in Costa Rica, as usual in all [of] Central America. The new are the Taiwanese and the old, well, are the old established [Cantonese] folks. In Panama, the story is different. The new are the newcomers from mainland China, who consist mostly of people who work in the *tienditas* [little stores], while the old are the established old-timers and their Central American-born descendants, who are not interested in this kind of infighting. [The old immigrants and their children] are the ones who wanted Miss Honduras to win.

Ricardo was careful to point out that in Costa Rica, the recent immigrants are mostly Taiwanese, while in Panama, they are mainland Chinese who work in or own small stores. However, in the context of this convention, both the Taiwanese and the store-owning mainland Chinese are categorized together as "recent immigrants" and are defined in opposition to the old immigrants and their Central American-born descendants.

A recent wave of Chinese immigrants to Panama in the 1980s has dramatically changed the demography of the Chinese population there, such that the recent immigrants now constitute about half of the total Chinese population in Panama. The two groups are characterized as complete opposites. While the old "Chinese Colony" (which includes the well-established Chinese immigrants and their descendants) are characterized as respectable, educated, and law-abiding citizens of Panama, the recent immigrants are portrayed as poor, uneducated, dirty, untrustworthy, and sometimes even criminal.

These negative images of recent Chinese immigrants are constructed alongside several other discourses, which may help elucidate how these images come into being and how the divisions between the immigrants and the Chinese colony are actualized and solidified. First, this group of newer arrivals is criminalized by being characterized as illegal immigrants. Shortly after the arrest of Manuel Noriega in 1990, the incoming government publicly announced that Noriega's military regime had sold Panamanian travel visas and passports to these immigrants. This information was then used to criminalize the immigrants, who quickly became scapegoats of Panamanian nationalism after the U.S. invasion. Second, the narrative of the immigrant-as-victim was set against the image of the established-Chinese-as-victimizer. A series of sensational newspaper articles showed that many recent immigrants came as either short-term contract laborers or as wage workers who took on low-paying jobs as maids, caretakers, and cooks for established Chinese. Immigrants and established Chinese were thus pitted against one another as victims and victimizers, respectively. Finally, recent immigrants were distinguished from the "Chinese Colony" along explicitly ideological lines, such that these immigrants were described as "communist Chinese," as if their undesirable behaviors were somehow inherently communist. These communist Chinese were deemed "a different breed of Chinese altogether," I was told repeatedly. The fact that many of the earlier immigrants and their families had been persecuted during the communist revolution in China partially contributes to their deep antagonism toward the recent immigrants, whom they associate with the communist regime. Another factor has to do with U.S. imperialism and its use of Cold War anticommunist rhetoric to justify its military presence and political repression throughout this region. Although *communism* and the *Cold War* may not exist in those same terms today, in this age of so-called globalization, ideological residues of the Cold War discourse are still firmly planted in people's memories and imaginations. Together, the three discursive constructions—the immigrant as criminal, as victim, and as ideological "deviant"—all feed into the formulation of the Chinese immigrant as an undesirable and dangerous subject.

Underlying these distinctions lies a certain fear that these new immigrants are transforming the "old Chinese Colony." According to Ricardo, the leadership of the Chinese Association in Panama is undergoing dramatic transformation. The representatives elected to office by the community are now reflecting the demographic changes in the Chinese population. More important, notions of Chineseness are changing faster than ever before. Since the 1980s, a number of new Chinese restaurants have opened, Chinese video rental stores have popped up in several places, cable television has given people easy access to Hong Kong media as well as American media, and Chinese karaoke performances are now being held regularly. In fact, at one of the Chinese Youth Association parties I attended, Chinese karaoke has now replaced salsa dancing, and a growing number of youth are speaking Cantonese with as much ease as Spanish. The members of the Youth Association convey their need to express their cultural pride and to affirm their difference. Salsa dancing no longer serves as a legitimate means of asserting their Chinese identity; rather, karaoke is their medium of choice to claim and reaffirm their Chineseness.

It does not matter what language they sing in—Cantonese, Mandarin, Span-ish, or English; what is significant is the act of singing karaoke and their par-ticipation in these performances. Karaoke has become the signifier of their Chineseness; it is the medium through which their diverse backgrounds and multiple identifications are enunciated. To be sure, this newfound Chinese confidence enacted by the recent immigrants threatens the established habi-tus of Panamanian Chinese who have survived culturally and economically by assuming a much more reserved and cautious comportment. The Chinese Colony, overwhelmed by these changes and challenges to their prescribed no-tions of Chineseness, feel as though they are losing control, losing their way of life, losing what was once an intimate community where everyone knew everybody else. To the extent that they are able to recreate their social net-works and imaginings of a community that is connected by no more than two degrees of separation, the Chinese Colony has maintained its distinctive identity. However, even these boundaries are quickly eroding.

The debate over who should be the beauty queen embodied these anx-ieties and tensions, articulating not only divisions within the existing dias-pora but also contrasting visions of what the diaspora should be. Discussions of standards of beauty are imbued with discourses of racial and cultural purity versus hybridity, discussions that express two divergent notions of Chi-neseness in the diaspora. I draw again from a conversation with Ricardo:

> This year [1998], Miss Nicaragua was the winner, and she was certainly the best fit for the job. . . . It is fair to say that she fits the Western standard of beauty, body, intelligence, and grace. Chinese standards are totally different. She has to speak [Chinese], look Chinese, her body doesn't matter, and above all [she] should and must be of Chinese [descent]. Costa Rica has always, to the best of my memory, chosen girls who met the Chinese standard. The Tai-wanese are almost pure in Costa Rica, or at least . . . they consider themselves as pure.

Ricardo claims that the recent immigrants prefer an aesthetic that is con-sidered racially and culturally "pure" Chinese, suggesting that other Cen-tral American Chinese do not share this preference, but rather one that fits Western standards of beauty. By Western, he means the Central American standard of beauty—that of a racially and culturally mixed woman (not the Western or European/North American idealized beauty). By preferring the Western, Central American standard of beauty himself, he is in a sense reaffirming his own positioning in Central America and Panama. His location in Panama, hence, is what informs his notions of Chineseness in the diaspora. In contrast, he would assert that the standards of beauty used by the recent immigrants are drawn from China, from what he considers to be the repository of "pure" Chineseness. Their notions are informed, he suggests, by their strong ties to the homeland, whether it is Taiwan or mainland China, not to Central America. Hence, Ricardo's preference for the Central American aesthetic is more than just a subjective reading of beauty. What he makes explicit is the politics of aesthetics in determining what it means to be Chinese in the diaspora. In stating his preference, he is asserting an ideological position as well as his resistance against hegemonic constructions of Chineseness.

In diaspora, notions of Chineseness change and evolve differently from those that are generated in China. Moreover, the play of difference within the diaspora also ranges tremendously. In the case of Chinese in Central America and Panama, these debates and contestations over Chineseness arise from the shifting power relations within the diaspora and the need for each community to assert belonging in relation to one another, to their nation of residence, and to the Chinese homeland. Indeed, at the center of the beauty contest controversy lies the struggle to determine what and who gets to represent diasporic Chineseness, at a time when the diaspora itself is undergoing rapid transformation.

*****

At the end of a very long evening, after most of the audience had retired to their hotel rooms, Miss Costa Rica was formally named queen of the Chinese Colony. In an almost empty banquet hall, the officials awkwardly presented her with the prize of U.S. $1,000 and a vacation package for two to Taiwan. The entire scene was somewhat surreal. The stage lights shone brightly on Miss Costa Rica, but there were only a few people left in the audience to witness her victory. Some people clapped, while others simply shuffled out of the banquet hall. With an awkward smile, Miss Costa Rica accepted her prize as if fulfilling an obligation.

Shortly after my return to Panama, I was told that the leadership of the Convention had decided to disqualify the 1996 competition altogether. Perhaps it was an admission of wrongdoing, but ultimately it was the only way to address the pain and hurt that had been inflicted on all those involved. The following year, Miss Costa Rica of 1996 did not attend the convention, and my cousin from Guatemala, the 1995 queen, crowned the incoming queen. It was as if the 1996 competition had never happened—but of course it had, and the tensions that erupted that night still persist within the diaspora today.

Conclusion

Initially established as a political and economic organization, the Federación de Asociaciones Chinas de Centroamérica y Panamá quickly incorporated an annual beauty contest to encourage multigenerational attendance at its annual convention and sociocultural interaction across the region. In doing so, the leadership transformed the convention into a project of diasporic reproduction in political, social, and cultural terms. Using gender as a category of analysis, I have shown that both the organization and the convention are highly gendered. Building on established diasporic associations whose membership is determined by patrilineal descent, this organization reinforces androcentric biases toward male participation and male dominance in formal spheres of diasporic politics. The beauty contest, however, offers an opportunity for women to articulate and negotiate the tensions and contradictions within the diaspora. Disguised as a seemingly harmless competition of beauty and femininity, the beauty contest in actuality incites and facilitates passionate and highly politicized debates about belonging and the meaning of diasporic Chineseness. Though working within the framework of the contest, the contestants not only reveal and disrupt dominant expectations of diasporic subjectivity but insist on difference and belonging in the diaspora by embodying and performing divergent ideals of diasporic femininity. For while the contest seeks to convey the shared triadic identification with the nation of residence, the homeland, and the larger diaspora—identifications that create the parameters of diasporic belonging and citizenship—it also unveils the differences and inequalities within the diaspora. Although it attempted to generate "a structure of common difference," the indeterminacy of the 1996 beauty contest reflects the enduring tensions within the diaspora—tensions that arise from a struggle for relatedness based simultaneously on shared identification with the Chinese homeland and the region of Central America/Panama and on difference along the lines of national context and racial and generational backgrounds. The idealism of diasporic egalitarianism is fractured by the realism of unequal access to material and cultural resources, both in terms of national economic development and of relations with the homeland and homeland state. Indeed, their emplacement in specific geopolitical entities matters in the diaspora, and recognizing this illuminates the complexities of diasporic belonging beyond the homeland/nation-of-residence binary.

Diasporic citizenship points to this dynamic and contested process of subject formation. To examine its nuances requires a temporary crystallization in historical time, as if putting a film in slow motion or freezing a frame just long enough to analyze its details. Indeed, while diasporic citizenship addresses relations across cultural and geographical terrain, it also insists on historical specificity. To understand the significance of the beauty contest controversy fully, one must situate it in the context of recent migrations to Central America and Panama. With the new influx of Chinese immigrants and the new technologies of transnationalism enabling different diasporic subjectivities to emerge, notions of Chineseness in diaspora along with the conditions of living in diaspora are being reconfigured. In the past twenty years, Hong Kong movie videos and karaoke discs have found their special niche market in diasporic Chinese communities all over the world, including those in Panama and Central America. Unlike the earlier generations of Chinese immigrants and Panamanian-born Chinese, who did not have easy access to such media, the children of recent immigrants today are conversant with Hong Kong popular music and culture. These rapid changes in transnational media distribution have expanded the resources of diasporic identification as well as complicated the process of identity formation. Hence, what one sees in the Chinese diaspora of Central America and Panama today is *not* a structure of common difference, but rather a debate, an ongoing argument about what the structure of common difference is or should be. Furthermore, membership in the Chinese diaspora is *not* defined by agreeing with this structure, but rather by participating in these debates and feeling that one has a stake in the argument.

While studies of diaspora have emphasized the popular mobilization of diasporic cultural productions (Gilroy 1987, 1993), they have not, for the most part, focused on the role of the homeland state in constructing diaspora. In the case of diasporic Chinese, the involvement of the Taiwanese state in transnational organizations such as the one discussed here underscores the state's influence in diasporic community formation. It not only shows the entrenched entanglement between the Taiwanese state and diasporic Chinese of this region but illustrates Taiwan's profound investment in ensuring the reproduction of both the diaspora and its identification with Taiwan via Chineseness. *Diasporic* Chinese serve as one vehicle through which Taiwan legitimates itself as a sovereign nation-state. The ongoing debates within the diaspora, therefore, also reflect and are produced by the conflict between mainland China and Taiwan. As long as the ROC continues to struggle for state status and the People's Republic maintains its claims that Taiwan is a "renegade province" of the mainland, Taiwan will continue to seek to influence the diaspora.

Notes

I thank Stanford University Press for giving me permission to reprint this chapter from my book *Memories of a Future Home: Diasporic Citizenship of Chinese in Panama* (2005).

1. The "national" dresses that the contestants wore and the "national" dances that they performed are often drawn from indigenous dress and dance forms that have been popularized as representative of the nation. For instance, Miss Guatemala would perform her nationality through Mayan dress and dance forms.

2. The term *Colonia China,* employed not only in Panama but throughout Central America since the late nineteenth century, suggests that diasporic Chinese are a satellite community of China, rather than being part of Panamanian society. It remains widely used today.

3. To a large extent, the ROC relies on diasporic Chinese to legitimate its claims to being the Chinese state. Conversely, the Chinese in Central America and Panama benefit from the financial and moral support of the ROC.

4. Throughout the nineteenth and twentieth centuries, Chinese communities in the diaspora have been subjected to varying degrees of persecution. Anti-Chinese movements have at one time or another been rampant in the United States, Mexico, Jamaica, Panama, Philippines, Indonesia, and Australia. Many of these movements led not only to mass destruction of property but also to intense physical violence and death. In some of these countries, communities of Chinese have emigrated, leaving few traces of their historical presence.

5. Different types of Chinese organizations are present in diasporic communities. The most prevalent ones include surname or clan associations, locality or native place associations, dialect group associations, consolidated benevolent associations, chambers of commerce, secret societies, and religious associations. For a more detailed discussion of this subject, see King (1994), Lai (1998), Sinn (1998), and Wickberg (1998).

6. This subject has been well documented by Chinese diaspora scholars. In this chapter, I restrict my discussion of locality associations to gender and kinship.

7. I am translating native place names from Cantonese.

8. Their long-standing differences have been further complicated by current political struggles within Taiwan over whether it should continue to seek reunification with the mainland or work toward independence. In the past ten years, the Beijing government has issued numerous warnings against Taiwanese independence. It has made official statements and even fired missiles across the straits as a show of non-

tolerance. On Taiwan's side, internal debates indicate that some support the "one China" principle (the idea that the two territories will reunify in the future), advocating for "status quo" or not changing the island's geopolitical status, while others support total independence from the PRC and official recognition as a nation. Despite their differences in strategy, most Taiwanese agree that neither China nor Taiwan is ready for reunification. The China-Taiwan issue is also debated among diasporic Chinese. For Chinese in Panama, the eventual reunification of the PRC and ROC has been a central impetus for their participation in specific diasporic organizations, and their support of the ROC is premised on that principle. With intensification of the China-Taiwan conflict, the ROC is more anxious than ever to recruit the support of diasporic Chinese, and this has aroused even more active and vocal participation among diasporic Chinese.

9. After losing relations with South Africa, the ROC has placed its priority on maintaining relations with Panama, its most important and influential supporter at the moment.

10. Panama's national dress is distinctly different from the other countries' national dresses because it is heavily influenced by Spanish colonial style. All the other Central American countries use indigenous dress forms to represent the nation.

11. At first, the masters of ceremony appeared uncertain about which languages to use, and after a few tries, they finally settled on speaking Spanish and Mandarin, with occasional interjections in Cantonese.

12. About twelve judges are selected every year. Some are local representatives of diasporic Chinese communities, some are local embassy people, and some are diplomatic visitors from the ROC.

13. The exceptions include Paul Gilroy and Jacqueline Brown, who explore connections among diasporic communities.

14. Manalansan (2003) explores the role of language among diasporic Filipinos in New York City. Besnier (2002) examines language use in beauty contests.

References

Anderson, Benedict. 1992. "The New World Disorder." *New Left Review* 143 (May–June): 3–13.

Ang, Ien. 1994. "On Not Speaking Chinese." *New Formations* no. 24 (Winter): 1–18.

———. 2001. *On Not Speaking Chinese: Living Between Asia and the West.* New York: Routledge.

Axel, Brian. 2001. *The Nation's Tortured Body.* Durham, NC: Duke University Press.

Basch, Linda, Nina Glick Schiller, and Cristina Szanton Blanc. 1994. *Nations Unbound: Transnational Project, Postcolonial Predicaments, and Deterritorialized Nation-States.* Longhorne, PA: Gordon and Breach.

Besnier, Nico. 2002. "Transgenderism, Locality, and the Miss Galaxy Beauty Contest." *American Ethnologist* 29, no. 3 (August): 534–566.

Brown, Jacqueline. 1998. "Black Liverpool, Black America and the Gendering of Diasporic Space." *Cultural Anthropology* 13, no. 3: 291–325.

Cohen, Colleen Ballerino, Richard Wilk, and Beverly Stoeltje, eds. 1996. *Beauty Queens on the Global Stage: Gender, Contests, and Power.* New York: Routledge.

Commission on Overseas Chinese Affairs, Republic of China. 1997. *Overseas Chinese Economy Yearbook (Huaquiao jingji nianjian).* Taipei: Commission on Overseas Chinese Affairs.

Duara, Prasenjit. 1997. "Transnationalist Among Transnationals: Overseas Chinese and the Idea of China, 1900–1911." In *Ungrounded Empires: The Cultural Politics of Modern Transnationalism,* ed. Aihwa Ong and Donald Nonini. New York: Routledge.

Gilroy, Paul. 1987. *"There Ain't No Black in the Union Jack": The Cultural Politics of Race and Nation.* Chicago: University of Chicago Press.

———. 1990. "It Ain't Where You're From, It's Where You're At . . . The Dialectics of Diasporic Identification." *Third Text,* no. 13 (Winter): 3–16.

———. 1993. *The Black Atlantic: Modernity and Double Consciousness.* Cambridge, MA: Harvard University Press.

Glick Schiller, Nina, and Georges Fouron. 2001. *Georges Woke Up Laughing: Long-Distance Nationalism and the Search for Home.* Durham, NC: Duke University Press.

Hall, Stuart. 1990. "Cultural Identity and Diaspora." In *Identity: Community, Culture and Difference,* ed. Jonathan Rutherford, 222–237. London: Lawrence & Wishart.

Helmreich, Stephan. 1992. "Kinship, Nation, and Paul Gilroy's Concept of the Diaspora." *Diaspora* 2, no. 2: 243–249.

King, Ambrose Yeo-Chi. 1994. "Kuan-hsi and Network Building: A Sociological Interpretation." In *The Living Tree: The Changing Meaning of Being Chinese Today,* ed. Tu Wei-ming. Stanford: Stanford University Press.

Lai, Him Mark. 1998. "Organization Among Chinese in America Since the Second World War." In *The Chinese Diaspora,* vol. 2, ed. Ling-chi Wang and Wang Gungwu. Singapore: Times Academic Press.

Lavie, Smadar, and Ted Swedenburg. 1996. *Displacement, Diaspora, and Geographies of Identity.* Durham, NC: Duke University Press.

Louie, Andrea. 2004. *Chinese Across Borders: Renegotiating Chinese Identities in China and the United States.* Durham, NC: Duke University Press.

Manalansan, Martin 2003. *Global Divas: Filipino Gay Men in the Diaspora.* Durham, NC: Duke University Press.

Muñoz, José. 1999. *Disidentifications: Queers of Color and the Performance of Politics.* Minneapolis: University of Minnesota Press.

Raj, Dhooleka. 2003. *Where Are You From? Middle-class Migrants in the Modern World*. Berkeley: University of California Press.

Sinn, Elizabeth. 1998. "A Study of Regional Associations as a Bonding Mechanism in the Chinese Diaspora: The Hong Kong Experience." In *The Chinese Diaspora*, vol. 2, ed. Ling-Chi Wang and Wang Gungwu. Singapore: Times Academic Press.

Scott, Joan. 1999. *Gender and the Politics of History*. New York: Columbia University Press.

Tu, Wei-ming, ed. 1994. *The Living Tree: The Changing Meaning of Being Chinese Today*. Stanford: Stanford University Press.

Wickberg, Edgar. 1998. "Chinese Organization in Philippine Cities Since the Second World War: The Case of Manila." In *The Chinese Diaspora*, vol. 2, ed. Ling-chi Wang and Wang Gungwu. Singapore: Times Academic Press.

Wilk, Richard. 1996. "Connections and Contradictions: From the Crooked Tree Cashew Queen to Miss World Belize." In *Beauty Queens on the Global Stage: Gender, Contests, and Power*, ed. Colleen Ballerino Cohen et al. New York: Routledge.

Yuval-Davis, Nira, and Floya Anthias, eds. 1989. *Woman—Nation—State*. London: Macmillan.

5 ## Ritual in Diaspora:
Pedagogy and Practice Among
Hindus and Muslims in Trinidad

Aisha Khan

Diasporic Consciousness and Religious Ritual

The subject of religious ritual is certainly one that has had its share, some
might say more than its share, of scholarly and popular attention. Thousands
of pages have been committed to analyzing religious rituals—their form,
function, and meaning—from various parts of the world, over centuries,
and by various kinds of observers, including social scientists, religious scholars, and practitioners. South Asian rituals are not only no exception to this
abiding fascination, they arguably have been central to the development of
contemporary academic analyses of rituals. Given the amount of preceding,
and ongoing, work in this area, and all the possible directions in which one
might train one's lens, my interest here is directed toward just one dimension of ritual practice. This dimension has to do with the degree of dynamism
in ritual practice, the ways in which this dynamism is interpreted both by
practitioners and external observers, and thus its ethnographic significance.
When we consider the persistence of rituals over time among local communities, it becomes clear that even when these communities have become permanently settled, certain cultural practices, such as religious rituals, can remain
characterized in terms of arrival, newness, rupture, loss, and uncertainty. In
other words, in diasporic contexts, such as those of the Indo-Caribbean, a
consciousness of diaspora can shape fundamental, ostensibly timeless and
fixed practices that define a community's identity.

As many scholars have noted, religious rituals have long been characterized as representing cultural convention, stability, and timelessness;

anthropologist Peter van der Veer (1996: 144) reminds us that still prevalent is the "formal point of view," where rituals are "characterized by convention-ality, condensation, and repetition." When viewed as unchanging and thus static, ritual is seen to represent "tradition" and the symbolic moral frame-work or charter of a society, which ostensibly needs to remain constant in order to hold the society together. Yet when viewed as contextually responsive and fluid in addition to representing conventionality and repetition, rituals become a different kind of object of analysis. In joining the scholarship that approaches ritual in terms of responsiveness and fluidity, what I hope to un-derscore in this chapter is that, as a multilayered phenomenon, religious ritu-als among Hindus and Muslims in Trinidad—one of two islands that comprise the Republic of Trinidad and Tobago—employ repetition and conventional-ity, but do so as part of ideological projects rather than always or necessarily in terms of customary tradition, and that, at the same time, dynamism and contingency are key aspects of Hindus' and Muslims' ritual practices. In the Indo-Caribbean diaspora as a whole, and in Indo-Trinidad in particular, we can see that context, ideology, dynamism, and conventionality in ritual prac-tice are linked and mediated through two powerful cultural motifs: *betrayal,* or "being fooled," and *exegesis,* access to and creation of knowledge through explanation or interpretation.

The material on which my discussion rests involves the ways Hindu and Muslim Indo-Trinidadians understand the importance of gaining religious knowledge by means of ritual and what the meaning and explanations of rit-ual and religious knowledge should be. Rather than examining specific rites, my interest here is in how people talk about and assess religious practice as a kind of metanarrative. Thus, I do not offer a description or study of religious content per se. What I would like to argue, at its broadest, is that we look at the concept of ritual as suggesting more than it defines, as guiding rather than cementing. In being more suggestive than definitive, rituals can offer a more ethnographically effective frame for understanding the shifting contexts in which local practitioners find themselves, particularly those who comprise diasporic communities. In short, ritual practice and diasporic consciousness are always in a mutually defining dialogue with each other.

A diaspora is a particular kind of historical experience, with far-reaching implications for cultural forms and social relationships. That is to say, the very fact of uprootedness has shaped the sense of self of entire communities; a consciousness emerges among members of a community that memorializes its displacement in everyday discourse and practice. This diasporic consciousness takes different forms of memorialization over time, in part because the historical conditions in which it is meaningful change over time, and in part because the discourses and practices in which it is expressed also change over time. Nonetheless, as varied as the theme of memorializing displacement may be, given different historical moments and cultural expressions, what remains a key constant is a community's emphasis on its awareness of its outsider-foreign origins, the struggle in local contexts to overcome the stigma with which outsider-foreign origins contend, and the eventual victories over local forms of social inequality that this stigma takes. Given these specifications we are able to understand that certain populations are diasporic. In other words, all peoples throughout human history have experienced migration in some form, and all cultural forms have undergone transformation over time—but only some populations have become communities based in large part on a shared ideology of deterritorialization that actively has inspired their culture and cultural production. The difference between "diaspora" and "migration" is not simply about retaining a feeling of belonging to a homeland or the creation over time of communities symbolically connected to ancestral origins. It is also about consciously interpreting one's culture as indelibly marked for all time by the experience of being uprooted. As such, diaspora represents among Indo-Caribbeans a monumental rupture in self-determination.

If a community's diasporic consciousness is necessarily always in a mutually defining dialogue with the historical conditions in which the community finds itself and with the cultural expressions it manifests, then it stands to reason that diasporic consciousness also shapes and is shaped by religious ritual, which is one form of discourse and practice that is part of a community's history and culture. A community's sense of self, and consciousness about how that self has been constituted historically and culturally, will both influence and reflect its core institutions, like that of religion and its rituals. Despite assumptions that religious rituals are ostensibly stable and timeless charters, which renders them impervious to, for example, the impact of practitioners' forms of consciousness about their identity, rituals are, rather, *presented* as stable and timeless charters by practitioners, as well as at the same time *interpreted* to the contrary (as being responsive to change). These presentations and interpretations of ritual work in concert with the community's particular consciousness about its identity; that is, they are in accord with how this consciousness informs ideas about the ways its identity is, or should be, defined and demonstrated. As I noted above and explore further below, two power-ful motifs in Indo-Caribbean consciousness of self are betrayal, or "being fooled," as the local parlance expresses it, and exegesis, access to and creation of knowledge through explanation or interpretation. Both of these themes are expressed discursively, as narratives about awareness, struggle, and victory. They are also registered in ritual, as the means of gaining knowledge and con-veying, through the "lectures," or sermons, of ritual specialists and the inter-pretation of religious rites, what the meaning and significance of ritual and religious knowledge should be, in its work as identity marker among Indo-Caribbeans. In a sense, rituals are constant commentaries on the condition and state of diaspora, and diasporic consciousness is always and necessar-ily a constitutive element of ritual practice and interpretation. Together they give rise to ritual's emphasis on overcoming disfranchisement through self-teaching: memorializations that assert Indo-Caribbean identity and thus force of presence in the region—thereby defying their historical marginality as uprooted, extraneous persons.

Constituted by the mutually defining dialogue between a community's (1) diasporic consciousness about its identity (tempered by historical and cultural transformations) and (2) the cultural expressions that represent that identity, religious ritual among diasporic Hindu and Muslim Indo-Caribbeans has be-come in the New World a site of instruction; religious ritual is not simply an anchor to the past but also preparation for the future. As such, ritual is ideo-logical as well as "cultural"; it is fluid as well as stable; it represents the projec-tion of "tradition" as well as the propulsion of "modernity."

Fooled into Submission

The Indo-Caribbean, which is part of the greater nineteenth-century South Asian diaspora to the Americas, is distinguished by the one and a half century presence of "East Indian," as they are still known, immigrants to the Carib-bean region from India. Beginning in 1838 to what was then British Guiana (today Guyana), and then in 1845 to Trinidad (now the Republic of Trinidad and Tobago), almost half a million Indians arrived in the region as "bound coolies," indentured laborers contracted by the British labor scheme to bolster sugar production on their colonial plantations after the emancipation of en-slaved Africans (or, by that time, Afro-Caribbeans). Today in Trinidad in par-ticular, as in the Indo-Caribbean more generally, memories, and memorializ-ing, of this movement are encapsulated in the powerful metaphor of betrayal, of being fooled. There are several elements to this metaphor of betrayal. One is being fooled into becoming indentured labor emigrants in the first place. The foundational moment for subsequent anxieties about being fooled is the initial luring away from home that indenture contracts may have represented to would-be immigrants gathered in the exit depots of Calcutta and Madras, and as they certainly represent among Indo-Caribbean peoples today.

Another element is being fooled into grossly subordinate positions as colonial subjects—as "coolie labor"—and then as ambivalently national citizens. From the perspective of the political, economic, and cultural authority exercised by colonial and postindependence governmental structures, Indo-Trinidadians were imagined as implicitly or overtly loyal to "Mother India" and therefore only uncertainly dependable and trustworthy in terms of their allegiance to colony and country. As a geographically and socially marginalized population for much of the indenture period, which officially ended in the Republic only in 1917, and well into the twentieth century, Indo-Trinidadians have been concentrated within grassroots communities where few opportunities for upward social mobility have been available. Most notable among these mobility opportunities was formal education, widespread access to which Indo-Trinidadians did not enjoy until the second quarter of the twentieth century, when Hindus and Muslims began to build their own schools. Until that time the only reliable educational opportunity came from attending Presbyterian schools, called Canadian Mission schools, whose missionaries first arrived in Trinidad from Canada in 1868. As late as 1946, however, census reports showed that over half (51 percent) of the Indo-Trinidadian population remained illiterate (see, for example, Singh 1996).

A final element in the metaphor of betrayal is being fooled in the sense of the difficulty Indo-Trinidadians see themselves as having experienced in successfully extricating themselves from their subordinate position. Reliance on local social institutions for support, from which historically they were kept apart, has been an exercise in tenacity, inventiveness, and alternative strategies. For example, Indo-Trinidadians' initially cautious embrace of Canadian Mission schools was represented by Euro-colonial and middle-class "colored" (Afro-Caribbean) sectors of the society, and well into the postindependence period, as indicative of Indian recalcitrance to assimilate and their general backward lack of appreciation of literacy and self-improvement. It was, however, indicative of indentured immigrants' reluctance to shed their religious heritage and accept Presbyterianism to the exclusion of Hinduism and Islam, which were, and remain, cornerstones of their identification of themselves as a particular community. Once they realized (and it took less than a generation) that they could "convert" to Presbyterianism, and thereby take advantage of the educational and employment opportunities (primarily in Presbyterian schools) such conversion offered, without necessarily eschewing their Hindu and Muslim worldviews and customs, Indo-Trinidadians shrewdly took advantage of this opportunity. Many, of course, became devout and exclusive Christians; many others practice, inclusively, heterodox forms of worship. Other examples of tenacity, inventiveness, and alternative strategies include Indo-Trinidadians' mid-twentieth century organizing and funding of Hindu and Muslim primary and secondary schools, and their continuous, energetic political participation (at times anticolonial or straightforwardly counter-hegemonic, and at other times not necessarily so), which preceded mid-twentieth century independence struggles and remain emblematic of their national presence today. Part of their diasporic consciousness, then, is an acute awareness of not simply the universal exigencies of life but the specific configuration of colonial hierarchies. As much as Indo-Trinidadians today may engage in a rhetoric of resignation about the circumstances of their New World diaspora (as many have said to me with a shrug, "wha' yuh go' do? That is how it was, we ent [didn't] know"), or of self-congratulations (for being the rescuers of empire after emancipation left the sugar plantations without local [read free] labor, and for overcoming the odds and enjoying significant upward social mobility), there is often at the same time an undercurrent of indignation, or at least an ironic appreciation of the workings of social inequality structured according to ethnic, religious, citizenship, rural/urban, and labor hierarchies. Built into diasporic consciousness, then, is a particular form of agency: a motivated and purposive engagement with power and authority.

Rituals, Agency, and Resistance in Context

At least three broad historical processes provided the conditions for the development of ritual practice and interpretation among Indo-Trinidadian Hindus and Muslims. First, founding generation indentured laborers "kept up we religion," as contemporary Indo-Trinidadians phrase it, often by covert means, taking unauthorized leaves from the estates to meet with fellow Hindus or Muslims and worship together. By the 1880s, as a means of curbing labor unrest, colonial policy enforced laws governing the movement of indentured laborers off their assigned estates. In addition to legalized punishments were controls in the form of contemptuous ridiculing of traditional forms of authority, commonly in the form of charges of chicanery and superstition rather than moral rectitude and divinely-inspired insight. The diaspora narratives that memorialize clandestine religious activities work to countermand the legacy of pejorative images of Indians as ignorant and pliable. In a conversation I had with Mr. Zayn, an older head imam (Muslim religious leader) and community elder who was born and raised in southern Trinidad, he spoke of his father, an indentured immigrant who arrived in Trinidad in the early twentieth century. A learned man, his father traveled among sugar estates surreptitiously in the night, in order to spread knowledge of Islam among fellow indentured and no longer indentured Indians. I heard virtually identical narratives from Hindus about their forebearers, as well. These kinds of activities were clearly forms of cultural resistance to plantation authority, surely strengthening the bonds and the resolve among immigrants.

The second of these broad historical processes was in plain view by the mid-1930s. Well underway was the consolidation of Hindu and Muslim identities among Indo-Trinidadians. For one thing, religio-cultural organizations, notably the Sanatan Dharma Maha Sabha (founded in 1932) and the Anjuman Sunnat-ul Jamaat (founded around 1931), that still represent Hindus and Muslims, respectively, were becoming increasingly institutionalized. They showed a growing investment in promoting certain doctrines of orthodoxy, as well as authorizing the pandits (Hindu religious leaders) and imams (Muslim religious leaders) that represented those doctrines. For another, a more formalized role for pandits and imams as community and religious leaders was developing. The overall effect of these processes was the attempt, in part in the spirit of teaching and learning to foster knowledge, to formalize and codify both Hindu and Islamic doctrine out of multiple and sometimes divergent traditions and pedagogies. This formalization and codification has at its discursive center the problem of "culture": the cultural heritage of India and its place in Caribbean contexts. In Indo-Trinidadians' parlance, "traditional," or "long time," or "grassroots" modes of understanding either hinder progress toward modernity or propel one forward, empowering one's group with forceful—plentiful and correct—knowledge of selected traditions, which were, for the most part, taken from religious practice.

Finally, compounding the processes of plantation-based strategies of resistance and organizational codification of religious belief and practice was the postindependence period's formation of Trinidadian political culture and party politics. Gaining independence in 1962, the Republic established parliamentary democracy based in part on universal suffrage and government distribution of patronage, in the form of resources and opportunities, on the basis of voting constituencies that are grouped according to ethno-cultural identities. These are tacitly understood to be "racially" constituted, and "culturally" represented primarily by "religious" diagnostic emblems. In Trinidad's self-proclaimed "rainbow" diversity of 40.3 percent Indo-Trinidadian, 39.6 percent Afro-Trinidadian, 18.4 percent Mixed, 0.5 percent Chinese/Syrian/Lebanese, 0.6 percent white/Caucasian, and 0.6 percent not stated (according to the national census) (Central Statistical Office 1990), Indo-Trinidadian and Afro-Trinidadian are the two salient politico-cultural entities. While Indo-Trinidadian Christians (Protestants and Catholics) are not defined as a political constituency in their own right, Hindus and Muslims, 24 percent and 6 percent of the total population, respectively (Central Statistical Office 1990), tend to be distinguished both from each other and from the entire Indo-Trinidadian population in political terms; that is, as distinct groups to be recognized and courted by the state. Thus, in sum, groups vie for state patronage in part within a discourse of deservedness based on "difference," or cultural alterity defined primarily by boundaries that are established through the practice of tradition and heritage.

Dimensions of Ritual Practice, and Ways of Knowing Them

There are numerous dimensions of ritual practice among Indo-Trinidadians. Many considerations (one might say variables) are pertinent to any discussion of Hindu and Muslim rituals in the Caribbean diaspora. Among the most important of these dimensions are the key interlocutors whose cultural practices, worldviews, and insistent interpretations shape ritual content. First are the different generations of Hindus and Muslims. Although now almost one hundred and seventy years after their initial arrival to the region, and thus constituting several generations, the most significant distinction among generations in terms of religious issues is between "older heads," as it is expressed locally, and "younger people." Older heads tend to be "grassroots," that is, poor or working class. Older heads symbolize a particular kind of religious and cultural authenticity and authority that celebrates forebearers who tenaciously struggled to keep their "traditional" worldview as a means of stabilizing a profoundly uncertain environment. At the same time, this kind of authenticity confronts other, "modern" notions of authenticity, underscoring the contradictory aspects of Indo-Trinidadians' past, both venerable and inglorious. Younger generations tend to be associated with modernity, largely through having experienced some degree of upward social mobility, primarily through greater access to formal education, both secular and religious. Yet "traditional" and "modern" do not simply denote past and present among Indo-Trinidadians. Each is itself a metaphor containing its own internal layers of meaning: authenticity can derive from traditions made genuine by being rooted in the pure and original India-based culture of indentured forebearers, or it can evoke spuriousness through a backwardness derived from those very same roots simply interpreted differently; authenticity can derive from traditions made genuine by being freed from the same roots, this time interpreted as untutored, ad hoc, contextually contingent beliefs and practices, and enlightened by rigorous formal training, or it can evoke a dangerous distancing from tradition toward a culturally diluted no-man's land of Westernized religious and cultural ambiguity.

Also an important part of the Indo-Trinidadian population are Christians, both Protestant and Catholic (about 3 percent of the total population). More numerous, Indo-Trinidadian Protestants in turn can be divided into old and new communities, in the sense of established congregations, such as the Presbyterians, and more recent (since about the 1970s)—and growing —congregations of evangelicals and Pentecostals. There are, as well, Afro-Trinidadian Muslims, who share certain Islamic philosophical and theological precepts with Indo-Trinidadian Muslims while they at the same time engage in debates over other doctrines and practices. Out of these multiple layers emerge discourses, at times incendiary, about what ritual practice should be and how it should be interpreted, what form of authenticity should be represented and what the distinctions between "religious" and "cultural" authenticity might be, and even whether or not rituals should be performed at all—that is, questions about whether they are atavistic and antimodern.

In addition to the material forces of social hierarchy and political culture in which rituals are performed, the cultural themes of betrayal and its recuperation through exegesis shape rituals' dynamic quality. Stories of betrayal are allegorical narratives that symbolize a dramatic reference point among Indo-Trinidadians that represents vulnerability through ignorance. I have heard many dozens of betrayal narratives from Indo-Trinidadians.

The general contours of the narratives, which are both apocryphal and historical, emphasize Indians' deception, being tricked into overseas indenture
in "Chinidad" (*chini* is *sugar* in Hindi/Urdu), where they were to sift sugar,
perceived as an easy task, for an inordinately high daily wage. The following
story encapsulates nicely the betrayal theme. It was told to me a few years ago
by Vishnu, who although only in his mid-thirties at the time, considers this
story as much a part of his identity as an Indo-Trinidadian as it was to the
man three generations earlier, to whom the story refers. As Vishnu recounted,
"Ninety-nine-point-nine percent of Indians tell the same story. They came [to
the Caribbean] with a willing mind, but they were fooled into thinking they'd
find a pot of gold there. Because that's the way the white people told them.
My great-grandfather's parents in India sent him to the grocery store to get
sugar. On his way to the shop, the people [indenture recruiters] came up and
they told him, he was a young boy, 'Come on this ship, there's lots of candies
there, so much things to eat.' The next thing you know, he was in Trinidad.
He grow up on the cane plantation. Then the time came to give people [time-
expired laborers] parcels of land [Crown lands in lieu of return passage fare or
a lump sum] . . . So that's how he ended up down there [in Trinidad]." Whereas
in Vishnu's version the protagonist is a child, the majority of the narratives
feature an adult—amenable, diligent, and gullible—who is led down an unknown path with false promises and left to fend precariously in unfamiliar
and disfranchising, hierarchical societies such as those of the Caribbean.

Both Indo-Trinidadian Hindus and Muslims rely on rituals as a key diagnostic emblem. They refer to rituals as "a prayers" or as a "function" (which
are interchangeable). The most common rituals among Hindus are the *puja*,
the *yagya,* and the *sat sangh.* Pujas and yagyas are devotional forms of worship
focused on one or more deities; in a sat sangh the focus is on the epic Rama-
yana. Among Indo-Trinidadian Muslims the most common "functions" are
the *maulood sherif* (Quranic reading), the *haqika* (pledging oneself to Allah),
and calendrical commemorations such as *Eid ul-Fitr* (feast breaking fast of
Ramadan) and *Milad ul-Nabi* (the birthday of the Prophet Mohammed).

In considering the recuperation of betrayal through exegesis (or access to
and creation of knowledge), I join the multilayered approach to ritual school
of thought specifically in distinguishing two important elements of Indo-
Trinidadian Hindu and Muslim ritual practice: the rites themselves, including
actions/movements, objects, sacred recitations (which as I noted at the outset
I do not address in this chapter), and the sermons, *kuttha* among Hindus and

kutbah among Muslims—or, as they are locally referred to, "lectures"—which are in essence tutorials that accompany the vast majority of ritual "functions" or "a prayers." Pandits and imams not only make rituals dynamic in the ways lectures register contemporary issues, but in the ways their debates about the diagnostic emblems of identity politics keep even the rites from being simply repetitive and conventional—even as practitioners strive to maintain their form as such. As I observed earlier, repetition, stability, and conventionality of rites not only must be distinguished from other elements of a given ritual, they also need to be understood as ideological projects of practitioners who are invested in demonstrating the timelessness of those rites, desires that always occur in conjunction with larger political, social, and cultural contexts.

By underscoring the distinction of these two prime elements of Hindu and Muslim rituals among Indo-Trinidadians (and the Indo-Caribbean in general), I am arguing against the idea, one that still remains influential in scholarly and popular discussion, that rituals are not geared toward intellectual pursuits, that they convey their messages through dramatic performance rather than through intellectual presentation. I would like to suggest instead that, at least in historically shifting and precarious environments of Indo-Caribbean diasporic communities, rituals are performances very much about intellectual pursuits and mental faculties, specifically the creation and apprehension of knowledge—as information and its interpretation. In other words, it is memories of movement, the conditions of movement, and the contexts of the changing present that shape the form and substance of ritual practice among Hindu and Muslim Indo-Trinidadians. Among these communities, religious rituals engage Indo-Trinidadian subordination by constituting the force by which being fooled / being foolish is countermanded. Rituals serve *simultaneously* (1) as tethers to heritage (which conforms to still-conventional scholarly and popular interpretations of ritual), though these tethers are constantly debated, and (2) as agentive exercises that prepare people for an improved future—specifically in terms of tutorials: self-edification lessons that both challenge and rectify social subordination through the attainment of certain forms of (religious) knowledge.

When Indo-Trinidadian Hindus speak about a heritage of "tradition," it is in a variety of contexts and often with a number of different referents. Two dimensions in particular are salient. One is the Great Tradition of Sanatan Dharm, which, even if at one level is understood to be located in India, transcends time and place as religious patrimony. The other dimension is an ancient cultural lifeway and worldview perceived as deeply rooted in place and time and thus able to provide the means to heal the ruptures of diaspora. The Great Tradition falls under the aegis of "lectures"; cultural roots are associated with older head, hence grassroots, pandits, both valorizing them and raising the issue of their being anachronisms in the current modern, middle-class moment of formally trained, younger generation pandits. Of course, participants in rituals as well as other community members weigh in on these evaluations in everyday conversations.

The pandit, older head or younger generation, has a double mission. This mission involves him being both a conduit of devotions to the deities and blessings to the devotees and a source of wisdom and tutelage both to his *chelas* (godchildren) and community of devotees. As one older head, Deo, told me about a prayers, "the people are mostly interested in the *text* being read and the pandit can provide it for the people." Yet in a conversation I had in my field site in Trinidad with Selwyn, a teenage boy, about the yagya his house-hold had recently sponsored, he remarked that older head pandits often lack sufficient breadth of scriptural knowledge—"what we can comprehend *these* days." Among the most important capabilities among people "*these* days" is the ability to distinguish between the literal interpretations of text and meta-phor and allegory. A younger-generation pandit offered me an example:

> The Gita is not a scripture, like the Ramayana. It is a philosophy, it goes to a higher level. Philosophy is not religion. Religion tells you how you should live in your religion. The Gita tells you there is a God . . . And that God could be anything . . . People don't understand that. For we have come from a grass-roots background. So when you sit down and you read the Gita, that God has a thousand arms and a thousand eyes . . . they [devotees] say you crazy! But now you interpret it. It mean that God can see everything, it doesn't literally mean something.

Here, then, where "a prayers" constitutes a pedagogical arena, learning what the correct rites are, their sequence, and their meaning, as well as the philosophical messages of the sacred texts (authorized by the pandit) increases cultural knowledge, where being informed about the subcontinental mother-land shores up the boundaries delineating religious and "racial" groups—that is, making oneself and one's group, in a sense, palpable, "real" in political terms. Another informant, Frank, put this very thoughtfully one evening when we were talking about the importance of Hindu rituals: "you must know where you coming from," he said. "To know how the religions were formed and how the people were living in India while English people were taking over. All we really know since we know ourselves here [in Trinidad] is how the English carrying on." For Frank, and many others, ritual participation is both the continuity of history and the awareness of historical change. And it is the connection between ritual and scripture that is at the heart of this relationship, and which forms of knowledge and expertise should have precedence, one based on "traditional ways," or one based on synchronicity with "modern" progress.

In contrast to Indo-Trinidadian Hindus' call for philosophical as opposed to literal interpretations, Indo-Trinidadian Muslims focus their attention on "pure" practices shorn of "cultural innovations." What constitutes purity and authenticity, however, are matters of serious scrutiny and are expressed in ritual. Embodied in the personas and practices of imams and other religious leadership, "functions" / "a prayers" are arenas of discourse and debates about correct religious knowledge, the definition and place of authentic cultural traditions in religious practice, and the implications these have for a Muslim identity that contends with an ambivalent relationship to ancestral India and ambiguous ties to Hindu kin and neighbors. As among Indo-Trinidadian Hindus, the effort to *know* sufficiently as well as correctly is a means to an end, rather than a final objective. That is, these efforts are always in dialogue with attempts to counteract the betrayal that renders them vulnerable, in sites still perceived as uncertain and under social conditions that still define them, in some important ways, notably in terms of local political culture, in terms of their foreign otherness as diasporic communities.

Let me briefly illustrate with the example of maulood sherifs. While they have always been integral to Indo-Trinidadian Muslim identity construction, one of my informants, Akeela, explained to me that today maulood sherifs are even more common because "people are hearing more about it through lectures." "People get smarter now," her sister added. In the effort to encourage jamaat (congregation) members and wider community residents to consistently attend and sponsor functions, hosts as well as imams (and a small but growing number of *maulanas,* or Islamic scholars) often remind participants why "a prayers" are imperative. At one annual household maulood sherif I attended, the masjid president gave the opening address, which included his statement that, "we have all attended today in order to honor a dear neighbor's invitation, to honor Allah, and to gain knowledge." At another I attended some time later, an honored guest invited to give an address asked rhetorically, "what is the purpose of this function today? To socialize in Islamic society and atmosphere . . . [and] to get education." Edification includes gaining greater familiarity with laws or scripture, Arabic script, correct enactment and understanding of rites, or related text-based knowledge.

Because Islam presupposes, at least ideally, a coherence that renders actual or possible variations in practice a matter of discussion on the part of clerics, lay practitioners, and scholars, "correct models" are subject to debates about interpreting the significance and modes of practices that belong to Islamic tradition (see, for example, Asad 1986, 1993). Embedded in these debates, and in the interpretations themselves, are relations of power (among groups and individuals) that shape the shifting hierarchies of value that designate, over varying periods of time, particular interpretations as being correct and as what must prevail. Counseling against blindly following religious traditions, my neighbor Dolly explained: "Just because you see your parents doing it [Muslim rites], maybe you don't know *why* or *what* it is . . . You can't just stay home again [any more]. You have to go out and look for it [knowledge about correct practice]. Who going to teach you [at] home?" Her older head neighbor Leila agreed: "even at my age we can still learn, as people will laugh at us in the masjid [mosque] and say, 'she is so old and hasn't learned the right thing?'" At still another maulood sherif I attended, the guest maulana urged in his address that, "unless we are educated and taught how to educate others, we are lost in a dark world. And we must save ourselves from corrupted doctrines coming into our religion and unnecessary arguments among ourselves. As the Prophet says, 'knowledge isn't compulsory, but to *seek* knowledge is compulsory.'" This guardianship of the correct, so to speak, is not to establish purity for purity's sake (simply for its iconic value) but to withstand inappropriate acts and beliefs whose untutored or improperly tutored "folk" versions maintained in diaspora from the subcontinent, or influences from Hinduism, can derail true Muslim practice. These folk Islamic or "Hinduized" practices are discredited as "innovations," characterized as "cultural" and "traditional," and traced according to their accretion through social and cultural influences rather than through demonstration by or dictum of the Prophet Mohammed.

Among the most common practices that foment ideological divisions among Indo-Trinidadian Muslims occur in ritual: saying prayers over food, celebrating the Prophet's birthday and *meeraj* (ascension to Heaven), singing *qaseedas* during rituals, and standing for the *tazeem* (praise sung for the

Prophet Mohammed). An Indo-Trinidadian Muslim man said to me, "way back in the fifties and sixties I just thought I was a Muslim, because I was *born* in a Muslim family . . . The practices in my environment, though, were different from what I later read . . . We had in the past, and we still have, a lot of practices that we got from our foreparents in India. We are grateful to them for keeping up Islam, but people are not trying to *learn* more. They are just *listening* to what is said . . . They go to functions and sit, but don't *educate* themselves." At the heart of the distinction between the legitimacy of customary or traditional religious practice and tutored religious practice guided by religious authority is the high value placed on self-conscious, achieved knowledge—in essence, doing something correctly and understanding its significance.

At one maulood sherif I attended, a woman present praised the officiating imam: "you must talk proper, make the sermon *meaningful.*" The quest for meaning may be heightened for individuals as they comprehend religiously charged moments in the Islamic calendar. One informant explained that Ramadan is a time when she is "always learning something *new,* whether it is a *sura,* a lesson, or whatsoever. She "soaks up the lectures" given during this period's numerous functions and tries to take time out every day to read; her bed is always "covered with books the whole month." As community residents invoke the idea of "meaning" in their reflections on an individual's attitude in undertaking rituals and on the nature of religious practice, *meaning* becomes both reified and a master symbol. In local usage, *meaning* encompasses distinct referents; in doing so it articulates these referents into what is familiar religious discourse. At another maulood sherif where I was present, the imam included in his remarks, "[it] is only when we get together like this [that] we can get the message. Our weakness is [lack of] knowledge, knowledge of Islam, and how to run our lives. Today a person talks [in order] to use you with *iklas,* in Arabic, ulterior motives. Trying to trick you. And it is only by practice [that] you can perfect your *salaat* [worship]." In the imam's comment, "meaning" addresses the theme of being fooled; here, worldly knowledge (not succumbing to trickery) and religious knowledge (perfecting salaat) enhance each other. Through group edification—"get together like this"—such as that which occurs during ritual functions, "meaning" ameliorates gaps, slippages that are threatening in both sacred and secular terms.

It is gaps like these that imams must fill as they work on the precision of their craft. The performances of older head imams and their "traditional" ways as they serve their jamaats are particularly susceptible to charges of engaging in practices that seem too much like meaningless, going through the motions (as many see it) ritual, and thus too Hindu-influenced, too India-derived, and therefore too innovative with mixed cultural, as opposed to purely religious, traditions. Imam Rahman, an older head "reformist" imam, as he identified himself, explained that:

> *traditional* practices are different from the handed-down practices of the Prophet . . . *Traditional* means practices of old . . . But the reforms were found through *research,* like [in] the Hadith . . . We don't make *naj* [prayers] over *sirni* [ritual sweets]. We question putting food for the dead, the dead cannot eat . . . and this was never done in the days of the Prophet. This was brought in as a innovation from India . . . a Hindu relic.

In the sense of being both a tie to ancestral heritage and a restraint on contemporary transformation (and therefore an authenticating medium), rituals are culturally stabilizing performances, reminding practitioners of their identity through connection with the past. They are, at the same time, however, culturally transforming tutorials, emphasizing identity through connections with the present. As sites where diacritic emblems are reproduced, rituals clarify the ambiguities of both heterodoxy (the local array of religious possibilities) and syncretism (when those possibilities converge into other, new, and debated, forms). They do this by repetition of certain rites, thereby establishing or fortifying boundaries between what is appropriate and what is incorrect. But rituals involve greater agency than mere reiteration, in their emphasis on the exegesis, and leadership, of the pandit and imam. In Hindu and Muslim rituals, therefore, there is a good deal of emphasis on correct performance. Participants make an effort to eschew spontaneity and innovation. As Peter van der Veer (1996: 144) observes, in Hindu ritual (and I would add in Muslim ritual), "despite all the evidence of change and consistency, the performers try their hardest to exclude creative innovation." Referred to as "lectures" by Indo-Trinidadian practitioners, the sermons that most Hindu and Muslim rituals highlight, however, are discursive spaces where formal continuity and creative innovation meet. While the issue of correct performance is always present, appreciation of the meaning and significance of performance is taught by the messenger (pandit or imam as learned authority) rather than simply through the medium (the rites). Different generations of leadership claim authority not simply through carrying out the rites, but through their ability to guide practitioners intellectually. Their claims reflect competing interpretations of Indo-Trinidadian cultural history and religious identity.

By teaching about religion, rituals augment educational opportunities more readily available to the socially privileged, but they also instruct in the way "religion" ought to be constituted, and why. Through the guidance of religious leadership and their lectures, a number of potential inadequacies can be alleviated: alienation from one's culture, underdeveloped piety, subordinate class position, or general naivete—a lack of sophistication and worldliness, and hence inability to assume the mantle of Western modernity. The multilayered dimensions within a given ritual, then, are always in dialectical tension.

In order to be effective, "a prayers" or "functions" must be seen as pure, in the sense of credibly sacred (indubitably "religion") and credibly authentic (indubitably "correct"). Yet at the same time, even if practitioners work to reinforce repetitiveness and conventionality, rituals still respond to the rhythm of political ideology and social striving. The performance of rituals must distinguish and announce distinctly Hindu and Muslim identities within a daily reality where rituals are "the busy intersections" where many distinct social processes converge (Rosaldo 1989). For Indo-Trinidadian Hindus and Muslims, rituals are intended to be revelatory and transformative as much as they are meant to reiterate and confirm. Thus they are sites of dynamism, not simply stasis, and can pedagogically rescue participants from the mental and material deprivations of diaspora's betrayal.

Conclusion

This chapter has told two distinguishable but articulated stories, one of diaspora and one of religious ritual. Its aim has been to argue five points. One is that as a way of understanding community identity and culture, "diaspora" must be understood as a particular kind of historical experience, one that has far-reaching implications for cultural forms and social relationships, and that necessarily involves a particular consciousness about the experience of migration on the part of those who constitute these communities, such as Indo-Trinidadians—one that both marks the very act of uprooting as shaping their sense of self and that memorializes displacement in everyday discourse and practice. Secondly, like all forms of consciousness, diasporic consciousness exists as a part of, and thus is responsive to, the changing historical and cultural contexts of Indo-Trinidadian life. My third point is that, like all discourses and practices, a community's religious rituals occur within these same contexts, making them also subject to the vicissitudes of history and culture, so that rather than ritual lying outside of these forces and pressures and thereby allegedly remaining stable, timeless, and the epitome of fixed "tradition," Indo-Trinidadian Hindu and Muslim rituals are context contingent, and their putative constancy is actually a matter of ideological projects emerging from the current moment. Fourth, these ideological projects are informed by modes of marking (defining and interpreting) Indo-Trinidadian identity which are a part of diasporic consciousness and are manifest in rituals as participants work to assert themselves politically and culturally by means of self-edification through competing forms of authorized knowledge. My final point is that the interplay of diasporic consciousness and ritual occurs at the nexus where identity, ideology, and cultural practice meet, intertwining diasporic consciousness and religious ritual together.

What does their connection tell us? Diaspora represents among Indo-Caribbeans monumental rupture in their self-determination. If we probe the discursive dimensions of diaspora—how it is envisioned and talked about among members of diasporic communities—rather than solely relying on it as an externally imposed (and, often, one-size-fits-all) analytical category, we get a clear idea of the agency that diaspora entails. By understanding diaspora as a dynamic phenomenon we are better able to understand the dynamism of cultural practices like religious ritual among diasporic communities. A key cultural practice in most communities and societies, religious ritual has been conventionally approached by both scholars and practitioners alike as static rather than dynamic and, linked to this idea of stasis, best characterized as dramatic performances rather than involving shifting consciousness and intellectual reflection. In the historically uneasy (in both senses: difficult and insecure) Caribbean environments with which Indian indentured immigrants and their diasporic progeny had to contend and make the best of, rituals are precisely about dynamism: agency and resistance through engagement with colonial and postindependence structures of social inequality. This engagement takes the form of *exegesis,* the creation and grasp of knowledge, conveyed through rituals. Although debated in terms of their respective degree of authority, Indo-Trinidadian Hindu and Muslim exegeses consistently evoke the theme of *being fooled,* challenging the forms of subordination that accompany, or are caused by, betrayal and marginalization. Among Indo-Trinidadian Hindus and Muslims, rituals are, in part, intellectual exercises that promote ideologies about the value of unchanging heritage that rituals are meant to demonstrate. At the same time, rituals are also intellectual exercises that acknowledge and actively engage the past, present, and future conditions of everyday life and well-being in this diasporic community.

Acknowledgments

I would like to thank Rhacel Parreñas and Lok Siu for inviting me to contribute to this volume and for their helpful editorial comments. This chapter is based on material taken from my book, *Callaloo Nation: Metaphors of Race and Religious Identity among South Asians in Trinidad* (Khan 2004). All names of individuals appearing herein are pseudonyms. A version of this chapter appears in *Cultural Dynamics* (in press, 2007).

References

Asad, Talal. 1986. "The Idea for an Anthropology of Islam." March. Occasional Paper Series. Center for Contemporary Arab Studies, Georgetown University, Washington, DC.

———. 1993. *Genealogies of Religion*. Baltimore: Johns Hopkins University Press.

Central Statistical Office, Republic of Trinidad and Tobago. 1990. *Demographic Report*.

Khan, Aisha. 2004. *Callaloo Nation: Metaphors of Race and Religious Identity among South Asians in Trinidad*. Durham: Duke University Press.

Rosaldo, Renato. 1989. *Culture and Truth*. Boston: Beacon. Singh, Kelvin. 1996. "Conflict and Collaboration: Tradition and Modernizing Indo-Trinidadian Elites (1917–1956)." *New West Indian Guide* 70(3–4): 229–53.

van der Veer, Peter. 1996. "Authenticity and Authority in Surinamese Hindu Ritual." In David Dabydeen and Brinsley Samaroo, eds., *Across the Dark Waters*. Pp. 131–46. London: Macmillan.

6 "Our Flavour Is Greater"

Sharmila Sen

What seest thou else
In the dark backward and abysm of time?

The Tempest, I.2.49–50

BETWEEN 1835 AND 1917, thousands of Indian indentured laborers crossed the kala pani (black waters) to fill the labor vacuum left by emancipated slaves in the Caribbean sugar estates. Today, almost half the population of Trinidad and Guyana are of Indian descent, forming an integral part of the global girmitiya (Indian labor diaspora) community. Using the form of the critical travelogue, this essay asks how the Indian diaspora remembers, forgets, and reconstructs tastes, cultures, identities, and affiliations in the twenty-first century. Shakespeare's final solo dramatic piece, *The Tempest,* is an important part of Caribbean cultural discourse. It is a play that has been rewritten and adapted to multiple ends by Caribbean authors as diverse as Aimé Césaire from Martinique to George Lamming from Barbados to Roberto Fernandez Retamar from Cuba. Yet, in Caribbean texts, *The Tempest* has so far been only critiqued through an Afro-Creole lens. This essay breaks from that tradition and posits a new relationship between the Shakespearean play that has been so crucial to twentieth-century Caribbean discourse and the Indo-Caribbean experience. More specifically, this essay draws a connection between the exilic subject in both Shakespeare's play and V. S. Naipaul's classic account of diasporic return in *India: An Area of Darkness.* This is a response to V. S. Naipaul's early Indian travelogues, an imagined dialogue between Shakespeare's Miranda and the Milanese, a record of shifting political and cultural attitudes of East Indians in the southern Caribbean, and as importantly, an exploration of the pleasures and disappointments that await the eater poised on the faultlines of multiple, overlapping diasporas of the Indian subcontinent.

Darwanji's Dal Puris

Our British West Indian Airways flight had barely landed in Port of Spain's newly renovated Piarco airport when I started looking for doubles. How can the Indian visitor in Trinidad look for anything else? Our secret sharers are everywhere. The faces, the names, the twenty-four carat gold jewelry all brought to mind the arrival of other Indians in another century. Sailing from Hooghly harbor in Calcutta, the Fath Al Razak (popularly known as the Fatel Rozack) arrived at Nelson Island on May 30, 1845 with 225 Indians on board. Account books kept by the British colonial administrators note that most of these indentured laborers began their journeys from villages deep in the Indo-Gangetic plains of northern India. In Port of Spain, the National Archives of Trinidad and Tobago are situated a few blocks away from the Savannah. The room where scholars can read manuscripts is a long narrow cell separated from the stacks of yellowing ledgers and documents by an iron grill. Elegant cursive writing in unevenly fading ink preserve for posterity the name, age, gender, caste, and village of each of the coolies who were brought to fill the post-Emancipation labor shortage in Caribbean sugar plantations. One place name caught my eye on the very first day I had walked into the National Archives. Basti. My great-grandfather was a schoolteacher in Basti. My grandmother had lived there until she married my grandfather in 1943. Basti, for me, is a place of my past, my grandmother's childhood home. It seems hermetically sealed from anything in my present life. I cannot imagine my grandmother or anyone in her family making a voyage from that small town in Uttar Pradesh to an unknown New World island, a tiny piece of the South American continent adrift in the Caribbean Sea. Yet, here was evidence that my grandmother's hometown was already linked to this Caribbean island.

Under what circumstances did the girl from Basti cross the kala pani and head for faraway Trinidad? What did fate have in store for her in the New World? Did her descendants settle somewhere in the Caroni plains? Perhaps, I fantasized for a minute, they live in Chaguanas, a vast family like the Tulsis in *A House for Mr. Biswas*. Staring at the page of that colonial logbook, I was faced not with the enigma of arrival, but with the enigma of departure. How does one ever leave a place fully? Did the girl from Basti have any family left in Basti? And if she did, what if their paths crossed with members of my own family even as I wrote this? As importantly, I wondered if it is ever possible for the migrant to arrive with a sense of uncompromised newness?

Trinidad refuses newness to the twenty-first-century Indian arrivant. The land holds deceptive similarities to the country left behind. Glimpses of half-remembered faces, fragments of partially comprehensible Bhojpuri, and whiffs of familiar spices lull us into a false sense of familiarity. The New World and the Old World have mutually transformed each other's ecologies enough to present an uncanny sense of continuity. And, of course, there are doubles everywhere in the southern Caribbean. A type of snack consisting of two pieces of fried bread with a spicy chickpea filling, "doubles" is the name of the working-class, "coolie" food, whose popularity is not diminished by the arrival of Kentucky Fried Chicken and McDonald's in the Caribbean. According to an article that ran in the *Express* on July 4, 2001, the average cost of a doubles is between $1.00 and $1.50. The cost of raw materials—flour, channa, spices, mango, pepper, shadon beni, chives, and salt—was estimated to be around 85 cents. Dee Balo's, a four-star doubles joint in Port of Spain, was about to become a franchise. As the newspaper article reported, there was good money to be made in doubles in Trinidad.

We drove to a roti shop in St. Augustine on our second day in Trinidad. Roberto, our driver, had chosen this place himself as the perfect introduction to everyday delicacies such as channa, curry goat, sada roti, buss-up-shot, dhallpourris, and doubles. All to be washed down with bottles of the ubiquitous Carib beer. Already a sense of disorientation was overtaking me. Everything was made slightly foreign—the pronunciation of words, the conventions of transliterating Indian words into the Roman alphabet. The extra *n* in a channa was only to be repeated in the extra *r* in the Bharrat of the Guyanese president Bharrat Jagdeo. Could these be the precursors of other excesses of East Indian culture in the West Indies?

The dhallpourri that Roberto promised—redolent, in my eyes, with its excessive *h, l, o,* and *r*—was a magical dish to me, doubly evocative of my Calcutta childhood and my early acquaintance with Indo-Caribbean writing. Some years earlier, I had concluded an essay on Indo-Caribbean literature with what seemed then to be a particularly clever allusion to Sam Selvon's discovery of a roti shop in London. Selvon once wrote, "In all my years in England, I never came across the kind of curry we ate in Trinidad, and I searched all over London for a dhall pourri, and never saw one until one enterprising Trinidadian started up a little cookshop."[1] In my essay on new Indo-Caribbean writing I went on to offer up the unsuspecting dhallpourri seller as a symbolic model for the kind of work doubly displaced Indo-Caribbean authors in metropolitan centers have to do in the twenty-first century. For those of us trained in American graduate programs in the past decade, it is easy to go on about diasporic cultures and metropolitan centers—all buzzwords of late-twentieth-century academia. Yet, like many literary critics, the gap between the words flickering on my computer screen and the ideas embedded deep in my brain, and even in my taste buds, is wide. Dhallpourris, or dal puris, I want to believe do not change across the distance of oceans, under the rigors of indentureship, through the inventiveness of courageous pioneers. And the best dal puris, I want to tell myself, are always made by Darwanji, our doorman at 18/10 Dover Lane in Calcutta.

Darwanji's real name was Hriday Singh. For as far back as I can remember, he rose at 4 A.M. every morning to wash our neighbors' cars in order to earn some extra money. He sent a money order to his village in eastern Uttar Pradesh every month. Once a year, Darwanji traveled to his village in order to visit his family. And in the time-honored Indian tradition of preparing a special meal for a long train journey, he made dal puris to take with him on the train. If we were inordinately lucky, he would share some of his dal puris with us once a year. Darwanji cooked the chana dal filling with great care in his makeshift kitchen over a kerosene stove. In an aluminium bowl marked with scratches and dents from years of use, he kneaded the whole wheat dough with the vigor of a man about to commence a long-awaited journey home. The final products were dark golden brown discs of fried dough filled with a spicy lentil mixture. Scented with cumin and asafetida, Darwanji's dal puris held the promise of a long journey, the romance of the railways, and the pleasure of returning home. And, years later, even as I was celebrating Selvon's discovery of Indo-Trinidadian food in London, I imagined the Trinidadian immigrant reversing the flow of time and history and biting into one of Darwanji's dal puris.

Years before I was born, Darwanji had left his village, Unnao, to find work in Calcutta. Unnao is located in the heart of the region from which nineteenth-century recruiters lured villagers to sign up for five-year indentureship periods in places like Trinidad and Guyana. Darwanji's village, I imagine, is not unlike Naipaul's own village of the Dubes, that repository of all that is anticlimactic and disappointing for the descendant of coolies looking for his roots. In the small university town of St. Augustine, under the sign of Turban brand curry powder, another disappointment lay in store for me. Roberto's choice for lunch was a modest roti shop filled with young university students and local residents. In the greasy, smoke-filled canteen buzzing with animated chatter, the sada rotis and buss-up-shots were disappearing at a furious rate. We ordered more than we should have. I ate less than I hoped to eat. From our table, past the whirring pedestal fans, I could see the canary yellow billboard with a crude drawing of a head, presumably Indian because of the eponymous red turban. Sprawled across the bottom of the billboard in a much less elegant cursive than the British administrator's faded writing was a proclamation that could also stand in for the new East Indian political and cultural resurgence to be witnessed in the southern Caribbean: "Our Flavour is Greater."

But the flavor of the St. Augustine dhallpourri was certainly not greater than Darwanji's railway specials. The lentils were vaguely spiced, the dough soggy. Instead of perfect little golden brown discs crisped at the edges, the Trinidadian dhallpourri was large, floppy, and pale in color. Not far from Roberto's roti shop, in the air conditioned comfort of the West Indian Special Collections of the University of West Indies, I decided to forego the rare manuscripts and colonial accounts of journeys to the New World and instead chose to settle down with a paperback account of a journey to the Old World, Naipaul's *An Area of Darkness*.

> To me as a child the India that had produced so many of the persons and things around me was featureless, and I thought of the time when the transference was made as a period of darkness, darkness that also extended to the land, as darkness surrounds a hut at evening, though for a little way around the hut there is still light. The light was the area of my experience, in time and place. And even now, though time has widened, though space has contracted and I have travelled lucidly over that area which was to me the area of darkness, something of the darkness remains, in those attitudes, those ways of thinking and seeing, which are no longer mine.[2]

Naipaul begins his first Indian travelogue with a Shakespearean formula. His darkness, the reader quickly realizes, is decidedly not Conradian. Rather, it is the darkness evoked by the exiled Prospero when he askes his daughter, "What seest thou else in the dark backward and abysm of time?" The Naipaul of *An Area of Darkness* is, of course, both Prospero and Miranda. He is both teacher and student, the one who has forgotten and the one who remembers, the one whose attention to the past wavers and the one who disciplines such wavering attention. And India is that area of darkness, the dark backward. India, in short, is the past. Simultaneously, India exists in the future. It exists in unrecognizable modernity, a sweeping betrayal of the more authentic diaspora by the debased homeland. In an uncanny moment in a taxi in

Georgetown a few weeks later, I was to hear a 1950s Hindi filmsong that would reshape my understanding of the relationship between India and its multiple overlapping diasporas.

> Waqt ne kiya
> Kya haseen sitam
> Tum rahe na tum
> Hum rahe na hum

It is hard to translate the pathos of Geeta Dutt's voice. But, the song goes something like this: "Time has committed such exquisite cruelty. You did not remain yourself. I did not remain myself." Looking for doubles, searching for the Caribbean secret sharer, was to suddenly take on the shades of a tragic Guru Dutt film. We were long lost lovers, familiar enough with each other to feel nostalgic for the mutual loss one represented to the other.

If according to Naipaul's scheme of things there remained in the dhall-pourri a touch of the ancestor from darkness, then, for me, Darwanji's dal puris came to represent the index by which to measure diasporic difference. Yet, not being fooled into looking for doubles, grasping the rupture in history, is the burden of the South Asian scholar studying Indo-Caribbean culture. Somewhere along the way, my distaste of Trinidadian doubles had turned into a fascination for the regularization of diasporic amnesia—a form of forgetting that works in all directions, past/future, home/elsewhere. It is a type of amnesia that deletes and creates memories, it binds and splits Unnao from Chaguanas, Basti from San Fernando, dal puris from dhallpourris.

To Be Larger than Life on Mount St. Benedict

A young V. S. Naipaul found English India on Kashmiri houseboats. "To be English in India," he wrote, "was to be slightly larger than life."[3] The ghostly larger-than-life English residents of those Kashmiri houseboats would be equally at home in the guesthouse on Mount St. Benedict in northern Trinidad. The cane chairs, the shady verandahs, the heavy wooden furniture, the high teas, the evening rum punch, the puddings after dinner, and the endless stream of British birdwatchers kept the guesthouse in a constant state of suspension in time and place: somewhere, sometime in the British Empire there was a guesthouse where one walked the hummingbird trail after drinking Darjeeling tea with coconut bread and guava jelly. If the anthropologist Sidney Mintz were to be sitting on the guesthouse verandah with me, he would not need to look far beyond his evening cup of Darjeeling tea to see the connection between the labor of Indian peasants in tea gardens and the labor of slaves and coolies on Caribbean sugar estates.[4] From our vantage point on Mount St. Benedict, we could see the vast green Caroni cane fields stretching to the horizon. At night, when darkness enveloped the hilltop, glittering lights stretched across the plain, and snatches of Hindi filmsongs drifted up from the Caroni villages to the very British guesthouse where I was living.

From the guesthouse suspended in time and place, we could see the land where the Indian indentured laborers and their descendants made their own time and place. The Indian villages in the Caroni plains find their doubles in similar villages in eastern Uttar Pradesh and Bihar in modern India. The new arrivants from the other end of the Empire had brought with them the architecture, clothes, flora, languages, and religions of the Indo-Gangetic plain. The Ganga was transposed upon the Trinidadian landscape and the Caroni invested with the properties of India's sacred river. What few people remember is that the crop that was at the root of this large-scale movement of peoples was itself a migrant. The earliest evidence of the use of cane sugar is found in India. The Sanskrit word for raw sugar, *khanda,* is the etymological root of both the Arabic and Persian words for sugar, as well as for the English *candy.*[5] Refined sugar, first introduced to Europe by traders from the Middle East and India, was later produced in the New World colonies and gained such immense following during the modern period that cakes, meats, and sauces became less spiced and more heavily sweetened in British cooking. By the mid-seventeenth century, the colonies in the West Indies, particularly Caribbean islands such as Barbados, Antigua, Jamaica, Trinidad, and Tobago, were producing large quantities of affordable sugar that slowly displaced the spices of the East Indies from the Empire's table.[6] Centuries after sugarcane came to the Caribbean, following the legal abolishment of slavery in the Empire in 1834–38, the British looked east again in order to find suitable agriculturists to tend to the valuable crop. It was no mere coincidence, then, that from 1835 to 1917 indentured laborers were largely recruited from the Upper Provinces and the Bengal Presidency—these were people who knew how to grow and cut cane.

This is history shrouded in darkness. For the young Naipaul, it is not India but the entire period of migration that is surrounded in darkness. Clearly, Sir Vidia never had the opportunity of attending lectures by the professors sent to the University of West Indies (UWI) by the Indian government. As part of a little-known plan to educate Trinidadian university students about South

Asia, the Indian government began sending scholars to UWI following a conversation between Jawaharlal Nehru and Eric Williams in the mid-1960s. These visiting professors, usually drawn from the social sciences, come to the St. Augustine campus for two-year periods.[7] Professor Brinsley Samaroo, a renowned historian of the Indian diaspora in the Caribbean, introduced me to Professor Gita Bajpai on my first day at UWI. Gita was a history professor from Baroda, Gujarat, sent by the Indian government for one of these two-year stints. It was as if the Milanese had sent a delegate to instruct Miranda about the land of her ancestors.

Exuding ferocious energy and resplendent in her oversized bindi, it was easy to see why Gita had so many fans among her diasporic students. She invited me to dinner within minutes of our introduction—our dislike of Trinidadian Indian food a guilty secret binding us in a criminal pact. That evening, I ate chicken curry and rice huddled over Gita's coffee table in the living room of her university quarters. The Indian diaspora had once again divided and realigned itself as a forty-something woman from Uttar Pradesh living in Gujarat and a twenty-something woman from Bengal living in the United States found themselves split from the Indian diaspora in the Caribbean over something as seemingly trivial as the proportion of cumin and coriander in a chicken curry.

With the notable exception of Naipaul's *A House for Mr. Biswas,* every Indo-Caribbean novel seems to celebrate the culinary exceptionalism of the East Indian home. David Dabydeen's Rohini and Vidia carry spices and cooking utensils from India to Plantation Albion. In the voyage from India to British Guiana—a second Middle Passage some would say—the decks of the British ships are memorably colored with "massala, turmeric, and dhall" as the coolies abandon their stomachs to the sea.[8] Dabydeen's friend Moses Nagamootoo continues the tradition of arming his East Indian immigrants with "a South Indian *massala* brick, a *bellna* and *chowkie*" as they make the transition from Plantation Albion to the village of Whim.[9] In the fictional island of Latanacamara, Shani Mootoo reserves for Mala Ramchandin's kitchen the most horrific scenes of incestuous rape and the most evocative scenes of East Indian cooking:

> Clutching a handful of hair at the back of her head, he shoved the bowl into her face again, twisting it back and forth. Her nose began to bleed. She concentrated on the sensation of enamel against her face as though taking notes on an experiment. With every clockwise twist he slammed his pelvis into

her, banging her into the counter of the sink. She felt no pain. She tapped her tongue against the roof of her mouth checking the stew for seasoning . . . She slipped her tongue out of her mouth and licked the stew on her face. The taste of garlic and anise erased his smell. The stew was indeed well-seasoned, perhaps the best she had ever cooked.[10]

It is no coincidence that Mala had been cooking a creole stew in her East Indian kitchen when her alcoholic father violently rapes her. Having lost his wife to her European lesbian lover, Mala's father attempts to reinforce the unspoken rules of racial contact in the kitchen. In Indo-Caribbean novels, the kitchen is the site of cultural and racial difference. It is here that the East Indian female subject asserts her difference from both the European colonizer and the Afro-Creole population. The way she might grind the masala, or use the belna to roll out the roti, or use the karhai to cook pumpkin all verge on the brink of becoming literary clichés employed to preserve India in the Caribbean. Violence in the East Indian kitchen must, then, also be read as the violence that erupts because of *and* in order to preserve rigid racial boundaries—the boundary between Indian curry and creole callaloo. Indeed, the term "creole" despite all its association with "mixing" is itself a border patrol in the Caribbean. In Trinidad, for instance, "creole" is clearly black, not Indian. Let us recall that the word *creole,* from the Spanish *criollo* signifies a New World provenance. In the eighteenth and nineteenth centuries, the slave born in the Caribbean plantation was labeled "creole" in order to distinguish her from the African-born slave. By excluding themselves from the creole, East Indians are forever nonnative, always arriving. And the kitchen is the deliciously dangerous site of that constant arrival.

In Caribbean anglophone writing, much as in Caribbean tourism catalogs, callaloo and creole stew are the commonplace exotica dished up for the delectation of the metropolitan West. Mala, Aplamma, and Rohini's curry messes up this easy arrangement. The East Indian curry is the inauthentic authentic; it is the foreign native. The birdwatchers in the guesthouse hardly noticed the Caroni villages lying below Mount St. Benedict. To them the island, with its prehistoric geological links to the Andes, was fascinating for the multitude of flora and fauna it offered. They consulted books on ornithology, updated their lifetime lists of birds viewed, and smiled politely at the locals. If they made any note of the local culture at all, it was only to reconfirm what the tourist guides promised all along—callaloo, calypso, and carnival. The red turban floating above the proclamation "Our Flavour is Greater" was an anomaly best ignored. Turbans and curries were after all signs linked to the jewel in the crown, not to the callaloo nation.

Mattai's

Where could Rohini, Aplamma, and Mala go if they ran out of cumin, coriander, turmeric, cinnamon, cloves, and cardamom? How long could their store of spices brought from India last? And if the belna broke, or the kadhai cracked, where could one find a replacement? In nineteenth-century Trinidad, there was a brisk business in what was then known as "coolie stores." The short-lived Indian *Koh-I-Noor Gazette* (published from 1898 to 1900) carried numerous advertisements for Lallapee, Indian and Colonial Merchant, Importers of Provisions and Indian Goods of all Kinds, situated at No. 1 Lower Henry Street, Port of Spain. Lallapee, as it happened, was also the owner of the Indian *Koh-I-Noor Gazette*.

Housed in the same building where the British colonial records of the first Indian arrivals are kept, the few remaining copies of the first Indo-Trinidadian newspaper survive in a fragile condition. In the editorial column, Thik Bat, the mysterious Effendi Beg,[11] offered a variety of contradictory views—the glories of Lucknow, the superiority of India over Britain, the necessity of British colonialism, the foolhardiness of Indian nationalists. Alongside intellectual offerings, literary competitions (which rarely came to fruition), international news (usually two months old), and political propaganda, the *Koh-I-Noor Gazette* informed the Rohinis, Aplammas, and Malas where to buy spices, kitchen utensils, and groceries. Here is an advertisement from Thursday, November 19, 1898:

Coolie Stores.
Sale on Tuesday 15th. Nov. 1898.
At the
Commercial Sale Rooms.
No. 1 St. Vincent St.
Surplus Stores Ex "Ems" from Calcutta
3 tins Cumin seeds, 2 tins ferragrek (sic), 5 Brls. tamarind, 3 bags turmeric, 2 bags black pepper, 1 bag mustard seed, 1 bag coriander seed, 1 bag garlic, 11 bags gram, 2 bags gram dhol, 9 bags moosor dhol, 3 bags moong dhol, 32 choora, 22 cases soap, 14 cases ghee, 3 cases mustard oil, 3 tins c. oil and sundries as may appear.

In neighboring Guyana, the modern equivalent of Lallapee can be found on Water Street in Georgetown. Harry Mattai runs Mattai's, the largest Indian grocery store in Guyana. He inherited the business from his father who ran the store in the days of Forbes Burnham. Today, upon entering Mattai's on Water Street, the visitor is greeted with sacks of spices—cinnamon sticks two feet long, nutmeg still in its shell, whole coriander, cumin, dried ginger, and Harry's very own dry roasted garam masala mix. Many of the spices are from Grenada. The lentils and rice are imported from India. The packaged foods are flown in from various nodes of the Indian diaspora: Gits gulab jamun mixes from India, Patak pickles and preblended spice pastes from Britain, Deep dosa and idli mixes from the United States. Mattai's business seemed brisk. He had left his home in Toronto with his wife and daughters to run the family business in Guyana. He had business contacts in New York, London, and Toronto. During a conversation in his private mezzanine office overlooking the store, Harry confessed that he preferred to buy Indian products through wholesalers in the Indian immigrant communities of North America and Europe. Although Mattai's looked just like any common grocery store in India, Harry felt there was too much of a cultural gap between himself and "real" Indians to conduct business directly with the subcontinent. Yet, he was hardly a cultural purist who claimed for himself a more authentic Indianness than those who never left India. Indeed, Harry was clearly inspired by the tastes and recipes he encountered among the newer arrivals from the old country in places like Southall in London, Jackson Heights in New York, and Prince Street in Toronto. He wanted to update the Guyanese Indian palate. He wanted them to try the cosmopolitan tastes of modern India. But abandoning the regional U. P./Bihari rural cooking modified and standardized over time in the southern Caribbean was proving to be difficult. If Harry wanted his customers to be adventurous and buy ingredients for a Bengali fish steamed in mustard, a Hyderbadi biryani sprinkled with kewra, a sweet and tangy Gujarati dhokla, or a crisp rava dosa, he needed to teach them how to prepare such "exotic" delicacies. During our last meeting, Harry and his wife were planning on starting an Indian cooking show on Guyanese television, as well as running a regular Indian cooking column in the local newspaper.

To see the dusty piles of Gits dosa mixes on Mattai's shelves was to be forcibly reminded of the power of diasporic amnesia and its twin, the desire for diasporic return. While the election of Bharrat Jagdeo had sparked notorious race riots in Guyana, it had also led to a new upsurge of East Indian

cultural pride. At the turn of the twenty-first century, to be a proud Indian in
Guyana meant many things: a suave member of parliament, who constantly
reproached me for not referring to India as Bharat, informed me that he was
a member of the Rashtriya Swayamsevak Sangh (RSS), a Hindu fundamentalist organization responsible among other things for demolishing the Babri
Masjid in Ayodhya in 1992, for inciting some of the worst religious riots in
Bombay in 1992–93, and for masterminding the genocide of Muslims in
Gujarat in 2002; an elderly university professor lectured me on the superiority of Indian arranged marriages over "Western love marriages" all the while
taking no pains to hide his disdain of contemporary India from me; a vet-
eran politician described his daughter's Indian dance programs on television
with great pride; Harry Mattai said that it was much easier to run an Indian
grocery store under the current government than it was for his father under
the so-called black government of Forbes Burnham. Under Bharrat Jagdeo's
government, it was apparently much easier to sell what Effendi Beg would
have dubbed "coolie stores." Faced with such signs of Indian pride, I experienced a desire for retreat almost Naipaulian in its violence. Looking for one's
diasporic double—the brother left behind, or the sister who went away—was
turning out to be as tricky as looking for Darwanji's dal puris in a Trinidadian
roti shop.

Amid the bags of cumin and coriander, the RSS members, the Hindi film
buffs, the devotees of arranged marriages, and Indian dancers on television,
one might forget that anyone other than Indians lived in Guyana. I might
have left Guyana, still misguidedly searching for doubles, blind to the other
half of the Guyanese population if it was not for Moses Nagamootoo. David
Dabydeen had introduced me to Moses, a former minister, a writer, and a
lawyer. One evening, Moses took me for a memorable drive past the Dutch
sea wall in Georgetown. The sea wall itself was a witness to the heterogenous
present and past of Guyana. Kentucky Fried Chicken signs vied for space with
Sujata Curry Powder advertisements. Once an ideal place for a picturesque
walk along the coast, the wall was no longer deemed safe at night. After Moses
showed me the village of Buxton, one of the recent riot sites, we stopped for
a drink at a small hotel off the main road running along the sea wall. On a
warm, dark evening, not unlike a Kerala evening along the Malabar coast,
Moses and I exchanged stories over beers and fish fingers, the snack food of
British colonials everywhere. My glass of beer arrived coyly wrapped in a
paper napkin, while Moses's glass seemed to need no such purdah. As an Indo-
Guyanese from a Madrasi family, Moses understood only too well the ten-

dency of the East Indian community in the Caribbean to erase all internal differences in favor of the hegemonic Bhojpuri Hindu culture. We spoke about India's internal others, about riverine Kerala, about communism, and about his name. At the time, Moses was trying to revive his original Tamil name Veeraswamy. "Where did you get the name Moses?" I asked. "The black midwife gave me that name," he replied with a smile. Later, at dinner in his house, Moses's wife Sita happily recounted her experiences with her black schoolteachers. Here, at last, was a fuller account of growing up East Indian in Guyana. Past the Hindutva, the Patak's pickles, and the Bharatnatyam programs, I caught a brief glimpse of the hand of a black midwife, of the childhood lessons imparted by a black teacher.

In 1996, the official soft drink of World Cup cricket was Coca Cola. That year the Indian ads for Pepsi featured a black cricket player, presumably from the West Indian team, who takes a swig of the cola and says naughtily, "Pepsi! Nothing official about it." That ad was very popular in India and the tagline was even incorporated into a Hindi filmsong in which Salman Khan sings "India! Nothing official about it." Abetted by a multinational's attempt to corner a lucrative market, the black face was once again India's popular vision of Caribbean exotica. Yet, the indigenizing gesture of the Salman Khan song shows how easily the intended consumer can manipulate a message and appropriate it for his own use. Abandoning the official lines of affiliation suggested by the departed colonial masters and the neoimperial multinationals, Indians might have to search for different sorts of doubles in the Caribbean. Could our secret sharer be the Afro-Creole, the ex-slave who worked alongside the coolie? This need not lead us to accept without reservations the facile callaloo nation theory foisted upon us by the Trinidadian government. After all, there are very real differences between people who celebrate Emancipation Day and people who celebrate Arrival Day.[12] Yet, to grasp the real link between the Amerindian, the African, and the Indian in the Caribbean is to understand South Asia's inextricable links not only with its scattered populations but also with other cultures with which it shares a history of colonialism, exploitation, and survival.

Indian Restaurant

I did not find my Indian double in the Caribbean; but I did find a fellow Bengali. During a brief visit to Tobago, the sky-high prices charged by the touristy restaurants around Black Rock had obliged us to rent a car and drive around the tiny island in search of a more modest meal. We were heading toward

Crowne Point when we spotted a sign for Mumtaz, an Indian restaurant. Not surprisingly, some British tourists had found their way to Mumtaz before us. A bit of curry can make any place seem like home to the British. As we perused the menu, the usual offering of vindaloos, tikka masalas, and kormas, we could not resist asking our hostess if the restaurant was truly owned by an Indian from India. As it turned out, our hostess was a muslim Trinidadian Indian married to a Bangladeshi immigrant. No wonder the British tourists looked so at home in this modest outdoor eatery. To be served "Indian Mughlai" food by a Bangladeshi must have made them feel like they never left England in the first place. Eventually, the Bangladeshi husband appeared, a little taken aback to find himself conversing with another Bengali on Robinson Crusoe's island. He told me about the only other Bengali family he knew of in Trinidad. Then, we chatted about some of the more unexpected corners of the world where one can find an Indian restaurant. "Have you ever been to the Moscow airport?" he asked me. "Try the Indian restaurant there." I promised him that if I ever went to Russia, I would surely try the curry at the Moscow airport.

Other than Indian and British visitors, who wants to eat in an Indian restaurant in Trinidad? While I was politely passing up the channa, roti, curry goat, and doubles in Trinidad, my diasporic brethren took no pains to hide their own fear of "real" Indian cooking. "Too spicy," they all said. So, I was a little surprised when Gerard, the manager of the guesthouse on Mount St. Benedict, took me to Chutney Rose, a posh Indian restaurant in Port of Spain, for a farewell dinner. Gerard's mother was Chinese and his father was Indian. Gerard himself was married to a Dutch woman who managed the guesthouse with him. The dinner was a special treat for all of us. Gerard and his wife had left the birdwatchers in the care of the guesthouse staff to spend the evening with me in an Indian restaurant. I tried to honor the importance of the occasion by wearing the only set of Indian clothes I had brought with me. I suspected the owner of the restaurant had named his place after the trendy Chutney Mary on King's Road in Chelsea, London. In the old imperial metropolis, the Anglo-Indian slang for a biracial woman had become the sign of bourgeois culinary sophistication. Chutney Rose was Mary's colonial cousin.

Gerard asked me to order—a real Indian would know what to eat in an Indian restaurant. I did my best by ordering all the standard stuff. I cannot remember what we ate that night. But, there was real joy in the air. We had dipped papadums in raita together; we had been ethnic together; we had been cosmpolitan together. We had both said goodbye and come home. A real friendship across the faultlines of diaspora was about to begin. The next night, my last night on the island, Gerard said that he had a surprise for me at dinner. He had asked his staff to prepare a Trinidadian Indian meal in my honor: channa, pumpkin, curry goat, rice, buss-up-shot. In short, everything I had secretly been avoiding since my first lunch with Roberto under the sign of the turban. Fighting off mosquitos on the grand colonial verandah shaded by an avocado tree, I ate as furtively as I could. When I left the next day, I promised to mail my hosts a silk sari from India.

Brave New World

The silk sari remains unsent. The attacks on the World Trade Center that occurred a few months after our departure were to rejigger multiple diasporic connections across the world. Certain existing networks that had remained surprisingly invisible to American eyes gained newfound visibility. Old connections were broken, new ones hastily soldered together. In the final act of *The Tempest,* upon meeting people from outside her island for the first time, Miranda who had led a rather insular life exclaims, "O brave new world/That has such people in't." Prospero corrects her immediately with a schoolmasterly zeal that I have always found irritating: "'Tis new to thee." Can the diasporic parent deny the thrill of brave new worlds to the diasporic child? I had traveled to Trinidad and Guyana prompted by cultural pasts. Four years later, I will return with an eye toward the future and with three new traveling companions. Our three children, all born after my encounter with the sign of the turban in St. Augustine, do not know India yet. Instead of a silk sari, Gerard's young daughter will receive a visit from three Indian children from New England. My youngest son will celebrate his first birthday on the grand verandah shaded by the avocado tree, overlooking the Caroni plains where the girmitya[13] tried to make the Indian Ocean meet the Caribbean Sea. For now, Trinidad will be the closest our children will get to India.

Notes

1. Sam Selvon, *Indian in the Caribbean,* eds. David Dabydeen and Brinsley Samaroo (Warwick: Hansib/University of Warwick, Centre for Caribbean Studies, 1987), 18.

2. V. S. Naipaul, *An Area of Darkness* (New York: Vintage Books, 1992), 24.

3. Naipaul, 214.

4. See, for instance, Sidney Mintz's classic work *Sweetness and Power: The Place of Sugar in Modern History* (New York: Viking, 1985).

5. Om Prakash, *Food and Drinks in Ancient India* (Delhi: Munshiram Manoharlal, 1961), 251. Prakash writes that the first sugar refineries were probably located in Bengal, a region famous for its high-quality sugarcanes.

6. Anne Wilson, *Food and Drink in Britain* (London: Penguin, 1984), 267.

7. Brinsley Samaroo informed me of this policy through personal correspondence.

8. David Dabydeen, *The Counting House* (London: Vintage, 1997), 70.

9. Moses Nagamootoo, *Hendree's Cure: Scenes from Madrasi Life in a New World* (Leeds: Peepal Tree Press, 2000), 15.

10. Shani Mootoo, *Cereus Blooms at Night* (New York: Avon Books, 1996), 205.

11. As far as I know, historical records of the erudite editor of the *Koh-I-Noor Gazette* are nonexistent. In a private conversation, Brinsley Samaroo conjectured that the reason there are no records of an Effendi Beg is that he does not, in fact, exist! It very well might be a pseudonym used by one of the local East Indian residents who feared persecution from the colonial authorities for some of the views presented in the newspaper. For a publication that explicitly aims to create an imagined East Indian community in Trinidad, it seems only appropriate that Effendi Beg himself is a figment of the Indian imagination.

12. May 30 is Indian Arrival Day in Trinidad. August 1 is Emancipation Day, which comes at the end of the month-long Tobago festival celebrating Afro-Caribbean culture.

13. *Girmitya* is the term for the Indian labor diaspora, spanning the globe from Fiji to Africa to the Caribbean. The word itself is an Indianized version of the English *agreement* which, in this case, signifies the agreement or contract papers signed by indentured labor.

7

Asian Bodies Out of Control: Examining the Adopted Korean Existence

Tobias Hübinette

Introducing the Adopted Koreans

During the past decade, there has been an upsurge in academic studies examining previously forgotten and unrecognized groups, identities, and experiences transcending antithetical and binary opposites of white/nonwhite, male/female, hetero/homo, and the like. Words like *borders* and *margins,* and prefixes like bi- (e.g., biracial), inter- (e.g., intersexual), and trans- (e.g., transgender) frequently turn up in this exciting and fascinating research trend challenging essentialist theories and notions and territorialized identities and collectivities. Based on a social constructivist and performative understanding of identity development and subject formation, this research trend takes place at the intersection of postcolonial, feminist, and queer theories. With this new research development in mind, this article sets out to examine one of these hitherto neglected and under-researched groups, namely the specific ethnic Korean diaspora of 160,000 children who since the end of the Korean War and during a period of over half a century have been adopted to fifteen different Western countries. The adopted Koreans have more or less up until now been overlooked and invisible in Asian and Korean studies, in migration and diaspora studies, and in race and ethnicity studies. This chapter may therefore offer new and valuable insights into the situation of a forced migration from Korea and a marginalized Asian diaspora growing up with white parents and in white families, and residing in predominantly white communities and white neighborhoods, contrary to the vast majority of other voluntary migrants from Korea and Asia living in Western countries.

For many years, governments and organizations and groups and individuals variously involved with international adoption were the only ones who spoke for and represented the adopted Koreans who were more or less deprived of their voice and agency. In this regard, I argue that the adopted Koreans can well be likened to subalterns in the sense of Gayatri Spivak (1988), as up until recently they could not speak for themselves, represented as they were as mute physical bonds by supplying and receiving governments and as grateful rescue objects by adoption agencies and adoptive parents. Furthermore, a Western multiculturalist ideology perceived international adoption as a left-liberal progressive act and a way of creating a rainbow family, and a Korean ethnonationalism utilized the adoptees as physical bonds to Western allies and made claims on them as part of its ethnoracial diaspora policy. For the adoption agencies, Korean adoption was marketed as the flagship of international adoption, while adoption researchers represented the group as the most perfect international adoptees in terms of adjustment and assimilation.

It was not until the end of the 1980s when adopted Koreans started to organize themselves, that the group for the first time was able to speak out about their own experiences and make themselves heard in a more pronounced manner. From the mid-1990s, there has been a veritable explosion of adopted Korean autobiographical works creating a cultural field of its own and encompassing such diverse genres as novels, plays, and poems; performances; art works and paintings; and documentaries and films. These previously subjugated self-narratives make it possible for the general public to hear the voices of the adopted Koreans themselves beyond what has been previously written and said about the group. The purpose of this chapter, then, is to understand the adopted Korean experience by reading and interpreting a selected corpus of written self-narratives, focusing on the ethnic subjectivities and identifications expressed within them. The autobiographical texts have been published since the end of the 1990s in connection with the emergence of a global adopted Korean movement and have been taken from journals and magazines, books and anthologies, or from Internet homepages and sites, as the adopted Korean movement is very much a virtual community.

This chapter argues that the adopted Korean existence is characterized by a white identification and a continuous performance of whiteness after having grown up in a white family and living in wholly white surroundings, suburbs or small towns, thereby making the group different from other urban- and community-based Korean and Asian immigrants and minorities in Western countries. In this chapter, I also go against the general celebratory hype of hybridity in postmodern writing, as this identification with and performance of whiteness is always interrupted, questioned, and disturbed by contradictory, unstable, and repeated passings and transgressions, in the form of a never-ending negotiation and navigation between the discourses of orientalism, immigrantism, and Koreanness. This ethnic instability leads to severe psychic violence and physical alienation and makes the inhabitance of this hybrid in-between space painful and not very easy to live in. I argue that this finding may help to explain the high preponderance of suicide rates, mental illnesses, and social problems among international adoptees as reflected in the depressing and worrying results of recent Swedish adoption research (Hjern and Allebeck 2002; Hjern, Lindblad, and Vinnerljung 2002; Hjern, Vinnerljung, and Lindblad 2004; Lindblad, Hjern, and Vinnerljung 2003). My interpretation therefore can be seen as a critique of postmodern concepts of nomadism and cosmopolitism, which tend to glorify liminal existences and border crossers like the adopted Koreans. After all, passing and transgressing like an ethnic chameleon is not always a self-liberatory act or a pleasant experience.

International Adoption from Korea

The practice of international adoption originated as a rescue mission immediately after the Korean War (1950–53). It was organized by Western individuals and voluntary agencies to transfer mixed-race children, who are fathered by American and other U.N. soldiers, to adoptive homes in United States and Western Europe (Chakerian 1968; Miller 1971). In 1954, it gained official status when Korea's first president Syngman Rhee (1948–60) initiated a government-sponsored program of international adoption with the purpose of cleansing the country of mixed-race children. Two years later, Harry Holt, a wealthy American farmer and a Christian fundamentalist, established the organization bearing his name. Since its founding, the organization has developed into a leading adoption agency in not only Korea but the world. Holt, believing he was taking part in a divine scheme, rapidly expanded his efforts in international adoption. His mission took on a massive scale, with full-race Koreans joining mixed-race children as eligible adoptees. By the end of the decade, the number of full-race Koreans eclipsed that of mixed-race children in Korea's international adoption program.

In 1961, Korea's modern adoption law was passed, laying the foundation for the most efficient institutional framework of international adoption unsurpassed in the world (Tahk 1986). Under the military regime of President Park Chung Hee (1961–79), Korea was industrialized with a terrible efficacy and at a furious and horrifying speed. Tens of thousands of children of young rural migrants turned into factory workers. Abandoned and betrayed by urban poverty, these children quickly replaced orphans from the Korean War. International adoption was integrated into the country's family planning and labor export programs to decrease the numbers in an over-populated country. It was also used as a goodwill strategy to develop political ties to and trade relations with important Western allies.

Since the end of the 1960s, adoptions from Korea started to rise dramatically as the domestic supply of white adoptable children almost disappeared overnight in the West as a result of changing mores and ideals taking place in connection with the social revolution of 1968. In this era of decolonization, antiracism, and civil rights movements—reinforced by left-liberating ideology prescribing multiculutralism—international adoption quickly came to be perceived as an antiracist and progressive act. Moreover, for radical feminists and sexual minorities, it also represented a liberating reproductive method (Kirton 2000; Solinger 2003). At the beginning of the 1970s, international adoption also played a role in the propaganda war fought between the two Koreas, as North Korea accused its southern neighbor of selling Korean children to Westerners (Hübinette 2002/2003). The accusation led to the entire adoption program being classified and transformed into something close to a state secret to avoid further embarrassment. In 1976, in response to escalating international adoptions and North Korean accusations, a plan for the gradual phasing out of international adoption by 1981 was announced to curb the massive outflow of children.

However, four years later the new military strongman President Chun Doo Hwan (1980–88) came to power and revitalized the country's adoption policy. International adoption was now directly linked to the expansion of the emigration program, and through a process of deregulation the adoption agencies were allowed to engage in profit-making businesses and to compete with each other to track down unrestricted numbers of "adoptable" children (Sarri, Baik, and Bombyk 1998). Consequently, a thriving and profitable adoption industry was created, resulting in the largest number of children ever sent abroad in a decade with 66,511 placements, and peaking in 1985 with close to 9,000 cases or "goodwill ambassadors" as the government preferred to designate them. At the end of the 1980s the country had accomplished a reasonable economic wealth, so from then on the children dispatched abroad were increasingly categorized as illegitimate because they were born to young unwed mothers rather than coming from poor working-class backgrounds.

In 1988, the Seoul Olympic Games showcased a newly democratized and industrialized Korea to the world. Suddenly, Western radio and television broadcasters and newspapers and magazines started to write about the adoption program and designated Korea as the leading global exporter of internationally adopted children. The unexpected attention was deeply humiliating and painful for the proud host country. As a result of the negative foreign media coverage, Korean society was finally forced to seriously address the problem. In 1989, the government decided to set the year 1996 as the deadline to end international adoption. This plan was revoked in 1994 in favor of the more distant deadline year of 2015, but during the tenures of Presidents Roh Tae Woo (1988–93) and Kim Young Sam (1993–98) the number of international placements gradually decreased as a result of deliberate efforts to phase out overseas adoption in the long run and replace it with increased government support to family preservation, economic incentives to encourage domestic adoption, and the establishment of a long-term foster home system. The adoption issue was particularly accentuated during Kim Dae Jung's (1998–2003) presidency, as international adoption started to increase again in connection with the Asian economic crisis and numerous family breakups resulting in so called "IMF orphans" (Hübinette 2003a). In 1998, President Kim Dae Jung delivered an official apology to the adopted Koreans for having sent them away for international adoption. At the same time, his wife Lee Hee-ho designated herself as a supporter and patron of the adopted Koreans. Hence the adoption issue was firmly placed on the country's political agenda during President Kim's term even if he was not able to stop the practice itself.

Every year around two thousand Korean children are still placed for adoption in eight different Western countries: the United States, Canada, Australia, Sweden, Norway, Denmark, France, and Luxembourg. All of the children, practically without any exceptions, are mothered by teenage high school pupils or young college students at secluded maternity homes and clinics affiliated with the adoption agencies. The task of these institutions is to secure a steady supply of infants for an insatiable adoption market in the West and to continue to uphold a patriarchal norm system of premarital chastity within the country (Hübinette 2006). The dominance of girls consisting of around 70 percent during the previous decades has slowly but steadily turned into a small preponderance of boys, reflecting changing family values in the Korean society. Over half a century of international adoption from Korea has produced a population of altogether 160,000 adopted Koreans. With Korea as the uncontested number one supplying country in the field of international adoption in modern history, the adopted Koreans make up approximately one third of all 500,000 estimated international adoption placements that took place between 1945 and 1949. The group constitutes the absolute or relative majority of all international adoptees in every country affected by Korean adoption. In many countries, regions, and cities they also make up the majority of ethnic Koreans or, in some cases, even ethnic Asians.

Of the 160,000 adopted Koreans, two-thirds or 100,000 have ended up in the United States, close to 25,000 in the three Scandinavian countries of Sweden, Denmark, and Norway, around 10,000 each in France and in the Benelux region (Belgium, the Netherlands, and Luxembourg), and the rest are spread out in Germany, Switzerland, Italy, and England, and in Canada, Australia, and New Zealand (Hübinette 2003b). The majority of the adoptees have been adopted by middle- and upper-class white couples or singles and have accordingly grown up in white suburban, countryside, or small-town communities and neighborhoods. Most are still living there as adults. Again, it is important to remember that this demographic background makes the group completely different from other urban-, family-, and community-based Korean and Asian diasporas in today's Western societies.

The Adopted Korean Movement

The first generation of adopted Koreans who were adopted primarily to the United States immediately after the Korean War started writing their life stories in the 1960s. In the early 1990s a couple of autobiographical texts were published in Korean. However, it was not until the mid-1990s with the breakthrough of the Internet that adopted Koreans started to be more visible and make themselves more audible in the public space. Ever since then, numerous cultural and autobiographical works written and produced by adopted Koreans—ranging from novels, poems, and art works to documentaries and films—have emerged (Kim 2000). For the first time, adopted Koreans are considered active agents capable of creating their own social spaces and expressing their own authentic voices instead of just being valuable commodities of Korea's adoption program, grateful and privileged children of Western elite families, or idealized and perfectly assimilated adoptees in academic research.

Simultaneously, adopted Koreans have also started to organize themselves both nationally and on a global level. Nowadays it is possible to talk about a specific adopted Korean movement and subculture, or even identity and community (Bergquist 2000; Harp 1999; Hübinette 2004; Johnsen 2002; Mackie 1999). The first adopted Korean association was formed in Sweden in 1986, and today there are equivalent associations in almost every Western country with a sizeable adopted Korean population, not to mention numerous city- and region-based local networks and circles. These associations function as affinity groups offering peer counseling, mentoring, and self-support. They organize a wide range of social activities, give out journals and publications, have their own home pages and list servers, and hold conferences and events. In addition, there are several Internet-based groups, which points to the fact that adopted Koreans have benefited greatly from the invention of the Internet, just like so many other deterritorialized and widely scattered groups (Hyon, 2004). The ethnogenesis of an adopted Korean community, with its extremely heterogeneous and diverse and completely deterritorialized character, takes place in response to both the birth country's nationalist vision of a global Korean community where the adoptees are automatically essentialized as Korean brethren and expected to reconnect with the "Motherland" and to a Western multiculturalism, which in reality means a more or less complete and compulsory adjustment and assimilation.

This organized movement reaching out to an estimated 5 to 20 percent of the adopted Korean populations in dispersed geographical locations started to interact globally in the 1990s. The most important international networking has occurred in three subsequent International Gatherings, the first one in Washington D.C. in 1999; the second two years later in Oslo, Norway; and the third in 2004 in Seoul, Korea. The concept of the Gathering has resulted in the frequent holding of regional minigatherings in the United States, while in Europe the annual Arierang weekend in the Netherlands functions as an informal pan-European gathering. Finally, a growing number of adopted Koreans who have resettled in Korea have created their own activist and affinity groups.

Performing and Mimicking Whiteness

Both my Danish and my American family are white, all my friends here in Denmark are white ... my husband is white ... and my two sons are often mistaken for being white. So whether I like it or not—and I actually don't—

I've developed a white identity. When I look in the mirror I'm actually surprised to see an Asian woman and I honestly don't know how to feel about the woman I see. I actually expect to see a white woman with rosy skin, blond hair and blue eyes. (Danish Asian 2001)

Growing up in a large Swedish community in the Midwest introduced me to the first criteria of what was considered the norm. Fair skin and blond hair were the standards I measured myself against. Honestly, I had no idea I didn't fit that description unless I saw my reflection in the mirror. I thought of myself as a Caucasian. What a shock to find out that I wasn't. (Rebecca Smith 1997)

I used to believe I was white. At least I was completely emotionally invested in this belief. Theoretically I was white, my family is white, the community I grew up in was white, and I could not point out Korea on a map, nor did I care about such place. The only thing I heard about Korea was that they ate dogs . . . However, my image starring back at me in the mirror betrayed such a belief . . . I hated myself, this betrayal, being given such a look without any knowledge of where it came from. (Young Hee 1997)

The first and foremost point of departure when examining the identity development and subject formation of adopted Koreans is that they have been subjected to a self-identity as white Westerners, having grown up with a white family and living in a wholly white surrounding and seldom in places and settings where the population is more diverse and multicultural. Because adopted Koreans identify themselves as white Westerners gives strong empirical support for the queer theorist Judith Butler's (1990, 1993) performativity theory, which claims that subject formation is not necessarily tied to material and bodily facts. It also supports the postcolonial theorist Homi Bhabha's (1994) hybridity theory, which says that the colonized and the colonizer are mimicking and contaminating each other, and that a new kind of subject arises out of the colonial encounter, which he calls the hybridized. For Butler and Bhabha, identity formation or subjectivization takes place on the level of the body regardless of anatomical features and biological differences, and the subject comes into existence by entering the social order and sustains its subject position or subjectivity through endless repetition or iterability of what is known as performatives.

In line with this, one could say that the adopted Koreans are upholding this white identification and subjectivity by constantly performing and mimicking whiteness on an everyday level, meaning that they are often able to pass as native Westerners in spite of having a physical Korean appearance. In this regard, adopted Koreans can be likened to ethnic drags and cross-dressers, transvestites, or even transgenders who are troubling, mocking and parodying supposedly fixed racial, ethnic, and national identities and belongings. This subversive and liberating interpretation of postmodern theory and the white subjectivization of adopted Koreans is indeed compelling and also appealing as it actually means that there is no authentic or original way of being a white Westerner. Rather, as adopted Koreans have acquired a white self-image and are able to perform and mimic whiteness more or less to perfection, they must also be considered as white Westerners.

So have adopted Koreans managed to break the walls of whiteness, which in the classical colonial era seemed to be so impregnable even for mixed race people who barely could pass as white? Unfortunately, I do not think so even if I still firmly adhere to a social constructivist and performative understanding of ethnic identities. Rather, I argue that to have a white self-identification as a nonwhite person coming from a non-Western country cannot be seen as unproblematic. The acquiring of a white subject position is also made mandatory in adoption research, and a white self-identification is even praised by an adoption ideology representing international adoption as a physical bond between cultures and a symbol for racial harmony and valorizing adoptees as living diversity tokens. It has also led proponents for international adoption to argue that a white subjectivity is exactly what diasporic nonwhites need to develop to be able to survive and compete in a world of white supremacy and white privileges and to conceptualize international adoptive families as ideal examples of postnational, postethnic, postracial or even nonracial kinship. This tendency is present in several recent works by Western adoption researchers inspired by postmodern theories (Howell 2002; Lal 2001; Yngvesson 2002).

Instead for me, to have a white self-image makes adopted Koreans together with other international adoptees absolutely unique in modern history as never before has any nonwhite group ever been subjected as white, probably with the exception of odd individuals among African slaves and Asian coolies who also were completely severed from their biological families and cultural communities and were allowed to grow up with and be educated by whites. This bizarre and by all means queer phenomenon of having a completely distorted physical self-image may easily lead to self-hate, self-contempt, and self-destructiveness. This makes adopted Koreans strangers to their own bodies. The Asian American scholar David Eng (2003) also conceptualizes the adopted Koreans as a queer diaspora in his extraordinary examination of the psychic realm of Korean adoptees. The distorted bodily self-image seems to haunt the adopted Koreans especially in the form of the reflection of the mirror, always betraying and rejecting the white identification of the adoptees, as evident in the three citations. In other words, the material body does matter in this case in spite of an almost complete identification with whiteness.

> While most people check in the mirror for renegade poppy seeds stuck between their teeth, I look to see if I am white: have my eyes formed wonderfully lazy lids to cover sky blue irises? Has my lost nose bridge reinstated itself to its true Nordic beauty? I do admittedly check my teeth but more to ignore my disappointment that this highly anticipated transformation has not yet occurred. I say "yet" because even though I am twenty four, I still harbour fantasies of having not been adopted, and more so, of being white like my adoptive family. As an international adoptee, I don't know what upsets me more: that I am indeed adopted or that I will never feel a part of any culture . . . Exchanging my Korean face for that of a German's is obviously a child's solution to a much more complicated issue . . . Once, when addressed in Korean by a stranger at the age of five, I asked my father why the person thought I was Korean. My question remains for me a sad punch-line to a confusing story and I cannot help feeling that I was somehow the victim of a cruel joke . . . It is difficult to know where to direct the pain . . . When I was encouraged to focus on Korea for school projects I would feign disinterest, while at other times, I would hide my shame at the distasteful association made between myself and that country. No one knew of my ambivalence. No one pressed beyond my fortress of silence. I was left to turn into a self-hating, introverted teenager who could not figure out what her reflection was trying to tell her. It has taken me many painful years to overcome my multitudinous methods of coping and I am by no means through with them . . . Perhaps the process of forgiving has to start with myself. I am not white but I never fooled anyone but myself . . . My reflection will never change but my vision is getting clearer. (Anonymous, u.a.)

Colonial subjects have of course historically always desired whiteness and wanted to have white bodies. Today this desiring of whiteness particularly concerns the descendants of slaves and coolies and postcolonial migrants living in Western countries. However, even if these groups can be said to be more or less Westernized on a cultural level, they are still racially subjected as nonwhites. Accordingly, they are desiring whiteness but they have not acquired a white subject position and bodily self-image. With this in mind, international adoption can truly be seen as the final triumph of the colonial project, as international adoptees must be the most whitened and Westernized subjects ever in the history of colonialism.

The Oriental Stereotype, the Asian Immigrant, and the Overseas Korean

Many have faced racial teasing and discrimination, looking different and being treated differently from their peers, taunts as children calling them "Chinks" or "Japs", "flat-face" or "squint-eye" . . . The harm is doubly intensified by the adoptee's ignorance of his or her own culture and origin, lack of having many, if any, models; having to explain that "No, I'm not Chinese or Japanese—I'm Korean" and not really knowing what that means. The difficulty that all adolescents face in trying to fit in with their peers is intensified in trying to look "white", act "white", and not looking like the people you are most likely to imitate—one's parents. (Kunya Des Jardins 1999)

I walk in this skin. And in this skin, I am any American. A single image has been etched inside of me . . . But my skin conflicts with me. The world sees me as a Color. Crossing the culture gap with other pioneers who are braving the elements of their own prejudices, I realize how much energy it takes to open the mind, however willing the spirit. And I slam up against the impenetrable wall. It hurts so much to still be on the outside. It is altogether a lovely pain, one with which I am intimate. (Su Niles 1997)

Adopted Koreans face cultural divide. We live lives of disjointed identity, balancing between what's seen and what's felt. Our minds belong in one universe, while our bodies exist in another. But as adopted Koreans, we can never truly call either sphere our own . . . Although the experiences of adopted Koreans range across the board, the zebra-like contrast between our culture and our beauty is at the core of us all. And each of us learns how to solder a unique link between our inner steel and our outer shell. (Samantha Pace 2000)

So the subject formation of adopted Koreans cannot be reduced to something as simple and unproblematic as the performing and mimicking of whiteness, which Butler's and Bhabha's theories may seem to promise at first sight. This might have been the case in an ideal world, but having a body marked and inscribed with a long history of otherness in a Western culture and society imbued with racist practices, regimes, and discourses actually does matter. In spite of being bestowed with a Western name and growing up in a white family, and in spite of only speaking a Western language and behaving like a Westerner, having a nonwhite body does create limitations to sustain a white subjectivity. The frequent, painful, and humiliating moments when adopted Koreans are revealed and exposed as a kind of ethnic pastiche and copycats are good examples of what Butler calls a misfire, meaning when a performative fails to reproduce its intended effect and instead ends up in an infelicitous performative. The performative character of the subject simultaneously constitutes its stability and its vulnerability, as it is always possible to oppose and subvert, and resignify and transform this iterability of performatives to create new subject positions, whether for good or for bad. So when are adopted Koreans failing to maintain a white subjectivity? When are they misfiring and performing infelicitously? What is exactly interrupting and fragmenting and destroying and crushing their white identification and self-image?

According to the autobiographical works of adopted Koreans, I have identified three principal and often sequential interventions when they are not being acknowledged, accepted, and taken as a white Westerner. These moments occur when the imagery of orientalism, the discourse of immigrantism, and the ideology of Koreanness intervene and they are imagined as an Oriental stereotype, addressed as an Asian immigrant, and interpellated as an overseas Korean. Here it is important to remember that performativity theory is not about advocating a strategy of individualistic or, even worse, neoliberal identity politics in the form of free role-playing and funny theatrical gestures, which some proponents may believe it to be. Butler also reminds us that subject formation is heavily constrained by a ritualized repetition or iterability of cultural rites and social norms policing and regulating the subject under the threat of marginalization or even death. Bodies sometimes do matter, as the surface of some bodies are inscribed with meanings and that these inscriptions have a history that makes such bodies particularly vulnerable to socially ingrained and historicized discourses, imageries, and ideologies.

> I was a "gook", a "chink", a "boat person" and a "V.C." (Viet Cong). My actual origin was not important enough to know. Conversely, to teachers, clergy and my own extended family, I was "adorable", a.k.a. "a little china doll". In the schoolyard, I was ridiculed and taunted, picked on and beaten up . . . I

ran from a boy who screamed in my ear, "pork fried rice", with the perceived stereotypical *Asian accent*. I was so deeply bothered by slurs about rice and chopsticks that I never wanted to be seen eating anything as such. Likewise with karate and kung fu, I would not agree to take karate lessons as my mother had wanted for my own protection. (Christine Jones Regan 1999)

Growing up, I was the perfect abducted daughter. Good, smart, considerate. I had a close relationship with my abductive parents, and I felt like I really loved them. So hearing them make comments like, "Our daughter is so obedient, it must be in her genes!" and listening to my abductive family use words like "Oriental", "Chinaman", and "China doll" to describe me and other Asians seriously sucked. (So Yung Kim 2002)

Sometimes my adoptive mother will see an Asian woman on tv and declare, "Oh she looks just like you!" Or when we eat in a Chinese restaurant the first thing they will comment on will be the "ching chong Chinese music." (Seoul One 2003)

With an Asian body constantly signifying orientalism, the sudden and powerful intervention of the orientalist imagery turning up at the most unexpected occasions always threatens to fetishize adopted Koreans into ethnic stereotypes. It is evident that this orientalization of adopted Koreans takes place even within the adoptive family, as having an adopted child from Korea does not stop one from being racist. It is perhaps no coincidence that So Yung Kim likens adoption to "abduction" and adoptive parents to "abductive parents" given her personal experiences within her own family. It is a well-known phenomenon that Asians and Asian children in many Western countries are perceived as being docile and submissive, clever and hardworking, and quiet and kind, and the fact that Asia is the dominating supplying continent of internationally adopted children from countries like Korea, Vietnam, Thailand, Cambodia, the Philippines, Taiwan, Indonesia, India, and Sri Lanka probably further underscores the orientalist imagery at work. Catherine Ceniza Choy and Gregory Paul Choy (2003) have also paid attention to this orientalization of Korean adoptee bodies in their textual analysis of adopted Korean poems and literary works.

Again coming back to the ever-present reflection in the mirror, it is important here to note that in practice for most adopted Koreans, the orientalist imagery is practically the only disposable mirror image at hand for physical self-identification besides the white bodies surrounding them during their upbringing and daily life. In this respect, there are of course similarities to other ethnic Koreans in Western countries like those living in interracial relationships or being of mixed race origin, as these groups usually are alienated from both their homeland and sometimes from the mainstream Korean and Asian diaspora communities as well. However, what makes the state of Korean adopteeness so unique is the complete severance of familial ties, cultural routes, and social connections to all kinds of Koreanness and Asianness whatsoever. This is also the reason behind an ambivalent response to the orientalist imagery as it at least offers a bodily mirror image, while other diasporic Koreans usually do not recognize themselves in it and even distance themselves and take it as a misrepresentation and as a distorted fiction. Accordingly, it is no coincidence that many adopted Koreans also perform orientalism, almost fully embodying the orientalist fantasies in their most gendered and heterosexual forms, as men often have taken on a nerdish lifestyle while women instead exoticize themselves. By this reading, I do not claim that this voluntary self-orientalization means that adopted Koreans are acquiring a false consciousness of some sort. Rather, I am assuming and proposing that orientalism may well be practically the only knowledge model adoptees have of Koreanness and Asianness, and of course it is very often mediated by way of popular culture.

> I remember feeling pulled between being white and being Asian when I watched "Miss Saigon" the first time . . . I didn't feel Asian, but as white as the friends who sat next to me. And yet the stirrings of identity were beginning, because I was emotionally drawn to the Asian American actors . . . Watching the play was exhilarating . . . It was like falling in love. I was giddy with the American dream it presented, tearful over the hardships of war, and became infatuated with the relationship between Kim and Chris, the lovers the story focused on. It was love, and I fell hard for "Miss Saigon" . . . I let myself be wooed by decent music, dramatic and lavish sets, and the story of a prostitute who was sold for a night of sex with an American Marine, fell in love, bore their child, and ended up killing herself in a star-spangled flame of sacrifice. (Holly Coughlin 1999)

> I didn't want to be like the Asian geeks I saw in movies . . . I'd watch with my lighter complexioned friends and laugh along with them. Laughing, I thought, would distance me from the popular Asian looking icons of American humor. I did not want to be another typical Asian overachiever, both praised as a model minority that other people of color should follow and denigrated as

an emasculated sex-starved wallflower. I tried to stay away from other Asian guys at school. (Peter Kearly 2002)

I am Korean but, God, do I wish I was white! To me, whiteness was the embodiment of everything good, everything pure. Who was always the good guy in the cartoons I watched after school? Why, the man in the white cowboy hat, of course . . . Thus, my idealization of the color white stemmed from my early experiences, and I ultimately succeeded in internalizing the dominant culture's standards and imprisoning myself in a cell of self-hatred. (Kristin Penaskovic 1992)

Furthermore, adopted Koreans always risk the threat of being taken for a non-Western immigrant of Asian origin by a discourse of immigrantism or perhaps just pure xenophobia, dividing phenotypically between native whites and immigrant and minority nonwhites in practically every contemporary Western society. With the background of being the most integrated and assimilated "immigrants" in any Western country, this might sound ironic as adopted Koreans are of course in no way a danger to the upholding of a perceived and threatened cultural homogeneity and social harmony in Western countries. In response, they often perform whiteness even more intensely, and often in combination with an over-exaggerated middle- or upper-classness with the hope of being taken for an Asian adoptive child to a white elite family and not mistaken as a working-class Asian immigrant, thereby asserting a certain belongingness both to family, class, and culture.

In my daily plan of achieving perfection, I made sure I was never associated with any of the other Korean adoptees at school. This worked out great because they were also hiding out in their other identities. What I hadn't anticipated was the first Hmong family that came to my school. I felt their stares in the hallway. They were immediately drawn to that thing I hated most about myself then—my Asian features. I avoided them like the plague. I figured they might blow my cover and actually call attention to the fact that I looked like them. (Sundraya Kase 1997)

During this period, there was no way I would be caught dead in a group of other Asian people. My perception of Asians at the time was negative because of what many of my peers said about Asian people who they assumed were immigrants—"Oh look they are fresh off the boat." Meaning, I'd probably look like someone who only spoke a foreign group of syllables and consonants that came out the same, "Me how ping pong." (Jamie Kemp 2001)

> I watched the way Americans moved, talked, used their hands; and I became a master at imitation. I had a better understanding of the language than the American-born children I went to school with. (Elizabeth Kim 2000)

An extreme example of this over-performed middle- or upperclassness and whiteness is apparently, according to the citations, to avoid the company of Asians and people of color, including other adopted Koreans, by any means. The other choice is to identify and socialize with Korean immigrants and Asian minorities, but this is not an easy option as adopted Koreans often end up as outsiders in both the white world and among diasporic communities. This interpretation is in line with Bhabha (1994), who argues that the hybridized person is usually rendered different both from the colonizer and the colonized and becomes an other in-between and beyond both cultures and worlds, namely both the white majority society and the nonwhite minority community. When prejudices, racism, and discrimination come from both sides, and racial expectations do not fit well with cultural experiences, adopted Koreans like Arthur Hinds express a frustrating feeling of incommensurability for never being able to unite and reconcile with both worlds at the same time.

> My Asian friends tell me that other Korean adoptees are too white, like bananas. They tell me it is good that I am learning about what it is to be Asian American. What it is to be a person of colour. And how white people think of me. I have white parents . . . Twinkie, banana, sell-out. I've heard them all before, and hate them just the same . . . I can see the racism from all my white friends, from my grandparents, and cousins . . . They say that my racism is internalized and that I have been tricked into believing the great white lie. Maybe I have. But what are they telling me? That I should hate my father? . . . White people think I'm just some gook. White people who don't know me, that is. Can you speak English? Oh your English is very good. Where are you from? How long have you lived in America? I didn't really know what to say to that. How can I say that I feel I am more American than you, you third generation European immigrant. My family has been here since the 18th Century. My great great great grandfather was making money in New York while yours was working some field in another country. Don't talk to me about speaking English. My mother is an English professor. That is what I think when white people are racist to me. What about Koreans? I'm one of them right? Wrong. Maybe it's just me, but I really feel out of place when I am around them. I also feel very . . . good. I'm one of them, yet there is always a sense of exclusion . . .

I need their acceptance. But I would rather not risk their rejection and simply just not have anything to do with them. (Arthur Hinds 2000)

Finally, recently Korean ethnonationalism has started to call for the adopted Koreans to "come back" and "return home." This lure of essentialism in the form of Koreanness by letting oneself be reclaimed and embraced by Korean ethnoracial body politics and visiting and resettling in Korea is naturally also threatening a white subject position. However, again this is not an easy alternative given the almost complete inseparability among race, language, and culture in Korean nationalism.

> This year in Korea has been a challenge for me particularly because I do not speak Korean well . . . Basically, people here think I'm some person who's trying to make them angry by deliberately not speaking what should obviously be my native language, based on my physical appearance. This is how most people react when they first meet me. And it always goes like this . . . : A guy in the street stops to ask me directions, speaking in rapid-fire Korean . . . After I clearly state that I don't speak Korean, the questions begin. First question: "Aren't you Korean?" Second question: "Well, then, don't you speak Korean?" Third question: "Why not? Didn't your mother-father-other Korean influences you had in your life growing up, teach you Korean?" How do you answer to this type of mentality? You can't. You will honestly go crazy if you try to. (Sunny Diaz 2000)

From the mid-1990s, adopted Koreans have increasingly been included as part of the Korean diaspora and treated as ethnic Koreans overseas, and they are nowadays regularly mentioned and included in official works and speeches dealing with the worldwide diasporic community of Koreans. However, it is one thing when the Korean government or president is addressing the adoptees as "Korean brethren and sistren," but in reality, on an everyday level, to not speak fluent Korean and to not behave like a native Korean create obstacles, as the experiences of Sunny Diaz point toward.

The Consequences of Psychic Violence and Physical Alienation

It is my conviction that this besieged subject position as a white Westerner, made fragile and questioned by having an Asian body that is perpetually under the threat of being fetishized, racialized, and essentialized, results in severe psychic violence and physical alienation in the form of an almost per-manent state of tremendous stress, rage, agony, and melancholia for never be-ing able to fit in and find a balance between racial expectations and ethnic and cultural identifications and experience, and to always feel like a social misfit and an ethnic outsider. Having nowhere to hide and rest, no place to find solace and no free zone or safe space, and no significant others to defend or at least understand and empathize with them—which other Asian and Korean immigrants arguably do have in their own families and communities—death in the form of suicide becomes the ultimate way for adopted Koreans to es-cape from this endless struggle to survive, negotiate, and navigate between all these self-identifications, imageries, discourses, and ideologies, and in the end to be left alone. This interpretation is in line with what Dani Isaac Meier (1998) observes in his dissertation based on interviews, where he illustrates how adopted Koreans are continuously and painfully negotiating their mul-tiple racial and ethnic subject positions.

By this interpretation, I am also consciously ignoring and leaving behind mainstream positivistic adoption research dominated by psychologists and psychiatrists, which instead wants to explain such "deviant" results as suicide among international adoptees only with genetic defects, low IQs, separation traumas, and attachment disorders. Instead, I suggest that it might be more productive to interpret the recent finding that suicide is five times more com-mon among international adoptees in Sweden than among native Swedes in light of the severe psychic violence and physical alienation expressed in the adopted Korean self-narratives (Hjern & Allebeck 2002).

> During childhood, this constant battle of acceptance of my heritage and the rejection of my looks created a kind of a constant, inner displacement, a gap which widened as I grew older. It helps when I can speak—because through my fluent Danish language, I can express my cultural heritage . . . But when I am silent, my appearance overpowers me and takes control. This dominance makes me feel, on the one hand, sad . . . On the other hand, I am sometimes overwhelmed by the longing to escape myself, which makes me extremely an-gry, because I feel predestined in a negative way. The result is a lack of bal-ance when it comes to identity. I was looking for white features, hoping I was biracial, longing for blond hair, blue eyes, and ultimately hating my body and avoiding mirrors. (Charlotte Yong-san Gullach 2003)

Our search for ourselves does not have an end—neither does the pain. You saw that, but what you couldn't see was a way to ease the difficulty of your earthly journey. Somewhere along the way, you forgot to open your eyes and catch a glimpse of hope. A friend recently commented that we, as adopted Koreans live a lie. In order to assimilate into not only a white society, but also our adoptive families, we learn to see ourselves as others want to see us. We turn our lies into betrayal—of ourselves. Maybe you got tired of wearing your mask. Maybe you forgot who existed beneath the weight of that façade. (Kari Ruth 1997)

Alienation, or the feeling that one is alien, is unavoidable when people ask incessantly, "So where are you from? No, where are you really from?" Since when is "I'm from Austin, Minnesota" not a good enough answer? ... Most adoptees have an "a-ha" moment at some point in their lives when they look in the mirror and realize, "I'm not white." A painful self-consciousness usually follows, with sometimes comical and sometimes tragic attempts to "fit in" with the majority. I know a few adoptees who, in their childhood, would have literally "whitewashed" themselves if physically possible. Feeling rejected for never being white enough, some adoptees turn their backs on the dominant culture and look for acceptance and affirmation in the Korean American community, or will even go visit the "motherland". Sadly, many discover even more hostility from the Korean people for not being "Korean enough" ... So the adoptee is left with the bewildering question: Who am I if I'm not white enough for America and not Korean enough for Korea? Where do I go from here? (Stan Wood 2003)

The adopted Korean existence is in other words not only characterized by a firm identification with whiteness, but also by numerous, constant, unwilling, and uncanny passings and transgressions. As Butler points out, the boundaries surrounding privileged subject positions like whiteness are governed by numerous regulatory and circumscribing juridical laws, cultural customs, and social conventions that delimit and constrain the potentialities for passing as a white Westerner and that punish those who dare to by social marginalization or biological death. So it may be that adopted Koreans are disembedded and free-floating Asian bodies who have gone completely out of place and out of control, and who constantly disturb and disquiet the taken-for-granted boundaries of race, culture, and nationality. Nonetheless, they always risk ending up being severely punished for their passings and transgressions.

To conclude, my main argument is that adopted Koreans have been fully acculturated and socialized to self-identify as white. At the same time, having a Korean body, they are incessantly liable to a whole regime of orientalist imageries trying to fetishize them into an ethnic stereotype. Furthermore, being a nonwhite person, an ever-present discourse of immigrantism wants to racialize them into an Asian and non-Western immigrant. Lastly, as an ethnic Korean, they nowadays are also warmly interpellated by a Korean diaspora policy essentializing them into and hailing them as an overseas Korean. Contrary to the liberationist interpretations of Butler's performativity theory and Bhabha's hybridity theory, I regard this acquiring of a white self-identification by adopted Koreans as a complete subordination to white hegemonic power and as a magnificent symbol of the final triumph of the colonial project. Here, again, it is important to note that this does not mean that I am advocating an essentialist understanding of what a nonwhite body should consist of, as I am aware of the fact that the white subjectivization of adopted Koreans may also be interpreted as a subversive undermining of whiteness itself. However, albeit its revolutionary potential on a theoretical level, I believe that this self-identification is highly problematic in real life for a nonwhite person of non-Western descent living in such a heavily racialized culture and society like the Western one. In this way, I also go against dominant normative adoption ideology where the acquiring of a white self-image is the primary goal of international adoption itself, conceptualized as adjustment, attachment, and assimilation.

Moreover, I am aware that hybridity is mostly linked to postcolonial diasporas and to second generation immigrants and mixed race people. However, for me it is the adopted Koreans who provide the best example of a hybridized existence that goes beyond all kinds of classical categories normally associated with *ethnies* and diasporas—like kinship and territory, culture, religion and language, and memory and myth—as they are completely severed and isolated from both the North and South Korean nation-states and other diasporized Korean immigrants. The uniqueness of the adopted Koreans, which makes them different from other Korean and Asian minorities, is precisely this estrangement from their biological families and ethnic communities, an estrangement that not only makes them self-identify as white Westerners but also compels them to respond differently to the discourses of orientalism, immigrantism, and Koreanness. However, even if many adopted Koreans understandably may feel like mistranslated white Westerners, misrepresented oriental stereotypes, misrecognized Asian immigrants, and misappropriated overseas Koreans, some of them have apparently come to accept that the only way to understand and accept the fate of being an adopted Korean is precisely to say that it is a never-ending story of misfiring and infelicitous performatives.

I have struggled much of my life to understand the complexities of my identity. At one point I believed I was white. Soon however, racist comments destroyed that misconception, and I grew to loathe the mirror's reflection and it's seeming contradiction. According to others, I was not American, yet in my mind neither was I Korean. After I grew to identify as Korean, I traveled to South Korea where I was promptly informed that I was actually American. In the end, I finally returned to the United States and became Korean-American . . . After such a complex path to self-discovery, I have now dedicated my life to helping redefine what it means to be "American." (Jennifer Arndt 2001)

Lately, I have had to confront a pastiche of labels: Asian, Korean, American, and adopted. A situation such as this has made me realize identity is not something that can be buried or ignored. I have too many hyphens to interconnect what it is that supposedly constitutes my existence that I have given up attaching any kind of "label". Ultimately, there is no term that will explain entirely that which makes me. So, call me what you will, but keep it clean. (Mark Keats 2003)

I don't fit into any pre-existing categories: I'm not Caucasian, Korean, Korean-American, or biracial . . . I can't choose an ethnicity intelligibly . . . Is ethnicity a question of choice? . . . But I've accepted my liminal status. I'll try to dance while trapped in this perpetual limbo. (Elizabeth Woyke 1998)

References

Primary Sources

Anonymous. U.a. "Thoughts of a Korean adoptee": http://www.adoption.on.ca/koreanadopt.html (July 2, 2004).

Jennifer Arndt. 2001. "Korean connection." *Mavin* 5/2001.

Holly Coughlin. 1999. "My breakup with Miss Saigon." *Minnesota Women's Press* July 7, 1999.

Danish Asian. 2001. "Adoptee's struggle between finding herself and fitting in": http://www.goldsea.com/Air/True/ILF/adoptee.html (June 20, 2004).

Kunya Des Jardins. 1999. "Finding Seoul." *Hongik Tidings* 3/1999.

Sunny Diaz. 2000. " 'Korean? American?! Hispanic???!!!.' An adoptee in Korea": http://www.fulbright.or.kr/eta/english/eta-perspectivs.html (July 2, 2004).

Charlotte Yong-san Gullach. 2003. "A Dane in a Korean shell." *Korean Quarterly* 2/2003.

Arthur Hinds. 2000. "Asian, Korean, adopted, American?" *Paradox* 1/2000.

Christine Jones Regan. 1999. "Carefully taught." *Bamboo Girl* 8/1999.

Sundraya Kase. 1997. "Mentoring." *Korean Quarterly* 4/1997.

Peter Kearly. 2002. "I'm Iwish." In *After the morning calm. Reflections of Korean adoptees,* edited by Sook Wilkinson and Nancy Fox. Bloomfield Hills, MI: Sunrise Ventures.

Mark Keats. 2003."A phone bill and the emergence of a Korean identity": http://www.akconnection.com/stories/keats2.asp?cat=4 (July 29, 2004).

Jamie Kemp. 2001. "The seeds of racial disparity." *Korean Quarterly* 3/2001.

Elizabeth Kim. 2000. *Ten thousand sorrows. The extraordinary journey of a Korean War orphan.* New York: Doubleday.

So Yung Kim. 2002. *I was abducted by white people.* Portland, OR: Confluere Publications.

Su Niles. 1997. "Obstacles and challenges." *We Magazine* 5/1997.

Seoul One. 2003. "A Korean adoptee's search for her identity": http://www.modelminority.com/article600.html (May 26, 2004).

Samantha Pace. 2000. "Adopted Koreans face cultural divide." *Minnesota Daily,* July 3, 2000.

Kristin Penaskovic. 1992. "Confessions of a banana." *Yisei* 2/1992.

Kari Ruth. 1997. "Dear Luuk." *We Magazine* 5/1997.

Rebecca Smith. 1997. "Unconventional Seoul." In *Seeds from a silent tree. An anthology by Korean adoptees,* edited by Tonya Bishoff and Jo Rankin. Glendale, CA: Pandale Press.

Stan Wood. 2003. "Jesus the adoptee": http://www.kpcmem.org/resources/article.asp?contentid=61 (July 2, 2004)

Elizabeth Woyke. 1998. "Growing up white." *Type* 2/1998.

Young Hee. 1997. "Laurel." In *Seeds from a silent tree. An anthology by Korean adoptees,* edited by Tonya Bishoff and Jo Rankin., Glendale, CA: Pandale Press.

Secondary Sources

Bergquist, Kathleen Leilani Ja Sook. 2000. *Racial identity and ethnic identity in Korean adoptees.* Ph.D. dissertation, College of William and Mary, Department of Counselor Education..

Bhabha, Homi K. 1994. *The location of culture.* London: Routledge.

Butler, Judith. 1990. *Gender trouble. Feminism and the subversion of identity.* New York: Routledge.

———. 1993. *Bodies that matter. On the discursive limits of "sex."* New York: Routledge.

Chakerian, Charles G. 1968. *From rescue to child welfare.* New York: Church World Service.

Choy, Catheringe Ceniza, and Gregory Paul Choy. 2003. "Transformative terrains. Korean adoptees and the social constructions of an American childhood." In *The American child. A cultural studies reader,* edited by Caroline F. Levander and Carol J. Singley, 262–79. New Brunswick, NJ: Rutgers University Press.

Eng, David L. 2003. "Transnational adoption and queer diasporas." *Social Text* 21 (Fall): 1–37.

Harp, Amy. 1999. *A life known and a history lost.* Master's thesis. San Diego State University: Department of Communication.

Hjern, Anders, and Peter Allebeck. 2002. "Suicide in first- and second-generation immigrants in Sweden. A comparative study." *Social Psychiatry and Psychiatric Epidemiology* 37(9), 423–429.

Hjern, Anders, Frank Lindblad, and Bo Vinnerljung. 2002. "Suicide, psychiatric illness, and social maladjustment in intercountry adoptees in Sweden: A cohort study." *Lancet* 360 (9331): 443–448.

Hjern, Anders, Bo Vinnerljung, and Frank Lindblad. 2004. "Avoidable mortality among child welfare recipients and intercountry adoptees: A national cohort study." *Journal of Epidemiology and Community Health* 58(5): 412–417.

Howell, Signe. 2002. "Community beyond place. Adoptive families in Norway." In *Realizing community. Concepts, social relationships and sentiments,* edited by Vered Amit, 84–104. London: Routledge.

Hübinette, Tobias. 2002/2003. "North Korea and adoption." *Korean Quarterly* (Winter): 24–25.

———. 2003a. "President Kim and adoption." *Korean Quarterly* 6 (Spring): 27–28.

———. 2003b. "The adopted Koreans of Sweden and the Korean adoption issue." *Review of Korean Studies* 6(1): 251–266.

———. 2004. "The adopted Koreans and an identity in the third space." *Adoption & Fostering* 28(1): 16–24.

———. 2006. *Comforting an orphaned nation. Representations of international adoption and adopted Koreans in Korean popular culture.* Seoul: Jimoondang Publishing Company.

Hyon, Sonjia. 2004. "Constellations of home: Korean adoptees making place and writing 'home' in cyperspace." Paper presented at the *7th Annual Sociology and Committee on Historical Studies Conference,* New School University, New York, April 24, 2004.

Johnsen, Sunny. 2002. *The creation and rise of KAD as a separate identity and nation.* Undergraduate term paper, Simon Fraser University, Department of Communication.

Kim, Eleana. 2000. "Korean adoptee auto-ethnography: Refashioning self, family and finding community." *Visual Anthropology Review* 16(1): 43–70.

Kirton, Derek. 2000. *"Race,"* ethnicity and adoption. "Race," health and social care series. Buckingham: Open University Press.

Lal, Barbara Ballis. 2001. "Learning to do ethnic identity: The transracial/transethnic adoptive family as site and context." In *Rethinking "mixed race,"* edited by David Parker and Miri Song, 154–172. London: Pluto Press.

Lindblad, Frank, Anders Hjern, and Bo Vinnerljung. 2003. "Intercountry adopted children as young adults—A Swedish cohort study." *American Journal of Orthopsychiatry 73(2): 190–202.*

Mackie, Elizabeth. 1999. *I am Korean but: Race and identity formation among adult Korean adoptees.* Senior honor thesis, Brown University, Department of American Civilization.

Meier, Dani Isaac. 1998. *Loss and reclaimed lives: Cultural identity and place in Korean-American intercountry adoptees.* Ph.D. dissertation, University of Minnesota, Department of Geography.

Miller, Helen. 1971. "Korea's international children." *Lutheran Social Welfare* 13 (Summer): 12–23.

Sarri, Rosemary C., Yeonoak Baik, and Marti Bombyk. 1998. "Goal displacement and dependency in South Korean-United States intercountry adoption." *Children and Youth Services Review* 20(1–2): 87–114.

Solinger, Rickie. 2003. *Beggars and choosers. How the politics of choice shapes adoption, abortion, and welfare in the United States.* New York: Hill and Wang.

Spivak, Gayatri Chakravorty. 1988. "Can the subaltern speak?" In *Marxism and the interpretation of culture,* edited by Cary Nelson and Lawrence Grossberg, 271–313. Chicago: University of Illinois.

Tahk, Youn-Taek. 1986. "Intercountry adoption program in Korea. Policy, law and service." In *Adoption in worldwide perspective. A review of programs, policies and legislation in 14 countries,* edited by R. A. C. Hoksbergen, 79–91. Lisse, Netherlands: Swets & Zeitlinger.

Yngvesson, Barbara. 2002. "Placing the 'gift child' in transnational adoption." *Law & Society Review* 36(2): 227–256.

8 Diasporic Politics and the Globalizing of America: Korean Immigrant Nationalism and the 1919 Philadelphia Korean Congress

Richard S. Kim

ON MARCH 1, 1919, Koreans from throughout the peninsula congregated in Pagoda Park in the capital city of Seoul to attend the national funeral of the last reigning Korean monarch, King Kojong, who had passed away earlier in the year. On that same afternoon, a young Korean man climbed atop a platform in the middle of Pagoda Park and read aloud a formal Declaration of Independence as Korean leaders simultaneously presented the written document to Japanese colonial officials. Upon the completion of the public reading, the large assembled crowd repeatedly chanted in unison *Taehan Tongnip Mansei!* (Long Live Korean Independence!), setting off waves of similar protests against Japanese rule throughout the Korean peninsula that lasted for months. Over two million Koreans from all walks of life participated in the nonviolent demonstrations, which subsequently became known as the March First movement. The Japanese, taken completely by surprise by the massive scale of the carefully orchestrated uprising, brutally repressed the demonstrations. Japan's powerful military police force arrested, imprisoned, tortured, and killed thousands of Koreans (Eckert et al., 1990, 276–79; Lee, 1984, 340–44).

Japan's harsh response to the March First movement necessitated that organized resistance against Japanese colonial rule would have to be coordinated and maintained in the Korean diaspora. Indeed, much of the trajectory of Korean nationalism occurred from beyond the Korean peninsula (Lee, 1963; Scalapino and Lee, 1972; Suh, 1967). Japanese repression, in particular, prevented the establishment of a base in Korea that could act with national authority. As a consequence, in April 1919, Korean nationalist leaders throughout the diaspora formed the Korean Provisional Government (KPG) in Shanghai, China. Created as a government in exile, the KPG represented a systematic effort to institutionalize a sovereign political entity that could be recognized as a legitimate actor within the international system of nation-states.

From its conception and inception, the KPG was a direct manifestation of the transnational, diasporic nature of the Korean nationalist movement. As a government in exile, the KPG struggled for power from outside the territorial boundaries of its claimed national territory (Shain, 1991). Moreover, its leadership positions were filled with individuals drawn from Korean communities throughout the diaspora in the United States, Manchuria, and Siberia. Japan's declaration of Korea as a protectorate in 1905 and subsequent annexation as a Japanese colony in 1910 spawned organized protest groups among Koreans abroad. For the most part, these exile groups conducted their activities independent of each other. The creation of the KPG in 1919, with headquarters in Shanghai, sought to unify this loose network of exiled nationalists into a more tightly knit structure (Eckert et al., 1990, 279–80; Lee, 1984, 344).

News of the March First movement and the establishment of the KPG quickly spread to Koreans living in the United States. As a diasporic community in exile, the 10,000 Koreans, who migrated to the United States in the years between 1903 and 1924, were continually involved in homeland politics as a result of Japan's colonization of Korea between 1905 and 1945 (Clifford, 1994; Cohen, 1997; Gabaccia, 2000; Safran, 1991). The mass movement for self-determination in Korea galvanized the Korean immigrant community in the United States. Shortly after the announcement of the creation of the KPG, Korean immigrants convened the "Korean Congress" in Philadelphia from April 14–16, 1919, to mobilize support for the Korean independence movement and the new Provisional Government.

By the end of World War I in 1918, the United States had emerged as the world's preeminent power, firmly establishing the twentieth century as what has come to be called the "American Century" (Eckes and Zeiler, 2003; Iriye, 1993; Ninkovich, 1999; Rosenberg, 1982). Heavily influenced by American political values and ideals, activities at the Korean Congress were imbued with the U.S. government's rhetoric of self-determination, democracy, and freedom as exemplified in U.S. President Woodrow Wilson's Fourteen Points. Given the strong sense of morality and mission that guided Wilsonian politics of the day, Korean nationalists found strong allies in American Protestant missionary groups. Accordingly, the language and ideology of Christianity were also integral to nationalist appeals for Korean independence.

The globalization of American power following World War I greatly heightened the significance of the U.S. polity for the diasporic political mobilization of the Korean independence movement, enabling Koreans in the United States to establish certain forms of political organizing that bolstered their prominence and visibility in and out of the United States. These homeland-related activities conducted by Koreans abroad provided the basis for the development of "long-distance nationalism" (Glick Schiller and Fouron, 2001) that created a political community extending beyond national boundaries and borders of the homeland.[1] In the process, Koreans in the United States forged strong transnational ties with their compatriots dispersed around the globe. Though their population was far smaller than the large number of Koreans living in Manchuria and Siberia, Koreans in the United States came to hold disproportionate political influence and power within the diaspora.[2] The Korean Congress in Philadelphia served to affirm the authority of the U.S. component of the Korean diaspora to define the movement's ideological frameworks.

In analyzing Korean nationalist rhetoric and politics at the 1919 Korean Congress and its immediate aftermath, this study pays close attention to the views and activities of nationalist leaders in the United States, who played a particularly dominant role in planning and directing the movement's tactics and strategies. The prominence of bourgeois nationalists and the intelligentsia in the leadership of anticolonial movements, especially in the formative stages, is well known (Breuilly, 1982; Hobsbawn, 1962; Marr, 1981; Robinson, 1988). The Korean nationalist movement was no exception. Many of the leaders at the Korean Congress were Western-educated elites and devout Christian converts. Such social and educational qualifications placed these individuals in privileged positions to define the ideological contents and political agenda of a burgeoning Korean nationalism within the context of American global power.

This article draws from a larger project that examines the challenges of defining and achieving coherent political action under the diasporic circumstances of statelessness and exile.[3] Following the March First movement, two major ideological camps emerged within the national liberation movement, both of which advocated competing policies and strategies for achieving Korean independence. One contemporary observer aptly referred to these two opposing ideological camps as the "American group" and the "Siberian-Manchurian group" (Kim, 1973, 113–14). The American group actively promoted international diplomacy as the primary means for gaining independence. Engaged in a variety of propaganda and lobbying activities, they aimed to enlist support for Korean independence from the United States and other Western powers. In contrast, the Siberian-Manchurian group argued that direct armed struggle against the Japanese was the only way to achieve unconditional independence for Korea. With Russian financial and military assistance, this socialist-oriented group sought to mobilize the large number of Koreans living in Siberia and Manchuria, who were in close geographical proximity to Korea, to conduct guerilla-style military attacks against the Japanese in the northern parts of Korea, believing that these attacks would kindle a revolution among the populace in Korea to overthrow Japanese colonial rule.

Given these multiple bases of nationalist activity within the diaspora, several different provisional governments were formed in the aftermath of the March First demonstrations. In launching the KPG in Shanghai, nationalist leaders consciously sought to unify the disparate elements of the Korean nationalist movement under a single authority headquartered in Shanghai (Hong, 1971; Kang, 1996, 2005). By the end of 1919, the KPG had forty-five major Korean organizations in and out of Korea under its authority (Ban, 1996, 412–13). In consolidating the multitude of nationalist groups under its leadership, the KPG expanded the scope and nature of its operational resources. Koreans in the United States and Hawaii, for instance, provided critical financial support and the ability to influence American politicians and public opinion while those in Manchuria and Siberia offered valuable resources in the form of manpower, arms, and geographical contiguity for military training and fortification.

While the diverse geopolitical bases of these varied resources called for multiple strategies and tactics in the struggle for Korean independence, the KPG emphasized diplomatic activities soon after its establishment. The Korean national liberation movement continued to revolve around the activities of the KPG until the mid-1920s (Kang, 1996, 2005). During this time, U.S.-based Koreans, who were strategically situated at the nexus of a complex web of geopolitical relations involving Korea, Japan, and the United States, emerged as vital actors in a diasporic movement that sought to free Korea from Japanese colonial rule. The KPG, however, was unable to develop a working consensus that could implement effective policies that addressed the multiple and diverse ideological and strategic perspectives to the liberation of Korea. By 1925, the socialist-oriented and armed struggle groups had completely withdrawn from the coalition government of the KPG, leaving the nationalist movement splintered into multiple competing factions (Kang, 1996, 2005; Lee, 1963). Nevertheless, the KPG and its embodiment of a new Korean nation based on republican principles remained important elements in the independence movement until the end of Japanese colonial rule in 1945 and became the precursor to the Republic of Korea established in 1948 (Zihn, 2002).

Although globalization processes, led by U.S. power and influence, situated Korean immigrants at the forefront of the nationalist movement, the same processes also ironically subordinated Korean voices and agency to a hegemonic American subjectivity that envisioned a new postwar international order modeled in its own image. In endorsing the United States as a global power and leader, Korean diasporic activities affirmed a thinly veiled imperialist drive that sought to propagate American political and cultural values abroad through economic investment and trade, missionary activity, and at times direct military force. By using the dynamics of Korean immigrant nationalism as an illustrative example, this chapter investigates the dialectical processes and consequences of diasporic political practices in globalization.

The Philadelphia Korean Congress, the Korean Independence Movement, and the "Globalizing of America"

Attended by nearly 200 delegates from Korean communities throughout North America and as far away as England and Ireland, the Korean Congress provided an opportunity for Korean immigrants to clarify and affirm their relationship to the recent events in the national independence movement. The presiding President of the Korean Congress, Philip Jaisohn, declared that neither the distant and remote location of the Provisional Government nor its absentee president Syngman Rhee, who was not in Shanghai but rather in attendance at the Korean Congress, should deter Koreans in the United States from supporting the new government. Jaisohn eloquently stated:

> It does not make any difference whether the President of the Provisional Government is in prison or whether he is in France; he may be in America; that does not make any difference . . . It does not make the government nonexistent, because it is not generally known where it is located. It is the will of the people that makes the government . . . If you read the history of this country [United States] when the Revolutionary War broke out, you will recall that the Government was not established in any one place, they were forced to move around. When the British chased them from one place, they moved their capital to another. They had a capital in Yorktown, and then they came to Philadelphia. That does not make the government illegal. As somebody has well expressed it in Korean, "the new Provisional Government of Korea is a

personification of the will of the people of Korea." It does not make any difference whether the Government is located in Manchuria, Philadelphia or Paris.
(Korean Congress, 1919, 27)

For Jaisohn and others at the Congress, the KPG represented the authentic
sovereign of the Korean nation, embodying the will and spirit of Koreans
not only in the homeland but also abroad as well. Another delegate, Henry
Chung, voiced similar views, asserting that the Provisional government was
part of a larger universal movement that represented all Koreans regardless of
class, gender, or religious beliefs. He also declared that the nationalist movement was an international one in that "every Korean both in and outside of
Korea is heart and soul back [sic] of this movement" (Ibid., 16). The Korean
Congress thus sought to establish Koreans in the United States as an integral
part of a diasporic political movement that was inextricably linked to their
compatriots in and out of their homeland.

In Jaisohn's impassioned speech about the location of the Provisional Government, he also made specific allusions to the American Revolution, whereby
he highlighted the similarities between the current situation facing the KPG
and the tumultuous beginnings of the American nation. Such comparisons
were a common rhetorical strategy among Korean nationalist leaders, who
perceived the creation of a new Korean nation-state akin to the birth of the
American nation-state, which had successfully liberated itself from colonial
rule. Referring to it as the "cradle of liberty," the very location of the Korean
Congress in Philadelphia even carried special symbolic significance for its
participants and observers. As home to the revolutionary government that
directed the war for independence from the British, the city of Philadelphia
was surely viewed as a particularly auspicious site for the christening of the
newly formed Republic of Korea (Ibid., 29).

Given these strong Americanizing tendencies, the Congress ceremoniously concluded on the third day of sessions with all of its participants joining
together in parade formation, headed by a platoon of mounted reserves and
a band. With participants carrying both Korean and American flags, the parade marched from the site of the Congress to Independence Hall. The parade
ended with all participants gathering in the room where the U.S. Declaration
of Independence and Constitution were both signed. Upon the final assembly
of all participants, KPG President Syngman Rhee read aloud the Korean Declaration of Independence and announced the establishment of the Provisional
Government of the Republic of Korea. The body of delegates enthusiastically

endorsed the Declaration of Independence and the newly formed Korean nation-state with three loud cheers for the Republic of Korea, followed by another boisterous three cheers for the United States (Ibid., 79–82).

The development of such forms of diasporic nationalism occurred within the processes of globalization driven by U.S. power and influence. Like many other peoples suffering under the yoke of colonialism, Koreans demanded immediate independence from the Japanese shortly after U.S. President Woodrow Wilson's Fourteen Points speech. In his famous speech presented before the U.S. Congress in January 1918, Wilson outlined the basic principles of his peace settlement plan for the end of World War I in which he championed the right of national self-determination for colonized peoples (DeConde, 1992; Iriye, 1993; Lauren, 1986).

The anti-imperialist implications embedded in Wilson's speech were accompanied by changing geopolitical circumstances, which further heightened the stature of the United States in the eyes of many colonized peoples around the world. As World War I came to an end in 1918, the American nation had emerged as the most dominant economic and military power in the world. Three years of American neutrality from the war in Europe and a government-sponsored program of war preparedness had enabled the United States to amass enormous economic wealth and to bolster its military strength to the most powerful in the world. Thus, at the eve of America's entry into World War I in 1917, the United States was in a prime position to supplant Europe as the world's premier leader. America's emergent leadership in global affairs, or what distinguished U.S. diplomatic and cultural historian Akira Iriye (1993) calls the "globalizing of America," would become further solidified in the decades following World War I.

The globalizing influence of Wilson's internationalism was clearly visible in the nationalist activities exhibited during the March First movement in Korea and the formation of the KPG in Shanghai. The Korean Congress in Philadelphia also reflected an astute awareness of the discourse of Wilsonian democracy. With the globalizing of America following World War I, the adoption and promotion of American democratic values displayed during the Korean Congress became central rhetorical and political strategies for the Korean independence movement. In the process, Koreans in the United States came to hold privileged positions, ideologically and organizationally, within the overall nationalist movement.

While the Congress successfully mobilized loyalty and support among Koreans in the diaspora, its primary objective was to draw international attention to Korean struggles for independence from Japanese colonial rule. Activities throughout the Korean Congress unabashedly championed American democracy and Christianity and the Korean people's ardent commitment to those ideals and values. However, the Philadelphia Korean Congress was simply more than uncritical, celebratory exaltations of American political values and ideals. Rather the proceedings indicated a high degree of political sophistication among the Korean participants as they demonstrated a critical and incisive engagement with the meanings and uses of American power in the new postwar world.

Korean leaders at the Korean Congress understood very well that international support, especially from the United States, was crucial to their quest for the independence of their homeland. In seeking to garner U.S. support, the Korean Congress consciously directed its energies toward influencing American public opinion regarding Japanese imperialism and Korean independence. Accordingly, most of the speeches and discussions at the Congress were in English. Written transcripts of the Congress proceedings were also published and distributed to the American public. Furthermore, prominent American religious and academic figures from the Philadelphia area were invited to speak on behalf of Korean independence at the Congress, all of whom expressed their sympathy and support for the Korean people's desire for freedom while denouncing Japan's motives and actions as tyrannical. The guest speakers also eulogized American values of democracy, freedom, and Christianity. As champions of justice and liberty, they asserted that the United States had a moral obligation to aid Korea in its emergent role as a global leader.

One of the first actions of the Korean Congress was to draft "An Appeal to America," in which Korean delegates at the Congress, claiming to represent the eighteen million Koreans living in Korea, requested American "support and sympathy because we know you love justice; you also fought for liberty and democracy, and you stand for Christianity and humanity. Our cause is a just one before the laws of God and man. Our aim is freedom from militaristic autocracy; our object is democracy for Asia; our hope is universal Christianity" (Korean Congress, 29–30). Clearly, references to Christianity were a salient aspect of the appeal. American Protestant missionaries had been instrumental in promoting Korean emigration to Hawaii at the turn of the twentieth century (Patterson, 1988). Moreover, the majority of Koreans residing in the United States were recent Christian converts themselves, and many had developed strong personal ties to Americans associated with Protestant missionaries in and out of Korea. Not surprisingly then, Korean nationalist appeals for U.S. support were often imbued with Christian ideals and imagery as exhibited in much of the proceedings of the Korean Congress.

At the same time, the conspicuous evocation of Christianity throughout the Congress also represented an important rhetorical and political tactic for Korean nationalists as they sought to frame Korean subjugation under the Japanese as a moral, humanitarian issue that demanded immediate international attention. In his insightful study of exile politics, political scientist Yossi Shain (1989) explains that exile groups often seek to attract international support for their struggles by "latching onto issues that the global international community finds symbolically resonant" (Shain, 27). Christian ideology certainly resonated with the universalistic moral imperatives associated with the prevailing Wilsonian discourse. In seeking U.S. sympathy for Korean independence, the Congress proceedings extensively chronicled Japan's brutal repression of the March First movement in which the Korean people had peacefully declared en masse their right to national self-determination. In this light, the active involvement of Korean Protestants in the nationwide demonstrations was undeniable. For instance, almost half, sixteen, of the thirty-three signers of the Korean Declaration of Independence were Christians, many of whom were Protestant pastors. Christian churches throughout Korea also provided essential networks in helping to plan and coordinate the uprising on such a massive scale. Moreover, a disproportionately large number of Korean Christians were among those arrested in the Japanese suppression of the protests. According to a Japanese military police report published at the end of 1919, more than 17 percent of the 19,525 persons arrested were Korean Protestants, who made up only 1 percent of the total Korean population in 1919 (Lee, 2000, 139; U.S. National Archives, 1919a). By appealing to Christian sensibilities, the Congress sought to make the struggle for Korean independence relevant and meaningful to the American people. As a result, the quest for Korean independence would not be perceived as just a "Korean" issue, but one based on universal humanitarian values represented by Christian principles, thereby highlighting the congruities between American and Korean interests and goals. In essence, Christianity provided moral justification for Korean independence.

Besides trying to sway American public opinion in favor of Korean independence, the Korean Congress also attempted to garner support from the U.S. government. In addition to appealing on moral grounds, the Congress also underscored the legal claims to Korean independence. In particular,

"An Appeal to America" directed attention to the 1882 Treaty of Amity between the national governments of the United States and Korea. Korean leaders maintained that they were justified in seeking assistance from the United States based on Article I of the Treaty, which read: "If other powers deal unjustly or oppressively with either government, the other will exert their good offices, on being informed of the case, to bring about an amicable arrangement, thus showing their friendly feelings" (Korean Congress, 30). With this in mind, leaders devoted a significant portion of the proceedings at the Congress to presenting the "true facts" of the oppressive nature of Japan's actions in Korea. Under the stipulations of the Treaty of Amity, the Congress claimed that the U.S. government was therefore obligated to uphold its responsibilities in aiding Korea.

Jaisohn and other leaders at the Congress believed the American government had already established official recognition of Korean sovereignty and its territorial integrity in the 1882 treaty agreement between the two nations. Accordingly, they asserted that the KPG's first order of action was to obtain official diplomatic recognition from the United States based on the terms of the international treaty (Ibid., 26–27). For nationalist leaders, the creation of the KPG in Shanghai was a major step in institutionalizing a sovereign political entity that could be considered a legitimate actor within the global community of nation-states. Diplomatic recognition of the KPG from a powerful sovereign government, such as the United States, would provide bona fide acknowledgment and validation of the KPG's claims to authority and power. Korean nationalists keenly understood that external recognition from other sovereign states was instrumental to the nation-state's authority and legitimacy. This understanding of the workings of an international system based on nation-states profoundly shaped the strategies and tactics of the Korean Congress and the overall independence movement.

"This is not old Korea; this is new Korea": Korean Nationalism and American Democracy

For Koreans throughout the diaspora, the establishment of the KPG following the March First uprising represented the beginnings of a new Korean nation. American political ideals and values were unequivocally central to the diasporic visions of this new nation. Inspired by the American Declaration of Independence and the doctrine of self-determination espoused in Woodrow Wilson's Fourteen Points, the Korean Declaration of Independence announced the birth of a new Korea in which "the old world of force has gone and out of the travail of the past a new world of righteousness and truth has been born" (Ibid., 80–82). The indelible imprint of U.S. political values and ideals was further evinced in the organizational structure of the KPG, which was conceived as a democratic republic. The establishment of the KPG, in fact, marked a sharp departure in the political history of Korea. Rather than seeking to restore the four-thousand-year old monarchy, Korean nationalist leaders endeavored to create a new democratic republic, modeled specifically after the United States (Lee, 1984, 344–45).

In its appeals for support from the international community, the Korean Congress sought to showcase the emergence of this new political consciousness. The delegates at the Congress drafted another lengthy resolution entitled "Aims and Aspirations of the Koreans" to articulate formally the guiding principles of the Korean independence movement. Though the Congress did not make any governmental claims to state power, Koreans in the United States hoped that "Aims and Aspirations of the Koreans" would provide a platform for legitimizing their authority in the diaspora to speak on behalf of the KPG and their compatriots in and out of their homeland. The resolution therefore carried great significance for the participants at the Congress because they believed it to be an official statement to the world of what the Korean people stood for. Philip Jaisohn emphasized this significance in declaring that "The very life of the whole nation has to depend on the questions embodied in this resolution" (Korean Congress, 36). Thus, the "Aims and Aspirations of the Koreans" not only served as a propaganda vehicle for the independence movement but also represented a political blueprint for an independent Korea. Jaisohn stated that a great number of the participants at the Congress would one day play a leading part in the reconstruction of Korea. Consequently, the ideas contained in the resolution were vital to the future of the Korean nation because they would likely be included in the national Constitution of a free and independent Korea (Ibid., 35). Indeed, many of the provisions in the Constitution of the KPG were incorporated directly into the Republic of Korea Constitution in July 1948 (Zihn, 2002, 66).

As part of the Congress's strategy to attract international attention and support for the cause of Korean independence while simultaneously affirming the authority of the Korean diaspora to lead the nation, "Aims and Aspirations of Koreans" also highlighted the Korean people's desire for freedom and a democratic form of government. The Congress sought to counter prevalent

Japanese propaganda that portrayed Koreans as incapable of self-rule. Due to the American public's general lack of knowledge about Korea, Jaisohn expressed his concern that Americans would likely question the Korean people's capacity to govern themselves. He then proceeded to extol Korean immigrants in Hawaii as exemplars of Korea's ability for self-government. He explained that the immigrants to Hawaii were not among the "elite class of Koreans," but rather laborers from rural areas of Korea "without any appreciable education." Despite their humble backgrounds, Jaisohn described how Koreans in Hawaii had successfully created and maintained numerous schools, churches, and benevolent organizations. They managed to raise large sums of money to support these institutions and their activities despite their meager earnings. Jaisohn also pointed out that they had already contributed a large amount of money for the cause of independence, totaling over $80,000 in bonds. He concluded that Koreans in Hawaii were "thoroughly democratic, religious and sincere in their mode of life and strictly obedient to the laws of the land." Jaisohn asserted that Korean immigrants were imbued with the values and spirit associated with American democracy and Christianity and thus stood as living proof of the Korean people's desire and propensity for self-rule (Korean Congress, 14–17). The Korean Congress attempted to highlight the prominence of Koreans in the United States as carriers of an American model of democracy that could be propagated abroad.

In this light, the Korean Congress was in itself a public performance of democratic decision-making processes. Before the first session, the delegates formally elected Philip Jaisohn to preside over the Congress proceedings. In his capacity as president, Jaisohn ceremoniously appointed delegates to serve on various committees, each of which were responsible for drafting a set of resolutions such as the aforementioned "An Appeal to America" and "Aims and Aspirations of the Koreans." The drafts were then presented to the entire body of delegates, whereupon the floor was open to every member of the Congress for discussion, suggestions, and debate. After the initial round of discussions, Jaisohn presented a motion to adopt a particular resolution. An incident early in the Congress revealed the self-conscious efforts to display itself as a democratic decision-making body. In serving as a committee chair, KPG President Syngman Rhee offered a motion to adopt a resolution without the need for any amendments. Jaisohn immediately interrupted Rhee stating that the Congress must abide by democratic principles. He exclaimed to Rhee, "You do not want to take any important action unless you get the views of the people. We would like to get the views of this Congress, who represent their people. This is not old Korea; this is new Korea. We want to go by the will of the people, by the majority present." The delegates enthusiastically expressed their agreement with Jaisohn. Soon thereafter, a discussion of the resolution commenced, after which the resolution was adopted with the unanimous approval of all in attendance (Ibid., 30–31). Aware that international patronage was integral to the authority of the Korean nation-state, leaders at the Philadelphia Korean Congress invested much energy into such symbolic activities in order to project a strong image of the diaspora's ability to represent and lead the new Korean nation.

Korean Diasporic Politics and the American "Missionary Mind"

The 1919 Philadelphia Korean Congress ushered in a period of extensive lobbying activities in the United States for Korean independence. Before the concluding ceremonies at the Congress, Philip Jaisohn announced plans for the opening of the Korean Information Bureau in Philadelphia that would carry on the work of publicizing and disseminating information about the Korean cause of independence (Ibid., 70–71). The diplomatic recognition of the KPG also continued as a focal point for diasporic political activities. Shortly after the Philadelphia Korean Congress, KPG President Syngman Rhee established the Korean Commission in Washington DC in August 1919. Overseeing its daily activities from Washington, Rhee designated the Korean Commission to be the sole diplomatic arm of the KPG (U.S. National Archives, 1919b).

The Korean Congress also had a stimulating effect on influential segments of the American public to assist the Korean independence movement. Soon after the Congress, prominent members of Philadelphia's religious, academic, and social circles created the League of the Friends of Korea. Formed in Philadelphia on June 16, 1919, the League sought to increase public awareness about Korea's situation under Japanese rule and to generate American support for democracy and Christianity in East Asia. With strong links to American Protestant missionaries in Korea, the League declared in its founding statement that the United States had a moral obligation to uphold its principles of justice, equality, and freedom throughout the world. The League asserted that its goals were based solely on humanitarian concerns to end the persecution of Korean Christians. The founding statement stressed that the League did not seek to interfere politically in the affairs of Korea, Japan, or China. Rather their mission was one of publicizing Japanese atrocities in Korea (*Korea Review*, 1919, 12–13).

The League coordinated its mission to publicize the plight of the Korean people with the Korean Information Bureau. Together, the two organizations published a monthly publication entitled the *Korea Review,* edited by Philip Jaisohn. The *Korea Review* declared itself the only English-language publication dedicated to covering political affairs in Korea, China and Japan. As the official organ of the League of Friends, the *Korea Review* published numerous articles and reports written by American missionaries that documented Japan's harsh treatment of Koreans. The *Review* also informed its readers of the activities of the League and the creation of new chapters around the country. The *Review* quickly found a sizable readership, revealing the American public's growing interest in the Korean political situation. By June 1920, the *Korea Review* reported that a total of eighteen branches of the League of the Friends of Korea had been established from Boston to San Francisco with a membership of ten thousand (*Korea Review,* 1920, 18).

Besides documenting missionary activities in Korea and elsewhere in East Asia, the *Korea Review* also reported on developments within the Korean independence movement in both Korea and abroad. Typical articles included updates on the status and activities of the KPG in China and columns such as the "Washington News" and the "Students' Corner" that covered nationalist activities among Koreans in the United States. Additionally, the *Review* provided a forum for nationalist leaders such as Philip Jaisohn, Syngman Rhee, and Henry Chung to reach out to a broader English-speaking audience. All three men traveled around America lecturing at schools and churches about Korea's plight under Japanese colonial rule and the need for U.S. assistance. Their writings and lectures reflected the views voiced at the Korean Congress, which championed American democracy and Christianity. Often providing astute analyses of the political situation in East Asia, contributors to the *Korea Review* asserted that U.S. political, religious, and commercial interests in Asia all hinged on the "Korean Question." They argued that peace and stability throughout East Asia was completely contingent on a free Korea. An occupied Korea provided an open entryway for the expansion of Japanese imperialism into the Asian mainland, thereby threatening another global conflict.

The creation of both the League of Friends and the *Korea Review* revealed the extent to which American missionaries figured so prominently in the Korean cause following the March First uprising. Since Japan's annexation of Korea in 1910, American missionary groups had maintained a strict policy of political neutrality in Korea to prevent political partisanship from affecting their evangelical endeavors. Japan's violent repression of the peaceful March

First demonstrations, however, brought their nonpartisan stance into serious question. Many missionaries witnessed firsthand the savage beating, torture, and killing of countless Korean civilians by the Japanese. Moreover, Korean Christians suffered especially harsh treatment at the hands of the Japanese, who were convinced that American missionaries had instigated the demonstrations.[4] Failing to persuade Japanese officials to discontinue the use of violent tactics against the Korean people, American missionaries refused to remain passive onlookers to Japan's policies. Asserting what they called "no neutrality for brutality," missionary groups began an extensive campaign to document and disclose Japanese acts of violence and cruelty in Korea (U.S. National Archives, 1919a). Aware that the Japanese government was extremely sensitive to international opinion, missionaries believed that the only recourse available to them was to publicize Japan's actions in Korea in the hopes that the court of world opinion would bring pressure upon Japan to stop its violent policies and methods.[5]

In response to the deluge of missionary reports of Japanese atrocities in Korea pouring into an array of religious, government, and media agencies in the United States, the Federal Council of Churches of Christ in America, the most influential voice of the American Protestant establishment at large, formed the Commission on Relations with the Orient in July 1919. After meticulously reviewing some one thousand pages of documents received from Korea, the Commission carefully compiled an assortment of reports, personal letters, and eyewitness affidavits from Korea, all of which described confirmed incidents of unwarranted brutality and extreme violence inflicted upon the Korean people by the Japanese. The compilation of documents was published as a lengthy 125-page report entitled *The Korean Situation: Authentic Accounts of Recent Events by Eye Witnesses*. Espousing political neutrality on the question of Korean independence, the report asserted that it only intended to bring public attention to the widespread prevalence of Japanese violence against the Korean people in the hopes that "every possible influence may be brought to bear" in ceasing the "brutality, torture, inhuman treatment, religious persecutions, and massacres" in Korea. The missionary report further stated the "need for a sound and enlightened public opinion here in America . . . to secure justice and fair dealing in Korea" (Commission on Relations with the Orient, 1919, 6).

Poised as objective experts on East Asian matters, American Protestant missionary organizations, such as the Federal Council of Churches and the League of Friends, were, in fact, uniquely situated to influence foreign policy and public opinion makers in America. Culminating in the presidency of Woodrow Wilson, American missionaries played prominent roles in American foreign policy issues regarding East Asia. Preoccupied with events in Europe, American attitudes toward East Asian affairs were marked by a general indifference during much of the second decade of the twentieth century. In *The Missionary Mind and American East Asia Foreign Policy, 1911–1915,* James Reed (1983) persuasively argues that a high degree of collective ignorance on East Asian matters permeated the circles of the American foreign policy opinion leadership. In this vacuum, Reed asserts that American missionaries came to play a vital and decisive role in shaping U.S. foreign policy opinions about East Asia. In contrast to the American foreign policy elite, Protestant missionaries had much firsthand knowledge of, and experience in, East Asian affairs. Consequently, the American foreign policy opinion leadership in the United States often consulted with what Reed called the "missionary mind" in formulating positions and policies pertaining to East Asia (1983, 41–105). Emerging as public authorities on Asia, American Protestant missionaries became the principal source of information about the region not only for government officials but for the general American public as well (Thomson, Stanley, and Perry, 1981).

American missionary activities on behalf of Korea did indeed have a discernable effect on American public opinion about Korea's plight under the Japanese. Soon after publication of *The Korean Situation,* articles sympathetic to Korea began to fill the pages of mainstream publications. For instance, on July 13, 1919, only one day after the release of *The Korean Situation,* the *New York Times* printed an article about the missionary report including excerpts from it. Similarly, the *Literary Digest* published portions of *The Korean Situation* in its July 26 issue with additional pieces about Japanese rule in Korea appearing in subsequent issues. In the ensuing months, articles in support of Korea and critical of Japan were published in *Current Opinion, Public, World Outlook,* the *Nation, Missionary Review,* the *North American Review,* and *Current History* (Baldwin, 1969, 150). Additionally, American newspapers throughout the nation printed numerous articles and editorials about Japanese actions in Korea and the Korean struggle for independence. According to one scholarly account, approximately 9,700 editorials sympathetic to the Korean cause appeared in American newspapers and periodicals between 1919 and 1921, while only fifty pro-Japanese articles were published during the same period (Kim, 1971, 132–33).

Missionary lobbying efforts had a decided impact on U.S. policymakers as well. In deliberating on the "Korean Question" as part of heated debates surrounding U.S. involvement in the League of Nations, the U.S. Congress invariably turned to the American "missionary mind." On July 15, Senator George Norris of Nebraska discussed at length the case of Korea before the U.S. Senate. Quoting extensively from the accounts of Japanese brutality reprinted in the recent *New York Times* article about *The Korean Situation,* Norris forcefully argued that Japan, if unchecked, would inevitably extend its expansionist policies and violent tactics onto the Asian continent (*Congressional Record* 1919a, 2594). Though he avoided directly addressing the issue of Korean independence, Norris insisted that the situation in Korea was therefore vital to collective efforts for international peace and stability. The senator from Nebraska concluded with a request that the *New York Times* article be included into the *Congressional Record,* which drew no objections (Ibid., 2594–97). Two days later on July 17, Senator William McCormick of Maryland received unanimous consent of the Senate to have the entire volume of *The Korean Situation* entered into the *Congressional Record* for future reference (Ibid., 2697).

On August 8, 1919, Senator Selden Spencer of Missouri, an ardent supporter of the Korean cause for independence, addressed the Senate, offering additional evidence that he believed demonstrated the need for U.S. assistance to Korea. Spencer presented a series of letters from the distinguished American missionary Homer Hulbert, who had served as Special Envoy to Korea's King Kojong in 1905. Hulbert reviewed Japan's policies toward Korea that had culminated in a protectorate agreement in 1905, which effectively transferred Korean sovereignty to Japan. In recounting the recent history of Japan's relations with Korea, Hulbert asserted that the Japanese protectorate over Korea in 1905 was illegitimate with no legal authority. He described in detail his attempts to deliver in person letters from the Korean king to U.S. President Theodore Roosevelt at the 1905 Treaty of Portsmouth negotiations, which officially ended the Russo-Japanese War on terms favorable to the victorious Japanese. Hulbert explained that these letters personally written by the Korean monarch himself revealed that Japan had seized control over Korea under the threat of direct military force and pleaded for U.S. intervention based on its 1882 treaty agreement with Korea. According to Hulbert, these letters therefore provided incontrovertible evidence against Japan's claims that the Korean government had voluntarily surrendered its national sovereignty to Japan. Hulbert believed that the Japanese government, aware of his intentions, had deliberately prevented him from meeting with President Roosevelt, who presided over the treaty negotiations at Portsmouth in 1905. Arguing that these actions by the Japanese government consisted of a carefully orchestrated conspiracy to conceal the true nature of Japan's belligerent actions, Hulbert concluded that the Japanese occupation of Korea had violated fundamental tenets of international law and therefore should not be recognized by the United States, irrespective of Japan's claims to the contrary (*Congressional Record* 1919b, 3924–26).[6]

Between June and December 1919, the U.S. Congress was presented with a sizable body of information and testimony regarding Korea's plight under Japanese colonialism, filling some sixty-four pages of the *Congressional Record*. Nevertheless, the U.S. Congress responded cautiously to the calls to aid the Korean cause. On October 1, 1919, Senator James Phelan of California introduced Senate Resolution 200, which was referred to the Committee on Foreign Relations, stating that the "Senate of the U.S. expresses its sympathies with the aspirations of the Korean people for a government of their own choice" (*Congressional Record* 1919c, 6172). On October 24, 1919, Representative William Mason of Illinois introduced an identical resolution, House Resolution 359 (Ibid., 7476). The carefully worded resolutions represented formal expressions of friendship toward the KPG, but fell far short of official recognition of the newly formed Korean government or any promise for future governmental action on behalf of Korean independence. As primarily symbolic gestures of nominal support, neither resolution moved beyond the deliberations of the Committees on Foreign Relations and Foreign Affairs. The actions of the U.S. Congress made it clear that government officials would not call for any dramatic changes to U.S. foreign policies concerning relations with Korea and Japan. However, the lobbying efforts of American missionary groups did generate sufficient publicity to draw the attention of policymakers in Washington DC, who devoted considerable time in deliberating on the Korean situation. After 1919, U.S. government officials, for the first time, were speaking openly against Japan's occupation of Korea.

The bureaucratic authority of the American missionary mind provided opportunities for Korean nationalists in the United States to create political spaces for themselves that greatly increased their overall visibility and prominence. By actively promoting homeland-related issues in a variety of arenas within the U.S. polity, Koreans emerged as a distinct political presence within the United States. Though Korean immigrants were largely excluded from formal political processes in the United States as aliens ineligible for citizenship, they managed to exert a viable foreign policy voice in the U.S. polity as their activities generated widespread discussions and debate among private citizens and government officials about U.S. policies toward Korea and Japan.

American missionary specialized expertise and involvement in Korean affairs, however, had a peculiar outcome for Korean nationalists. Missionary groups held an abiding faith in the moral responsibilities of America's moral leadership in the world. Guided by these convictions, they stressed the U.S. government's obligation to uphold its principles of democracy, liberty, and Christianity in Korea. In the process, Korean democracy became equated with Korean Christianity for many Koreans and Americans alike. With its direct links to American forms of democracy and Christianity, this formulation elicited some supportive responses from the American public and U.S. government officials. However, it also ironically effaced Korean political agency. This irony was particularly evident in the glaring absence of Korean immigrant figures or perspectives on the Korean situation throughout the U.S. Congressional hearings in the weeks and months following the Korean Congress. The conflation of Korean democracy with Korean Christianity ended up privileging the perspectives and experiences of American missionaries, who emphasized publicizing Japanese atrocities and brutality in Korea in their demands for an end to Japan's policies of violence and terror. In the process, the voices of Korean diasporic leadership conspicuously disappeared from the lobbying activities conducted before American government officials. Ironically then, the concerns and demands of American missionaries came to overshadow the nationalists' basic goal of Korean independence. The close alliance with American missionaries ultimately eclipsed Korean voices under the shadow of U.S. political hegemony.

In advocating changes in U.S. foreign policies, missionaries, along with other Progressives, believed that reform should occur on the international front as well as within the domestic arena. Indeed, missionary support for Korean struggles against the Japanese was consonant with the crusading zeal of Wilsonian internationalism that emphasized self-determination, pacifism, and the protection of the exploitation of the weak by stronger nations. Although both ideological models were rooted in universalistic rhetoric and principles, they were nonetheless imbued with a strong sense of an exceptionalist American nationalism that sought to propagate American political and cultural values at home and abroad. For missionary groups and American foreign policy makers alike, global well-being and American leadership went hand in hand. American missionary involvement in Korean affairs ultimately served to advance the expansion of American domestic and foreign power, helping to inaugurate the globalizing of America at the end of World War I.

Conclusion

The year 1919 marked a decisive moment in the development of Korean diasporic nationalism. As a result of Japan's violent suppression of the 1919 March First movement in Korea, it was clear that nationalist activities would have to be carried out from abroad. Shortly after the March uprising, nationalist leaders established the KPG in China. At the same time, the U.S. polity emerged as a key arena for the articulation of transnational practices associated with the project of Korean nation building, inaugurated by the Philadelphia Korean Congress in April 1919. With the globalization of American political power, embodied in the form of Wilsonian internationalism, the U.S. component of the Korean diaspora became the key actor in charting the overall vision of a new Korean nation-state.

American Protestant missionaries played an instrumental role in facilitating the diasporic political mobilization of the Korean independence movement. American missionary involvement in Korean affairs reinforced the independence movement's emphasis on democratic processes and Christianity, which helped attract widespread attention from the American public and government officials. Moreover, the special status of American missionaries within the infrastructures of the U.S. nation-state provided Korean immigrants in the United States with some leverage to influence foreign policy issues through official and nonofficial channels of the U.S. polity.

In extending well beyond the national borders of a single nation-state, the transnational activities of both American missionaries and Korean nationalists countered territorially bounded notions of identity and political participation. At the same time, these activities were also fundamentally nation based as they were intrinsically grounded in territorialized constructions of the modern nation-state system. Though transcending national boundaries and borders, transnational and diasporic processes thus served to reify the hegemony of the nation-state in globalization, rather than undermining it.

Given these dialectical tensions, the close alliance between the Korean independence movement and American Protestant missionaries had a paradoxical effect for Korean nationalists. While the processes of U.S.-led global-ization enabled the Korean diaspora to achieve a certain degree of political agency, these processes also ironically subordinated Korean agency to the workings of American political hegemony. Most notably, Korean immigrant voices and participation within the U.S. polity were overshadowed by the in-terests and claims of American Protestant missionary groups, who were in-extricably linked to the institutional and ideological mechanisms associated with an expansionist American nationalist project that actively promoted the Americanization of the globe. Korean diasporic political activities thus helped to affirm and reinforce U.S. global hegemony and power during much of the twentieth century. In the end, Korean diasporic nationalism could never fully liberate itself from the power structures of imperialism that it so fervently struggled to free itself from.

Notes

This essay is a revised version of an article, "Inaugurating the American Century: The 1919 Philadelphia Korean Congress, Korean Diasporic Nationalism, and American Protestant Missionaries," published in the *Journal of American Ethnic History* 26, no. 1 (Fall 2006): 50–80. Copyright by the Immigration and Ethnic History Society. Re-printed by permission.

I would like to thank coeditors Rhacel Salazar Parreñas and Lok Siu for their criti-cal feedback on various drafts of this article. The anonymous reviewer for Stanford University Press also provided useful criticism.

1. My analysis of diasporic nationalism is broadly consistent with what Glick Schiller and Fouron (2001) call "long-distance nationalism" in their insightful study of Haitian immigrants in the United States. In formulating the theoretical premises of long-distance nationalism, the co-authors argue that the concept of diaspora does not adequately capture the transnational experiences of Haitian immigrants because dia-sporic groups make no claims to nation-state building. In contrast, this study suggests that the concept of diaspora is intrinsically founded upon a nation-based discourse to demonstrate that Korean diasporic nationalism was fundamentally a state-building project.

2. Large-scale Korean migrations to nearby Manchuria and Siberia occurred dur-ing the 1860s, much earlier than the organized mass emigration of laborers to Hawaii and the continental United States, which commenced in 1903 and came to a virtual halt in 1924. As a result, the Korean community in the United States, including Hawaii, remained much smaller in size than their counterparts in Manchuria and Siberia. While Koreans in the United States numbered no more than 10,000, Manchuria and Siberia were home to some 600,000 and 200,000 Koreans, respectively, by the 1920s.

In all, approximately 3.7 million Koreans, or roughly 12 percent of all Koreans, lived abroad by the end of Japanese rule in 1945.

3. Richard S. Kim, *Diasporic Dilemmas: Korean Immigrant Nationalism and Transnational Statemaking, 1903–1945* (manuscript in progress). It is currently under review with Oxford University Press.

4. Consistent with their disavowal of political involvement in Korea, American Protestant missionaries actually had little or no involvement in the planning or implementation of the March First uprising, contrary to Japan's vehement accusations. Most missionaries were, in fact, as surprised as the Japanese when the mass demonstrations first broke out on March 1.

5. The March First demonstrations, along with the subsequent negative international publicity surrounding Japan's use of excessive violence, did indeed force the Japanese government to modify its colonial policies in Korea. The new policies abandoned the repressive military police system and liberalized certain social and politi cal activities. These changes, however, were superficial, intended only to give the appearance of a more tolerant system of rule while actually tightening Japanese control over Korea.

6. Unbeknown to Hulbert as well as most members of the U.S. Congress at the time, the United States in 1905, under the initiative of President Theodore Roosevelt, had actually accommodated Japan's colonial ambitions in Korea. Prior to the beginning of the peace negotiations at Portsmouth, the United States and Japan had secretly signed the Taft-Katsura agreement, in which the United States agreed to Japanese control in Korea in return for Japanese acceptance of American dominance in Hawaii and the Philippines. American acquiescence to, and complicity in, Japan's control over Korea removed all remaining obstacles for Japan to assume full control over the Korean peninsula, precipitating Japan's declaration of Korea as a protectorate in November 1905 and formal annexation as a colony in 1910.

References

Baldwin, Frank P., Jr. 1969. "The March First Movement: Korean Challenge and Japanese Response." Ph.D. dissertation, Columbia University.

Ban, Byung Yool. 1996. "Korean Nationalist Activities in the Russian Far East and North Chientao (1905–1921)." Ph.D. dissertation, University of Hawaii.

Breuilly, John. 1982. *Nationalism and the State*. Manchester, UK: Manchester University Press.

Clifford, James. 1994. "Diasporas." *Cultural Anthropology* 9, no. 3: 302–336.

Cohen, Robin. 1997. *Global Diasporas: An Introduction*. Seattle: University of Washington Press.

Commission on Relations with the Orient. 1919. *The Korean Situation: Authentic Accounts of Recent Events by Eye Witnesses*. New York: Federal Council of the Churches of Christ in America.

Congressional Record: Proceedings and Debates of the 1st session of the 66th Congress. 1919a. Vol. 58, pt. 3. Washington, DC: Government Printing Office.

———. 1919b. Vol. 58, pt. 4. Washington, DC: Government Printing Office.

———. 1919c. Vol. 58, pt. 6. Washington, DC: Government Printing Office.

DeConde, Alexander. 1992. *Ethnicity, Race, and American Foreign Policy: A History.* Boston: Northeastern University Press.

Eckert, Carter J. et al. 1990. *Korea Old and New: A History.* Seoul, Korea: Ilchokak Publishers and Korea Institute, Harvard University.

Eckes, Alfred E. Jr., and Thomas W. Zeiller. 2003. *Globalization and the American Century.* Cambridge: Cambridge University Press.

Gabaccia, Donna R. 2000. *Italy's Many Diasporas.* Seattle: University of Washington Press.

Glick Schiller, Nina, and Georges Eugene Fouron. 2001. *Georges Woke Up Laughing: Long-Distance Nationalism and the Search for Home.* Durham, NC: Duke University Press.

Hobsbawm, Eric. 1962. *The Age of Revolution.* London: Weidenfeld and Nicolson.

Hong, Soon-ok. 1971. "The Legitimating of the Shanghai Provisional Government." *Korea Observer* 3:3 (April): 41–64.

Iriye, Akira. 1993. *The Globalizing of America, 1913–1945.* The Cambridge History of American Foreign Relations, ed. Warren I. Cohen, III. Cambridge: Cambridge University Press.

Kang, Man-gil. 1996. "The Nature and Process of the Korean Liberation Movement during the Japanese Colonial Period." *Korea Journal* 36:1 (Spring): 5–19.

———. 2005. *A History of Contemporary Korea* [Koch'yŏ ssŭn han'guk hyŏndaesa]. Folkston, Kent, UK: Global Oriental.

Kim, San, with Nym Wales. 1973. *Song of Ariran: A Korean Communist in the Chinese Revolution.* San Francisco: Ramparts Press.

Kim, Warren Won Yong. 1971. *Koreans in America.* Seoul: Po Chin Chai.

Korean Congress. 1919. *First Korean Congress.* Philadelphia: Korean Information Bureau.

Korea Review. 1919. "League of the Friends of Korea," 1:4 (June 1919): 12–13. Philadelphia: Korean Information Bureau.

Korea Review. 1920. "Be Informed on the Far East," 2:4 (June 1920): 18. Philadelphia: Korean Information Bureau.

Lauren, Paul Gordon. 1986. *Power and Prejudice: The Politics and Diplomacy of Racial Discrimination.* Boulder, CO: Westview Press.

Lee, Chong-sik. 1963. *The Politics of Korean Nationalism.* Berkeley: University of California Press.

Lee, Ki-baik. 1984. *A New History of Korea.* Cambridge: Harvard University Press.

Lee, Timothy S. 2000. "A Political Factor in the Rise of Protestantism in Korea: Protestantism and the 1919 March First Movement." *Church History* 69, no. 1: 116–142.

Marr, David G. 1981. *Vietnamese Tradition on Trial, 1920–1945*. Berkeley: University of California Press.

Ninkovich, Frank. 1999. *The Wilsonian Century: U.S. Foreign Policy since 1900*. Chicago: University of Chicago Press.

Patterson, Wayne. 1988. *The Korean Frontier in America: Immigration to Hawaii, 1896–1910*. Honolulu: University of Hawaii Press.

Reed, James. 1983. *The Missionary Mind and American East Asia Foreign Policy, 1911–1915*. Cambridge: Council on East Asian Studies, Harvard University.

Robinson, Michael Edson. 1988. *Cultural Nationalism in Colonial Korea, 1920–1925*. Seattle: University of Washington Press.

Rosenberg, Emily S. 1982. *Spreading the American Dream: American Economic and Cultural Expansion, 1890–1945*. New York: Hill and Wang.

Safran, William. 1991. "Diasporas in Modern Societies: Myths of Homeland and Return." *Diaspora* 1, no. 1 (Spring): 83–99.

Scalapino, Robert A., and Chong-sik Lee. 1972. *Communism in Korea—Part I: The Movement*. Berkeley: University of California Press.

Shain, Yossi. 1989. *The Frontier of Loyalty: Political Exiles in the Age of the Nation-State*. Middletown, CT: Wesleyan University Press.

——, ed. 1991. *Governments-in-Exile in Contemporary World Politics*. New York: Routledge.

Suh, Dae-Sook. 1967. *The Korean Communist Movement, 1918–1948*. Princeton, NJ: Princeton University Press.

Thomson, James C., Jr., Peter W. Stanley, and John Curtis Perry. *Sentimental Imperialists: The American Experience in East Asia*. New York: Harper & Row, 1981.

U.S. National Archives. 1919a. *Records of the Department of State Relating to Internal Affairs of Korea (Chosen), 1910–29*, reel 3, Decimal File 895.00/639.

——. 1919b. *Records of the War Department General and Special Staffs*, Record Group 165, Military Intelligence Division, Decimal File 1766–1391.

Zihn, Choi. 2002. "Early Korean Immigrants to America: Their Role in the Establishment of the Republic of Korea." *East Asian Review* 14:4 (Winter): 43–71.

9 When Minorities Migrate: The Racialization of the Japanese Brazilians in Brazil and Japan

Takeyuki (Gaku) Tsuda

SCHOLARS EMPHASIZING THE SITUATIONALIST APPROACH to ethnicity have stressed that ethnic identity, an individual's group identification based on awareness of cultural and/or racial characteristics, is not simply a matter of primordial attachments of shared descent but is constructed in response to varying social contexts. This is especially the case with diasporic subjects who negotiate multiple ethnicities as they are displaced by transnational migration to different societies and subjected to radically different local perceptions not only of their cultural characteristics, but of their racial features. Since the experience of race is ultimately based on socially relative perceptions of physical difference, various immigration scholars have documented how the same ethnic group can be racialized quite differently when they migrate to other societies. For instance, peoples of African descent from the Carribean and Latin America who were considered creole, mulatto, or mestiço back home are quite surprised when they migrate to the United States and are racialized as "black" and grouped together with African Americans (Basch, Schiller, and Blanc 1994; Charles 1992; Freeman 2000) (the category of black was used to refer only to people of very dark complexion in their homelands). In this manner, the experience of race is de-essentialized through the migratory process, causing immigrants to realize that their ethnicity, which seemed to be partly based on primordial physical characteristics, is contextually relative and subject to redefinition in a different society abroad.

This chapter examines the impact of different racial ideologies on the ethnic identities of transmigrants by examining the ethnic "return" migration of second and third generation Japanese Brazilians to Japan as unskilled foreign workers. The Japanese Brazilians began migrating to Japan in the late 1980s because of a severe economic crisis in Brazil coupled with a severe shortage of unskilled labor in the Japanese economy. Even though they are relatively well educated and mostly of middle-class background in Brazil, they still earn five to ten times their Brazilian salaries in Japan as factory workers. The return migration flow was enabled by an open Japanese immigration policy toward the *nikkeijin* (Japanese descendants born and raised abroad), which was based upon an assumption among Japanese government officials that the Brazilian nikkeijin would assimilate smoothly into Japanese society, providing much-needed immigrant labor without disrupting Japan's cherished ethnic homogeneity. Although most Japanese Brazilians migrate to Japan with intentions of working only for a couple of years and then quickly returning home with their savings, many have already brought over their families, and the process of long-term immigrant settlement has begun. Because a vast majority of them are of the second and third generations who were born and raised in Brazil, do not speak Japanese very well, and have become culturally Brazilianized to various degrees, they are ethnically marginalized in Japan despite their Japanese descent and have become the country's newest ethnic minority.

As their lives have increasingly become transnational in scope, the Brazilian nikkeijin have constructed multiple situated ethnic identities in the different racial contexts of Japan and Brazil. Like other transmigrants in the Asian diaspora, they do not assert a uniform ethnic identity (as "Japanese Brazilian") across the different countries in which they reside, but emphasize different sides of their dual identity depending on the local racial context in which they are embedded. Although they are racialized as "Japanese" in both Brazil and Japan, the cultural meanings attached to this category are quite different, causing the Japanese Brazilians to ironically feel ethnically "Japanese" in Brazil, but quite "Brazilian" in Japan. In Brazil, they tend to embrace their Japanese identities instead of insisting on their status as Brazilian nationals when they are ethnically differentiated by their Asian phenotype as *japonês* because of some of the positive stereotypes associated with this racial category. In contrast, when the Japanese Brazilians return-migrate to Japan, their racialization as Japanese becomes a means of assimilationist homogenization by the Japanese who expect them to be culturally Japanese because of their appearance. Since the nikkeijin are culturally Brazilianized and cannot meet such standards, they ethnically differentiate themselves from the Japanese by asserting their Brazilianness in order to avoid ethnic confusion and resist assimilationist Japanese pressures. In this manner, the different meanings attached to the same racial category can produce different processes of racialization among transmigrants in varying localities, causing them to develop different situated identities.

This chapter is based on over twenty months of intensive fieldwork and participant observation in the mid-1990s in both Japan and Brazil. Nine months were first spent in Brazil among two separate Japanese Brazilian communities in the cities of Porto Alegre (Rio Grande do Sul) and Ribeirão Preto (São Paulo). During my one-year stay in Japan, I conducted fieldwork in Kawasaki (Kanagawa-prefecture) and Oizumi/Ota cities (in Gunma-prefecture), where I worked for four intensive months as a participant observer in a large electrical appliance factory with Japanese Brazilian and Japanese workers. Close to one hundred in-depth interviews (in Portuguese and Japanese) were conducted with Japanese Brazilians and Japanese workers, residents, and employers, as well as local and national government officials.[1]

The Racial Essentialization of Japanese Ethnicity in Brazil

Racial Markers of Difference

Japanese emigration to Brazil began in 1908 and continued in significant numbers until the early 1960s. Many of the emigrants were farmers suffering from difficult conditions in Japan's rural areas, which were plagued by overpopulation, declining agricultural prices, increasing debt and unemployment, as well as harsh climatic conditions. Others were second and third sons who did not inherit land from their parents under the old Japanese household system and had limited economic opportunities. In addition to such factors that "pushed" the Japanese out of Japan, the expanding, labor-deficient Brazilian coffee plantation economy served as the necessary "pull" factor that drew them to Brazil.

As Brazil's oldest and by far largest Asian minority (population over 1.2 million), the Japanese Brazilians are now relatively well integrated in Brazilian society, both socioeconomically and culturally. Most of them live in large cities in the most economically developed states of São Paulo and Paraná and have become part of Brazil's middle class as professionals and business owners with educational levels and incomes that are considerably higher than the Brazilian average. Considerable cultural assimilation has also occurred among the second and third generations, most of whom do not speak Japanese very well or maintain Japanese customs at home.

Despite their high level of sociocultural integration however, the Japanese Brazilians continue to be racialized as a Japanese ethnic minority because of their distinctive Asian appearance. In Brazilian society, the nikkeijin are immediately recognizable because of their *traços orientais* (oriental features), which are seen as markedly different from those of whites, blacks, and mixed-descent mestiços of all types (cf. Maeyama 1984:455). Much attention is given by Brazilians to these phenotypic differences because of the high Brazilian sensitivity to racial characteristics, including slight differences in skin color.[2] Therefore, the Japanese Brazilians are always referred to as japonês by other Brazilians simply because of their facial features, not only in unfamiliar contexts when names are not known (such as in the streets, stores, and public areas) (cf. Maeyama 1984:448), but also when they are talked about among familiar acquaintances. Their distinctive racial appearance is much more prominent as an ethnic marker of Japaneseness in Brazil than for the Japanese Americans in the United States, where there are many Asian Americans of non-Japanese descent. As a result, an Asian phenotype does not denote Japanese ancestry as it usually does in Brazil, where most Asians are of Japanese descent.[3]

The experience of being racially identified as japonês is undoubtedly familiar to anyone of Japanese descent who has lived in Brazil. It happened to me for the first time a few days after I had arrived in Brazil. I was walking innocently down the street in downtown Porto Alegre (state of Rio Grande do Sul), when suddenly:

"Oi, japonês!" (Hey, Japanese!)

Startled, I turned around to find a Brazilian street vendor beckoning to me, trying to interest me in his goods.

"Só três mil cruzeiros, japonês," he was holding up a bag of apples. "Mais barato do que nas lojas." Realizing that he had caught my attention, he continued his upbeat sales pitch, telling me how fresh and delicious his apples were. I hesitated before the proper words in Portuguese came out.

"Não obrigado" (no thank you).

My hesitation was less the result of my still inadequate Portuguese than the way I had been addressed directly by my race. It was the first time in my life that I had been greeted by a stranger in such a manner.

I reached the downtown bus station where a row of buses waited, the open doors beckoning passengers inside. I checked the signs designating the various routes. My bus had not yet arrived. However, because I was still unfamiliar with the bus system, I approached the attendant to confirm that I was waiting at the right spot (and also to practice my Portuguese). After indicating that I had the correct bus stop, he gestured toward the bench.

"Espera aqui, japonês" (Wait here, Japanese).

There it was again. I was beginning to realize that this would be a common occurrence in Brazil. In the following days, I would experience it numerous times—strangers calling me japonês in public (sometimes for no apparent reason), store clerks referring to me as japonês, a pedestrian muttering "japonês" as I walked past, questions ending with the ethnic designation, japonês.

"You might as well get used to it," one of my Japanese Brazilian friends told me. "There are so few Japanese living in Porto Alegre that you have Brazilians here who have hardly ever seen a Japanese person."

Of course, children are merciless in this regard since they react with an unrefined spontaneity that adults have politely learned to suppress. I will never forget the little Brazilian boy who grabbed his mother's skirt as he pointed to me as I walked past and said, "Mommy, Mommy. Look! A japonês!" Nor will I ever forget the group of smiling Brazilian children who surrounded me on the street and greeted me with every Japanese word they knew. *Sayonara, arigato.*

The other experience that remains vividly in my mind was a particular bus ride I took from downtown Porto Alegre. A little girl who sat next to her mother across from me spent most of the bus ride staring at me, her large and cute eyes studying my features intently. I shifted uncomfortably in my seat, averted my eyes for awhile, then glanced back at her. The stare continued. After a few minutes, I realized that it was hopeless—there was no way I could shake her probing eyes off of me. My Japanese ethnicity was being located and essentialized by the silent gaze of a mere child! Yet, the gaze was more powerful and meaningful for me than any utterance. I could easily fill the absence of words with my own imagination: "So, this is what a Japanese looks like. The slanted eyes, the flat face, the small nose. How intriguing." Even after I got off the bus, the gaze seemed to follow me relentlessly. In contrast to children, the ethnic curiosity is expressed in a more muted form among adults as concerns for decorum intervene and the novelty wears off after numerous ethnic encounters. Yet, the gaze was always there, making me acutely aware of my peculiar Japanese racial appearance that clearly differentiated me from the surrounding blend of Brazilian faces.

In fact, this racial designation as japonês is not simply confined to places like Porto Alegre where the sight of a Japanese descendant is quite rare. It prevails throughout Brazil, including the city of São Paulo, which has the highest concentration of Japanese Brazilians in the country. Of course, in such areas it is less frequent and more of a confirmation of ethnic difference than a reaction to ethnic novelty. Nonetheless, when ethnic appellations are based on physiognomy, it inscribes a racially constituted ethnic awareness (cf. Fanon 1967:109–12). Although my distinctive Asian appearance had never been a real focus of attention in the United States, my race was suddenly thrust into my self-consciousness in Brazil, becoming a prominent component of my Japanese ethnic identity.

Was it ethnic prejudice? For a moment, I was reminded of Frantz Fanon's experience in France as a black man from Martinique:

"Look, a Negro!" It was an external stimulus that flicked over me as I passed by. I made a tight smile.

"Look, a Negro!" It was true. It amused me.

"Look, a Negro!" The circle was drawing a bit tighter. I made no secret of my amusement.

"Mama, see the Negro! I'm frightened!" . . . Now they were beginning to be afraid of me. I made up my mind to laugh myself to tears, but laughter had become impossible.

I subjected myself to an objective examination, I discovered my blackness, my ethnic characteristics; and I was battered down by tom-toms, cannibalism, intellectual deficiency, fetishism, racial defects, slave-ships . . .

What was it? Color prejudice. (1967:111–12, 118)

Of course, the issue is one of subjective interpretation. The external ethnic stimulus I received in Brazil was somewhat similar, but unlike Fanon I was not ethnically burdened by a historical legacy of colonialism, exploitation, and slavery at the hands of the Brazilians. Even during my first week in Brazil, I had fully realized that Japaneseness did not have the negative connotations that blackness had in France for Fanon. For me, the Brazilian insistence on racially inscribing me as japonês was simply a recognition of *diferença* and not a prejudicial reaction in which difference is negatively perceived (cf. Park 1999:682). At worst, there may have been a tint of ridicule or banter at times, but never overt denigration or dislike. In general, I was much more amused than offended. After awhile, it became routine, expected.

Yet, the emphasis placed on racial difference in Brazil is not always this subtle. I soon realized that certain Brazilians pull their eyes upwards with their fingers to indicate the *olhos puxados* (slanted eyes, or literally "pulled eyes") of the Japanese Brazilians. However, this ethnic gesture is not necessarily intended as an affront directed at the nikkeijin, but as simply an amusing commentary on their different physiognomy. In contrast to the United States, where the gesture is considered to be an ethnic insult, when it was used in Brazil to refer to people or things Japanese, the context was basically neutral or playful. One of the most typical examples I observed was when my landlady in Riberão Preto (state of São Paulo) described the children of her Japanese Brazilian friend to an acquaintance. "Their father is Brazilian, but they still look very Japanese," she remarked, pulling her eyes up with her fingers for emphasis. I have also seen the gesture used when referring to products made by the Japanese. The worst case that I encountered was actually personally solicited—one of my many attempts to gather derogatory ethnic humor about the Japanese Brazilians. "Why do the japonês have eyes like this?" my Brazilian friend asked, repeating the now familiar gesture. "Because they spend all their time frying pot-stickers."

The peculiar Japanese physiognomy has even been conveniently appropriated by Brazilian commercials. A television ad for Toshiba products ends with a magnifying glass passing over the eyes of a Japanese face. "Abre os olhos" (Open the eyes), the ad exhorts. The commercial undoubtedly pokes fun at the Japanese, but seemingly has a double connotation which asks consumers to open their eyes to the quality of Japanese products. Again, local context is everything, making an unmitigated ethnic insult in one society a good-humored advertising gimmick in another.

My Japanese Brazilian informants seemed to generally share my interpretation of such ethnic experiences in Brazil. In fact, most were very accustomed to their constant racial designation as japonês in Brazil, whether by appellation or gesture, and very few were bothered by it.[4] "It's simply how people behave here in Brazil," one nikkeijin man explained. "And it happens to other ethnic groups as well. Brazilians frequently say, 'Hey, black! Hey, German!' Or 'Hey, Jew!'" A few mentioned that they would be offended if they were called "Jap," but most claimed it did not happen.

Others even read positive meanings into the experience. "My kids came home from school one day somewhat bothered that they are always called japonês by the other kids," one Japanese Brazilian mother remarked. "I told them that the Brazilians are not making fun of them. I told them that being Japanese is a source of pride. The Japanese are respected and admired in Brazil."

Even the slanted eyes gesture was taken in stride as simply ethnic humor. "It's just a joke. No one takes it seriously," one man expressed a common opinion. It was quite remarkable that only one informant was personally offended by the gesture, claiming that behind the jovial exterior was a serious attempt to ridicule the funny appearance of the Japanese. Yet, even she admitted that the Brazilian tendency to express ethnic prejudice in a jocular manner takes much of the bite out of ethnic discrimination in Brazil.

Despite the apparent lack of pejorative connotations, the tendency among mainstream Brazilians to single out the Brazilian nikkeijin by their race essentializes them as an ethnically different, Japanese minority. As some Japanese Brazilians mention, regardless of how culturally Brazilian they may become, they will be forever marked as *japonês* because of their distinctive physical appearance (see also Reichl 1995:47). "Even if we become completely Brazilian and act as Brazilian as possible, we will always be seen by Brazilians as Japanese because of our faces. There's no way to avoid this," a young Japanese Brazilian student said, a hint of resignation in his voice. "We can go to a soccer game and cheer on our favorite São Paulo team, or even dance samba in the streets, and in the midst of it, someone will say, 'Oi, japonês.'"

Since minority identities always imply a certain amount of ethnic marginalization, by racially essentializing the Japanese Brazilians as Japanese, many Brazilians partake in a discourse of ethnic exclusion (whether inadvertently or not). Despite the cultural assimilation of the Japanese Brazilians in Brazil, mainstream Brazilians continue to find it difficult to conceptualize them as part of majority society because they do not belong to one of the three "founding" races of the Brazilian nation (white, black, Indian), a notion popularized by the famous Brazilian scholar, Gilberto Freyre (Capuano de Oliveira n.d.:18). As a result, those Brazilian nikkeijin who wish to be fully accepted as majority Brazilians and do not want to be treated as an ethnic minority sometimes say, "a cara não ajuda" (the face does not help) (cf. Smith 1979:59).

However, most of them have no problem with being racially differentiated as *japonês*, since they do not wish to discard their minority Japanese ethnicity in favor of a Brazilian national identity in the first place. In fact, their Japaneseness is less of an ethnic stigma to be avoided than a positive asset to be maintained.

The Positive Cultural Meanings of "Japonês"

The racial category of japonês in Brazil is associated with various positive cultural meanings about Japan and Japaneseness. Because their racialization involves such favorable images, the Japanese Brazilians have become a "positive minority" in Brazil who are respected, if not admired, for their Japanese cultural attributes, in contrast to most minority groups, which usually suffer from low socioeconomic status, prejudice, and discrimination (e.g., see Giddens 1989:245; Ogbu 1978:21–25). As a result, many of them take pride in their ethnic heritage and have developed a rather strong Japanese ethnic identity while generally distancing themselves from what they perceive negatively as Brazilian.

These favorable cultural perceptions of Japaneseness in Brazilian society are undoubtedly a product of Japan's prominent and respected position in the global order as an economic superpower. Plenty of positive images about Japan's industrial development, prosperity, and advanced technology have been transmitted to Brazil through global mass media and telecommunications networks (see Tajima 1998:191). Reports and stories about Japan in Brazilian newspapers, magazines, and television programs have saturated Brazilian society with favorable impressions and information.[5] In addition to current news, there are plenty of stories featuring Japan's economic accomplishments and prosperity[6] as well as new Japanese products and technological innovations. The effectiveness of these images is further enhanced by the limited but increasing availability of high-quality Japanese products in Brazil (video/electronic equipment as well as automobiles), which are admired for their reliability and technological superiority.

This favorable Brazilian perception of Japan is based not only on specific knowledge and commodified images about the country but also on general impressions of the First World (*primeiro mundo*) that come mainly from the United States, which dominates the global flow of mass media and popular culture. In fact, when specific knowledge about Japan is lacking, generalized and rather idealistic images about the First World are quickly substituted as if they were synonymous with Japan. Although very few of the Brazilians I spoke with had a clear idea of the actual living conditions in Japan, since images of relatively privileged and luxurious Euro-American standards of living are readily available through American movies and television shows, they were automatically applied to Japan by virtue of the country's First World status. Although the First World continues to be associated with the white (Caucasian) race in Brazil (and is one reason why whiteness continues to be valued in Brazilian society), the racial category of japonês has now come to also have strong First World connotations, even though it may not be seen as a physically attractive racial type.

This global dissemination of positive impressions about Japan as a technologic and economic power and First World nation has greatly enhanced the amount of ethnic respect the Japanese Brazilians receive in Brazil. In fact, the ethnic status of the Japanese in Brazil has fluctuated historically depending on the changing position of Japan in the global order (see Tsuda 2001). The nikkeijin were not held in high ethnic regard in the past when Japan's international status was unfavorable and negative images of the Japanese prevailed. In the early twentieth century, when Japan was still a backward Asian nation attempting to catch up with the West, Japanese immigrants were perceived by the Brazilian political elite as an "inferior race" who would have negative effects on Brazilian racial composition. Although the ethic of hard work among the Japanese was always admired by some Brazilian officials, they were generally regarded as a problematic immigrant group with inscrutable customs and habits who simply refused to be assimilated. During the period of Japanese imperialist expansion and World War II, the Japanese in Brazil were seen as a serious threat to Brazilian national security (the "yellow peril") and were subject to considerable ethnic repression, leading to Japanese ultranationalist fervor within the immigrant community.

However, because of Japan's global emergence as a preeminent First World nation after World War II, the Japanese Brazilians have experienced a dramatic improvement in their minority status. Although this is partly a result of their notable success as a socially mobile immigrant group, virtually all of my older informants agreed that their ethnic status in Brazil has increased considerably with Japan's postwar rise in the world order. The observations of a nikkeijin woman were representative of her contemporaries: "Although we were not involved in Japan's postwar growth, we have certainly benefited from it. Japan's great success has always reflected well on us and as a result, our standing in Brazil has improved dramatically. Indeed, some act as if we actually participated in Japan's economic miracle."

The influence of Japan's global stature on the Japanese Brazilians is especially strong because of the Brazilian tendency to closely associate them with Japan by virtue of their racial appearance. "Some Brazilians don't clearly differentiate the Japanese in Brazil from the Japanese in Japan," one informant observed. "For them, a Japanese is a Japanese, regardless of whether he lives in Brazil or Japan. Therefore, what the Japanese [in Japan] do instantly becomes a reflection of who we [Japanese Brazilians] are."

Indeed, the Japanese Brazilians have capitalized on the currently pro-Japanese climate by asserting and embracing their racialized Japanese distinctiveness. In fact, because Japan is now part of the First World, there is a certain prestige in being associated with the country in contrast to Third World Brazil. In this manner, by developing a strong transnational ethnic identification with Japan, the Japanese Brazilians are able to distance themselves from negative images of Brazil (cf. Linger 2001:25; Reichl 1995; J. Saito 1986:246). Undoubtedly, with the development of modern communications and mass media, which reach out to people across national borders, it has become easier for second and third generation immigrant minorities to identify transnationally with distant ethnic homelands by appropriating positive images that circulate in the global ecumene (cf. Gupta and Ferguson 1992:10–11; Harvey 1989:289).[7]

In addition, being racially Japanese in Brazil also has various positive *cultural* connotations associated with Japanese culture and Japaneseness. The dissemination of positive images about Japan in Brazil has been accompanied by favorable portrayals of Japanese culture. In fact, there is considerable interest among some non-nikkeijin Brazilians in Japanese culture, which has lately come to be seen as refined, fashionable, chic, and exotic (Maeyama 1996:491; Moreira da Rocha 1999: 289, 295; Reichl 1995:45). As Moreira da Rocha remarks, "Lately, it has become fashionable in Brazil to know about Japanese things, to learn cookery, to be able to read some *kanji* [Japanese characters], and to sit *zazen* [and to] learn . . . *chanoyu* [Japanese tea ceremony]" (1999:295). Although many of these Brazilians are introduced to Japanese culture by their Japanese Brazilian friends, much of their interest is also generated by their exposure to Japanese cultural images through television, films, and print media. When I lived in Porto Alegre (which has only a small Japanese Brazilian population), the local catholic university held a series of demonstration classes on Japanese culture, including tea ceremonies and flower arrangement. I was surprised to find not only that these classes were well attended but consisted overwhelmingly of non-nikkeijin Brazilians (cf. Moreira da Rocha 1999:290–291). Indeed, Japanese language classes offered both at the university and in more informal contexts consist not only of nikkeijin, but a good contingent of Brazilian students as well. "It's amazing how many Brazilians want to learn Japanese," one Japanese Brazilian university student remarked. "It has no practical value for them—they just do it out of personal interest in Japanese culture. I am frequently asked by my [Brazilian] friends how long it will take them to learn the language."

Although most Japanese Brazilians are culturally assimilated and have not retained Japanese cultural practices, they have attempted to preserve their cherished Japanese cultural heritage through the symbolic re-creation of Japanese festivals, rituals, food, music, and dress within their ethnic communities, which run a multitude of ethnic activities and events ranging from festivals, large dinners, and performances featuring Japanese karaoke, theater, traditional music, and dance to various sporting events and Miss Nikkei beauty pageants (see also Cardoso 1973). In fact, the Japanese Brazilians show much more interest in Japanese music and other aspects of Japanese culture than Japanese Americans (Centro de Estudos 1992).

In addition, the Japanese Brazilians are regarded by majority Brazilians as having inherited various positive Japanese cultural qualities by virtue of their racial descent and ancestry. There is notable consensus among Brazilians that the japonês are hard-working, honest, intelligent, trustworthy, and responsible (cf. Saito 1986; Smith 1979:58–59), which is partly the result of their notable success as a socially mobile and highly educated immigrant minority. The Japanese Brazilians are also sometimes seen as more timid, reserved, and calm than Brazilians, characteristics that can have positive connotations. Such positive stereotypes and attitudes were quite evident in my interactions with mainstream Brazilians, which resulted in numerous unsolicited ethnic comments about the Japanese Brazilians such as the following:

"The japonês are very respected. They do the work of ten Brazilians," a Brazilian waiter told me, when he found out that I had interviewed a Japanese Brazilian woman in his restaurant.

"Japonês, eh?" an agent at a Brazilian bus terminal confirmed when I gave him my name, mistaking me for a Japanese Brazilian. "They are good people. Very intelligent, hard-working."

"We trust the japonês very much, much more than Brazilians," an old Brazilian lady told me. "I have many Japanese friends and they are always honest, responsible."

"You see, he is japonês" my professor in Porto Alegre observed when one of his students showed up unexpectedly to fulfill an obligation he did not need to honor. "He has a sense of responsibility lacking among Brazilian students."[8]

In addition to such stereotypic ethnic images of the nikkeijin, many Brazilians directly racialize the perceived cultural differences of the Japanese
Brazilians in positive terms (cf. Maeyama 1984:448, 1996:312). There is a strong
tendency among a good number of Brazilians to favorably interpret many of
the distinctive aspects and behaviors of the Japanese Brazilians (such as their
high academic achievement, politeness, greater social reserve, cleanliness,and
so forth) as positive Japanese cultural qualities which are a product of their
different racial descent and ethnic heritage. A Japanese Brazilian mother gave
a typical example of this type of Brazilian ethnic reasoning in regard to her
son: "When my son gets good grades in school, they say, 'Of course, it's because he's Japanese.' When he does a really careful and neat job on a class as-
signment, they say, 'Of course, it's because he's Japanese.' When he keeps his
desk clean in the classroom, they say, 'Of course, he is Japanese.'" In fact, as a
Japanese descendant in Brazil, my behavior was also sometimes attributed to
essentialized Japanese cultural traits. My Japanese intelligence was credited
for my relatively quick mastery of Portuguese more than a few times. On the
day I left Porto Alegre, I told my Brazilian friends who drove me to the bus
terminal that I had spent much of the previous night cleaning my apartment
before I moved out. Again, the inevitable ethnic conclusion: "Ele é japonês"
(He is Japanese).

These racialized cultural definitions of Japaneseness are not only hegemonic constructs that are simply imposed on the self-consciousness of the
Japanese Brazilians. Because of their positive connotations, they are actively
asserted by the Japanese Brazilians themselves. When talking about their
cultural differences, my nikkeijin informants agreed with the way they were
ethnically characterized in Brazilian society and claimed that they *are* indeed more hard working, diligent, honest, educated, intelligent, and responsible than most Brazilians, who they stereotypically portrayed as lazy, easy-
going, irresponsible, immature, and dishonest (see also Flores 1975:95; Reichl
1995:49, 51, 55;, T. Saito 1986; Smith 1979:58).[9] In fact, it was remarkable how
the comments that they made about their positive cultural qualities were frequently accompanied by negative images of majority Brazilians. For example,
consider the reflections of one young Japanese Brazilian man:

> We feel lots of cultural differences in relation to other Brazilians. Lots. Our
> cultural level is higher. We work harder, are more diligent, and intelligent.
> Brazilians like the beach too much and spend too much time partying and
> enjoying themselves. If you ask a Japanese [Brazilian] to do something, you

can be assured it will be done. If you ask a Brazilian . . . who knows what will happen? They aren't serious about work and are unreliable.

In this manner, although the racial differentiation of the nikkeijin as Japanese in Brazil prevents them from being considered as part of majority Brazilian society, it apparently has its advantages because it invokes a positive contrast between First World Japan and Third World Brazil and between Japanese and Brazilian cultures. In fact, the Japanese Brazilians have themselves become all too willing participants in their positive racialization by asserting a culturally distinct Japanese ethnic identity while distancing themselves from the negative aspects of Brazilianness. For many of them, their ethnic minority status is a source of much pride and self-esteem, and for some, it even leads to a sense of superiority over what is considered Brazilian.[10] The result is a relatively strong self-identification as ethnic Japanese, which continues to take precedence over their identities as Brazilian nationals.

Racial Homogenization and Ethnic Differentiation in Japan

Essentialized Racial Perceptions of Japanese Brazilians

When the Japanese Brazilians return-migrate to Japan, they are forced to resituate their ethnic identities in a completely different social and racial environment. In Japan, race obviously loses its power of ethnic differentiation. However, the lack of phenotypic difference between the migrants and their hosts[11] does not mean that the Japanese Brazilians are no longer subject to racial ideologies in Japan. Although they are not racialized as culturally different, they are still racialized in Japan, but this time as culturally *similar* Japanese. Needless to say, however, what it means to be culturally Japanese in Japan is very different from what it means to be culturally Japanese in Brazil. These different cultural meanings attached to the racial category of Japanese causes the Japanese Brazilians to negotiate a different situated ethnic identity in Japan.

When the Brazilian nikkeijin are racialized as culturally Japanese in Japan, they are obviously held to much more stringent standards than in Brazil. According to one of my Japanese Brazilian friends in Japan: "We think we are Japanese in Brazil, but in Japan, we find out that we were wrong. If you act differently and don't speak Japanese fluently, the Japanese say you are a Brazilian. To be considered Japanese, it is not sufficient to simply have a Japanese face and eat sushi with chopsticks. You must think, act, and speak just like the Japanese. Another informant had similar feelings : "In Brazil, we are considered Japanese because we speak some Japanese, eat Japanese food, and maintain some Japanese customs from our parents. This is Japanese enough for Brazilians, but for the Japanese, it means nothing. We appear quite Brazilian to them and are seen as foreigners."

Japanese ethnic perceptions of the Japanese Brazilians are based on a presumed correspondence between race and culture that seems to develop in nations such as Japan in which an ideology of ethnic homogeneity is maintained. In other words, since all Japanese are seen as the same race and all Japanese are perceived as culturally similar in thinking and behavior, those who are "racially" Japanese (i.e., who have a Japanese face) are assumed to be culturally Japanese as well (see also Kondo 1986). The comments of a local neighborhood doctor who treats foreign workers was quite representative of this type of essentialized ethnic perception: "When you live in Japan, you come to take this for granted. Everyone looks Japanese and we all think and act in more or less the same way. So when we see someone who has a Japanese face, we end up thinking that they are like the Japanese—that they will speak and behave like the Japanese."

This perceived correlation between racial descent and culture applies not only to the Japanese in Japan, but also to a lesser extent to those of Japanese descent born abroad, because it is assumed that Japanese culture will be transmitted through family socialization to those of Japanese descent regardless of national boundaries. Therefore, there was a strong expectation among most of my Japanese informants that the Brazilian nikkeijin should be culturally similar since they are expected to have literally inherited Japanese customs from their parents, even if they were born in a foreign country. The Japanese undoubtedly realize that the Japanese Brazilians have become culturally foreign to a certain extent, and some are not sure how much of the Japanese language and behavioral patterns they have retained abroad. Despite this, however, the anticipation is that there will be strong cultural similarities. Such ethnic attitudes toward the nikkeijin are clearly expressed in the following statement by a local storeowner, which echoes the feelings of many of my Japanese informants: "We think the Brazilian nikkeijin, as descendants of Japanese, must have retained good Japanese traditions because even if born abroad, they grew up in Japanese families. So they must be like the Japanese, at least a little . . . if their face is pure Japanese, we have the idea that their customs and attitudes will be at an above average Japanese level."

Because of such essentialized Japanese ethnic understandings in which those of Japanese descent are assumed to be culturally similar, the Japanese Brazilians come under considerable assimilative ethnic pressure in Japan. However, most cannot meet such Japanese cultural demands because they lack sufficient Japanese linguistic and cultural competence. Jefferson, a young second-generation nikkeijin man spoke about such frustrations:

> The Japanese make many more demands on us than on whites or other foreigners in Japan because of our Japanese faces. They think we should speak the language and understand Japanese ways because we are Japanese descendants. They must realize that we can't understand and act like them because we are from a foreign country. But the Japanese always demand this. They say: "you are nikkei, why don't you speak Japanese?" Our adaptation is harder because of this pressure.

The greater cultural demands on the Japanese Brazilians affect even their children in Japanese schools. One Japanese teacher noted how nikkeijin students, because of their Japanese faces, suffer more than those of mixed descent (cf. Hirota 1993:31) because they experience greater pressure to culturally conform at school. However, Japanese cultural standards are sometimes imposed even on the mixed-descent mestiços. Maria, a second-generation mestiça woman, spoke about how the Japanese women at her factory during one social outing told her not to sit Indian style on the *tatami* floor but to sit *seiza* style,[12] as is expected of Japanese women. "I just can't sit on my legs," she complained. "I'm simply not used to it. I always get leg pains after a few minutes." Maria was also reminded by her female Japanese co-workers not to use the rough Japanese to which she was accustomed, which is unbecoming of a Japanese woman.

Acting Brazilian in Japan

A number of Japanese Brazilian immigrants therefore decide to resist such assimilative Japanese cultural pressures by acting in conspicuously Brazilian ways in Japan in order to demonstrate to the Japanese that they are *not* Japanese despite their Japanese racial appearance and therefore cannot be held to Japanese cultural expectations. By asserting the Brazilian side of their multiple identities, they are able to ethnically differentiate themselves from the Japanese, therefore challenging their racialization as Japanese and relieving themselves from the essentialized and unreasonable cultural demands that are placed on them.[13] Therefore, although they had previously emphasized their Japaneseness in Brazil because of its positive racialized connotations in that country, they situate their ethnic identity quite differently in the assimi-lationist racial context of Japan.

A common way in which the nikkeijin display their Brazilianness to the Japanese is through dress, which is among the most frequent emblems used to symbolize ethnic difference. Although their manner of dress is normally different from the Japanese, some Japanese Brazilians deliberately wear dis-tinctive Brazilian clothes to catch the attention of the Japanese. Jefferson was quite explicit about his intentions:

> At first, I tried to dress like the Japanese. I knew that the Japanese manner of dressing was different from ours, so I went out and bought new clothes at the department store. But now, whenever I go to the bank or to stores, I wear Bermudas or Brazilian T-shirts. The Japanese never dress like this, so they can always tell I am Brazilian. I feel better this way because I don't want to be seen or mistaken as Japanese.

The ethnic effectiveness of clothes as an identifying marker of Brazilian-ness has actually increased the demand for Brazilian clothes in Japan. As a result, Brazilian clothing stores have opened in areas with high concentra-tions of nikkeijin in Japan. Of course, some Japanese Brazilians wear Bra-zilian clothes in Japan purely out of physical comfort or habit, but for oth-ers it is a prominent ethnic display of cultural difference. The manager of a Brazilian clothing store explained that the clothes she sells have distinctive designs, fashions, and colors that cannot be found in Japanese department stores. Jeans have colorful ornamental features and those for women tend to be tighter around the hips (as the buttocks, not the breasts, are the primary lo-cus of female sexual attention in Brazil). Shirts have strong (even loud) colors and may have mosaic patterns, while T-shirts with the Brazilian flag, national colors, or the country's name prominently displayed are also popular. Many of these Brazilian styles are undoubtedly exaggerated constructions that have appropriated stylistic images of Brazil without necessarily representing any particular cultural style in Brazil. When national symbols are appropriated by migrants abroad, they are frequently culturally decontextualized and re-constructed. Such clothes are meaningful as symbolic makers of ethnicity only in Japan, where the Japanese Brazilians suddenly feel a desire to express their cultural identities as Brazilians.

The Japanese Brazilians also culturally differentiate themselves as Bra-zilians through the use of language and greetings. Although some nikkeijin are sensitive to Japanese opinions and social pressures and lower their voices when speaking Portuguese in public areas, others take the opposite approach. For instance, Martina mentioned that although she speaks Japanese well, whenever she walks into a store, she makes a point of speaking Portuguese loud enough so that the Japanese will notice. "I don't want to be confused as Japanese," she said. "So I always show them I am Brazilian." Likewise, the tendency of some nikkeijin to greet each other loudly and affectionately in public by embracing or kissing is similarly a display of Brazilian behavior, which is completely incongruous with Japanese culture and thus serves as another means of ethnic differentiation.

Some individuals take their cultural resistance further by exaggerating their Brazilian behavior in Japan in a rebellious, exhibitionist manner by purposefully acting more Brazilian in Japan than they ever did in Brazil. As one informant observed a bit cynically, "Some of these Brazilian youth have this attitude toward the Japanese: 'Hey, I'm Brazilian and I am going to act Brazilian in Japan. And if you don't like it, screw you.' As a result, they are seen less favorably by the Japanese. However, in Brazil, they would never have acted like this and do it only in Japan." Even among those who do not take such a rebellious approach, the public assertion of their Brazilian identities is frequently a way to tell the Japanese that despite their racialization as Japanese, they are Brazilians who cannot be expected to behave like Japanese and speak the language fluently.

Others engage in much more subdued performances of their Brazilian identity. This is especially true among the more acculturated nikkeijin, who are more accommodating toward Japanese cultural expectations and feel more pressure to act in accordance with Japanese norms. For such individuals, the assertion of their Brazilianness is much less ostentatious than their peers and is usually limited to introducing themselves as Brazilians or foreigners. Of course, the need to make self-introductions is not as relevant to those Japanese Brazilians who do not speak much Japanese, since it is apparent to the Japanese that they are foreigners when they open their mouths. However, for nikkeijin who can speak Japanese well enough to communicate, the issue becomes critical when they meet Japanese who are unfamiliar with them and therefore assume that they are native Japanese because of their racial appearance. In such cases, their imperfect Japanese leads to some confusion and disorientation among the Japanese. Therefore, by introducing themselves as Brazilians when meeting Japanese for the first time, such individuals are able to avoid being mistaken as Japanese and therefore relieve themselves of the resulting Japanese cultural expectations that are then imposed. Geraldo spoke about how he finds it beneficial in this regard to introduce himself as a Brazilian in order to avoid cultural embarrassment or ill-treatment:

> If I just ask simple questions at a store, there is no problem, but if they start using technical terms or the conversation continues, they are surprised at my lack of comprehension and find my accent really strange because they think I'm Japanese. So it's better to say from the beginning that I am Brazilian, so that the Japanese will understand and explain things to you more carefully without looking down on you. When I first got to Japan, I would try to act like a Japanese, but now I always say I'm Brazilian. It's a way to apologize beforehand for my inability to understand Japanese perfectly.

Such concerns are most salient among those nikkeijin who speak fluent Japanese and are students or office workers in Japan. These individuals are the most likely to be mistaken as Japanese because of their cultural and linguistic abilities and their unwillingness to overtly display Brazilian behavior. Therefore, they sometimes find subtle ways to culturally differentiate themselves as Brazilians and avoid being held to the same social standards as the Japanese. This includes not only introducing themselves as nikkeijin, but writing out their Japanese last names in *katakana* (a phonetic alphabet used for foreign names) instead of using Japanese characters. Those who have both Brazilian and Japanese first names sometimes intentionally use their Brazilian name in Japan, although they may have been called by their Japanese name in Brazil. "It is my way of identifying myself as someone who is not Japanese," a Japanese Brazilian graduate student remarked. "It is my way to ask permission from the Japanese to forgive me because I behave differently from them."

Other individuals use not only public symbols such as names and self-introductions, but also personal symbols in order to ethnically mark themselves as Brazilians in Japan. For instance, Marcos, a Japanese Brazilian journalist, wears a goatee as his "little rebellion against the Japanese," an idiosyncratic emblem of his ethnic differences with Japanese men, whom he believes do not like facial hair. He also told me that he was clean-shaven in Brazil, again showing how his goatee is a symbol of his Brazilian identity that has significance only in Japan. In order to resist the cultural pressures of Japanese society, Marcos, like many others, finds a need to assert his Brazilianness—a desire he had not had in Brazil. In this manner, there is considerable variation in the conscious expression of Brazilian cultural difference ranging from aggressive displays of cultural difference in public to the subtle use of introductions, names, and other personal symbols for proper identification in order to avoid Japanese cultural pressures and ethnic embarrassment.

The enactment of Brazilian identities in Japan occurs not only in individual behavior, but in collective ritual performances as well. The most important example is the samba parades that the Japanese Brazilians organize in local communities with high nikkeijin concentrations. Although most Japanese Brazilians never participated in samba in Brazil and even scorned it as a lowly Brazilian activity, they find themselves dancing the samba for the first time in their lives in Japan and actually finding it a lot of fun. However, as was the case with the emblematic use of Brazilian clothes, considerable decontextualization and modification again occur when nationalist symbols from back home are conveniently appropriated for ethnically demonstrative purposes by Japanese Brazilian migrants in Japan.

Since the nikkeijin never really danced the samba in Brazil, the nikkeijin have insufficient cultural knowledge of this national Brazilian ritual. As a result, their ethnic performance in Japan is not structured or regulated by preordained cultural models of the samba, but is a spontaneous cultural form generated by them in the context of enactment. For example, the samba parade I observed (in Oizumi-town, Gunma prefecture) was a somewhat random cultural performance that was improvised, haphazard, and casual. The "samba costumes" the Japanese Brazilians wore were randomly chosen and ranged from simple bathing suits, clown outfits, festival clothes with Brazilian national colors (yellow and green), to T-shirts and shorts. Apparently, few of the nikkeijin knew how to design or construct any real Brazilian samba costumes or had the resources to do so. In addition, most of them did not seem to know how to properly dance the samba, and even if some of them were familiar with the dance form, almost no one had the experience or will to execute it properly. Therefore, instead of properly schematized body movements, most of the participants seemed to be moving and shaking their bodies randomly, some in a lackadaisical manner. The general result was simply a potpourri of costumes and individuals moving their bodies randomly without any pattern, definition, or precise rhythm that resembles the actual Brazilian samba. The only part of the parade that required any explicit cultural knowledge was the singer of the samba theme and the *bateria* (the drum section that beats out the samba rhythm), both of which were composed almost exclusively of non-Japanese-descent Brazilians.

Therefore, the final cultural product that emerged had little in common with the samba as it is practiced in Brazil and would have been barely recognizable back home. Nonetheless, given the Japanese context in which this samba was being enacted, it was seen as very Brazilian because of its cultural distinctiveness in Japan. In other words, as long as the nikkeijin could find some costume that looked vaguely Brazilian and could shake their body in one way or another, the performance remained effective as a collective assertion of their Brazilian ethnic identity. This process of cultural authentication is also unintentionally supported by the presence of attentive Japanese spectators, who showed active interest in the unusual and different festivities of another nation. Since the Japanese have even less knowledge about the samba than the Japanese Brazilians, they are unable to provide any cultural critique of the performance as "inauthentic" like a Brazilian audience. For them, anything that seems culturally different and novel is accepted and appreciated as bona-fide Brazilian samba. Therefore, the implicit collusion between participant and observer in a foreign context validates and authenticates the spontaneously generated and random performance as a true display and assertion of a distinctive Brazilian culture.

Conclusion: Racialization and the De-essentialization of Ethnic Difference

As the case of Japanese Brazilian return-migration demonstrates, the making of ethnic identities is an ongoing negotiation between individuals and the constantly changing racial ideologies and sociocultural forces in which they are embedded. Even if the same racial category is used to classify immigrants in both the home and host societies (as black, Asian, Mexican, Japanese, and so forth), they can construct very different situated ethnic identities in response to the different cultural understandings attached to race in specific local contexts. For the Brazilian nikkeijin, what it means to be racially Japanese is quite different in Brazil and Japan. In Brazil, Japanese racial appearance was automatically associated with positive images and cultural stereotypes, which enabled them to claim a respected Japanese minority identity almost by fiat. As a result, their Japanese ethnic distinctiveness could easily be validated by their perceived behavioral characteristics and their symbolic deployment of Japanese tradition and ethnic festivities. When they migrate to Japan, however, the nikkeijin find that having a "Japanese face" is an ethnic burden because of the Japanese insistence that they be culturally Japanese by virtue of their shared descent. This causes the Japanese Brazilians to assert their Brazilianness in order to resist and defy such unreasonable, assimilationist cultural demands. Therefore, although the nikkeijin touted their distinctive Japanese cultural qualities when racialized as Japanese in Brazil, they ironically find themselves asserting their Brazilian cultural differences when racialized as Japanese in Japan. In this manner, the same racial category can produce different processes of racialization in different societies, causing migrants to respond in ethnically divergent ways.

As a result, diasporic peoples tend to develop multiple situated identities that constantly shift based on their experiences in different societies. However, which identity they choose to deploy in a specific local context is not merely a response to hegemonic processes of racialization, it is also an attempt to maintain a positively construed ethnic distinctiveness as they are displaced to multiple localities. This may cause diasporic peoples to be more willing to acquiesce to their racialization in one society but adamantly resist it in another. In Brazil, the Japanese Brazilians have maintained their ethnic distinctiveness by accepting, if not promoting, their racialization as Japanese in Brazilian society, laying personal claim to positive Brazilian images of Japanese culture by virtue of their Japanese descent. However, because they do not actively challenge racially essentialized Brazilian perceptions of their cultural differences, they are forever defined as a culturally Japanese minority regardless of their level of cultural assimilation. Indeed, some Japanese Brazilians themselves continue to insist that the positive Japanese cultural qualities they have inherited from their parents and grandparents have persisted despite generations in Brazil, a claim made partly credible by symbolic re-creations of Japanese tradition in their communities. As a result, both majority Brazilians and minority nikkeijin were somewhat blinded to their substantial cultural similarities, which greatly outweigh any lingering differences.

Although race in Japan no longer inscribes cultural difference, the Japanese Brazilians are still confronted by essentialized notions of ethnicity in which Japanese culture is closely related to notions of Japanese racial essence. However, because their racialization in Japan is used to assimilate them under a homogeneously constituted Japanese majority ethnicity, the Japanese Brazilians resist their cultural essentialization as Japanese this time. Through assertive demonstrations of their Brazilian cultural differences, they insist on their ethnic distinctiveness despite their Japanese racial appearance. By disassociating culture from race in this manner, they effectively de-essentialize racialist conceptions of Japanese ethnicity among both the Japanese and themselves, causing them to mutually question their previous assumptions of cultural similarity based on common descent (see Tsuda 2003:chapter 5). If anthropology has attempted to de-essentialize the self by disengaging it from notions of biological or universal essence (Kondo 1990:34),[14] my nikkeijin and Japanese informants seemingly came to the same conclusion in their ethnic encounters, although few of them attain this level of theoretical reflexivity.

In this manner, ethnic identity for Japanese Brazilian immigrants changes from something that is racially inscribed (essentialized) to something that is culturally contingent and actively negotiated in various social contexts (de-essentialized). Racially essentialized ethnic identities become harder to sustain under transnational migration because it disengages relatively static ethnic meanings from a certain locale and re-engages them in a new social context, causing them to be challenged and redefined. As a result, the multiple and situated nature of ethnic identity becomes more apparent among diasporic peoples, making it subject to continued contestation and renegotiation.

Notes

1. See Tsuda (2003: introduction) for a detailed analysis of my fieldwork experiences.

2. Because of the considerable racial intermixture in Brazil, Brazilians (unlike Americans) have a wide array of racial categories. Harris and Kottak (1963), in their study of racial categories among Brazilians in a fishing village in coastal Bahia, uncovered 40 categories used to describe phenotypic differences.

3. It is interesting to note that those of Korean and Chinese decent in Brazil are also called japonês and frequently have to correct this misnomer (cf. Maeyama 1984:455).

4. Maeyama claims that many Japanese Brazilians become angry when they are called japonês and say "I am not japonês. I am brasileiro" (1996:322). However, his impressions seem to be based on earlier postwar experiences and are no longer true today.

5. Some have even claimed that favorable images of Japan, fostered by the mass media, prevail throughout Latin America (e.g., see Nakagawa 1983:63).

6. When the author was in Brazil, Japan's serious and prolonged recession did not receive prominent media coverage.

7. Some researchers have noted a desire among second and third generation immigrant minorities to explore and assert their past ethnic heritage (e.g., Hansen 1952).

This type of "ethnic revival" occurs not just because they feel that they are losing their ethnic distinctiveness due to assimilation. Since they are now well established and secure in the majority society, they are able to assert a minority ethnic identity without compromising or threatening their social position.

8. In fact, the only notable negative image of the Japanese Brazilians that I encountered in Brazil was a sense that the japonês are somewhat unreceptive toward ethnic outsiders. I have also heard Brazilians mention how the japonês are too timid and restrained and that the women are too submissive to men, although the reference was more to Japanese in Japan. Although much of Brazilian ethnic prejudice is expressed through joking behavior, the jokes about the japonês that I actively collected from Brazilians tended to emphasize the positive aspects of the Japanese Brazilians such as their high academic achievements (although my own Japanese ethnic status undoubtedly made complete access to any nasty jokes difficult). The most popular ethnic joke in Brazil about the Japanese Brazilians is undoubtedly the following: "If you want to enter the University of São Paulo [the Harvard of Brazil], kill a Japanese" (like Asians in the United States, the Japanese Brazilians are overrepresented at top Brazilian universities). The other joke of this type I heard involves plugging a Japanese into an intelligence measuring machine. The reading goes off the scale, causing the machine (made in Brazil) to break and the Japanese to come out stupid like a Portuguese (in contrast to American attitudes toward the British, the Portuguese are frequently portrayed in Brazilian jokes as bumbling idiots). Other jokes poked fun at either the facial features or strange and complicated last names of the Japanese Brazilians. Also, the stereotype of Asians in the United States as geeks or nerds seems to be much less prominent in Brazil.

9. Many Japanese Brazilian respondents in T. Saito's survey (1986) characterized Brazilians in this unfavorable manner. Few saw Brazilians as educated, hard working, intelligent, or responsible. In fact, according to a 1995 *Datafolha* poll of Japanese Brazilians living in São Paulo, 59 percent admitted that they are prejudiced against Brazilians, whereas only 35 percent felt that Brazilians were prejudiced against them (cited in Linger 2001:25).

10. Studies have shown very high levels of self-confidence and esteem among the Japanese Brazilians (J. Saito 1986:249–250). In fact, Kitagawa's study of two Japanese Brazilian communities found that 86 percent of those surveyed have lots of pride in their Japanese descent and 11 percent have some pride; rates are higher than for the Japanese *in Japan* (Kitagawa 1996:188, 1997:133).

11. There are relatively few Japanese Brazilians of mixed descent in Japan.

12. Seiza is when one sits on folded legs with the knees together. The sitting position is very uncomfortable for those who are not accustomed to it, and the author himself cannot endure seiza for more than several minutes, although men are allowed to sit Indian style on the tatami floor.

13. It is very important to note that the desire to resist Japanese cultural pressures is not the only reason the nikkeijin express their Brazilian identities in Japan. See Tsuda (2003) for an extensive analysis of the development of Brazilian migrant nationalism among the Japanese Brazilians in Japan.

14. This has also been emphasized by those studying the cultural construction of emotion as part of the self (e.g., see Lutz 1988; Rosaldo 1980, 1984).

References

Basch, Linda, Nina Glick Schiller, and Cristina Szanton Blanc. 1994. *Nations Unbound: Transnational Projects, Postcolonial Predicaments, and Deterritorialized Nation-States.* Amsterdam: Gordon and Breach Publishers.

Capuano de Oliveira, Adriana. N.d. Migration and Identity: Brazilian Dekasegi in Japan. Unpublished manuscript.

Cardoso, Ruth Corrêa Leite. 1973. "O Papel das Associações Juvenis na Aculturação dos Japoneses" (The Role of Youth Associations in the Acculturation of the Japanese). In Hiroshi Saito and Takashi Maeyama, eds., *Assimilação e Integração dos Japoneses no Brasil* (The Assimilation and Integration of the Japanese in Brazil), pp. 317–345. Petrópolis, Rio de Janeiro: Editora Vozes.

Centro de Estudos Nipo-Brasileiros (Center for Japanese-Brazilian Studies). 1992. *Pesquisa de Comportamento e Atitude de Japoneses e seus Descendentes Residentes no Brasil.* São Paulo: Centro de Estudos Nipo-Brasileiros.

Charles, Carolle. 1992. "Transnationalism in the Construct of Haitian Migrants' Racial Categories of Identity in New York City." In Nina Glick Schiller, Linda Basch, and Cristina Blanc-Szanton, eds., *Towards a Transnational Perspective on Migration: Race, Class, Ethnicity, and Nationalism Reconsidered,* pp. 101–123. New York: The New York Academy of Sciences.

Fanon, Frantz. 1967. *Black Skin, White Masks,* Charles Lam Markmann, trans. New York: Grove Press.

Flores, Moacyr. 1975. "Japoneses no Rio Grande do Sul" (The Japanese in Rio Grande do Sul). *Veritas* no. 77: 65–98.

Freeman, Carla. 2000. *High Tech and High Heels in the Global Economy: Women, Work, and Pink-Collar Identities in the Caribbean.* Durham, NC: Duke University Press.

Giddens, Anthony. 1989. *Sociology.* Cambridge: Polity Press.

Gupta, Akhil, and James Ferguson. 1992. "Beyond 'Culture': Space, Identity, and the Politics of Difference." *Cultural Anthropology* 7(1): 6–23.

Hansen, Marcus. 1952. "The Third Generation in America." *Commentary* 14: 492–500.

Harris, Marvin, and Conrad Kottak. 1963. "The Structural Significance of Brazilian Racial Categories." *Sociologia* 25: 203–209.

Harvey, David. 1989. *The Condition of Postmodernity.* Cambridge, MA: Blackwell.

Hirota, Yasuo. 1993. "Toshi Esunikku Comyunitei no Keisei to 'Tekiyo' no Iso ni Tsuite: Tokuni Yokohama-shi Tsurumi no Nikkeijin Comyunitei o Taisho to Shite" (About the Construction of Urban Ethnic Communities and the Phase of Adaptation: Especially within the Nikkeijin Communities in Tsurumi, Kanagawa-ken). *Shakai Kagaku Nenpo* 27:289–325.

Kitagawa, Toyoie. 1996. Hamamatsushi ni Okeru Nikkei Burajirujin no Seikatsu Kozo to Ishiki: Nippaku Ryokoku Chosa o Fumaete (The Lives and Consciousness of the Brazilian Nikkeijin in Hamamatsu City: Based on Surveys in Both Japan and Brazil). *Toyo Daigaku Shakai Gakubu Kiyo* (Bulletin of the Department of Sociology at Toyo University) 34(1): 109–196.

———. 1997. Burajiru-taun no Keisei to Deasupora: Nikkei Burajirujin no Teijyuka ni Kansuru Nananen Keizoku Oizumi-machi Chosa (Diaspora and the Formation of Brazil-town: A Continuing Seven-year Oizumi-town Survey about the Settlement of Brazilian Nikkeijin. *Toyo Daigaku Shakai Gakubu Kiyo* (Bulletin of the Department of Sociology at Toyo University) 34(3): 66–173.

Kondo, Dorinne K. 1986. "Dissolution and Reconstitution of Self: Implications for Anthropological Epistemology." *Cultural Anthropology* 1(1): 74–88.

———. 1990. *Crafting Selves: Power, Gender, and Discourses of Identity in a Japanese Workplace*. Chicago: University of Chicago Press.

Linger, Daniel T. 2001. *No One Home: Brazilian Selves Remade in Japan*. Stanford: Stanford University Press.

Lutz, Catherine. 1988. *Unnatural Emotions: Everyday Sentiments on a Micronesian Atoll and Their Challenge to Western Theory*. Chicago: The University of Chicago Press.

Maeyama, Takashi. 1984. "Burajiru Nikkeijin ni Okeru Esunishitei to Aidenteitei: Ishikiteki Seijiteki Genjyo to Shite" (The Ethnicity and Identity of the Nikkeijin in Brazil: Politico-Cognitive Phenomena). *Minzokugaku Kenkyu* (Ethnicity Research) 48(4): 444–458.

———. 1996. *Esunishitei to Burajiru Nikkeijin* (Ethnicity and Brazilian Nikkeijin). Tokyo: Ochanomizu Shobo.

Moreira da Rocha, Cristina. 1999. "Identity and Tea Ceremony in Brazil." *Japanese Studies* 19(3): 287–295.

Nakagawa, Fumio. 1983. "Japanese-Latin American Relations Since the 1960s: An Overview." *Latin American Studies* 6:63–71.

Ogbu, John U. 1978. *Minority Education and Caste: The American System in Cross-Cultural Perspective*. New York: Academic Press.

Park, Kyeyoung. 1999. "'I Am Floating in the Air': Creation of a Korean Transnational Space among Korean-Latino American Remigrants." *Positions* 7(3): 667–695.

Reichl, Christopher A. 1995. "Stages in the Historical Process of Ethnicity: The Japanese in Brazil, 1908–1988." *Ethnohistory* 42(1): 31–62.

Rosaldo, Michelle, Z. 1980. *Knowledge and Passion: Ilongot Notions of Self and Social Life*. Cambridge: Cambridge University Press.

———. 1984. "Toward an Anthropology of Self and Feeling." In Richard A. Shweder and Robert A. LeVine, eds., *Culture Theory: Essays on Mind, Self, and Emotion*, pp. 137–158. Cambridge: Cambridge University Press.

Saito, Júlia Kubo. 1986. "Auto-Estima e Auto-Conceito entre os Jovens Descendentes de Japoneses" (Self-Esteem and Self-Concepts among Japanese-Descent Youths). In Massao Ohno, ed., *O Nikkei e Sua Americanidade* (The Nikkei and their Americanness), pp. 241–255. São Paulo: COPANI.

Saito, Toshiaki. 1986. "Brasileiros e Japoneses, Confronto de Identidade" (Brazilians and Japanese, Confrontation of Identity). In Massao Ohno, ed., *O Nikkei e Sua Americanidade* (The Nikkei and their Americanness), pp. 199–224. São Paulo: COPANI.

Smith, Robert J. 1979. "The Ethnic Japanese in Brazil." *The Journal of Japanese Studies* 5(1): 53–70.

———. 1998. "Socio-Cultural Differentiation in the Formation of Ethnic Identity and Integration into Japanese Society: The Case of Okinawan and Nikkei Brazilian Immigrants." *JCAS Symposium Series* 8: 187–197.

Tsuda, Takeyuki. 2001. "When Identities Become Modern: Japanese Immigrants in Brazil and the Global Contextualization of Identity." *Ethnic and Racial Studies* 24(3): 412–432.

———. 2003. *Strangers in the Ethnic Homeland: Japanese Brazilian Return Migration in Transnational Perspective*. New York: Columbia University Press.

10 Legal Servitude and Free Illegality: Migrant "Guest" Workers in Taiwan

Pei-Chia Lan

PRISCILLA FIRST CAME TO TAIWAN as an overseas contract worker (OCW). She worked in a private household, caring for two children, cleaning a three-story house, and cooking three meals a day. Sometimes she was asked to clean the house of her employers' parents, with only a small extra payment. She had only two days off each month. The employers did not like her to mingle with other Filipinas and would rather pay her overtime for staying home on Sundays. Priscilla was exhausted, lonely, and worried. The male employer sometimes came home during the day while his wife was at work. Once when the wife was out of town for business, he came to Priscilla's door around midnight. "It was a long long knock. I had to drag the cabinet against the door and hide myself in the closet. I was afraid what he wanted from me," recalled Priscilla with lingering fear in her eyes. In addition to the worry about sexual harassment from the husband, Priscilla was also concerned about the wife's reaction. She was afraid that the female employer might send her home out of jealousy. She thought of her children in the Philippines who need money to pay off their tuitions; she thought of her debts borrowed from a loan shark to cover the placement fee. She bit her lips and told herself, "I cannot go home, not now."

Priscilla decided to "run away," more exactly, she left her employers without notice. She moved into a small two-bedroom apartment with three other Filipinas—one is also a runaway OCW and two have agreements with their contract employers for a live-out arrangement.[1] Through the referral of friends, Priscilla found part-time cleaning jobs. When she has a sufficient supply of jobs, she is cleaning ten houses a week and earning more than twice what she did as a live-in contract worker.[2] After going undocumented, she lost some of the legal protection that regular migrants get, such as health insurance ("I pray for my health. God is my insurance!" said Priscilla). And she has to avoid the public gathering of Filipino migrants, especially during the times of police crackdown. Nevertheless, she gains more autonomy at work and more freedom in life in comparison with her documented days.

The flows of transmigration within Asia accelerated in the early 1980s and reached unprecedented levels in the last decade. The oil boom in the Gulf countries and the rapid industrialization in East Asia have attracted a growing number of migrant workers from the Philippines, Indonesia, Thailand, Sri Lanka, Bangladesh, and Vietnam. Temporary migration of semiskilled and unskilled workers is the most significant category of labor migration in this region. It is estimated that the stock of temporary migrant workers in Asia, with or without legal documents, reached 6.1 million by 2000 (Battistella 2002).

The adoption of the "guest worker" regime is a salient feature of state regulation in Asian host countries. Legal channels are open for foreigners placed in the so-called "Three D" jobs (dirty, dangerous, and difficult), but state policies position them exclusively as contract workers and transient residents. The legal channels of migration sometimes lead to routes of irregular migration. Some documented migrant workers may "run away" from the employers as an escape from debts shackles and contract bondage. Ironically, these irregular migrants become "free" in the domestic labor market and improve their working conditions, as in the case of Priscilla. Such situations contest the common ideas about improved security within legal realms and prevalent vulnerability in irregular migration.

Why are migrant contract workers trapped in this system of "legal servitude" while undocumented migrants gain higher wages and enjoy more freedom? This puzzle leads us to examine several critical dimensions in the "guest worker" system of labor migration in Asia. I offer the case of Taiwan[3] to examine how Asian states intervene in the process of international labor migration and how their policies impact the recruitment process and conditions of migrant contract workers. In such a highly regulated market, brokers are trading not only labor power but also quotas and passports for profits. For migrant workers, the legal status and contract bonds become more mechanisms of servitude than measures of protection. As a result, stringent state regulations punish those who abide by the law and induce the formation of irregular migration.

Guest or Alien?

The guest worker regime is widely adopted in Asian destination countries, in which migrant workers are employed on temporary contracts and are prohibited from immigrating or becoming naturalized. Historically, more strict modes of labor migration have existed, such as indentured workers (the "coolie" system) who were recruited, sometimes by force, to work on plantations in European colonies or the United States during the second half of the nineteenth century. Indentured workers were bound by strict labor contracts for a period of several years and subject to rigid discipline and poor wages (Castles and Miller 1993). To ease labor shortages after the second world war, several Western European countries systematically recruited foreign guest workers from Southern Europe or former colonies; these programs stopped in the mid-1970s, shadowed by the oil crisis and the subsequent recession (Castles 1986).

Today, guest worker contracts are still a common mode of employment for recruiting migrant workers from overseas. They are especially predominant in European and Asian countries that lack a history of immigration or an ideology that favors permanent settlement (Massey et al. 1998: 5). In Europe, the scheme of guest worker is prevalent in spite of national variation in methods of incorporating migrants (Soysal 1994). The European Commission also proposed a policy plan in 2005 to expand legal venues for temporary labor migration (Castles 2006). The presence of guest workers challenges the universalistic principle of European welfare states, who find it difficult to deny migrant workers their entitlements to economic and social rights. In some countries, noncitizen migrants are also granted the right to vote in local elections. Migrant workers, in theory yet not always in practice, are eligible to rights and benefits associated with the residency-based status of "denizenship" (Hammer 1989).

In Asia, more restrictive immigration policies are enforced on the basis of state concerns about geographic constraints, population densities, and nationalist agendas. Quota controls, work permits, and levies are widely adopted to control the volume and distribution of migrant workers (Cheng 1996). No immigration is granted for unskilled workers in any Asian host country so far; the Singapore government even prohibits residency to migrant workers married to Singaporean citizens.

Behind the euphemism of guest worker lies the cruel fact that the receiving state treats migrants as disposable labor, as they live in the country of destination only during a restricted term of employment. Through prohibiting migrant workers from permanent settlement and family reunification, the host state externalizes the cost of renewing labor to the economies and states of origin (Burawoy 1976). Such an arrangement allows the host country to enjoy the labor power of migrants while they are young and healthy. They are, however, sent back home after they age, fall ill, or suffer injury.

The sending state also favors the guest worker system, which positions migrants in the frame of temporary visits rather than permanent immigration. The sending state often invests in ideological work to secure the loyalty of its overseas nationals as well as the flow of their regular remittances. For example, the Philippine government has promoted the notion of "national heroes" in a media campaign based on the nationalist imagery of "homeland." In addition, many sending states have established special financial programs to attract overseas remittances, such as offering tax breaks, setting up banking facilities in receiving countries, and requiring the remittance of a fixed share of earnings into government-controlled accounts (Athukorala 1993).

Direct involvement of governments in promoting international migration is a major feature that distinguishes the Asian system from its counterparts in North America and Western Europe (Massey et al. 1998: 191). Many states of origin actively facilitate and channel the export of their nationals as profitable commodities. Several Asian governments, for example those of the Philippines and Indonesia, have established special labor export agencies within their national bureaucracies to regulate flows, train potential migrants, and promote their workers to receiving countries. Vietnam, previously a communist regime, has now established state-owned companies to handle the recruitment and placement of all overseas workers.

In addition to promoting and facilitating emigration, the sending state may also use policy tools to control certain kinds of labor outflow. Nana Oishi (2005) found that many emigration policies in Asia place specific restrictions upon overseas employment of women such as age and occupational regulations, while allowing men to leave their country almost freely. She argues that the policies for male migration are generally driven by economic imperatives, while the policies for female migration tend to be more value driven, which curtail women's freedom of movements under the moral banner of protection. I will later discuss how migrant women may circumvent these rules in practice.

In sum, we have envisaged the interlocking processes of "denationalizing economies" and "renationalizing politics" in contemporary labor migration (Sassen 1996). One the one hand, the integration of market economy, region-ally as well as globally, has facilitated and expedited the trade in migrant workers; on the other hand, nation-states continue to play an essential role as gatekeepers to regulate inflows and outflows of migration. Being incorporated into the host labor market, migrant workers are nevertheless excluded from the political collective, whose policy frameworks in the distribution of rights and benefits make migrant workers, even with legal documents to work, marginalized and vulnerable to abuses. As Michael Waltzer (1983: 58–59) describes, the market for guest workers is created based on the political prem-ise that migrants as a group constitute a "disfranchised class"—"without the denial of political rights and civil liberties and the everpresent threat of de-portation, the system would not work."

Border Control and State Regulation

In October 1989, Taiwan's government, for the first time, authorized a special order that allowed foreigners to work legally for a national construction proj-ect. Two years later, the release of working permits for migrant workers was expanded to the private sector, including construction, labor-intensive manu-facturing, and the employment of domestic helpers and caretakers. This pol-icy emerged primarily as a response to a labor shortage, or more exactly, a lack of cheap labor for low-skilled positions not in high favor by locals. The current number of documented migrant workers exceeds 360,000, about 2.5 percent of the national workforce.[4]

When Taiwan's government legalized the employment of foreign work-ers in the early 1990s, it copied a great deal from the policy frameworks in Singapore and Hong Kong, both of which had established a guest worker sys-tem in the late 1970s. The case of Taiwan is a microcosm for a trend of policy convergence in East Asia.[5] It also constitutes a significant case for the discus-sion of the guest worker program, because the state has adopted rather strict regulations on the granting of work permits and the maximum duration of the workers' stay.[6]

Vic Satzewich (1991) identifies three forms of state intervention in the pro-cess of labor migration. First, the state, by setting up a standard of *exclusion,* determines who is eligible for entry into the geographic national boundar-ies. Second, the state stipulates who is *included* within the symbolic bound-aries of the nation by regulating access to civil rights. Third, the state also determines how migrant workers are *allocated* and *incorporated* into specific sites in the relations of production and the organization of the labor process. I use this theoretical framework to examine Taiwan's foreign labor policy, whose aim, in a nutshell, is to ensure that migrant workers are temporally transient and spatially fixed. Against such policy backdrop, undocumented migrants break loose the state regulations with their mobile bodies and potential to stay permanently.

As early as the beginning of the 1980s, some Southeast Asians entered Taiwan as tourists and overstayed their visas. The estimated number of undocumented foreign workers in the late 1980s exceeded 50,000 (Tsay 1992). The legalization of migrant labor in 1989 should be read not only as a response to capitalist demands for cheap labor but also as a turning point in border control —total exclusion became limited and regulated inclusion. The Council of Labor Affairs (CLA) has adopted a quota system to control the quantity of migrant workers and their distribution in selected occupations and industries.[7]

This quota system has created an interest liaison among the state, employers, and employment agencies. The procedures of releasing quotas and granting admissions have provided a breeding ground for bribery and corruption. Taiwan's newspapers have uncovered several scandals in which employers mobilized political networks for quotas, or placement agencies paid off CLA officials to speed the bureaucratic procedures for granting admissions.

Although migrant workers are included within the geographical national boundaries, the state has taken some measures to *exclude* them from *symbolic* national boundaries. As the CLA officials have repeatedly announced, one of the crucial principles in Taiwan's migration policy is to strictly prohibit the permanent settlement of migrant workers. In the beginning, Taiwan's government mandated that the maximum duration of a migrant worker's contract was three years (two years plus a one-year extension), and each worker could work in Taiwan only once. In order to reduce the number of runaway migrants, the new legal regulation effective since January 2002 allows migrant workers "with good records" to reenter once more and work in Taiwan up to six years (including both contracts).

The inclusion or exclusion of foreigners is nevertheless selective on a class basis. While blue-collar migrant workers are not eligible for permanent residence or citizenship, white-collar professional migrants, including professionals, managers, and teachers, are subject to distinct rules. Their work permits are granted on an individual basis and not subject to quota controls. There is no limitation on length of stay in the country, and they are eligible to apply for permanent residence or citizenship after residing in Taiwan and working legally for five years or more.

The third dimension of state intervention places migrant workers in a vulnerable position by depriving them of the right to circulate in the domestic labor market. The government dictates that a migrant worker can work for only one particular employer during a stay in Taiwan. No transfer of employer is allowed except under the following conditions: if the original employer goes bankrupt, closes business, or cannot pay wages to the worker; if the care recipient of a migrant worker dies or moves to another country; or if a worker is abused by the employer or illegally placed with an employer different from the one stipulated in the contract.

By depriving migrant workers of the right to freely circulate in the domestic labor market, the government monitors the whereabouts of these ethnic others. This measure deprives workers of the proletariat's trump card—market mobility—thus helping employers stabilize the relations of production and aggravating inequality in the worker-employer relationship (Liu 2000). As I will detail later, migrant workers, in consequence, are tied to a contract of personal subordination and forced to tolerate hardship or mistreatment.

Taiwan's government also places migrant workers in the custody of employers as a way of externalizing management costs. Each employer is requested to pay a monthly levy,[8] a fee designed to subsidize government expenses for managing migrant workers and retraining local workers. If a migrant worker disappears from the custody of her or his employer, the latter is still obligated to pay the fee every month until the worker is caught or the contract expires. Another more serious punishment to the employer entails temporarily freezing the quota associated with the runaway worker so that the employer cannot hire a replacement. In other words, the employer suffers not only the loss of labor power once provided by the runaway worker, but also the loss of a more precious commodity, the quota, the capacity for replenishing migrant labor.

Brokering Labor and Quotas

In countries like Canada and the United States, where migrant workers with legal documents are entitled to acquire permanent status, contractors usually emerge within ethnic communities ("bottom-up" intermediaries). Yet in Asia, where the contract workforce is constantly replenished with new blood, both employers and workers lack sufficient information about the other party and tend to rely on private agencies as intermediaries (Martin 1996; Okunishi 1996). Placement agencies in receiving countries, together with recruitment agencies in sending countries, become major gatekeepers in the process of migration.[9] This section looks at the brokering of migrant labor in Taiwan, a market practice greatly constrained by the "visible hands" of state policy.

The placement fees charged to migrant workers for coming to Taiwan is higher than elsewhere in Asia. A migrant worker has to pay a placement fee ranging from NT$90,000 to NT$220,000, an amount that equals five to fourteen months of migrant wages in Taiwan. This charge varies by industry and nationality of workers: the job offers in construction and manufacturing cost more than domestic jobs; migrants from Thailand, Indonesia, and Vietnam usually pay more than their Filipino counterparts.

What explains the emergence of exorbitant placement fees in Taiwan? The economic model does work to some extent, but we have to consider multiple markets under the regulation of the state as a visible hand. First, there is a supply-demand imbalance in the migrant labor market. Taiwan is one of the most attractive destinations for migrant workers because of its relatively attractive wages. The minimum-wage regulation has made the average wage offered to migrants higher than that in other Asian host countries. Yet opportunities to work in Taiwan are relatively scarce owing to quota controls. Labor brokers are therefore able to appropriate a significant cut in the process of recruiting and placing workers.

The second and more crucial reason comes from the brokerage market in Taiwan. There are currently about six hundred licensed placement agencies competing to do business with a limited number of employers possessing quotas. The figure does not even include unlicensed companies or individuals, which account for about 15 percent of the market, according to a broker I interviewed. Excess capacity and limited demand have increased volatility and competition in the brokerage industry. Placement agencies in Taiwan have a notable "organizational death rate," estimated to be as high as 18 percent per year (Tsai and Chen 1997: 80)

To compete for job offers held by factory employers, placement agencies usually have to pay employers a kickback, estimated to be NT$20,000 to NT$30,000 for recruiting each migrant worker into Taiwan. In this way, it is the *service provider*, rather than the *service user*, who pays for the costs of labor recruitment (Tsai and Chen 1997: 82). The kickback burden on placement agencies also includes expenses in socializing with employers, arranging free trips for employers to interview foreign applicants, and even hiring prostitutes or escorts for employers during their stay in Southeast Asia.

A Filipino agency in Manila offered a historical account of the rising place-ment fees in Taiwan. In 1991, there were only a limited number of Taiwanese agencies and the "service fee" collected from a worker basically complied with the amount stipulated by the Philippine government, 5,000 pesos (equivalent to US$200 then). The situation changed after 1993 when Taiwan's brokerage market was opened to more participants:

> Now there are more brokers and more competition. New brokers need to get niches in the market, so they develop new marketing strategies, which is, I am the broker, you are the employer, you are dealing with agency A, you pay them this much, but agency B said, "You don't have to pay me." The employer thinks, "Yes. Why do I have to deal with agency A, if I can get free service from agency B?" Then the third broker came in, "You don't even have to pay me, I will pay you, I will send you to Manila on my expenses, you can even bring your family in and I will pay you shopping money." So these brokers got their job orders without money, but since they have invested their capital, they need to convert the job orders into money.

The kickback practice emerged out of the supply-demand imbalance in Taiwan's brokerage market: there are more brokerage services than employ-ers who want to buy (and so the prices to employers go down), while there are fewer job offers than workers who want to buy (and so the prices to workers go up). A staff in a Taiwanese agency complained bitterly about this situation: "Now the factory (employer) is the boss. Who has the quota, who is the boss . . . Trust doesn't count anymore. When another broker approaches the employer offering a higher kickback, do you think the employer will take it or not?"[10]

Placement agencies are willing to pay the kickback because they can still appropriate significant profits in the process of "converting job orders into money." Taiwanese agencies "buy" job orders from employers at the costs of the kickback and then "sell" these job orders to foreign recruiters. The prof-its generate from the placement fees collected from migrant workers. Labor brokers in both sending and receiving countries accuse the other of demand-ing excessive money, so they had no choice but to raise charges to workers. A manager in a Taiwanese placement agency said, "We cannot do anything about this. Foreign agencies want to have a share. Taiwanese employers don't want to pay. We brokers have to make money, so workers are the ones who are out of luck!" The owner of a Filipino recruitment agency, however, pointed his finger at Taiwanese brokers:

Now, 5,000 pesos became too little money, because the [Taiwanese] brokers were demanding money. So we started to lobby with our government: Why don't we increase the fee that we can collect from our workers to one month? Our government was hesitant, because NGOs [non-governmental organizations] were not happy about this. In the end, our government sugarcoats the money: they said the placement is still 5,000, but the agency can collect a "mobilization fee" that is equivalent to one month salary. It is only playing with words. Although both the Philippine and Taiwanese governments have set the maximum amount of placement fees collected from a migrant worker,[11] labor brokers invent payment categories such as mobilization fees, entrance fees, and service fees to cover the actual charge of placement fees. Some agencies require workers to sign a receipt before their departure to Taiwan to disguise wage deductions as money the worker "borrowed"—for instance, a loan "for my family's immediate expenses while waiting for my salary here in Taiwan." Some canny brokers collect cash from workers to avoid records shown on the pay slips; as such, the workers could not hold any evidence for illegal wage deduction.

The reason that placement agencies hold different attitudes toward their two sets of clients (employers and workers) owes partly to Taiwan's migration policy. A migrant worker is allowed to work in Taiwan only once or twice, but the quotas used by employers are renewable. Quota, as an abstract capacity of recruiting and replenishing workers, becomes an even more valuable commodity than migrant workers themselves. Some business associations and employers who possess the privileges to distribute or monopolize the limited number of quotas can even make extra profits by selling the quotas or subcontracting migrant workers to other employers. In favor of quota-owning employers, labor brokers burden migrant workers with most of the recruitment cost. As a result, migrant workers become victims to loan sharks and debt shackles.

Contract Bondage and Debt Shackle

The primary feature that distinguishes migrant workers from local workers is the bondage of contract employment. Many Taiwanese employers report that the total expenses for hiring a migrant worker, including food, boarding, and levies, are only slightly lower than hiring a local worker. Migrant workers are yet considered much more *hao-yong* (Chinese: easy to use) than local workers. Migrant workers reduce costs for employers not only through their lower wages, but also through their powerlessness in the organization of labor process associated with their foreigner status and lack of citizenship (Sassen 1988).

With the exception of domestic workers and caretakers, most migrant workers in Taiwan are entitled to rights and benefits stipulated in the Labor Standards Law.[12] However, the policy is motivated less by the desire to safeguard the welfare of migrants and more by the wish to appease trade unions. Universal labor standards help protect the job security of Taiwanese workers by reducing the gap between the cost of hiring a local worker and a migrant worker. The pressure from local unions explains why Taiwan's government has been hesitant to change the policy even in the face of widespread complaints among employers.

The legal protection of migrant workers is, after all, more a symbolic statement than a set of enforceable measures. The CLA has failed to supervise actual working conditions or provide effective legal assistance. Many migrant workers receive partial benefits only, having no paid vacations or receiving no overtime pay. They are often given unfavorable assignments, such as night shifts and the use of hazardous equipment in substandard conditions. For instance, Anru Lee (2002) found that Thai workers in a textile factory were assigned to double shifts and paid at a fixed rate (the minimum wage) that was lower than the wages for local workers paid on a piece-rate system.

A riot broke out on August 22, 2005, in which about a hundred Thai migrants working on Kaohsiung's mass rapid transit railway project protested against stringent labor management. The conflict was initiated when a guard stopped some workers from entering the dormitory while carrying a few bottles of beer. The riot opened up an oppressive apparatus full of human rights violations to the public scrutiny. In the name of "life management," Thai workers in this project were banned from smoking, drinking alcohol, and using mobile phones in the very confined living space. They suffered from wage docking and underpayment; they received only forty-six hours of overtime pay for the one hundred hours of overtime they worked each month. They were also subjected to other forms of exploitation because they depended on the employers to provide food and lodging. They received tokens instead of cash as their allowances, and the charges for snacks and groceries in the dormitory were much higher than market prices.

In fact, open confrontation like the described case rarely happens among foreign workers in Taiwan. When I asked, in a focus-group discussion, why migrant workers do not take action to assert their rights, the answers of the migrant participants centered on the financial burdens of debts and placement fees: "Placement fees tie our arms from fighting." "We still have five-six[13] to pay at home!" "We are afraid if we speak out, we will be sent back to the

Philippines. We don't want to spend money on placement fee again. We rather stay in Taiwan, at least making money."

Migrants are usually told by recruiters that job offers in Taiwan are valid for two or three years. In fact, their contracts are renewed annually. Those who fail to extend their contract after one year rarely get their placement fees refunded. Workers usually pay the down payment of their placement fees to recruitment agencies in their home countries. Placement agencies in Taiwan collect their share through monthly deduction from workers' wages. During their first year contract, migrant workers receive only partial wages after the subtraction of a placement-fee deduction and "forced saving" (NT$3,000–NT$5,000; a deposit held to prevent workers from running away). Their three-year stay in Taiwan is divided into three phases: the first year is to pay the debt, the second year is to balance the costs, and the third year finally nets a profit for the worker (Powpee Lee 1995).

Migrant workers, who are short of bargaining power and eager to earn money during their limited stay, grant their employers enormous flexibility in organizing the pace of production. Burdened by substantial debts, migrant workers tend to agree to work on Sundays in order to earn extra income and to save on expenses. Said two Filipina domestic workers: "If I go out, I lose money. I need more money to pay the broker." "I didn't have even one single day off the whole year! But I didn't want to, either. How can I have my days off? I don't have money at all!" The overworked migrant workers also attempt to demonstrate their loyalty and diligence to their employers to ensure the renewal of their second-year or third-year contract. One Filipina domestic worker explained to me why she voluntarily gave up her days off during her first eleven months in Taiwan: "I want to take the time to show my employers I will be good . . . I want to win their trust."

Migrant workers, bound by financial shackles, exercise overt resistance only when a contract's termination is inevitable. Open confrontation mostly happens toward the end of a contract or when employers attempt to terminate a contract. For example, Jenny was recruited as a caretaker for one patient but illegally placed in a nursing home taking care of fourteen patients, working a night shift without extra pay. She did not complain until the employer attempted to terminate her contract. Jenny then filed a complaint with the Manila Economic and Cultural Office (MECO) in Taipei[14] to seek compensation for overtime with the evidence of time cards and pay slips she had carefully collected during the whole time.

Contract bondage and debt shackle depoliticize migrant workers not only through self-discipline but also by depriving their rights of collection organizing. Although migrants are legally entitled to union membership, their alien status and fear of termination often prevent them from getting involved in similar activities. Some migrant factory workers are requested to sign an agreement that stipulates prohibition from participating in protests and rallies (Wu 1997). Another reason that discourages migrant workers from asserting their legal rights is the restriction on employment during legal proceedings (Cheng 1996). They are not allowed to work for new employers while having cases against their previous employers in court; many drop their cases when facing financial pressure during the lengthy legal process.

Lacking the opportunity to switch employers, some migrant workers manage to run away from their contractual employers. The deprivation of freedom among documented migrant workers presents a striking contrast to undocumented migrant workers, who are free to switch jobs and gain increased bargaining power in relation to unauthorized employers.

Causes and Risks of Running Away

The total number of irregular migrants in Taiwan is still unknown, which includes those who entered Taiwan with a tourist visa and overstayed and others who came as contract workers and ran away from the jobs stipulated in their work permits. According to the police, the accumulated number of runaway contract workers in Taiwan from 1994 to 2005 was 91,421. More than 76 percent of these workers have been repatriated or left the country voluntarily, and 21,679 still reside in Taiwan.[15] In 2004, about 4.35 percent of migrant contract workers left their designated employers without notice.[16] Domestic workers are reported to have the highest runaway rate among all categories of migrants, occupying almost a quarter of the total number of runaway workers.[17]

Why did migrant workers run away? I have interviewed eight migrant domestic workers without legal documents to stay and work in Taiwan. Two entered Taiwan as tourists and overstayed; the others escaped from their contract employers for various reasons. Some became undocumented to avoid abuse, maltreatment, and unreasonable workload. Some did so for more personal reasons, such as disputes with co-workers and problems in marriage or relationships. Another common incentive for escaping was workers' wish to stay in Taiwan longer than the period granted by their contracts or their employers. Otherwise, they would have to pay another large amount of placement fees and stay unemployed at home for several months prior to applying for another overseas job. This explains why many escaping cases happen near the end of contracts or when employers break or decline to renew contracts.

Runaway workers usually have developed some local connections in Taiwan. They locate new jobs either through referrals of friends or through the placement of unlicensed brokers, mostly bilingual ethnic Chinese migrants (*huaqiao*), with a charge of NT$5,000 to NT$7,000.[18] The supply of undocumented migrant labor emerges to meet the substantial demand for unauthorized employment. A two-tiered migrant labor market has thus been established: on the top are registered employers who recruit migrant labor overseas through legal venues; on the bottom are those employers who are not qualified for granting with quotas and so hire migrants without proper documents.

The undocumented status renders migrants vulnerable in many aspects, in particular to threats of deportation. Filipino migrants call runaway workers TNT (*Tag nang Tago* in Tagalog, meaning "hide and hide") or, with some black humor, *artista* (celebrity). A runaway worker explained the latter's meaning: "We call ourselves artista because we have so many fans—those policemen, they are always running after us!"

Irregular migrants may also suffer from a lack of legal protection and health insurance. NGOs in Taiwan have reported cases in which undocumented migrant women were raped by their boarding house roommates or abused by their unlicensed brokers. These victims were often afraid to seek legal assistance due to their clandestine status. Because irregular employment is not contract bound, undocumented migrants are at risks of "working for nothing" if employers or brokers maliciously withhold their wages. In addition, a number of occupational injuries happened to undocumented migrants, who mostly worked in small, unlicensed factories with hazardous environments and substandard conditions of safety. These employers could often waive their legal liability to pay a full coverage of medical expenses and indemnification for the injured migrants, a situation clearly marking the status of undocumented migrants as "disposable labor."

Illegal on Paper, Free in the Market

Despite the risks involved in irregular employment, undocumented migrants paradoxically become free in the labor market. That is, they are free to determine which of the positions offered by potential employers they will fill or leave.[19] Madeline, a Filipina who ran away one year ago and has shifted among three employers, compared her experiences as a documented and undocumented worker: "They [employers] treat illegal [workers] better. Because they have the need, they want you to stay. If they treat you bad, you will just go out. And they are afraid you will point them out [to the police that] they are illegal bosses."

The exit option empowers irregular migrants to negotiate better terms and work conditions with unauthorized employers. They are not like documented employers, who are the sole legitimate employers endorsed by the state authority. The monthly wage of an undocumented worker is about NT$5,000 to NT$10,000 higher than the wage of a legal contract worker, plus no further deductions. A survey study reports that more than half of the migrant informants enjoy raised pay, increased days off, and relaxed labor management after going undocumented (Sheu 2001). The precondition for the comfort and security of irregular migrants is that there is a sufficient supply of jobs for them. Some runaway migrants complained to me that it had become more difficult to locate factory jobs due to the recent economic depression in Taiwan. The discrepancy in working conditions across the legal and illegal realms is most significant in the sector of domestic service, where the demand continues to rise and yet employer qualification is highly regulated.

Undocumented domestic workers are able to choose arrangements accommodating more privacy and autonomy, such as day work, part time, and live out. Migrant part-timers, in particular, enjoy improved working conditions in many respects compared to the live-in documented worker. They are paid by the hour with an increased wage rate, and their working hours and tasks are clearly defined. The job content amounts to house cleaning and usually excludes laundry, ironing, and dishwashing. Part-time cleaners have minimal interaction with their employers, a situation that allows domestic workers autonomy and flexibility in arranging the procedure and pace of work (Romero 1992). It also assists domestic workers in avoiding risks involved in a live-in condition, such as abuse, maltreatment, sexual harassment, and excessive demands.

The live-out arrangement also protects freedom and privacy of workers and lessens isolation and monotony prevalent in a live-in condition.[20] Migrant part-timers usually share a rental apartment. Access to a private space shelters their lifestyles and habits from employers' regulation. They can freely smoke, drink, dance, and invite friends to stay over. They hold frequent social activities in their apartments with other migrants, including ethnic Chinese and spouses of Taiwanese. With more social connection to the local society, many of them are able to run sideline businesses, such as selling Levis jeans, cellular phones, internet phone cards, and direct-selling products to other migrant workers.

As a consequence of these live-out benefits, undocumented part-timers could develop a more balanced relationship with employers than the live-in documented workers. They have stronger bargaining power to negotiate working conditions, to control the labor process, and to arrange their schedules and days off in a flexible way. Once Priscilla invited me to a Sunday party in her apartment. While we were eating adobo and singing karaoke, her cellular phone rang. One of her employers called begging her to squeeze a service into her busy schedule so that the employer's house would not become a mess. After hanging up, Priscilla proudly said to me:

> If you are part-timer, you are the boss! If you don't want to work, it's OK. Not like stay-in, you feel lazy but you still have to do it. You get only one day free. Part-timer, you can have everyday free. It's just you don't earn. Sometimes we have appointments; then we set another date. That's why I told you we are the bosses! We choose the day, choose the time. We have more freedom and power!

A symmetrical dynamic of employment relationship is reflected in the titles part-time workers use for their employers. Unlike live-in migrants who call their employers "Madam" indicating an undisputable class hierarchy, part-time workers call their employers by their last name or first name on a more equal basis. When asked how they addressed their employers, Cecilia, an undocumented part-time cleaner expressed a clear aversion toward the term *Madam* and emphasized her capability to negotiate an equal-footing position in the symbolic struggles of calling names:

> I call them names, like Mrs. Chang. I never call them Ma'am. Why do I call them Ma'am? I think it's not good to call them Ma'am, because we are the same. If I call them Ma'am, they look down on me. So I just call her Mrs. Wang. But many of my employers have the same last name, so I asked them, "What is your English names?" They said, "I don't have any." I said, "OK, I will give you a name. You look sexy, so I call you 'Sexy'!" When she calls me, I said "Who is this?" She said, "Sexy!"

While Cecilia was telling me this, Trina, a contract domestic worker, cut in and said, "You can do that, because you are part-time, you are not live-in!" Migrant workers are victimized in a live-in arrangement not only because they are physically confined in the residences of employers, but also because they are legally bound to their contract employers. As noted earlier, Taiwan's government prohibits migrant workers from transferring employers and circulating in the local labor market. These legal constraints exacerbate a status of personal subordination. Fey, a Filipina domestic worker who for years had overstayed as a tourist, came back to Taiwan in 1999 as a contract worker. She compared her different work experiences:

> If you are an OCW, you are controlled by your employers in two or three years. If they are not good, you still have to stay with them. If you are a tourist, you can just leave and find another employer. For example, I ask for an over night stay. If they don't agree, I just transfer to another employer. But now OCWs can't, so if their employer is bad, they just run away.

When irregular migrants surrender to or get caught by the police, they are obligated to point out at least one employer before repatriation.[21] A couple of undocumented migrants I visited in a detention center were held there for a while only because they refused to report any names of their previous employers. One told me, half jokingly and half seriously, "My last employer was bad. I am going to give her name to the police!" To avoid being pointed out and charged for government fines, unauthorized employers are compelled to treat their undocumented employees with some kindness because both of them are located outside the legal realm.

Passports as Fictitious Commodities

Another common illegal practice among migrant workers in Taiwan is the use of counterfeit documentation. To avoid the rule of working only once or twice in Taiwan, many migrant workers reenter Taiwan with forged passports. They are called "ex-Taiwan" by fellow migrants. In some cases, returning with a falsified name is acknowledged or even encouraged by employers, especially household employers who wish to keep the employees they have grown accustomed to instead of recruiting and training new ones. Many ex-Taiwan migrants borrow the names of their siblings or cousins, who have decided not to work overseas and are willing to lend them their legal identities. Others, through recruitment agencies, purchase names of people they have never met. A Filipina migrant, who had used passports under three different names during her ten-year stay in Taiwan (with one overstayed tourist visa and two working contracts), mocked herself: "I have so many names. Now I don't even remember what my real name is!"

Migrant workers need passports with falsified information not only to bypass the rules of host states but also to avoid the restriction of their own governments. Most sending Asian states have placed age restrictions on female migration. Women in the Philippines must be at least twenty-one years old to work abroad as domestic workers and eighteen as entertainers. The age restriction is even stricter in South Asia; for example, the Indian government only allows women over thirty to carry on domestic work in western Asia and northern Africa (Oishi 2005: 60). Despite the existence of these rules, it is a common practice for underaged women to work abroad by using forged passports with falsified age records.

The passport, as a means for the documentation of individual identity, is fundamental to the operation of nation-states. It represents the state's documentary control over the movements of people in a national community that is geographically bounded and bureaucratically guarded (Torpey 2000). The passport as a tag of membership bestowed by the state of origin allows the bureaucracy to identify and track those who travel across borders. It also provides an essential document of personhood required for one's entrance and circulation in the global labor market. The practices of using forged passports or reporting falsified information reveal how migrants maneuver the institutional channels of nationhood and citizenship to improve their prospect in the bounded global market. Although counterfeit documents indicate a malfunction of the bureaucratic apparatus, sending governments often turn a blind eye to covert violation in order to facilitate labor export.

The varied strategies that migrants develop to circumvent the documentary control of nation-states reveal grave inequality in the resources available to different class groups. Aihwa Ong (1999) found that business and professional migrants from Hong Kong and Taiwan seek passports from different countries to facilitate their business and social ties across national borders and to achieve a metropolitan lifestyle in multiple continents. In contrast, lower-status migrants obtain multiple passports from their home nation to recycle quotas and repeat entry into destination countries. For these mobile workers, "nationality is no more than a means to facilitate travel" (Harris 1995: 221). In poor sending countries, where many nationals cannot afford to travel abroad unless working overseas, the passport becomes a commodity that can be bought and sold between locals and overseas migrants.

Karl Polanyi (1944/1957) wrote about the "great transformation" in the beginning of the nineteenth century: labor, land, and money—three elements that were the subsistence of human and societal existences in feudalism—turned into "fictitious commodities" in the new market economy. The self-regulated market, seemly an invisible hand on the surface, could not sustain itself without the intervention of the state by regulating finance, trade, labor markets, and conditions of work in alliance with growing trade unions. The insights of Polanyi remain helpful in sorting out the relationship between market and state in contemporary global capitalism and revealing the complex modes of commodification in the nexus of international labor migration.

Aristide Zolberg (1991) describes contemporary nation-states as the "bounded states in a global market," which continues to guard the porous borders based on the model of state sovereignty and nation-based citizenship. I would like to further point out that migrant workers are situated in a bounded global market. Transnational labor recruitment exacerbates the commodification of migrant workers, who are treated as profitable objects of exchange by labor brokers and disposable labor power by receiving countries. Meanwhile, the global labor market space is shaped and patterned by bilateral links between state agencies, whose visible hands direct and channel movements of migrant workers, domestically and internationally.

In this bounded global market, multiple forms of fictitious commodities have been created against the backdrops of state sovereignty and territorialized regulations. First, *quotas,* privileges granted by the host government to a small proportion of employers, become a valuable commodity that can be bought and sold between employers and agencies and between qualified employers and unqualified employers. Quotas, with the capacity to renew migrant labor, are converted into economic values even before they are used to employ a migrant worker who actually creates productive values. Second, *job offers,* which refer to overseas employment opportunities, are monopolized by the transnational brokerage industry. Agencies purchase jobs from employers at the cost of kickbacks and then convert job offers into profits by collecting exorbitant placement fess from migrant applicants. Finally, *the passport,* a symbol of one's national membership, is turned into a lucrative item purchased by migrants to multiply their job opportunities in the global labor market.

Conclusion

The "guest worker" policy in Asia has created a highly exploitative system of labor migration. Migrant workers not only lack political rights and civil liberties but also are deprived of the economic right of market mobility. They constitute a new form of slave labor tied to temporary contracts and personal subordination. The oppressive labor conditions and excessive placement fees, coupled with uncertainties in the renewal of contracts, contribute to the increasing number of runaway migrants in Taiwan. State regulations, hence, have resulted in a two-tiered labor market for migrant workers. Indeed, as we have seen, undocumented, or irregular, migrants can nevertheless escape the circumstance of "legal servitude" and enjoy some "free illegality" in the underground economy.

The problem of runaway migrants signals an erosion of state sovereignty, indicating that the government fails to monitor the whereabouts of foreigners who are supposedly slotted in the country only for a transient period. Without dealing with the root causes of irregular migration, the government only tries to iron out the problem with temporary bans on employment[22] and severe penalties on unauthorized employers. The system also holds contract employers liable for the escape of their employees, leading to control strategies such as wage withholding, surveillance, and even confinement (see Lan 2006). And yet, the stricter the measures of personal control the employers adopt, the more likely migrant workers will choose to escape them.

Recently, some countries, including the United States, have turned to the guest worker program as a solution to the prevalence of irregular migration. The Bush government advocates this system as the best model of "managing" labor migration to strike a balance between easing labor shortages and patrolling borders. However, as I have shown in the case of Asia, the guest worker program often becomes an oppressive regime of labor control and social exclusion. Similar situations have also happened to foreign workers recruited to do farm work in the United States under short-term contracts, many of whom suffer from low pay, exorbitant fees, and broken promises (Greenhouse 2007). State regulations in the name of management may only subject migrant workers to legal servitude if there is no sufficient protection of civil rights or enforcement of universal labor standards. Scholars have also criticized the exclusion of guest workers from family unification and naturalization as an immoral policy against the ideals of justice and democracy (Waltzer 1983).

In reality, the presence of guest workers has become relatively permanent in many host countries. In Asia, migrants make up some 29 percent of the workforce in Singapore; Malaysia has about 16 percent; in the Persian Gulf countries, migrant workers outnumber national workers (Asia 2004). Although their contract-bond overseas stay is inevitably transient, it often prolongs into a sojourn of migration. The trajectory of circular migration may involve a series of movements across countries. For example, many Asian migrants first work in the Middle East, later move to East Asia where higher wages are offered, and then seek immigration to Canada as the final destination. Other migrants use false documents or overstay visas to extend their residence in the same country. They may not become permanent citizens in host countries, but their active participation has greatly contributed to the economic, social, and cultural life of the host societies.

In facing the situation of the "provisional diaspora" of migrant workers (Barber 2000), we need alternative policy frameworks beyond the conventional ideas of membership and sovereignty. If the host country really treats migrants as guests, it must break loose the dichotomy between citizen and alien. Migrants, who contribute their labor and tax to host societies, should enjoy substantial rights and benefits based on a "membership without citizenship" (Brubaker 1989). International conventions and transnational migrant movements have also advocated the protection of migrant workers based on the global discourse of universal human rights (Soysal 1994). As labor equals and human fellows, migrant workers should be granted the freedom to change jobs and extend residency, as well as the rights to participate in civil politics in the residence country; their family should be entitled to public education and other social services. In the dire strait of globalization, we have to remap the course of national sovereignty by anchoring on the shores of moral obligations and human rights. After all, the essential values of membership are not based on blood ties or formal identifications but are constituted by equality, solidarity, and participation of members in a community, be it a city, a society, or the world.

Notes

I am grateful for the comments of Rhacel Parreñas and Lok Siu. The completion of this article was sponsored by a research grant from the National Science Council in Taiwan (NSC 93-2412-H-002-004-SSS).

1. These documented workers are able to conduct part-time work under the sponsorship of their contract employers. They usually have worked in Taiwan before and their sponsors were their previous employers. Some of them provide free cleaning services in exchange for the sponsorship of employers.

2. The monthly wage of a migrant contract worker is NT$15,840, equivalent to the amount of the minimum wage in Taiwan. The overtime pay is NT$580 per day. Part-time cleaners are paid by the hour; the market rate is NT$250–300 per hour. The exchange rate at the end of March 2007 for one U.S. dollar to one NT (New Taiwanese) dollar is NT$33.

3. This chapter is part of a larger project on Filipina and Indonesian domestic workers in Taiwan. See Lan (2006) for a comprehensive discussion of the foreign labor policy and ethnographic details of the situation of migrant workers in Taiwan.

4. Council of Labor Affairs, Executive Yuan, Taiwan, R.O.C, http://statdb.cla.gov.tw/statis/webproxy.aspx?sys=100&funid=alienjsp, accessed on April 10, 2007.

5. South Korea started admitting unskilled foreign labor and adopted a similar guest worker policy in August 2004. Japan has allowed the employment of foreign contract workers in particular occupational categories, including entertainers and caregivers (the latter is a new policy implemented in 2006).

6. In Singapore and Hong Kong, the employment of foreign domestic workers is granted as long as the income of the household is sufficient; foreign workers could extend their contracts without a maximum duration but they are by no means entitled to permanent residence or naturalization.

7. Based on investigations into an alleged labor shortage, the CLA determines the size of quotas, selects the industries or occupations that may enjoy quotas, and releases the quotas on an irregular basis. The qualification for the employment of domestic helpers and caregivers is based on the "urgent need" of employers, measured by the number and age of the children in a household or the physical condition of the elder or patient.

8. The size of the levy, officially called an "employment stabilization fee," is NT$1,500 for the employment of caretakers and NT$5,000 for the employment of domestic helpers.

9. Recently, some Taiwanese agencies have bought out agencies in sending countries to minimize transaction costs. Because the sending governments outlaw foreigner-owned agencies, these Taiwanese brokers purchase management rights and register under the name of local owners.

10. Anonymous brokers interviewed by Lin Chia-li (Aldrich 2000, appendix: 3-2B: 3) and translated by the author.

11. In Taiwan, an agency can legally collect a placement fee up to the amount of a worker's monthly wage, plus a monthly service fee (NT$1,800 during the first year, NT$1,700 during the second, and NT$1,500 during the third). Accordingly, the maximum amount of legal placement and service fees collected from a worker during three years totals NT$75,840.

12. According to the current law, the maximum working hours are eight hours a day and fory-eight hours a week; workers are entitled to one weekly leave plus seven days of annual leave. In terms of copaying health insurance, the employer is responsible for 60 percent, the government for 10 percent, and the worker for 30 percent.

13. A short-cut expression refers to loans borrowed from loan sharks in the Philippines: as one borrows 5,000 pesos, he or she has to return 6,000 pesos in a month (monthly interest rate equals to 20 percent).

14. Given the absence of formal diplomatic relationship between Taiwan and the Philippines, MECO serves as a proxy institution for the Philippine embassy in Taiwan. The labor office in MECO is an overseas branch of the Overseas Workers' Welfare Agency (OWWA).

15. Statistics provided by the National Police Agency, Ministry of the Interior, Executive Yuan, Republic of China, August 18, 2005.

16. Police Statistics Report, no. 8, 2005 (February 22, 2005), available at: http://www.npa.gov.tw/stats.php?page=content06_1&id=72&tr_id=&pages=1, accessed on March 24, 2006.

17. Statistics provided by the CLA, August 1998. Unfortunately, similar occupation-based statistics are not available for recent years. Chao (2004) estimated that the proportion was getting even higher after 2000.

18. It should be noted that licensed and unlicensed brokers are not necessarily exclusive categories. Chao (2004: 78) reported that one Indonesian Chinese, working as a freelance recruiter for a licensed manpower company, places jobs for undocumented migrants on the side. Sometimes he even makes extra money by turning in undocumented migrants and earning rewards from the police.

19. My definition of "free labor" and "unfree labor" draws on Vic Satzewich (1991), who points out these two ways in which foreign workers are incorporated into host economies. By free labor, he follows Karl Marx to describe that workers in capitalism are "free to determine which of the positions offered by potential buyers of wage labour they will fill, a decision which lends a degree of personal determination within the limits set by market forces" (Satzewich 1991: 41).

20. It should be noted that not all undocumented migrants prefer live-out, part-time jobs. Some prefer a live-in condition that saves the costs of lodging and food expenses and the trouble of locating multiple employers. In addition, live-out workers face a higher risk of being caught by the police, because they are more visible when renting a boarding house together.

21. The current law stipulates that an unauthorized employer is subject to a fine as much as NT$750,000 and could be sentenced to jail for recommitment within five years.

22. Taiwan's government has imposed several temporary bans on the recruitment of Indonesian and Vietnamese workers as a warning against their rising runaway rates.

References

Aldrich, Louis. 2000. *A Comparison of the official and Unofficial Systems for Foreign Workers in Taiwan: the Present Situation and an Ethical Analysis* (in Chinese). Taipei: Fu-Jen University.

Athukorala, Premachandra. 1993. "Improving the Contribution of Migrant Remittances to Development: The Experience of Asian Labor-Exporting Countries." *Migration Review* 24:323–346.

Asis, Maruja. 2004. "When Men and Women Migrate: Comparing Gendered Migration in Asia." Paper presented to United Nations Division for the Advancement of Women (DAW) Consultative Meeting on "Migration and Mobility and How this Movement Affects Women," Malmo, Sweden, December 2–4, 2003. Available at: http://www.un.org/womenwatch/draw/meetings/consult/CM-Dec03-EPI.pdf, accessed on June 2, 2005.

Barber, Pauline Gardiner. 2000. "Agency in Philippine Women's Labor Migration and Provisional Diaspora." *Women's Studies International Forum* 23(4): 399–411.

Battistella, Graziano. 2002. "International Migration in Asia Vis-à-vis Europe: An Introduction." *Asian and Pacific Migration Journal* 11(4): 405–414.

Brubaker, W. Rogers. 1989. *Immigration and Politics of Citizenship in Europe and North America.* Lanham, MD: University Press of America.

Burawoy, Michael. 1976. "The Functions and Reproduction of Migrant Labor: Comparative Material from Southern Africa and the United States." *American Journal of Sociology* 81 (5): 1050–1087.

Castles, Stephen. 1986. "The Guest Worker in Western Europe: An Obituary." *International Migration Review* 20(4): 761–778.

———. 2006. "Guest Workers in Europe: A Resurrection?" *International Migration Review* 40(4): 741–766.

Castles, Stephen, and Mark Miller. 1993. *The Age of Migration: International Population Movements in the Modern World.* New York: The Guilford Press.

Cheng, Shu-Ju Ada. 1996. "Migrant Women Domestic Workers in Hong Kong, Singapore and Taiwan: A Comparative Analysis." *Asian and Pacific Migration Journal* 5 (1): 139–152.

Chao, Jimmy. 2004. *Suppressed Labor Rights of Migrant Domestic Workers in Taiwan* (in Chinese). Masters thesis, National Chengchi University, Taipei, Taiwan.

Greenhouse, Steven. 2007. "Low Pay and Broken Promises Greet Guest Workers in the U.S.," *New York Times,* February 28, 2007, A-1, 16.

Hammer, Thomas. 1989. "State, Nation, and Dual Citizenship." Pp. 81–95 in *Immigration and the Politics of Citizenship in Europe and North America.* edited by William Rogers Brubaker. Lanham, MD: University Press of America.

Harris, Nigel. 1995. *The New Untouchable: Immigration and the New World Workers.* London: I. B. Tauris Publishers.

Lan, Pei-Chia. 2006. *Global Cinderellas: Migrant Domestics and Newly Rich Employers in Taiwan.* Durham, NC: Duke University Press.

Lee, Anru. 2002. "Guests from the Tropics: Labor Practice and Foreign Workers in Taiwan." Pp. 183–202 in *Transforming Gender and Development in East Asia.* ed. Esther Ngan-ling Chow. New York: Routledge.

Lee, Powpee. 1995. *Why Don't They Take Actions? A Study on Different Acting Strategies of Foreign Workers* (in Chinese). Masters thesis, Fu-Jen Catholic University, Hsin Chuan, Taiwan.

Liu, Mei-Chun. 2000. "A Critique from Marxist Political Economy on the 'Cheap Foreign Labor' Discourse (in Chinese)." *Taiwan: A Radical Quarterly in Social Studies* 38: 59–90.

Martin, David. 1996. "Labor Contractors: A Conceptual Overview." *Asian Pacific Migration Journal* 5 (2–3): 201–218.

Massey, Douglas G., Hugo J. Arango, A. Kouaouci, A. Pellegrino, and J. Taylor. 1998. *Worlds in Motion: Understanding International Migration at the End of the Millennium.* Oxford: Clarendon Press.

Okunishi, Yoshio. 1996. "Labor Contracting in International Migration: The Japanese Case And Implications for Asia." *Asian and Pacific Migration Journal* 5 (2–3): 219–40.

Oishi, Nana. 2005. *Women in Motion: Globalization, State Policies, and Labor Migration in Asia.* Stanford: Stanford University Press.

Ong, Aihwa. 1999. *Flexible Citizenship: The Cultural Logics of Transnationality.* Durham, NC: Duke University Press.

Polanyi, Karl. [1944] 1957. *The Great Transformation: The Political and Economic Origins of Our Time.* Boston: Beacon Press.

Romero, Mary. 1992. *Maid in the U.S.A.* London: Routledge.

Sassen, Saskia. 1988. *The Mobility of Labor and Capital: A Study in International Investment and Labor Flow.* Cambridge: Cambridge University Press.

———. 1996. *Losing Control?: Sovereignty in an Age of Globalization.* New York: Columbia University Press.

Satzewich, Vic. 1991. *Racism and the Incorporation of Foreign Labor: Farm Labor Migration to Canada Since 1945.* London: Routledge.

Sheu, Wen-Yuan. 2001. *The Study of Illegal Foreigner Worker Regulative Policy in R.O.C.—From Aspect of Policy Implementation Theory* (in Chinese). Masters thesis, National Chengchi University, Taipei, Taiwan.

Soysal, Yasemin Nuhoglu. 1994. *Limits of Citizenship: Migrants and Postnational Membership in Europe.* Chicago: The University of Chicago Press.

Torpey, John. 2000. *The Invention of the Passport: Surveillance, Citizenship and the State.* Cambridge: Cambridge University Press.

Tsai, Ming-Chang, and Jia-Huei Chen. 1997. "The State, Foreign Worker Policy, and Market Practices: Perspective from Economic Sociology (in Chinese)." *Taiwan: A Radical Quarterly in Social Studies* 27: 69–96.

Tsay, Ching-Lung. 1992. "Clandestine Labor Migration to Taiwan." *Asian and Pacific Migration Journal* 4(4): 613–20.

Walzer, Michael. 1983. *Spheres of Justice: A Defense of Pluralism and Equality.* New York: Basic Books.

11 Asian Diasporas, and Yet . . .

David Palumbo-Liu

THE ESSAYS COLLECTED HERE provide ample evidence of the tremendous variety of ways diasporic subjects are interpellated by a multiplicity of regimes—those of the state, of national ideologies, of market forces, labor demands, ethnic and religious affiliations, and by gendering, familial, and other roles. The essays are for the most part scrupulously historical and empirically substantiated, but beyond that, what is laudable is their effort to excavate and debate new and unexpected histories and evidentiary objects, often located at the seam of the dominant discourses with and through which we have grown accustomed to producing knowledge of others. The instantiations of a new Chinese diasporic *habitus* in Cuba and Peru; the Japanese communities in Brazil; the role of the state in evoking, reinventing, and exploiting gender and nationalist identifications in migrant laborers; the elasticity of Korean national identity as propounded from various exiled spaces; the reinvention of spousal relations and their relation to diasporic national identifications; the liminal yet functional identifications of adopted Koreans; and the mobile, global community of Filipino seafarers whose diasporic sites are the chronotopes of ships and oceanic voyages all provide a wealth of information with which to test the capaciousness of theories of diaspora. Cultural rituals around beauty, religion, food, and femininity, rituals that are commonly regarded as both articulating and consolidating social identity, position, distinction, and value, are discovered to be crosshatched by shifting and hybridizing forces of location, power, intent, and reception. And yet . . . perhaps *because* of this wealth and variety of case histories, one cannot help but wonder, "Why *Asian diasporas*?" What is the conceptual, historical, theoretical, and political jus-tification for subordinating each of these cases beneath that rubric? Posing this question inevitably leads us to core questions about the very ability to conceptualize diaspora.

The editors of this volume recognize and address this question, yet the answers remain only partially satisfying. And the incompleteness of these an-swers again points to the inherently difficult and entirely provocative nature of theorizing diaspora. My thesis will be that diaspora as transported into the modern and postmodern periods contains a basic contradiction. The ru-bric, Asian Diasporas, evinces—as well as any other naming of a diaspora or diasporas—this contradiction. Let me briefly consider first the notion of dias-pora and then of Asian diasporas. The editors write, with regard to diaspora: "We view the experience of diaspora to entail one's (1) displacement from the homeland under the nexus of an unequal global, political, and economic sys-tem; (2) the simultaneous experience of alienation and the maintenance of affiliation to both the country of residence and homeland; and finally (3) a sense of collective consciousness and solidarity with other people displaced from the homeland across the diasporic terrain." I think that this emphasis on "experience" and "consciousness" captures well the intent of the volume, especially if we look at how the terms are traditionally defined. The Oxford English Dictionary (OED) defines *experience* as "the fact of being consciously the subject of a state or condition, or of being consciously affected by an event. Also an instance of this; a state or condition viewed subjectively; an event by which one is affected." Here the editors' comments jibe well with the OED's definition—subjects are "conscious" of their being in a state of diaspora, and their actions and behaviors manifest that consciousness. But this is only the OED's fourth definition of *experience*. The first few focus rather on experience as "testing": "The action of putting to the test; trial, *to make experience of.*" The second entry takes this further: "A tentative procedure; an operation per-formed in order to ascertain or illustrate some truth; an experiment."

If we take these definitions together, alongside the comments of the editors of this volume, then we can regard these essays as documenting the testing out of the notion of diaspora, of stretching its designation and empirically, through the actions and behaviors of the subjects documented here, putting the meaning of the term under trial. I suggest that we follow this spirit and put the notion of diasporic experience and consciousness to a series of other tests. One such test would be to confront head-on the following statement from the editors' Introduction: "We stress that the diasporic condition is produced by the partial belonging of subjects to both their place of residence and the homeland, and more specifically by the displacement caused by their placement outside the logic of the racially and culturally homogenous and territorially bounded nation-state." I take seriously the wording here—the editors are not claiming that the state is in fact homogeneous; I take them rather to be deploying the word *logic* as a way to avoid such a claim. We seem to be instructed to look at the operationalizing of that logic in practice. Indeed, the spatialization that founds the very opening gambit of this project ("outside") would seem to beg our attention, dividing the terrain of analysis into a binary opposition of inside/outside, even as the sentence is introduced by the notion of "partial" belonging. This binary is precisely that which these studies seek to explode, and yet the analytic frame persists as the enabling backdrop—diaspora has to name both a difference and a sameness at once, and inside *and* an outside, a *co*-occupation, and this is its tension. Seen from this angle, diasporic subjects are thus located dialectically both inside and outside the logic of the "racially and culturally homogenous and territorially bounded nation-state," and concomitantly, that state must be recognized as riddled with difference, and its boundedness secured dialectically as well, and secured by hegemonic identifications that admit an unruly and unsettled and unsettling space for difference within, and by geopolitics and notions of sovereignty as well.

These specters of "homogeneity" and boundedness haunt the logic of this collection of essays that so well and so convincingly offer evidence of heterogeneity and flexibility. Seeming to sense this spectral presence, the editors seek to justify the unifying modifier, *Asian:* "We do not claim the formation of an all-encompassing or singular Asian diaspora . . . we are not proposing a pan-ethnic Asian diaspora but rather insist on referring to Asian diasporas as well as the fragmentation of ethnicity, gender, race, nation, sexuality, and class in and across diasporas." But we are still faced with the question, why retain *Asia*? Why not let free rein to these phenomena? What holds these discrepant phenomena together? Why restrict them to Asia? Are "Asian" diasporas accidents (coincidences) of location, of geography? Or is it not a racial term, and thus a way of relying on some family resemblance among the subjects under scrutiny and relegating others outside? If that is the case, is this not to erase one of the main effects of diaspora, which is mixedness? And then why lean toward the "Asian" side of things?

The racial seems to be abandoned in favor of an oppositional definition, one that differentiates Asia from the West. The trouble with adopting such a formulation is that, while we can perhaps accept it as a strategy, it seems again to accept and thereby reinforce precisely those categories in (to my mind) too broad and undifferentiated a fashion. Not only does this formulation rely upon a reification of West and Rest, but it also makes it hard to account for the diasporic populations that were the product of the conquest of the Philippines, Korea, and parts of China by the Japanese in the first half of the twentieth century, or the civil and national wars in Korea, Cambodia, and other parts of Indochina. Each of these acts of conquest, national division, and inter-Asian strife created exiled subjects. Think too of the Islamic communities in Malaysia and the Philippines, whose presence there stands in a vexed relation to the West and Rest formula. I am wondering then if we might get a fuller and more precise sense of what "Asian" diasporas might mean if we bring in case histories that are less fixated upon the West and Rest. And some of the essays here do just that.

Besides an appeal to us to extend our working definition of *diaspora* historically and outside (or in senses other than) the West and Rest division, I would suggest a wider inquiry into the driving forces behind the movement of populations outside the homeland. Besides the familiar agents of expulsion and out-migration of national, ethnic and racial, and national subjects, let's also think about the relegation of the insane, the deviant, the illegal, the variously abject, outside national borders. This points to a potentially rich field of inquiry and stands both within and alongside the racial, ethnic, and economic. Hitler went after communists, Jews, and queers, after all. Wong Kar-wai's brilliant film, "Happy Together" captures precisely this sense of a queer, class-bound, Chinese, Hong Kong, Argentinian locatedness and displacement, in which the West is but one part (and a minor one at that) of a complex intersection of identifications and desires. In each of the above arguments, rather than simply "critiquing" the aim or agenda of this collection, I am attempting to demonstrate how the term *diaspora* holds within it a series of contradictions that the name itself seeks to elide. The most general way to name this contradiction is to locate it at the nexus of similitude and difference. Each articulation of diaspora (home, yet not home; national subject, yet not subject to the nation; Asian, yet not Asian) rehearses this dialectical negation of the negation as well, and we should, I believe, extend it both more broadly and self-reflectively as well.

My next point returns to the discussions of "experience" and "consciousness." To me, it would be essential to build in a discussion of what might be called "intensities" or calibrations of affect and action. What I mean by this is that we need to somehow distinguish the degree to which any particular instance of "diasporic consciousness" is made or registered. This would be a critical element of any testing of the actual form of diaspora. And this leads to my final point, which is at once etymological and historical.

If we look to the Jewish (and here specifically Zionist-inflected) notion of *galut,* from which the term *diaspora* is derived, then we have precisely the notion of not only diasporic longing for a home, but political strategizing for a nation-state. Hence, to argue that diaspora is not state bounded or delimited is not only to present a partial reading of its designation but to neutralize a key historical and political fact. As I have written elsewhere, historically the notion of diasporic identity (a shared disseminated/dispersed identity) was in large part a compensation for the loss of a state: diaspora was precisely the condition of statelessness read as homelessness. It mourned deeply that loss, yet retained the possibility of its recovery or re-creation. The Jews felt this; the Palestinians still do. The right to return is a *fundamental* and to many nonnegotiable right. I do not mention the case of the Palestinians to be politically correct, nor to disavow the call found in these pages, to think outside the nation-state, but rather I wish to remind us always of the historical location of our pronouncements and theorizations. This is exactly what I meant above when I said that the transposition of diaspora from the premodern to the modern and postmodern historical moments cannot completely slough off the historical and foundational element of disenfranchisement and statelessness that drives the identification with home. If we substitute for that political identification a kind of vestigal form of cultural identification, we should realize not only what we are doing and the historical context that deeply affects our so doing, but we should also consider that there is an abiding possibility that the cultural identification with home is more than (merely) sentimental. I want to read these essays as much for that abiding sense of loss as for the empowering sense of making a difference, or at least, so as not to homogenize, make us sensitive to the possibility that for some diaspora is a loss of something real and irrecoverable. And the recombinatory poetics we find in these essays might well be read for the ratio of compensation/liberation they may evince.

In short, what I would ask us to do is to recognize and grapple with the ideological richness of the term in order to account better for its saliency, to recognize its modification and function under different circumstances. We should be working together to arrive at a more finely tuned optic that would, again, realize the historically produced and actually lived heterogeneity behind and within seemingly homogeneous categories, but also the ideological and practical lure and demand for claims to sameness, in other words, to identity (idem). Because that is what *identity* signifies—sameness through time. The experience of diasporic identity may be seen to be the testing out of the conditions of articulating identity after the historical rupturing of locatedness. And this collection of essays gives us more than enough material with which to debate the parameters of the terms and the legitimacy of labels. And for that, we must congratulate the editors and each of the authors.

12 Beyond "Asian Diasporas"

Ien Ang

THIS COLLECTION OF ESSAYS brings together a range of diverse and divergent histories, experiences, and practices of "Asian diasporas" in a volume that gives us astute insights into, among others, the gender politics of transnational marriages between Vietnamese migrant men and women from the Vietnamese homeland, the problematically racialized diasporic identities of Korean adoptees in the West, the ambiguous and shifting racialization and ethnicization of Japanese Brazilian migrants as they "return" to Japan, the role of the Filipino state in the management of the labor diaspora of Filipino seafarers, the contradictory experiences of "legal" and "illegal" Filipina domestic workers in Taiwan, and the politics of religious ritual among Hindu and Muslim Indians in Trinidad. The sheer diversity of subject matter addressed by these rich essays indicates that the movement of peoples from parts of Asia to other parts of the world (and back) has had a long-standing and complex history, a history that cannot be told in any singular, one-dimensional, or teleological manner. As the editors put it in their Introduction, "essays in this volume illustrate the ongoing social relations, memories, and imaginaries, and cultural production of diasporic Asians that construct multiple links to places, cultures, and communities." Indeed, the notion of Asian diasporas to bring these diverse histories, experiences, and practices together can be no more than a facilitating device—a strategically essentializing and homogenizing move that is designed to focus our analytic eye on particular, historically and geographically specific *ethnoscapes* (to use Arjun Appadurai's term) that may not have received sufficient scholarly consideration so far. In this respect, the value of this edited collection is beyond contestation. Moreover, this very move—this speaking of Asian diasporas —enables us to look at ways in which we can go *beyond* the artificial boundaries that any categorical concept creates: ultimately, the histories, experiences, and practices that we are fortunate to learn about in this book cannot be contained within the singular category of Asian diasporas.

The historical association of *diaspora* with the archetypical Jewish case points to the deeply emotional and political connotations of the term. The diasporic experience is often described negatively in terms of exile, isolation, and loss, of displacement from the ancestral homeland as a traumatic experience, where some catastrophic event—often but not always of a political nature—is collectively remembered as the starting point of the original dispersion. Concomitantly, a longing for a *return* to the homeland is classically assumed to be integral to diasporic consciousness. In the Jewish case, this longing for return has been expressed politically in the Zionist struggle for the creation of a new Jewish homeland, that is, the modern nation-state of Israel in 1947. This development highlights an important assumption in the modern meaning of diaspora, namely, that all peoples must have a territorially specific homeland and that living away from it is an unnatural and undesirable condition. This meaning of diaspora as deviant is strongly associated with the lingering dominance of the modernist global nation-state system and its ideological assumption of perfect overlap of nation, people, territory, and culture.

Today, however, the term *diaspora* is increasingly used in a more generalized sense to refer to all kinds of groups who have a history of dispersion, groups variously referred to as immigrants, expatriates, refugees, guest workers, exile communities, overseas communities, ethnic minorities, and so on. Overall, the term is reserved to describe collectivities who feel not fully accepted by, and partly alienated from, the dominant culture of the "host society," where they do not feel (fully) at home. In other words, where the classic definition of *diaspora* emphasized the traumatic past of the dispersed group, in today's usage *trauma* is located as much in the present, in the contemporary experiences of marginalization or discrimination in the nation-state of residence. The essays in this collection eloquently speak to these experiences in a variety of contexts.

At the same time, the very explosion of global migrations in the past few decades, not only from the Rest to the West but also laterally, back and forth between any different parts of the world, signals a weakening of the hold of the modern nation-state on the identities and identifications of the populations who have come to live within their borders. Diasporic groups imagine themselves increasingly not as "ethnic minorities" *within* nation-states, but as transnational subjects whose affiliations and loyalties reside in the interstices *between* nation-states: they cannot be contained within the boundaries of any nation-state, be it the homeland, the host society, or any other country (e.g., where coethnics live). In this sense, diasporic movements, cultures, and politics today are very much associated with the rising significance of transnational flows and migrations of people as a consequence of the heightened process of globalization in the closing decades of the twentieth century. In this context, the term *diaspora* has increasingly lost its paradigmatic association with exile from home and the myth of return and has become much more widely and unspecifically used to describe the condition and experience of dispersion as such, which may not necessarily involve trauma and marginalization but also empowerment, enrichment, and expansion. An important example is the rise to prominence of what Aihwa Ong and Donald Nonini (1997) call "modern Chinese transnationalism," referring to the role of powerful diasporic Chinese business networks in the racial/cultural/economic profile of contemporary global capitalism.

To put it differently, the burgeoning language and consciousness of diaspora is itself a manifestation and effect of intensifying cultural globalization. While migrations of people have taken place for centuries and have been a major force in the creation of the modern world since the nineteenth century, it is only in the past few decades—with the increased possibilities of keeping in touch with the old homeland and with coethnics in other parts of the world through faster and cheaper jet transport, mass media, and electronic telecommunications—that migrants are individually and collectively more inclined to see themselves, and act, not as minorities within nation-states, but as diasporic subjects who routinely cross national boundaries and go back and forth between their home and host lands. In other words, the rise to prominence of diasporic discourse is a sign of the decentralization and unsettling of nation-states in the contemporary globalized world. This does not mean that nation-states are no longer powerful or "in decline"—far from it; what it means is that nation-states, as discrete territorial and governmental units within a much larger world of global flows and exchanges, are no longer in full control of the composition of their populations or capable of commanding people's movements in and out of their territories. All nation-states now have to own up to their internal diversity, often referred to in terms of multiculturalism or pluralism. Moreover, no nation-state these days can maintain absolute "sovereignty"; instead, international interdependence and interconnection are now the order of the day, whether in terms of trade, military cooperation or, indeed, people exchanges and relations.

Diasporas, then, are now an index of the profound *unsettling* of (national) identities rather than the antithetical pointers to their confirmation and consolidation. What it means to be Chinese, Filipino, Japanese, Indian, or Vietnamese is increasingly pluralized, transnationalized, and, indeed, diasporized, even if the nation-states that command institutional ownership of these national identity labels still attempt to monopolize the legitimate right to circumscribe them and, to a certain extent, have the disciplinary powers to impose their corresponding inclusions and exclusions (e.g., through citizenship laws and border patrol regimes). As Arjun Appadurai has observed, "state and nation are at each other's throats, and the hyphen that links them is now less an icon of conjuncture than an index of disjuncture" (1996: 38). As quintessentially deterritorialized social formations, diasporas not only disturb prevailing territorial modes of nationalism; more importantly, they problematize the quest for nationhood as such (even though the desire for nation-state status is still an important political rallying point for some diasporized people).

But if the nation-state as the predominant discrete unit of analysis of area studies is now deeply contested, then the status of a larger, more encompassing unit of analysis—Asia—should also be put under erasure. As we know, there is nothing ontologically discrete about Asia at all: the very idea of Asia as a separate, demarcatable region of the world was developed within the imperializing European geographical imagination, with its preoccupation of mapping and carving up the globe in terms of distinct "continents" (Lewis & Wigen 1997). Asia is an imagined construct, and as a construct it has become part and parcel of how we see the world, with real effects on how the world is organized. In today's globalized world, for example, Asian nation-states are increasingly drawn toward integrating themselves within pan-Asian regional organizations such as the Association of Southeast Asian Nations and the Asia-Pacific Economic Cooperation—modeled after, for example, the European Union. But it is clear that, however we wish to draw a boundary around this region called Asia—a much more difficult and fraught task than it seems—it will always be a construct that suppresses the huge internal heterogeneity of peoples, histories, economies, polities, and cultures it is assumed to take in. In other words, to paraphrase Raymond Williams, there are no Asians, only ways of seeing people as Asians.

In this sense, the term *Asian diasporas* in the title of this volume points to a basic contradiction. There are no Asian diasporas, only ways of seeing diasporas as Asian. But precisely by bringing these two terms—*Asian* and *diasporas*—together, the volume is also suggestive of a project that would usefully deconstruct and take apart the notions of Asia and Asians as discrete categories of identity. In other words, looking at Asia and Asians from a diasporic angle—that is, from an angle that emphasizes displacements, flows, and movements—opens up a critical perspective that would highlight the shifting and situated multiplicity of identities and trajectories that now characterize the lives of millions of people with regard to whom the term *Asian* says both too much and too little. Some of the essays in this volume astutely illuminate this double insufficiency. Thus, in a study of Filipina or Indonesian domestic workers in more wealthy countries such as Taiwan or Singapore, the category "Asian" would hardly be able to do any analytical work: it is the differences (economic, social, political) between the (Asian) countries involved that would need to be accentuated. For Koreans in Japan, the nominal Asianness they presumably share with the dominant culture is neither here nor there: indeed, in the tumultuous history of the region the Japanese claim to Asia has been a manifestly contentious and violent affair—a historical legacy that still reverberates in lingering antagonisms and hostilities today, impeding any smooth integration of Asia as a harmonious whole. At the same time, what Asian diasporic movements across the world also demonstrate is how they tend to exceed their categorization as Asian. In the process they strip the category of its apparent solidity and discreteness. Thus, Korean adoptees in the West or Vietnamese migrants in the United States are, to all intents and purposes, both Asian and Western, while Chinese in Panama, and Japanese-Brazilians or Indians in Trinidad harbor identities that are perhaps nominally Asian, but also Latin American. In other words, diasporic subjects everywhere embody multiple histories and identities, maintaining contradictory linkages with the past yet experiencing disconnects that are uncontainable within some "origin," Asian or otherwise.

In short, "Asian diasporas" works toward its own productive analytical undoing—an enormously important contribution to our understanding of the complex and variegated transnational experiences of people on the move in and out of and beyond Asia.

References

Appadurai, Arjun. 1996. *Modernity at Large.* Minneapolis: University of Minnesota Press.

Lewis, Martin W., and Wigen, Karen E. 1997. *The Myth of Continents: A Critique of Metageography.* Berkeley: University of California Press.

Ong, Aihwa, and Nonini, Donald. eds. 1997. *Ungrounded Empires: The Cultural Politics of Modern Chinese Transnationalism.* New York: Routledge.

Contributors

Ien Ang is Professor of Cultural Studies and Australian Research Council Professorial Fellow at the Centre for Cultural Research, University of Western Sydney, in Australia. She has published numerous books and articles in media and cultural studies. Her latest book is *On Not Speaking Chinese: Living Between Asia and the West* (2001).

Tobias Hübinette (Korean name: Lee Sam-dol) is a researcher at theMulticultural Centre, Botkyrka, Sweden. His Ph.D. thesis in Korean Studies from 2005, "Comforting an Orphaned Nation," examined the Korean adoption issue and representations of adopted Koreans in Korean popular culture. He is researching issues concerning transnational adoption and transracial adoptees.

Evelyn Hu-DeHart is Professor of History and Ethnic Studies, and Director of the Center for the Study of Ethnicity and Race in America (CSREA) at Brown University. During the academic year 2005–06, she was Distinguished Freeman Visiting Professor in Asian/Asian American Studies at Wesleyan University, an initiative to bridge area studies (Asian studies) and ethnic studies (Asian American studies) around the themes of diaspora and transnationalism. Her most recent publication is *Voluntary Associations in the Chinese Diaspora* (coeditor with K. E. Kuah-Pearce, Hong Kong University Press, 2006).

Aisha Khan teaches anthropology at New York University. Her research interests include New World diasporas, Atlantic studies, postcolonial societies, and the construction of identities, particularly racial, ethnic, and religious. She has conducted ethnographic research among the Garifuna (Black Carib) in Honduras and among South Asians in the Republic of Trinidad and Tobago. Her books include *Callaloo Nation: Metaphors of Race and Religious Identity Among South Asians in Trinidad* (2004).

Richard S. Kim is an Assistant Professor in the Asian American Studies Program at the University of California, Davis. He has recently published articles in the *Journal of American Ethnic History, Amerasia Journal,* and *Seoul Journal of Korean* Studies and is currently completing a book on Korean diasporic nationalism.

Pei-Chia Lan is Associate Professor of Sociology at National Taiwan University. She has published articles in journals such as *Social Problems, Feminist Studies, Gender & Society, Identities, The Sociological Quarterly,* and *Journal of Family Issues.* Her book, *Global Cinderellas: Migrant Domestics and Newly Rich Taiwanese Employers* was published by Duke University Press in 2006. She was a postdoctoral fellow at UC Berkeley in 2000–2001 and was a Fulbright scholar at New York University in 2006–2007.

Steven C. McKay is Assistant Professor of Sociology at the University of California, Santa Cruz. He is the author of *Satanic Mills or Silicon Islands? The Politics of High-Tech Production in the Philippines* (Cornell/ILR Press 2006) and coeditor of *Routing Diasporas: Labor, Citizenship and Empire* (forthcoming). He is currently completing an ethnographic study of Filipino seafarers onboard merchant ships, addressing work and racial formation in the global labor market.

David Palumbo-Liu is Professor of Comparative Literature at Stanford University. He is currently writing a book on the status of literary narrative under contemporary globalization, editing a collection of essays on rational choice theory and the humanities, and coediting a collection of essays assessing attempts at theorizing on the world scale. His articles have appeared in *boundary 2, diacritics, New Literary History,* and *New Centennial Review.* He is the author of *Asian/American: Historical Crossings of a Racial Frontier* (1999).

Rhacel Salazar Parreñas is Professor of Asian American Studies and the Graduate Group of Sociology at the University of California, Davis. She has written extensively on issues of women's migration, migrant domestic workers, and gender and intergenerational relations in transnational migrant families. She is currently working on a book project about Filipino migrant entertainers in the nightlife industry of Tokyo.

Sharmila Sen is the Editor for the Humanities at Harvard University Press. Prior to joining Harvard University Press, she was an assistant professor of English at Harvard where she specialized in postcolonial literature from Africa, the Caribbean, and South Asia. Her publications include essays on Caribbean fictions, francophone African novels, popular Bombay cinema, language politics in contemporary India, and border culture in South Asia.

Lok C. D. Siu is Associate Professor of Anthropology and Asian/Pacific/American studies in Social and Cultural Analysis at New York University. Her work focuses on diaspora, citizenship, transnationalism, migration, and Asians in the Americas. Her book, *Memories of a Future Home: Diasporic Citizenship of Chinese in Panama* (2005), won the 2005 Social Science book award from the Association for Asian American Studies. She is currently coediting a volume on gender and cultural citizenship and starting a new project that explores the cultural-social formation of Asian Latino restaurants in New York City.

Hung Cam Thai is Assistant Professor of Sociology and Asian American Studies at Pomona College in Claremont, California. He has conducted research in Vietnam and in the United States, with a special focus on Vietnamese transpacific marriages. His forthcoming book *For Better or for Worse: Marriage and Migration in the New Global Economy* will be published by Rutgers University Press.

Takeyuki (Gaku) Tsuda is Associate Professor of Anthropology at the School of Human Evolution and Social Change at Arizona State University (Tempe). Previously, he was a Collegiate Assistant Professor at the University of Chicago and then served as Associate Director of the Center for Comparative Immigration Studies at the University of California at San Diego. His primary academic interests include international migration, diasporas, ethnic minorities and identity, transnationalism and globalization, ethnic return migrants, the Japanese diaspora in the Americas, and contemporary Japanese society.

Index

Acculturation, 14
Adoption. *See* International adoption from Korea; Koreans, adopted
Advertising, Japanese physiognomy and, 231
African slave labor, in Cuba, 32, 51
Afro-Creole population, 162, 173
"Aims and Aspirations of the Koreans," 211–212
"American Century," 202
American Dream ideology, 91
American missionaries. *See* Missionaries, American
Anjuman Sunnat-ul Jamaat, 147
Anti-Asian movements, 51, 52, 136*n*3
"An Appeal to America," 208–209, 210, 212
An Area of Darkness (Naipaul), 165–166
Arranged marriages, 85–102; dangers of, 94–95; gender configuration of, 20; "highly marriageable" category for, 89; Indian, 172; international views on, 85; intimate details of, 89–94; moment of encounter, 96–100; personal interviews, 87–89; politics of kinship in marital choice, 94–96; successful, 94–95; support from older generation, 95; transpacific marriage market and, 86–87, 89; "unmarriageable" category for, 89
Asia: colonial history of, 9–10; connection with Latin America, 29; homogeneous view of, 8–9; identification against West, 9; inter-Asian strife/conflict and, 16–17; nonhomogeneous view of, 8; producing/sustaining diasporic connections, 8

Asian American population: American-born, 3; demographic shifts in, 3–4; disembodiment of, 5; foreign-born, 3
Asian American studies: denationalization of, 4–5; diaspora in, 3–7; panethnic coalition-building spirit of, 5; self-determinism and, 7; transnational approaches in, 4
Asian diasporas: colonialism and, 21–22; communication within, 3; conceptualization of, 14; epistemology of, 11–12; ethnic-specific/transnational, 3; framework of, 6–7; globalization and, 21–22; homeland-place of settlement relationship, 6; inter-Asian strife/conflict and, 16–17; labor demands and, 20–22; multiple/varied formations of, 7; vs. other diasporas, 8; outside United States, 2–3, 23–24; place-specific/cross-ethnic, 3; production of, 9; pursuit by Asian states, 8; racializing-gendering process and, 9; *See also specific Asian diasporas*
Asian labor: contemporary migrations, 10; coolies (*see* Coolie labor, Chinese); Easter Islanders, 50; in Latin America, 31, 51
Asianness, multinational collective politics of, 11
Asia-Pacific region, 51–57; El Norte phenomenon, 53–54; Latin American migration, 52; in the 1990s, 54–57
Asiento, 34
Assimilation, cultural, 14, 245
Authentication, cultural: Chinese diaspora and, 126; Indo-Trinidadians and, 149,

295

Authentication, cultural (*continued*)
153, 154, 157; Japanese Brazilians and,
245; Vietnamese women and, 97, 99
Aztec empire, 30

Bagong Bayani ("new hero"), 72–73, 76–77, 79
Baja California, Chinese immigrants in,
49–51
Balboa, Vasco Núñez de, 30
Basadre, Jorge, 33
Beauty contests, cultural meanings and,
106–107. *See also* Queen of the Chinese
Colony beauty contest
Beauty standards; "pure" Chinese vs. racially
mixed, 132–133; Vietnamese, 96, 97
"Being fooled." *See* Betrayal
Belonging, sense of: of adopted Koreans,
191–192; cultural barriers to, 12;
diasporic, 12–13, 134, 143; triadic
relationships and, 12–13
Betrayal (being fooled): metaphor of,
Indo-Caribbeans and, 142, 144–145;
recuperation through exegesis, 150–151
Bhabha, Homi, 184, 187–188, 192, 196
Bolivia, Japanese labor in, 50
Brazil: coffee plantation economy, 227;
commercials in, Japanese physiognomy
and, 231; cultural differences of
population, 245; "founding" races
of, 232; Japanese immigrants in (*see*
Japanese Brazilians)
Brazilianness, of Japanese Brazilians in
Japan, 19, 240–245
Brazilian nikkeijin. *See* Japanese Brazilians
Britain. *See* Great Britain
Butler, Judith, 184, 187–188, 196

Cabrillo, Juan Rodríguez de, 30
California, ethnic/racial minority population
in, 49, 54
Canadian Mission schools, 145–146
Cantonese language, 128–129
Caribbean anglophone writing, 169
Caribbean cultural discourse, 161
Caribbean sugar plantations, labor for, 161,
162, 167
Cheongsam, Chinese, 120, 121, 122
Chicanery, formal charges of, 147
China: labor migrations (*see* Coolie labor,
Chinese); Manila galleon trade route, 30
China poblana, 30
Chinese Association in Panama, as all-male
organization, 112, 123

Chinese Association of Costa Rica, 118
Chinese diaspora, 127–136; "brotherhood
of patrilineages," 110–111; in Central
America and Panama, 107–110;
Chineseness concept (*see* Chineseness,
diasporic); collective consciousness of,
116; coolies or contract laborers, 31–41;
in Costa Rica, 117, 128–130; as criminals,
victims, and deviants, 130–131; in Cuba,
20–21; cultural formation in, 22–23;
differences in, 124–126; embodied
differences in, 124–126; histories of, 126;
homeland state and, 114–117; "impurity
or inauthenticity" of, 126; inequalities,
127–129; irreconcilable tensions in,
126–127; kinship relations in, 111; labor
immigrants, 29; language differences
in, 128–129; in Latin America, 50–51;
in Mexico, 41–49; migration of labor
immigrants, 10, 31; national differences
in, 127–129; in Panama, 21, 111;
patrilineality in, 111; persecution of,
136n; in Peru, 20–21; regional differences
in, 106–107; relations with ROC,
114–116; in seafarer labor market, 68;
shared sense of being, 18–19; tensions in,
134; unequal power relations in, 127; in
United States, 127
Chinese Exclusion Act of 1882, 41
Chinese Fraternal Union, 45
Chinese languages, privileging of, 128–129
Chineseness, diasporic: changes in, 132–133,
135; karaoke and, 131–132; language
differences and, 122–123; meaning of,
134; measuring, 126–127; "pure," beauty
standards of, 132–133
Chinese organizations, in diasporic
communities, 136n5
Chinese Panamanians, at 1996 convention, 117
Chinese restaurants (*chifas*), 51
Christianity: democracy in Korea and,
219–220; Korean independence
movement and, 202, 203, 208–209, 212,
213, 219; missionaries (*see* Missionaries,
American)
Christians, Indo-Trinidadian, 148, 149
Chung, Henry, 214
Citizenship, diasporic, 18, 134–135
Clothing: Brazilianness of Japanese Brazilians
in Japan and, 241, 244; symbolism of,
in Queen of the Chinese Colony beauty
contest, 120, 123–124, 136n1
Cold War rhetoric, remnants of, 131

Colonialism, Asian diasporas and, 21–22
"Communist Chinese" immigrants, 130
Community, diasporic consciousness of, 143
Congressional Record, 217, 218
Consciousness, diasporic; of community, 143;
   host country relationship and, 14; racial
   exclusion processes and, 10; rejection
   of, 7; religious practices and, 23,
   142–144, 146; tension from, 126–127
Convention of Chinese Associations of
   Central America and Panama: in 1996,
   117–119; beauty contest (*see* Queen of the
   Chinese Colony beauty contest); Chinese
   collective consciousness and, 116; costs
   of attending, 118; as diaspora-building
   project, 116–117; expansion of activities,
   108–109; gender imbalance in, 112–113;
   language differences of members and,
   128–129; politics of, 115–116, 129;
   purpose of, 107–108; social ties and, 127;
   tourism and, 113
Cooking: "coolie" food, 163, 164–165; East
   Indian, 168–169
Coolie labor, Chinese: vs. African slave
   labor, 31, 51; "coolie food," 163, 164–165;
   "coolie stores," 170–171; in Cuba (*see*
   Cuba, Chinese coolie labor in); forced
   recontracting of, 36–37; Indo-Caribbean,
   144, 145; international criticism of,
   34; labor contractor/brokers and, 38;
   transition to free workforce, 39–40, 51
Coronado, Francisco Vázquez de, 30
Cortés, Hernán, 30
Costa Rica, Chinese diaspora in, 117, 128–130
"Creole," use of term, 169
Cross-cultural translation, of migrants, 14
Cross-ethnic alliances, 10, 11
Cross-national alliances, 10, 11
Cuadrilleras, 38–39
Cuba: abolishment of slavery in, 33: Chinese
   coolie labor, 10, 34–41, 51; cuadrilleras
   and Chinese labor, 38–39; demographic
   shifts in, 32–33, 37; Junta de Fomento,
   33–34; labor migration of ethnic Chinese
   in, 20–21; Manila galleon trade, 31;
   migration of Cuban middle class, 52;
   plantation agriculture, dominance of, 32;
   revolution of 1959, 52; sugar production,
   35*t*, 36
Culture: assimilation of, 14, 245; centrality
   in diaspora, 22–24; meanings of racial
   categories and, 226–227; stereotypes,
   positive images and, 245

Dance: Japanese Brazilians and, 244;
   national, in Queen of the Chinese
   Colony beauty contest, 119–121, 136*n*1
Democracy, Korean, 219
Dhallpourris (dal puris), 163, 164
Diasporas: affiliation with homeland, 14–24;
   as analytical category, 3; consciousness
   of, 142–143; cross-ethnic/cross-racial
   political alliances and, 11; culture,
   centrality of, 22–24; definition of,
   1–2, 127; development of multiple
   situated identities, 245; displacements,
   see Displacement; ethnicity, salience
   of, 19–20; exclusionary practices
   and, 13–14; gendered identities in,
   19–20, 64; historical experiences of,
   157; as liberatory concept, 13; making
   of, 9, 12–14; masculinist projects of
   transnational community formation, 110;
   vs. migration, 143; nation-state and,
   108; networks, institutionalization of,
   114–115; persistence of nation-state and,
   17–19; processes in, 10–11; racialization
   and, 10–11, 245; reproduction of,
   109–110; as resistance strategy, 10–11,
   245; sexuality, salience of, 19–20. *See also*
   specific diasporas
Díaz, Porfirio, 41
Disidentification, of diasporic people, 15
Displacement: double, 13; external forces
   and, 12; marginalization from, 19;
   multiple forms of, 12; nationalism
   and, 11
Division of household labor, in Vietnamese
   families, 92–93
"Double marriage squeeze," 87
Dual identification: "home" concept and,
   14–24; rejection of, 7; tension from,
   126–127
Dynamism, in religious rituals, 141

Easter Island population, in Peru, 50, 51
East Indian laborers, export of, 32
Economic relations, East-West, 9
Education, of Indo-Trinidadians, 145–146
Eid ul-Fitr (feast breaking fast of
   Ramadan), 150
Elías, Domingo, 34
El Norte phenomenon, 53–54
El Salvador: Chinese population in, 117;
   San Marcos Free Trade Zone of San
   Salvador, 57
Emigration, facilitation of, 9–10

Empowerment, 72–73
Endogamy, 109
Eng, David, 186
Enganchador, 38
ERP (*Ejército Popular Revolucionario*), 54
Ethnicity: Asian differences in, 8;
  differences, de-essentialization of,
  245–247; identification with, 225, 226,
  247; prejudice of Japanese Brazilians
  and, 248n8; racialization of, 225–226,
  245–247; salience of, 19–20
European colonialism, 10
Exegesis, 142, 144, 150–151
Exogamy, 109

Facial hair, Japanese Brazilians and, 243–244
Family: "normative structures" in, 91;
  Vietnamese (*see* Vietnamese families)
Father, Vietnamese respect for, 92
Federal Council of Churches of Christ in
  America, 215–216
Federation of Chinese Associations in
  the Americas, 114, 134; Convention
  of Chinese Associations of Central
  America and Panama, 107–108;
  founding of, 107; members of, 111;
  Republic of China and, 107
Females: in Convention of Chinese
  Associations of Central America and
  Panama, 112, 113; Filipina domestic
  workers, 16, 71, 72; traditional "women's
  work," 92–93
Femininity: Chinese, 122; diasporic ideals
  of, 134
Feminism, 96
Filipina domestic workers, 16, 71, 72
Filipinoness: competing claims of, 80; construction of, 64; masculinity and, 71, 73
Filipino seafarers: age of, 74; American
  colonial policies and, 64, 67; collective
  wage complaints, 71–72; construction
  of work meanings, 79; dominance of,
  67–68; high respect for, 77–78; history of,
  65; image of, 70–71, 75–77; labor market
  niche, 63, 78–80; marketing of image
  for, 70–71; masculinities, multiple, 17,
  75–79; new heroism rhetoric and, 72–73,
  76–77, 79; nonofficers, 68–69; officers,
  underrepresentation of, 68–69; personal
  identities of, 73; pride/experience of,
  75, 78; as problem solvers, 75; public
  acknowledgment of, 76–77; racial

discrimination, onboard, 74–75, 79–80;
  recruitment of, 68; reemergence in
  international shipping, 65, 66; return
  to homeland, 76; rural working-class
  background of, 74; sexuality of, 78;
  status in homeland, 76–78; training/
  certifications for, 67, 68, 69; view of their
  jobs, 76; wages of, 71; workplace status
  of, 69–70, 76, 78–80
First World nation concept, 233–234, 235
Flags of convenience (FOC), 66–67
Fourteen Points of Woodrow Wilson, 202,
  207, 210
France, export of Asian labor and, 32
Freyre, Gilberto, 232
Fujimori, Alberto, 29, 52
FZLN (*Frente Zapatista de Liberación
  Nacional*), 54

Gadsden Purchase, 53
Gender: of adopted Korean children,
  181–182; as category of analysis, 134;
  diasporic community identity and,
  106–107; labeling of jobs and, 66, 74;
  material performances of Vietnamese
  peers and, 90–91; salience of, 19–20;
  traditional arrangements of, 92–93
"Gendered geographies of power," 89
Geopolitics, complexities of, 124
Germany, second registers, 66
Global Association of Cantonese, 114–115
Global capitalism, Asian diasporas and,
  11–12
Globalization, Asian diasporas and, 21–22
"Globalizing of America," 207
Great Britain: coolie labor trade, 33–34;
  export of Asian labor and, 32; labor
  scheme, indentured laborers in, 144
Great Depression, 51
Great Tradition of Sanatan Dharm, 151–152
Guatemala, Chinese population in, 117
Guyana, Indian diaspora in, 144, 161,
  170–173

Haqika (pledging oneself to Allah), 150
Hawaii, Koreans in, 212
Hee, Park Chung, 180
Heroism, Filipino seafarers and, 72–73,
  76–77, 79
Hindu fundamentalist organization, 172
Hindu Indo-Trinidadians: consolidation
  with Muslim identities, 147; heritage of

"tradition," 151–153; Hindu and Muslim schools and, 146; identity of, 157; Presbyterian schools and, 145–146; ritual practices, 23, 142, 148, 150-151, 152–153, 156, 157, 158

Holt, Harry, 179

Homeland: diaspora affiliation with, 14–24, 114–117, 135; politics, transnational migrant participation in, 115; return to (see Return-migrations); sense of belonging to, 143

Honduras, leadership of Chinese associations in, 128

A House for Mr. Biswas (Naipaul), 162, 168

Hulbert, Homer, 217–218, 222n6

Hwan, Chun Doo, 180

Hybridity theory, 184, 196

Idealized diasporic subjectivity, 123

Identity formation process, in current Chinese diaspora, 135

Illegal immigrants, in Panama, 130

ILO (International Labor Organization), 71

Imams (Muslim religious leaders), 147, 151, 153, 155–156

IMF orphans, 181

Immigration and Naturalization Service, Marriage Fraud Amendment Act of 1986, 102n7

Immigration laws, granting exclusive license to Chinese coolie labor, 34, 36

Immigration Reform Act of 1965, 3

Indentured laborers: East Indian, 144, 161; Indo-Trinidadian, 146–147. See also Coolie labor, Chinese

India: diasporic economic investment in, 8; Great Tradition of Sanatan Dharm, 151–152; multiple overlapping diasporas, 166; seafaring labor force, 66

India: An Area of Darkness (Naipaul), 161

Indian diaspora: cultural formation in, 22; in Guyana, 144, 161, 170–173; professors for University of West Indies, 167–168. See also Indo-Caribbean diaspora

Indian restaurant, in Trinidad, 173–175

Indian words, transliterating in Trinidad, 163, 166

Indo-Caribbean diaspora: cultural expressions, 144; cultural motifs of exegesis and betrayal, 142, 144–145; as "East Indians," 144; historical marginality of, 144; literature from, 163–164, 169; memorialization of displacement, 144–145

Indo-Chinese, situated loyalties of, 15–16

Indonesia, seafaring labor force, 66

Indo-Trinidadians: betrayal or being fooled theme, 144–145, 158; consolidation of Hindu and Muslim identities, 147; cultural history and religious identity, competing interpretations of, 156–157; cultural resistance to plantation authority, 147–148; diasporic consciousness, 157; educational opportunities for, 145–146, 157; employment opportunities for, 146; extrication from subordinate position, 145; first generation indentured laborers, 146–147; first newspaper for, 170; Hindu and Muslim schools for, 146; identity, 158; marginalization of, 158; memorialization of displacement, 157; mobility opportunities of, 145; population diversity of, 145, 148; religious and cultural authenticity of, 149; rhetoric of resignation about New World diaspora, 146; selected traditions of, 147; subordination, 158; uprooting, in shaping identity of, 157. See also Hindu Indo-Trinidadians; Muslim Indo-Trinidadians

International adoption from Korea: as antiracist/progressive act, 180; from Korea, 179–182; negative foreign media coverage, 180; as profit-making business, 180. See also Koreans, adopted

International Labor Organization (ILO), 71

International marriages. See Arranged marriages

Iriye, Akira, 207

Islamic Muslim scholars (maulanas), 153

Jaisohn, Philip, 205–206, 210, 212–213, 214

Japan: capital investment in Mexico, 55–56; effect of March First uprising on, 222n4; favorable Brazilian perception of, 233–238; Manila galleon trade route, 30; occupation of Korea, 214–215, 217–218; open immigration policy, 226; postwar status of, 234; racial homogenation and ethnic differentiation in, 238–245; racialization in, 245–246; response to March First movement, 201; Taft-Katsura agreement, 222n6

Japanese Brazilians, 225–247; Brazilianness
in Japan, 240–245; characteristics of,
236, 237; collective ritual performances,
244; cultural assimilation of, 227–228;
cultural definition of, racialized,
236–238; cultural heritage of, 236; de-
essentialization of ethnic difference,
246–247; essentialized racial perceptions
of, 238–240; integration into Brazilian
society, 227–228; negative images of,
248n; personal symbols of, 243–244;
population growth of, 49–50, 52, 227;
positive cultural meaning of japonês,
233–238; public symbols of, 243;
race categories, positive stereotypes
with, 226, 231–232; racialization of
ethnic differences, 19, 226, 228–230,
245–247; racial markers of difference,
227–232; respect for, 236–237; return-
migrations, 17, 21–22, 225–226, 238;
second-generation, 240, 247n–248n11;
self-confidence and esteem of, 248n10;
self-introductions of, 242–243; situated
loyalties of, 16, 19
Japanese diaspora: labor migration in Latin
America, 31, 49, 52; racial descent-
culture correlation, 239; seafarers, 74–75
Japaneseness, positive cultural meaning in
Brazil, 233–238
Japanese Peruvians, during WW II, 52
Japonês: Japanese Brazilian view of term,
247n4; of Korean and Chinese decent,
247n3; positive cultural meaning of,
233–238. See also Japanese Brazilians
Jobs, for Mexican immigrants, 53

Karaoke, Chineseness and, 131–132
Kashmiri houseboats, 166
Katakana, 243
Kim Dae Jung, 181
Kim Young Sam, 181
Kinship networks, native place associations
as, 111
Kinship politics, arranged marriages and,
94–96
Knowledge access or creation (exegesis), 142,
144, 150–151
Koh-I-Noor Gazette, 170
Kojong, King, 217
Korea: adoption law in, 179–180;
capital investment in Mexico, 55–56;
international adoption from (see

International adoption from Korea);
nationalism of, American democracy
and, 210–213; national self-determination
(see Korean independence movement);
propaganda war in, 180
Korean Commission, 213
Korean Congress in Philadelphia, 202, 203,
205–210
Korean Declaration of Independence,
210–211
Korean diaspora: displacement after Korean
War, 21; in Hawaii, 212, 221n2; Korean
Provisional Government and, 202;
long-distance nationalism of, 18, 203,
207, 221n1; in Manchuria and Siberia,
221n2; Philadelphia Korean Congress and,
202, 203, 205–210; politics of, 213–220.
See also Koreans, adopted
Korean independence movement: ability
for self-government and, 211–212;
American group, 203–204; American
influence on, 202–203, 206, 207–208,
210, 211; Christian ideology and, 202,
203, 208–209; establishment of, 205,
206–207, 211; Korean consciousness
and, 18; legal claims for, 209–210;
Manchurian group, 204; March First
uprising, 201–204, 207, 209, 220, 222n4.
See also Korean Provisional Government
Korean Information Bureau, of Philadelphia,
213
Korean Provisional Government (KPG):
diplomatic activities, 204–205;
diplomatic recognition of, 210, 213,
218; formation of, 202, 207, 220; sole
diplomatic arm of, 213
Koreans, adopted: as Asian immigrants, 191–
193; association for, 183; demographics
of adoptive families, 182; ethnogenesis
of, 183; gender of, 181–182; as "goodwill
ambassadors," 180; identity formation or
subjectivization, 183–184; International
Gatherings for, 183; Korean ethnonationalism and, 193; mental illness/
social problems of, 179; number of,
177; organized movement for, 182–183;
orientalist imagery and, 188–191;
physical alienation, consequences
of, 193–197; placement in Western
countries, 181–182; psychic violence,
consequences of, 193–197; as queer
diaspora, 186; racial discrimination of,

187; self-hate, self-contempt and self-destructiveness, 185–186; self-identification as white, 19–20, 178–179, 183–187, 195–197; self-narratives of, 178, 182, 188, 194–195; subject formation of, 187–188; suicide rates of, 179

The Korean Situation: Authentic Accounts of Recent Events by Eye Witnesses, 215, 216, 217

Korean War, 21

Korea Review, 214

KPG. *See* Korean Provisional Government

Kuomintang Chinese Affairs Commission, 118

Labor diasporas: Chinese (*see* Coolie labor, Chinese); Filipina domestic workers, 16, 71, 72; Filipino (*see* Filipino seafarers); gendered identities in, 64; shaping of, 63–64

Labor market segmentation, nationality, gender and, 69–70

Labor niches, gendered, 66

Language: Brazilianness of Japanese Brazilians in Japan and, 241–242, 243; Chinese, privileging of, 128–129; differences, in Chinese diaspora, 117, 122–123, 124, 128; double meaning of words in Trinidad, 163, 166; Japanese, in Brazil, 235–236; Sanskrit, 167; Spanish, 128; transliterating of Indian words in Trinidad, 163

Latin America: Asia-Pacific labor in, 31, 49–54; connection with Asia, 29; Japanese communities in, 52; limitations on Asian immigration, 51; in the 1990s, 54–57. *See also specific Latin American countries*

"Latin America-Pacific," 31

League of Friends of Korea, 213–216

Lee, Alberto, 107–108, 109

Liberia, 66

Long-distance nationalism, 115

Macao, European coolie traders in, 34

Males: Filipino (*see* Filipino seafarers); provider/patriarch role of, 73; traditional "men's work," 92–93

Manchuria, Korean diaspora in, 221*n*2

Mandarin (language), 128–129

Manila galleon trade, 30, 31

Manilamen, 65

Maquiladora program, 55–56, 57

March First movement, 201–204, 207, 209, 220, 222*n*5

Marginalization, 12, 13, 15

Marriage Fraud Amendment Act of 1986, 102*n*7

Marriages: within Chinese culture, 109; internationally arranged (*see* Arranged marriages)

Marriage squeeze, 100*n*

Masculinity: *Filipinoness* and, 71, 73; of Filipino seafarers, 17, 74–79; hegemonic, 74, 75; labor diasporas and, 64; types of, 74

Mason, William, 218

Mattai, Harry, 171

Maulood sherifs (Quranic readings), 150, 153, 154, 155

McCormick, William, 217

Meier, Dani Isaac, 194

Memorialization of displacement, 143–145, 147

Mexican immigration, into United States, 52–53

Mexican Revolution of 1910–1917, Chinese merchants and, 42

Mexico: anti-Chinese persecution, 48, 51; Asian capital investment in, 55–56; Asian diaspora in, 20; business enterprises, 42–49; Chinese laborers in, 41–49, 50–51; female labor in, 54; international border with U.S., 53; Japanese labor in, 49; manufacturing labor in, 55–56; postrevolutionary land reform, 54; poverty in, 55; Spanish colonial influences, 30–31; territorial losses to United States, 53; "trilateral strategy of," 55–56

Middle class, whiteness as, 91

Migrations: Asian, 7; family-forming Vietnamese, 86; labor-demanded, 20–22, 29; material or symbolic capital from, 94. *See also* Asian diasporas; *and specific population migrations*

Milad ul-Nabi (birthday of Prophet Mohammed), 150

Minority identities, ethnic marginalization and, 232

Mintz, Sidney, 166–167

Missionaries, American, 213–220; Korean diasporic politics and, 218–221; *The Korean Situation: Authentic Accounts of Recent Events by Eye Witnesses*, 215;

Missionaries, American (*continued*)
  March First uprising and, 222*n*5; "no
  neutrality for brutality" groups, 215;
  shaping of U.S. foreign policy opinion,
  215–217
*The Missionary Mind and American East Asia
  Foreign Policy, 1911–1915* (Reed), 216
Muslim Indo-Trinidadians: of African
  descent, 149; consolidation with Hindu
  identities, 147; Hindu and Muslim
  schools and, 146; identity of, 153–154,
  157; Presbyterian schools and, 145–146;
  ritual practices, 23, 142, 148, 150–151,
  153–155, 156, 157, 158

NAFTA (North American Free Trade
  Agreement), 54–57
Nagamootoo, Moses, 172–173
Naipaul, V. S., 166, 167–168; *An Area of
  Darkness,* 165–166; *A House for Mr. Biswas,*
  162, 168
Name change, by Vietnamese, 89–90, 101*n*6
National dance, cultural meanings of,
  120–121
Nationalism, diasporic displacement and, 11
National Seamen Board (NSB), 70, 80*n*2
Nation-states, 17–19, 64, 108, 115
Native place associations, in Panama,
  111–112
Nicaragua, leadership of Chinese
  associations in, 128
Nikkeijin, Brazilian. *See* Japanese Brazilians
Norris, George, 217
North American Free Trade Agreement
  (NAFTA), 54–57
Norway, second registers, 66
Norwegian sailors, 75
Norwegian seafarers, 67, 68
NSB (National Seamen Board), 70, 80*n*2

Okinawans, in Latin America, 49
"One China" principle, 137*n*8
Oriental stereotype, adopted Koreans and,
  188–191

Pacific region, initial formation of, 30–31
Panama: Chinese diaspora in, 21, 111, 117,
  128, 129, 131; Chinese-owned businesses in, 131; flags of convenience,
  66; illegal immigrants in, 130; kinship
  networks in, 111; leadership of Chinese
  Association in, 131; national dress of,

137*n*10; native place associations in,
  111–112; "Old Chinese Colony" in, 129,
  131, 132; recent vs. earlier immigrants,
  129–131; Republic of China and, 114,
  137*n*8
Pandits (Hindu religious leaders), 147,
  151, 152
Patriarchy, 95, 99, 100
Patrilineality, diasporic organizations and,
  110–112
Patrono, 37
People's Republic of China. *See* Taiwan
Performativity theory, 184, 196
Peru: abolishment of slavery in, 33; anti-
  Japanese sentiments during World War II,
  52; Chinese coolie labor, 10, 20–21, 31–41,
  50–51; Chinese Peruvians, 51–52; Easter
  Island population in, 50, 51; *enganche*
  system, 39–40; gold, in Loreto Province,
  41; guano trade, 33; Iquitos, 41; Japanese
  labor in, 31, 49–50, 52; native Peruvian
  workers, 39; rubber business, 41; slave
  trade, 33; Spanish influence in, 30, 31;
  sugar production, 33, 35*t*, 36; War of the
  Pacific and, 38
Phelan, James, 218
Philadelphia Korean Congress of 1919, 202,
  203, 205–212, 220
Philippine Merchant Marine Academy
  (PMMA), 67
Philippine Nautical School (PNS), 67
Phillippine Overseas Employment
  Administration (POEA), 70, 71, 72, 80*n*2
Philippines: gender balance of migrants
  and, 72; gross domestic product,
  80*n*1; heroism concept and, 72–73,
  79; Manila galleon trade route, 30;
  migrant abuse and, 71–72; out-migration
  encouragement, 18; promotion of
  Filipino seafarers, 70–71, 73, 79; sea-
  faring labor force, 66
Philippine Seafarers Promotion Council
  (PSPC), 71
Physical alienation, consequences for
  adopted Koreans, 193–197
PMMA (Philippine Merchant Marine
  Academy), 67
PNS (Philippine Nautical School), 67
POEA (Philippine Overseas Employment
  Administration), 70, 71, 72, 80*n*2
Political relations, East-West, 9
Prayers, Indo-Trinidadian, 152–154

PRC (People's Republic of China). *See* Taiwan
Presbyterian schools (Canadian Mission schools), 145–146
PRI (*Partido Revolucionario Institucional*), 55
Protestant missionaries, American. *See* American missionaries
Psychic violence, consequences for adopted Koreans, 193–197
Puja (Hindu ritual), 150
Push-pull labor migration, 227

Queen of the Chinese Colony beauty contest of 1996, 105–137; clothing, symbolism of, 120, 123–124, 136n1; dances, national, 119–121, 136n1; differences in Chinese diasporic identifications and, 107–108, 110–111, 119–120, 124–128; to encourage multigenerational attendance, 134; female kinship and, 113; immigration, competing claims of belonging and, 129–134; judges for, 137n12; language in, 137n11; Miss Costa Rica, 105, 117, 119, 121, 122, 124–126, 133; Miss Honduras, 105, 119, 120–121, 122–126; outcome, confusion/indeterminancy of, 105–106, 107, 133–134; Panamanian-Chinese view of, 129–130; public identity of women and, 114; purpose of, 110; self-introduction category, 119, 121–123; shared triadic identification, 134; sponsorship (*see* Convention of Chinese Associations of Central America and Panama); transnational networks and, 107–108, 110–111
Quranic readings (*maulood sherifs*), 150, 153, 154, 155

Race: categories, 226–227, 231–232; de-essentialization through migratory process, 225–226; differences, recognition of vs. prejudicial reaction to, 230–231; salience of, 19–20
Racial identification, of Japanese Brazilians, 228–230
Racializing-gendering process, place-specific, cross-ethnic study, 9
Racial marginality, 91
Racism, as marginalizing force, 13
Ramadan, 155
Rashtriya Swayamsevak Sanagh (RSS), 172
Reed, James, 216
Religious rituals; cultural motifs, 142, 144; of diasporic communities, 158; diasporic

consciousness and, 23, 143–144; dynamism in, 141; metaphor of betrayal and, 149–150; older vs. younger generations and, 148–149; political culture and, 149; social hierarchy and, 148–149; South Asian, 141; as stable and timeless, 141–142, 143. *See also* Hindu Indo-Trinidadians, religious practices; Muslim Indo-Trinidadians, religious practices
Religio-cultural organizations, 147
Reproduction, of racial and cultural purity, 109–110
Republic of China (ROC): "Chinese identity" and, 126–127; conflict with Taiwan, 114, 116, 117, 135–136; Federation of Chinese Associations in Central America and Panama and, 107; Ministry of Overseas Chinese Affairs, 118; Panama and, 114; relationship with Central America and Panama, 124; relations with diasporic Chinese, 114–116, 123, 135–136, 136n8
Republic of Korea, Constitution of, 211
Republic of Trinidad and Tobago, 144
Return-migrations: adopted Koreans and, 193; ethnic identity and, 245–247; of Japanese Brazilians, 17, 21–22, 225–226, 238–245; Vietnamese, 94–96
Reunification of China, 137n8
Rhee, Syngman, 179, 205, 206, 212, 213, 214
Rizal, José, 72
ROC. *See* Republic of China
Rodríguez, Juan, 34
Roh Tae Woo, 181
Roosevelt, Theodore, 217, 218, 222n6
RSS (Rashtriya Swayamsevak Sanagh), 172
Russians, in seafarer labor market, 68
Russo-Japanese War, 217
Ryukyu Islanders, in Latin America, 49

Salinas de Gotari, Carlos, 54–55, 56
Samba, Japanese Brazilians and, 244
Sanatan Dharma Maha Sabha, 147
Sanskrit, 167
Second registers, 66
Seiza, 240, 248n12
Senate Resolution 200, 218
Sexual division of labor, 19–20, 66
Shipping industry, international: changes in, 65–69; cost-cutting measures, 66–67; flags of convenience, 66–67; labor demand in, 65–66; labor market restructuring, 66–67; labor unions, 67;

Shipping industry, international: (*continued*)
positions, stratification by nationality,
67–70, 74–75; second registers, 66–67. *See
also* Filipino seafarers
Shipping vessels, foreign ownership of, 66
Siberia, Korean diaspora in, 221*n*2
Situated loyalties, 15–16
Slave labor: African, in Cuba, 32, 51; Chinese
coolie labor (*see* Coolie labor, Chinese);
legal abolishment of, 167
Sobretiempo, 37
Sonora: Chinese occupations in, 46–48,
46*t*; Chinese population in, 42–43, 44*t*,
45–46
South Asian diaspora, Indo-Caribbeans. *See*
Indo-Caribbeans
South Korea, seafaring labor force, 66
Spanish America, initial formation of Pacific
region, 30–31
Spanish language, 128
"Spanish-Pacific," 31
Spencer, Selden, 217
Stigma, of outsider-foreign origins, 143
Sugar, Sanskrit word for, 167
Sugar production, in Cuba and Peru, 35*t*, 36
Superstition, formal charges of, 147

Taft-Katsura agreement, 222*n*6
Taiwan: capital investment in Mexico, 55–56;
"Chinese identity" and, 126–127; conflict
with ROC, 116, 117; demographic shifts
from coolie labor trade, 37; diasporic
community formation and, 135;
independence, 136*n*8; legitimization
as sovereign nation-state, 114, 135–136;
"partial citizenship" in, 18
Tanedo, Benjamin, 70
The Tempest (Shakespeare), 161, 175
Texas, independence of, 53
Toshiba, 231
Tourism: Convention of Chinese
Associations of Central America and
Panama and, 113; Việt Kiều, 100*n*
Transnationalism, 7, 9
Transnational media distribution, Chinese
diaspora and, 135
Transnational organizations. *See* Federation
of Chinese Associations
Transpacific marriages, Vietnamese. *See*
Arranged marriages
Treaty of Amity, 210
Treaty of Guadalupe Hidalgo, 53

Treaty of La Mesilla, 53
Treaty of Portsmouth, 217–218
Triadic relationship, of diasporic experience,
12–13
Trinidad: "coolie" food in, 163; Indian labor
diaspora, 144, 161; Indian restaurant
in, 173–175; Indian tourists in, 162–163,
175; Indo-Gangetic plain, 167; Mount
St. Benedict, 166–170; population diversity in, 148; religious diversity in, 148;
transliterating of Indian words in, 163.
See also Indo-Trinidadians

Ukranians, in seafarer labor market, 68, 69
United Kingdom, second registers, 66
United States: Asian population in (*see*
Asian-American population); California,
ethnic/racial minority population in,
49, 54; capital investment into Mexico,
53–54; commercial ties with Mexico,
42–43; expansion into Mexican territory,
53; family as place with "normative
structures," 91; Hawaii, Koreans in,
212; imperialism of, 124, 131; influence
on Korean Independence, 202–203,
206–208; international border with
Mexico, 53; lobbying activities
for Korean independence in, 213;
newspapers/periodicals, articles
on Japanese actions in Korea, 216;
Protestant missionaries from (*see*
Missionaries, American); Taft-Katsura
agreement, 222*n*
United States Exclusion Act, 51
United States-Japan trade imbalance, 56–57
University of West Indies, Indian professors
for, 167–168

Van der Veer, Peter, 142, 156
Việt Kiều (overseas Vietnamese): age, double
marriage squeeze and, 100*n*3; interviews with brides and grooms, 101*n*4;
money and, 98–99; "real," 99; return to
homeland, 100*n*
Vietnam: *doi moi* socioeconomic policy, 86;
"female revolt" in, 100; out-migration,
85–86; resistance to local marriages,
100; return migration, 94–96; socioeconomic ties with United States,
normalization of, 86; transpacific
marriage market, 86–89
Vietnamese double gender revolution, 87

Vietnamese double marriage squeeze, 100*n*3

Vietnamese families, 91–92; approval of marriage, 96–97; in bride-receiving communities, 95; celebration of arranged marriage, 98–99; division of household labor, 92–93; as ethnic model, 92; good, concept of, 93; mothers, 96, 99–100; parents, gender practices of, 91–92; remittance-receiving, 98

Vietnamese men: arranged marriages for (*see* Arranged marriages); average size of, 90; economic protection in traditional gender arrangements, 95; gender, class and ethnic paradox, 93; marriage to Vietnamese women, 93–94; meetings in diaspora, 94; middle-class privilege and, 91; peers, "material performances" of, 90–91; postmigration jobs for, 90, 92; provider role for, 93, 95; sense of belonging of, 91; traditional gender arrangements, 95

Vietnamese out-migration, 85–86

Vietnamese Student Association (VSA), 90

Vietnamese women: arranged marriages for, 20; "authentic" femininity of, 97, 99; "bad girl" reputations of, 94; beauty standards for, 96, 97; brides, credentials of, 95; educational mobility of, 96; exchange of submissiveness/propriety for economic protection, 95, 97; husband's surname and, 89–90, 101*n*6; "listen and respect" repertoire, 97–98; meetings in diaspora, 94; "passport chasers," 95; role of wife, 98; sense of belonging of, 91; status, from marriage, 95–96; traditional gender arrangements, 95

VSA (Vietnamese Student Association), 90

Wang, David, 57

War of the Pacific, 38, 39

West, identification against Asia, 9

Wilson, Woodrow, 202, 207, 210, 216

"Women's work," traditional, 92–93

Wong, Sau-ling, 4–5

World War I: American entry into, 207; Chinese immigrants in Mexico and, 42–43

World War II: Japanese imperialist expansion, 234; Japanese Peruvians and, 52

Xenophobia, 13

Yagya (Hindu ritual), 150

Yapa, 37

Zapatista National Liberation Front, 54

Zulueta, Julián, 33, 34